Personality-Guided Therapy
in Behavioral Medicine

Personality-Guided Therapy in Behavioral Medicine

Robert G. Harper

Series Editor Theodore Millon

AMERICAN PSYCHOLOGICAL ASSOCIATION
WASHINGTON, DC

Published by
American Psychological Association
750 First Street, NE
Washington, DC 20002
www.apa.org

To order
APA Order Department
P.O. Box 92984
Washington, DC 20090-2984
Tel: (800) 374-2721
Direct: (202) 336-5510
Fax: (202) 336-5502
TDD/TTY: (202) 336-6123
Online: www.apa.org/books/
E-mail: order@apa.org

In the U.K., Europe, Africa, and the Middle
East, copies may be ordered from
American Psychological Association
3 Henrietta Street
Covent Garden, London
WC2E 8LU England

Typeset in Goudy by World Composition Services, Inc., Sterling, VA

Printer: Sheridan Books, Ann Arbor, MI
Cover Designer: Berg Design, Albany, NY
Project Manager: Debbie Hardin, Carlsbad, CA

The opinions and statements published are the responsibility of the authors, and such opinions and statements do not necessarily represent the policies of the American Psychological Association.

Library of Congress Cataloging-in-Publication Data

Harper, Robert Gale, 1944–
    Personality-guided therapy in behavioral medicine / by Robert G. Harper.—1st ed.
        p. cm.—(Personality-guided psychology)
    Includes bibliographical references and index.
    ISBN 1-59147-043-9 (alk. paper)
        1. Psychology. 2. Personality disorders—Treatment. 3. Medicine and psychology.
    4. Sick—Psychology. 5. Clinical health psychology. 6. Behavior therapy. I. Title.
    II. Series.

RC480.5.H315   2004
616'.001'9—dc21   2003044348

British Library Cataloguing-in-Publication Data
A CIP record is available from the British Library.

Printed in the United States of America
First Edition

This book is dedicated to my parents,
Lawrence and Anna Harper,
who shaped and guided my life;
Michael and Mildred Kotik,
who so positively influenced my life;
and to my family—
Doreen, Mikah, and Reina, who *are* my life.

CONTENTS

SERIES FOREWORD

The turn of the 20th century saw the emergence of psychological interest in the concept of individual differences, the recognition that the many realms of scientific study then in vogue displayed considerable variability among "laboratory subjects." Sir Francis Galton in Great Britain and many of his disciples, notably Charles Spearman in England, Alfred Binet in France, and James McKeen Cattell in the United States, laid the groundwork for recognizing that intelligence was a major element of import in what came to be called *differential psychology*. Largely through the influence of psychoanalytic thought, and then only indirectly, did this new field expand the topic of individual differences in the direction of character and personality.

And so here we are at the dawn of the 21st century, ready to focus our attentions ever more seriously on the subject of personality trait differences and their impact on a wide variety of psychological subjects—from how they impinge on behavioral medicine outcomes, alter gerontological and adolescent treatment, regulate residential care programs, affect the management of depressive and PTSD patients, transform the style of cognitive–behavioral and interpersonal therapies, guide sophisticated forensic and correctional assessments—a whole bevy of important themes that typify where psychologists center their scientific and applied efforts today.

It is toward the end of alerting psychologists who work in diverse areas of study and practice that the present series, titled *Personality-Guided Psychology*, has been developed for publication by the American Psychological Association. The originating concept underlying the series may be traced to Henry Murray's seminal proposal in his 1938 volume, *Explorations in Personality*, in which he advanced a new field of study termed *personology*.

It took its contemporary form in a work of mine, published in 1999 under the title *Personality-Guided Therapy*.

The utility and relevance of personality as a variable is spreading in all directions, and the series sets out to illustrate where things stand today. As will be evident as the series' publication progresses, the most prominent work at present is found with creative thinkers whose efforts are directed toward enhancing a more efficacious treatment of patients. We hope to demonstrate, further, some of the newer realms of application and research that lie just at the edge of scientific advances in our field. Thus, we trust that the volumes included in this series will help us look beyond the threshold of the present and toward the vast horizon that represents all of psychology. Fortunately, there is a growing awareness that personality variables can be a guiding factor in all spheres of study. We trust the series will provide a map of an open country that encourages innovative ventures and provides a foundation for investigators who wish to locate directions in which they themselves can assume leading roles.

Theodore Millon, PhD, DSc
Series Editor

ACKNOWLEDGMENTS

This book would not have been possible without the seminal contributions of Theodore Millon to personality theory. His latest contribution, *Personality-Guided Therapy*, provided the framework for the organization of this book and the basis for understanding medical patient behavior from a personological standpoint. I am grateful to Susan Reynolds and Linda McCarter of the American Psychological Association for their patience and acumen, and to the unnamed reviewers for their kind, constructive critiques of early approximations of this final version.

Personality-Guided Therapy
in Behavioral Medicine

INTRODUCTION:
BEHAVIORAL MEDICINE

With the beginning of a new millennium, expectations of a longer life span and greater wellness have risen with scientific forecasts and widely publicized cutting-edge medical advances (e.g., organ transplantation and therapies generated by the human genome exploration). Although no one expects that disease eradication or prevention will be feasible in the near future, Americans' demand for quality health care still appears likely to greatly outstrip the national health care system financial resources to realize those expectations. Antoni, Millon, and Millon (1997) have observed that "at the close of last decade, it was apparent that chronic medical diseases— those maladies that are the most expensive to treat, were the major health challenge in United States" (p. 409). It has been estimated that 75% of all fatalities from cancer can be linked to behavior (Doll & Peto, 1981) and 50% of other fatalities to the 10 major medical causes of death (Ogden, 2000).

Behavioral medicine has at its disposal considerable technology that has been developed to facilitate habit and behavior change. The notion of self-management (Creer & Holroyd, 1997), active participation by patients in their health care, has been identified as critical to reducing health care costs. This was the conclusion of a blue ribbon panel commissioned by the government (National Heart, Lung and Blood Institute, 1992). This requires productive collaboration between patient and physician to ensure each has sufficient information concerning the medical condition and treatment requirements and a full understanding of the obstacles to compliance and adjustment challenges imposed by the medical condition. It then becomes the patient's responsibility to manage his or her illness except for appropriate monitoring and modifications provided by the physician. In some instances, clear-cut guidelines have been established concerning diagnostic and treatment strategies for managing the disease. This goal of patient responsibility, a laudable objective, assumes that these individuals have the capacity for self-management. Although many patients benefit from general behavioral medicine self-management interventions with efficacy demonstrated in group studies, many are not successful, and some even contribute to deterioration in patients' health. In turn, these patients contribute disproportionately to health care expenses. It is these outliers or "difficult" cases that deserve notice, as well as the problems these patients experience in effectively pursuing the best quality their genetic endowment confers on them.

An important recent development in the field of mental health treatment has been Millon's proposal (Millon, 1999) that a patient's personality characteristics play a defining role in the selection and organization of treatment interventions. This takes into account differences in individual's coping styles and vulnerabilities as a function of their deeply ingrained attitudes, beliefs, action tendencies, and habits. What follows is an effort to extend this orientation to the field of behavioral medicine, in which psychological knowledge is applied to medical problems in the context of the specific personality characteristics of patients. It is hoped that this methodology will increase providers' understanding of what different patients experience when faced with threats to their well-being and how this can translate into either a facilitation or impeding of health care intervention efforts. In recognition of the many disciplines that participate in behavioral medicine, the material presented in this volume is intended for the benefit of not only psychologists but also physicians interested in the psychological and psychosocial aspects of medicine, medical social workers, nurses, occupational therapists, and other health professionals involved in the care of patients who would benefit from behavioral medicine interventions.

The domain of behavioral medicine is dauntingly broad and involves the interface between medicine and many subdisciplines of psychology, including social psychology, personality psychology, clinical psychology, and clinical neuropsychology. Managing the knowledge base of these many fields may represent the greatest challenge and weakness of this book. Practitioners of behavioral medicine face the same dilemma in their practices, because it is impossible to know everything about specific medical syndromes and all the psychosocial aspects of that illness, especially how a particular illness may be experienced by specific individuals, considering their unique personality makeup. The primary objective of this book is to develop a conceptual framework for systematically considering the most important personological issues that may be raised by different illnesses and the health care efforts generated by them. This can be best accomplished through using Millon's evolutionary theory of personality applied to the *DSM–IV* (American Psychiatric Association, 1994) defined personality types, which in turn will be interwoven with some basic behavioral medicine concepts and perspectives.

BEHAVIORAL MEDICINE AND HEALTH PSYCHOLOGY

Behavioral medicine has been variously described as knowledge from the behavioral science disciplines (such as psychology, sociology, health education), focusing on health care, treatment, and disease prevention (Schwartz & Weiss, 1977); and as the use of the experimental analysis of behavior, such as behavior therapy, applied to the evaluation, treatment, and primary prevention of physical disease (Pomerleau & Brady, 1979). Behavioral medicine's obvious precursor was the field of psychosomatic medicine, elegantly refined by the work of Engel (1977, 1980). Engle's biopsychosocial model of health and illness linked the traditional medical model of health to psychological and social factors contributing to, interacting with, and causing illness.

An increasingly appreciated, complementary notion offered by Matarazzo (1980) has been the concept of behavioral health. This is the pursuit and maintenance of wellness and illness prevention behavior in healthy persons, especially pertinent as we witness the spread of SARS in mid–2003. In 1980 the concept of health psychology was introduced, defined as the "aggregate of the specific educational, scientific and professional contribution of the discipline of psychology to the promotion and maintenance of health, the promotion and treatment of illness and related dysfunction" (Matarazzo, 1980, p. 815).

Behavioral medicine in clinical practice involves psychologists or other mental health professionals providing services to individuals seeking health care by applying the collective knowledge contributed by diverse disciplines, including medical and psychiatric physicians; social workers; professionals in public health; health care economists; and the psychology subdisciplines of clinical, social, personality, developmental, and neuropsychology. Typically the behavioral medicine practitioner is working cooperatively with primary care physicians and other medical specialists. Various designations of psychologists working in this area have been proposed, such as "clinical health psychologist" (Belar & Deardorff, 1995) or "professional health psychologist" (Ogden, 2000), as used in Europe. It will be for others— professional associations and licensing boards—to determine the correct designation, definition, and professional credentialing standards for such practitioners. It is hoped that the knowledge summarized will have broad application to the many professional disciplines involved in health care.

MENTAL HEALTH SERVICES WITH MEDICAL PATIENTS

The delivery of psychological services to medical patients differs from the traditional mental health setting practice. The medical patient understandably may be preoccupied by his or her health problem, to the extent that the patient has little interest or emotional energy to address the psychological aspects of his or her illness. Such an individual may also be threatened by the introduction of a "shrink" in his or her care. Medical patients may question the relevance of "behavioral medicine" to their condition, a view that unwittingly may be reinforced by the referring physician, who may not have provided a cogent rationale for a behavioral medicine approach. Where most patients seeking psychotherapy are in some form of personal or situational distress, the immediacy, urgency, and timing for a behavioral medicine intervention may differ greatly, creating different levels of receptivity or resistance to such efforts. Some patients are referred for "wellness" interventions involving adoption of healthy habits and behaviors before development of a serious illness for which they may be at future risk. Other patients may be newly confronted and overwhelmed with a life-threatening diagnosis. Still others will be in the stage of coping with a chronic illness, or even facing the end of a terminal disease. The behavioral medicine practitioner can intervene at any of these stages and contribute meaningfully to illness prevention, health maintenance, or reduction of suffering.

Although psychiatric factors, such as depression and anxiety, are quite common with medical illness, they are not a necessary condition for introduction of behavioral medicine services. Subclinical manifestations of emotional distress and character trait pathology can play a significant role in the genesis of illness and its management. Recognizing the specific nature of even subtle problems by a behavioral medicine specialist can contribute to patient and provider comfort and the efficiency of health care delivery. At the other extreme, patients with personality disorders do become physically ill and require care that is typically more problematic in an obvious way for the physicians treating them.

Even with healthy individuals, the behavior change too often involved in wellness programs can be a daunting challenge to the practitioner. Although illness amelioration and symptom reduction may be an important motivator of lifestyle alteration, smoking cessation, exercise, modification of drinking patterns, and so forth, these are among the hardest behavior patterns to modify, especially if there is great effort (as in exercise) or restraint of appetitive–addictive cravings (e.g., caffeine, tobacco, alcohol) required in vulnerable individuals.

For both the patient and behavioral medical practitioner, the intervention can be more complicated than traditional therapy. For example, treatment typically will involve coordination of psychological and behavioral care with the medical treatment regimen, which in many cases may define the nature of the psychological intervention. The goal of therapy may also be more circumscribed, limited to facilitating certain medical treatment objectives rather than producing generalized insight, attitude, or behavior change. Involvement of family may be similar to traditional treatment for serious psychiatric conditions, where education and some supportive and monitoring roles may be called for.

The behavioral medicine practitioner may engage in both primary–secondary prevention activities ("wellness behaviors," lifestyle improvement, and risk prevention), as well as tertiary interventions with individuals in various stages of a disease process. Although individuals vary greatly with regard to their genetic predisposition for many conditions, disease prevention and health maintenance can be promoted by reducing risk behaviors. Antoni et al. (1997) have noted that risk behaviors are influenced by self-appraisals that include a person's sense of self-worth, his or her investment in maintaining health, his or her perception of disease susceptibility, and his or her sense of confidence in the capacity for making change.

Important to risk reduction is also appropriate help-seeking, which includes obtaining recommended medical consultations and diagnostic tests, as well as adhering to appropriate health care guidelines. Although there is only a limited understanding of the immune system, it appears clear that stress, if only defined in terms of life events requiring adaptation (both positive and negative), and chronic affective distress exert a subtle effect over time, undermining health by increasing susceptibility to common illnesses (e.g., respiratory infections). Conversely, "healthy " attitudes, expectations, and coping can buffer one from development of a disease or degenerative influences on the immune system. Similarly, all of these influences play a role once a disease develops or becomes chronic.

Psychosocial supports may be even more essential, as will be the patient's ability to deal with the physical discomfort, fatigue, and disruption to life routines imposed by illness. The context in which health maintenance efforts are occurring is thus very important. A high degree of life stress affects a person not only physiologically but also diverts or distracts from efforts to maintain wellness, if only reducing sleep time, dietary changes, and leisure relaxation time. Interacting with these factors are the material, psychological, or social supports available to the person. Obviously, a combination of poor genetic predisposition, inadequate social support, high life stress, and low self-esteem–poor coping will increase the likelihood of poor health and reduce the opportunities for recovery from illness. All of these issues represent potential opportunities for meaningful intervention and follow-up for the behavioral medicine practitioner.

Professionals functioning in such roles tend to work in nonpsychiatric facilities such as rehabilitation centers, internal medicine practice groups, or treatment settings dedicated to specific medical diseases such as cancer, neurological disorders, HIV, diabetes, chronic pain, and the like. However, this activity does not exempt them from being confronted with patients with serious and complicated psychiatric conditions. Indeed, individuals with Axis I or Axis II psychiatric conditions are probably overrepresented in many settings (e.g., brain injury, rehabilitation settings) given the association between those conditions and risk-taking behaviors. It is important to keep in mind that much of the theory and empirical work discussed in this volume is based on development of an understanding of how nonpsychiatric individuals think and behave with regard to their health and illness. The relationships between psychosocial factors and physical illnesses is based on group differences concerning specific individual difference characteristics or treatment interventions. This is how behavioral science is able to demonstrate its contribution to the understanding of the genesis and treatment of physical disease states. On the other hand, it is the application of this general knowledge to a given individual that defines clinical work.

BEHAVIORAL MEDICINE AND PERSONALITY

This section will briefly and selectively touch on some recent efforts to link personality variables to the genesis of disease states and, conversely, to the prevention of illness or promotion of health. The examples chosen are intended to illustrate empirically generated work demonstrating this critical interface, and by no means represent all of the important contributions to this area.

Personality and Illness

McCrae and Stone (1997) wrote that "personality refers to features of the individual that are enduring, pervasive, and distinctive; an accurate description of personality tells us what the person is really like" (p. 29). Attempts to examine personality and diseases in relationship to one another in behavioral medicine for the most part have focused on only certain personality attributes, dispositions, or traits that influence or predispose one to development of an illness. Space does not permit exploration of the rich history of psychosomatic medicine as it relates to this topic. However, even in the past decade a multitude of personality variables have been investigated as possible factors in response to stress, illness precursors or reactions to illness, or predictors of health-damaging behaviors. In their authoritative review of this issue, Contrada and Guyll (2000) have listed no less than 55 different temperamental characteristics; mood dispositions; cognitive, coping, or defensive style characteristics; and motivational states or orientations. However, only three met criteria for personality risk factors (Siegal, 1984). That is, they should be (a) identified via prospective research designs, (b) linked to objectively determined manifestations of disease states, (c) replicated in different studies, (d) of sufficient magnitude to be of practical significance, and (e) of "biological plausibility"—in other words, support for a physiological mechanism linking personality to a disease state.

Drawing on the heuristic value of the Type A behavior pattern, much additional investigation has been devoted to anger–hostility–aggressiveness as playing a role in development of heart disease (e.g., as reviewed by Helmers, Posluszny, & Krantz, 1994; Scheier & Bridges, 1995); smoking, blood cholesterol, and obesity (Siegler, 1994); and hypertension (Suls, Wan, & Costa, 1995). This behavior pattern has even been related to mortality in cancer (Carmelli et al., 1991). Anger displays among marital couples have been associated with reduction in immune functioning (Kiecolt-Glaser et al., 1993). In addition to physiological consequences to health, trait hostility has been associated with unhealthy behaviors such as smoking, obesity, alcohol use (Siegler, 1994), reduced activity–exercise, dental hygiene, and poor sleep hygiene (Leiker & Hailey, 1988). It has also been negatively linked to chemotherapy compliance in cancer treatment (Ayres, Hoon, Franzoni, Matheny, & Cotanch, 1994), medication adherence in hypertension (Lee et al., 1992), cardiac rehabilitation participation (Digenio, Padayachee, & Groeneveld, 1992), and recovery from cardiac surgery (Jenkins, Stanton, & Jono, 1994). Given that anger as an emotion is disinhibiting and may reduce restraint or control over impulses, one might speculate that the chronically angry or quick to anger individual is predisposed to impulsive acts and has less emotional–motivational resolve to exert discipline over needs when aroused.

Conversely, emotional suppression–repression broadly embraces the notion that feelings overcontrolled or held in can be deleterious to health, either if they are recognized and not expressed or are outside of conscious awareness. This view harkens back to the analytical writings of Alexander (1930), who considered hypertension might be related to anger suppression, a supposition supported by more recent research (Suls et al., 1995). The Type C personality pattern of overcontrol of emotion has been proposed as a cancer risk factor (Temoshok, 1987), although findings in support of this perspective are mixed (Scheier & Bridges, 1995).

Another promising concept, that of disengagement (Schieier & Bridges, 1995), refers to a giving up orientation involving feelings of pessimism, fatalism, helplessness–hopelessness, and dysphoria–depression. An aspect of this concept, pessimistic explanatory style, or the propensity to attribute uncontrollable stressors to internal factors, has been negatively associated with coronary disease survival (Buchanan, 1995) and longevity after diagnosis of breast cancer (Levy, Morrow, Bagley, & Lippman, 1988). Depression, a mood state that is cognitively characterized by a negative future orientation, has been related to cerebrovascular accident, risk of occlusive artery disease (Carney, Freedland, Rich, & Jaffe, 1995) and risk of heart attack and death following it (e.g., Frasure-Smith, Lesperance, & Talajic, 1993). With cancer, the concept of fatalism, a passive orientation to negative expectations about the future, has been associated with poorer prognosis (Pettingale, Morris, & Greer, 1985), as it also has been with AIDS (Reed, Kemeny, Taylor, Wang, & Visscher, 1994).

These factors emphasize trait-like characteristics of an individual that are believed to be linked to the genesis of different disease states. Smith and Gallo (2000) have noted, however, that "care must be taken to avoid mistaking an association between personality traits and illness behavior for an association with actual illness" (p. 142). They have encouraged consideration of a cognitive–social or transactional approach to personality, which focuses not only on the trait characteristics but also on the social contexts and eliciting circumstances that produce a chain of reciprocal events between an individual and the environment. As such this view overlaps with stress and coping and self-regulation models of illness. It also provides a basis for more readily understanding intervention possibilities in relation to the person–situation and person–environment interactions that are taking place continuously. Personality traits can be viewed as moderators of the stress–illness interaction (Baron & Kenney, 1986) or as a determinant of the coping mechanism used. Buss (1987) has observed that personality characteristics may have a stress-creating influence in leading an individual to gravitate to or select certain situations that evoke reactions by provoking environmental responses that will elicit it. Thus, the Type A individual may not only appraise situations as competitive and elicitive of aggressive–hostile behavior, but they may actively seek out or manufacture situations that fit with their dispositional views and tendencies. Houston (1994) has noted that hostility can be linked more strongly to interpersonal than nonsocial stressors and provocations. Conversely, Lepore (1995) demonstrated that in nonhostile but not hostile individuals social support reduced cardiovascular reactivity to stress.

Personality and Wellness

If certain aspects of personality confer risk, a reasonable question is whether there are "characteriological immunogens." In fact, there is a small body of thought that has looked at the opposite side, that of positive characteristics and feeling states and health or wellness. Kobasa (1979) introduced the concept of hardiness, the capacity of a person to experience commitment, meaning, and involvement in what he or she does; have a sense of control or influence in his or her life; and approach change flexibly with positive anticipation and curiosity. These qualities are viewed as protecting an individual from the toxic effects of stress in resisting a sense of helplessness and loss of purpose and meaning. Hardiness has been inversely related to symptoms of ill health (Wiebe & Williams, 1992). It has been linked to buffering stressful events (Funk, 1992; Ouelette, 1993) and has predicted vigor in elderly individuals (Magnani, 1990). Lower burnout rates are reported by individuals high in hardiness in nursing (e.g., Rich & Rich, 1987; Topf, 1989) and by school teachers (Holt, Fine, & Tollefson, 1987). High commitment elements of hardiness (Florian, Mukuliner, & Taubman, 1995) have been linked to reduced threat appraisal and emotion-focused coping and a greater sense of anticipation that stresses could be mastered. The sense of control component was associated with greater problem-solving coping and support-seeking activities (Florian, Mikuliner, & Taubman, 1995).

A related notion is the concept of sense of coherence, which refers to a person's experiencing his or her life as comprehensible, manageable, and meaningful (Antonovsky, 1987, 1993). This dispositional orientation has been related to fewer symptoms of ill health (Bowman, 1996), less physiological distress among homeless women (Ingram, Corning, & Schmidt, 1996), less distress and pain following surgery (Chamberlain, Petrie, & Azariah, 1992), more health-enhancing behaviors such as social skills use (Margalit & Eysenck, 1990), and reduced need for emotion-focused coping (Larsson & Setterlind, 1990).

Dispositional optimism (Scheier & Carver 1985, 1992) has been described as an anticipation by an individual that positive events will occur in his or her life, which in turn generates favorable outcome expectancies that generate adaptive coping and motivate goal attainment. Negative expectancies tend to lead to giving up. Optimism has been related to effective coping and college students' physical well-being (Aspinwall & Taylor, 1992) and to healthiness in cardiac bypass patients (Scheier et al., 1989). This construct has also been associated with healthy behaviors in heart patients, such as use of vitamins (Scheier & Carver, 1992) and exercise and diet (Shepperd, Maroto & Pbert, 1996). It has also been linked to safer sex practices in women (Morrill et al., 1996).

Explanatory style has been used to describe pessimistic or optimistic attributions to events. An optimistic explanatory orientation views negative events as being determined by external, specific, discrete events that are unstable or uncontrollable in nature. Conversely, positive events are attributed to internal factors that are viewed as stable and global in nature (Abramson, Seligman, & Teasdale, 1978; Peterson, Seligman, & Valliant, 1988). Harvard graduates measured to have a positive rather than negative explanatory style at age 25 were found to be in better health than those with a pessimistic orientation some 20 years later. A motivational construct, that of affiliative trust, has been related to indexes of immunocompetence (McKay, 1991). Individuals who harbored internalized object relations characterized by malevolence and harmfulness and anticipation of mistreatment and abandonment, as inferred from content analysis of Thematic Apperception Test (TAT; Murphy, 1943) stories, had lower helper-to-suppressor T-cell ratios.

Although all of these efforts have empirically linked aspects of personality to medical conditions, the findings have been applicable more to research contexts rather than applied health care. What is needed for clinical practice is a bridge or preliminary integration between a general theory of personality and behavioral medicine.

MILLON'S EVOLUTIONARY THEORY OF PERSONALITY

In keeping with the school of thought developed by Theodore Millon (1969, 1981, 1990, 1999), it is the premise of this book that behavioral medicine interventions can be made more meaningful to patients, and in turn more effective, if interventions are organized around or take into account the personality of the individual.

The theory of personality adopted in this book is based on Millon's notion of three phases or polarities: those of pleasure–pain, passive–active, other–self dimensions, which "have been used to construct a theoretically anchored classification system of personality styles and clinical disorders" (Millon, 1999, p. 97). This theory specifies that to evolve, humans must pursue pleasure (gratification of needs) and avoid pain (or potential annihilation). This is regarded as an individual's existential aim. A person's adaptation mode is seen in the extremes of passivity, conforming or adjusting to environmental circumstances, or activity, aggressively seeking to modify circumstances to one's advantage. Finally, an individual's expression of his or her replication strategy can be manifested through the (prototypical male) self-orientation, which involves singular pursuit of reproduction, or the (prototypical female) other polarity position, involving an inherent investment in having–raising young.

From the three basic polarities, 11 different prototypes and 3 severe variants were derived, 10 of these corresponding to the different personality disorder types specified in the *DSM–IV*. Normal variants of all these types are present, although some combination of the polarity qualities will make for a healthier adjustment than others. It would be assumed that a reasonable balance between all of the active–passive, pleasure–pain, self–other polarities would be present in a normally functioning individual and skewed or distorted in pathological individuals. Temperament, an inborn characteristic, can be transformed by environmental or contextual influences to manifest certain traits or dispositions that constitute certain personality characteristics or styles expressed in these polarity combinations. Whereas other theories have adopted a dimensional model of personality involving a continuum of characteristics (e.g., McCrae & Costa, 1990), the categorical approach (such as *DSM–IV*) favors a qualitative approach and requires a threshold level of pathological characteristics to constitute a diagnosis (American Psychiatric Association, 1994). A combination of both categorical and dimensional models would characterize the prototypal model for assessing personality.

Millon's theory of personality emphasizes common elements or denominators to each type. A distinction is made between "functional" domains of personality—that is, those aspects of adjustment between the individual and his or her environment, and "structural" aspects or domains of personality—that is, those that represent the inner, organizing influences that regulate a person's functioning. Earlier personality theories might represent one or more aspects of a single domain. Behavior theories would emphasize the expressive actions from the functional domain, whereas interpersonally based theories would focus on only those aspects of the functional domain. Cognitive theories or psychodynamic object relations theories might constitute more structurally relevant domains.

A tradition in psychology has been for proponents of different theories to compete with each other on the grounds that their view was sufficient to understand and define personality. This is a requirement to meet the rigor of science, which ensures that only the essential or unique, necessary and sufficient explanatory features of each theory survive to contribute to a final body of knowledge. Obviously, this is an ongoing process, because psychological knowledge of personality, especially from a biological and genetic standpoint, is incomplete, awaiting input from contributions from the neurosciences and the human genome project.

These considerations are not an argument for the clinical sciences to halt their application of existing knowledge to current treatment needs until new breakthroughs clarify existing theories. However, it does make sense to pursue an integration of existing knowledge from competing sources, consistent with the thrust of the effort of this book and the allied series of works on personality-guided treatments. Millon's theory of personality is particularly suited to this purpose because it embraces the benefits of knowledge gained from the behavioral, cognitive, interpersonal, and psychodynamic views of psychopathology and its treatment.

AXIS I/II COMORBIDITY: COMPLEX CLINICAL SYNDROMES

Whereas *DSM–IV* makes rigorous delineation between Axis I and Axis II syndromes, there is at best an awkward effort to acknowledge "comorbid" patient states, where there is a basis for both diagnoses in the same individual. Millon makes the important distinction between complex syndromes and simple reactions. The latter are comparatively specific responses to specific events that do not engage an individual's personality traits. Complex clinical syndromes in their manifest form may be indistinguishable from simple clinical reactions, especially because they can be elicited by the same external event. However, they are quite different in that the event has disturbed a vulnerable personality characteristic or coping style that complicates the process of recovery from a distressing event. Individuals with personality disorders or personality trait disturbances may experience specific thoughts and emotions that determine their response to a precipitating event. This results in very complicated presentations that require considerable unraveling, given the patients' histories of painful experiences, faulty learning, conflicted relationships, and confused emotions during their developmental–formative years. When contemporaneous relationship conflicts or losses occur, these histories activate convoluted reactions and defenses that even tend to intensify or perpetuate the problems they face. This is in contrast to the relatively straightforward expression of anxiety or depression in otherwise well-adjusted individuals reacting to clear-cut eliciting events and their uncomplicated response to treatments. Extension of this notion to medical conditions, adding or substituting an Axis III condition, would seem to offer a natural opportunity to understand problematic, vexing, or outlier presentations of garden-variety medical conditions.

In complex clinical syndromes, coping responses, or those instrumental or emotional transactions designed to deal with challenges and stresses, are used to deal with either perceived external threats or inner emotions or impulses, recognition of which would disturb one's psychic equilibrium, self-image, or views of significant others. Unless the practitioner is aware of the certain sensitivities or predispositions and coping styles of an individual, the significance of his or her behavior and *meaning* of the physical illness or symptom can be misunderstood. In general, more complex clinical syndromes manifest themselves in such a fashion as to encourage individuals to seek support, regard or sympathy from others, and avoid social rejection or humiliation that undisguised display of an unacceptable feeling or impulse would elicit. Depression (or presentation of physical illness) accompanied by anger can inhibit others from counteraggression and simultaneously achieve some satisfaction by frustrating or constraining others who may feel guilty over the depressed individual's apparent distress. The form and content of the complex clinical syndrome will of course vary from individual to individual, whose different life experiences will shape the meaning and significance of even a common threat that may be faced (e.g., job loss). Axis I (or Axis III) conditions such as depression and anxiety can thus take on drastically different forms and express themselves in very different ways depending on the Axis II diagnosis. Just as with emotional conditions, it follows that medical conditions, even if they do not produce anxiety or depression, may be expressed quite differently depending on the coping style–personality determinants of the particular individual.

PERSONALITY-GUIDED INTERVENTIONS

Personality is based on the notion that individuals each process and exhibit core dispositions, action tendencies, and characteristics expressed consistently across different situations and contexts. This provides a predictability by which knowledgeable clinicians can anticipate what stressed medical patients may do, so that prophylactic interventions can be designed to minimize disruption in their care. When consulting on cases where there has already been significant disruption to treatment and interpersonal disaffection between patient and medical staff, an accurate understanding of the patient's traits and coping tendencies can be invaluable in getting treatment back on track. For medical practitioners and nurses used to following the medical model approach, a personality diagnosis can promote psychological distance and facilitate a "clinical" posture, as opposed to a personalized countertransference reaction, in response to the intense and aversive personal experiences a "difficult" patient can produce in his or her interactions with providers.

Adjustment Domains

Personality can be considered in terms of its behavioral manifestation, with regard to (a) observable or expressive behaviors and (b) interpersonal–relational conduct. There is also a phenomenological level, which includes (a) cognitive modes of functioning, (b) self-image, and (c) internalized object representations. A third level of personality functioning is the intrapsychic, which consists of two aspects: (a) the predominant regulatory coping or defense mechanism and (b) the "morphological organization." Millon speaks of morphological structures that "represent deeply embedded and relatively enduring templates of printed memories, attitudes, needs, fears, conflicts . . . which guide experience and transform the nature of ongoing life events" (Millon, 1999, p. 141). Finally, mood and temperament are also critical variables, often working in the background to predispose certain dispositions, sensitivities, and reaction tendencies given the personalities.

Treatment Considerations

As opposed to eclectic therapy approaches, it is argued that personality-guided treatments permit synergistic and integrated interventions, because the theory permits different levels of analysis and points of intervention in the behavioral, cognitive, and experiential–intrapsychic domains. Millon has proposed two important concepts, that of potentiating pairings and catalytic sequences. Potentiating pairings involve simultaneous combining treatment methods to address maladaptive behavior patterns that might be refractory to change if each intervention were used alone. Catalytic sequences, in turn, would consist of carefully selected interventions that would address different aspects of a patient's complex clinical syndrome in an orderly or sequential fashion, where each previous gain facilitates a progress in and dealing with the subsequent targets of intervention. The value of personality-guided strategy is that it permits a systematic and reasoned basis for treatment planning and selection. A workers' compensation patient with a histrionic personality disorder, propensity for somatization, and symptom amplification may not be a suitable candidate for a chronic pain or rehabilitation program given the risk that suggestion could engender greater illness behavior, at least until issues of dependency and social secondary gain are first addressed.

Millon's theory also lends itself to targeting patients' specific adjustment domains—in other words, interpersonal, vocational, and physical, the latter in such instances where there may be some medical disability. Millon makes an important distinction between strategic and tactical considerations in treatment. The former has to do with the broad conceptual understanding of the case and the plan of action; the latter involves the operational specifics of a given intervention. All too often managed care objectives dictate only tactical interventions that may produce immediate symptom relief but no protection against recurrence of a conflict or symptom because the underlying or broader issues have been ignored, at the expense of maintenance and relapse issues. For treatment to have the highest likelihood of success and permanence, an understanding of the strategic issues and a coherently derived tactical plan taking into account the individuals personality will be required.

Another distinction that is important is between interactions and transactions that take place in treatment. Interaction refers to the exchange and interplay of information and feelings between patient and therapist, whereas transaction implies activity directed at change or realization of some goal. Therapy that consists of only interaction is likely to be unfocused and wandering, perhaps leaving the patient feeling better but unchanged. With a transaction, there is an immediate target goal in sight, to which patient–therapist interaction is devoted. This can be a subtle distinction in therapy easily lost sight of, but a useful reference point to revisit periodically to ensure the intervention is actually progressing toward its objective. Medical physicians and even trained behavioral medicine practitioners may mistake patient–provider interactions for transactions, with consequent surprise that little has been accomplished in the way of treatment adherence.

PERSONALITY DISORDER PATTERNS

The first step to understanding the personality disorders is specification of the basic features of each condition according to the previously introduced polarity model proposed by Millon (1999). This includes a review of the clinical domains at the behavioral, phenomenological, intrapsychic, and biophysical levels. The implications of these characteristics can then be considered in relation to patient diagnosis, management, and treatment in the behavioral medicine setting. The reader familiar with psychiatric diagnostic criteria will recall that the *DSM–IV* defines a personality disorder as "the enduring pattern of inner experience in behavior that deviates markedly from the expectations of the individual's culture" (p. 275). To meet threshold criteria for such a condition, an individual must manifest at least two deviations in the following domains: (a) cognitive: an individual's way of perceiving experiences, themselves, and others; (b) affective: an individual's range, intensity, lability, and degree of appropriateness of emotional responses; (c) individual's interpersonal style of functioning; and (d) the nature of his or her impulse control. These characteristics in turn must (a) have a widespread impact on the individual's personal and social functioning, leading to (b) significant disruption or distress in social, vocational "or other important areas of functioning" (p. 275) and (c) it cannot be exclusively manifested as a feature of an Axis I condition, including schizophrenia, depression anxiety, or organic mental disorders and substance abuse.

The 10 recognized disorders have been grouped into three different clusters, based on their most salient characteristics. Cluster A disorders all involve social withdrawal in deviant modes of social functioning. These include paranoid, schizoid, and schizotypal personality disorders. Cluster B conditions, the antisocial personalities, borderline, histrionic, and narcissistic disorders are all characterized by difficulties with impulse control and excessive emotionally. Cluster C conditions have in common a prominent sensitivity to social rejection, preoccupation with conformity, and anxiety proneness. There are actually four other patterns derivable from polarity theory but not incorporated into the *DSM–IV*. These include depressive, negativistic, sadistic, and masochistic types. Although important theoretically, because of space requirements and a need for correspondence with currently used nomenclature, they will not be discussed as separate entities.

The discussion of personality disorders in terms of Millon's formulations will have obvious overlap with these descriptive features of personality disorders. However, given that there is an underlying "evolutionary" theoretical basis for the disorders, they also can be distinguished by the variation in endowed biopsychosocial tendencies, as defined by the three different polarity systems.

CONCLUSION

Although behavioral medicine and health psychology have made significant contributions to the general understanding of the role of behavioral and psychological factors in disease states and health care, the applicability of this knowledge to individuals, especially "difficult" clinical cases, has been rather limited. This volume is intended to represent a first approximation to systematic consideration of the implications of personality disorder in different medical contexts. The chapters that follow will reference the *DSM–IV* criteria and then proceed with an elaboration of the theorized polarity imbalances as they apply to each condition and implications for treatment and their expression in behavioral medicine clinical situations. All of this first must be placed in the context of a behavioral medicine perspective and the *universal* challenges patients experience in dealing with illness and trying to stay well.

1

BEHAVIORAL MEDICINE THEORY AND MEDICAL DISEASE

Appropriate application of personality theory to behavioral medicine will require at least selective consideration of some general behavioral medicine concepts and the psychological implications of diseases as they affect individuals in general. Interested readers seeking a broader view of the field may want to consider such excellent general references as Ogden (2000); Baum, Newman, Weinman, West, and McManus (1997); and Baum, Revenson, and Singer (2000).

STRESS AND COPING

Fundamental to the field of psychosomatic and behavioral medicine has been the notion of stress as a causal factor in disease development. The concept of stress is one of the most ubiquitous but difficult to define terms in the psychology literature. Most would agree that it is something that requires adaptation or change and that it often involves a sense of being threatened and unpleasant feeling states. A recent definition of stress generally reflecting these views is as "a negative emotional experience accompanied by predictable biochemical, physiological, and behavioral changes that are directed towards adaptation either by manipulating the situation to alter the stressor or by accommodating its effects" (Baum, 1990, p. 653). Because it involves both physiological and behavioral consequences, health problems can develop at a biological level through chronic demands placed on the sympathetic, hypothalamic–pituitary–adrenal cortical systems (Seyle, 1956, 1984), and the immune system (Herbert & S. Cohen, 1993), or they can be behaviorally induced through health-damaging behavior such as drug use, overeating, inactivity, or risky–dangerous behavior (e.g., road rage). Another perspective is that life events, simply defined as consensually shared significant experiences, both negative and positive (e.g., death of a family member, or, conversely, birth of a child), can require major adjustments, placing physiological and behavioral demands on an individual (Holmes & Rahe, 1967).

The concept of coping, in contrast, deals with efforts to manage threats to well-being. Coping often refers to adaptive actions that confer benefit to the individual, whereas "defenses" represent maladaptive efforts to deal with threat that can lead to unfavorable consequences. Coping involves "the process of managing demands (external or internal) that are appraised as taxing or exceeding the resources of the person" (Lazarus & Folkman, 1984, p. 283). Use of the term *management* implies something less than mastery of the threat. Successful management has been exemplified by greater tolerance or endurance in the face of hardship, such as chronic or terminal illness. Another important aspect of coping involves a recruitment and mobilization of effort and purposeful activity. Coping can be distinguished from adaptation, a person's typical adjustment and routine modes of functioning. Coping assumes some degree of stress. As such, coping can be a form of adaptation under difficult circumstances.

A primary cognitive process involved in coping with stress is the evaluative process a person goes through when faced with a new, typically ambiguous event. If the event is viewed as a challenge rather than a threat involving certain loss or harm, this view is likely to elicit very different emotions, motivations, expectations, and actions. Cognitive appraisals as such are at the heart of individual differences in responding to specific situations. Lazarus and colleagues (Lazarus, 1975; Lazarus & Cohen, 1973, 1977) have emphasized the importance of cognitive appraisal of threat to stress and coping. Appraisal can be regarded as primary, in terms of evaluation of the external potential stressor, which can be considered benign, potentially harmful, or irrelevant. Secondary appraisal refers to the individual's analysis as to his or her capacity to deal with the threat, if it is so evaluated. Coping can pertain to actions in response to events that have already occurred, but there can also be "anticipatory coping" involving important expectations and appraisals that will determine the future behavior. The element of ambiguity can play an important role, as well as the presence of information specific to the threat (diagnosis of a disease) that may either intensify or reduce emotional distress, depending on the nature of the individual.

Billings and Moos (1981) have described three different coping styles, active–cognitive, active–behavioral, and avoidance. Problem-focused coping involves direct action, oriented at modifying or ameliorating whatever threatens or is injurious to the person. Emotion-focused coping in contrast pertains to efforts to regulate the experience or expression of a feeling state. Often both processes occur in dealing with acute or chronic illness, either in succession or simultaneously. In addition, effective coping in one form can benefit the other. For example, seeking social support successfully can provide tangible benefits (monetary loans, cooking or cleaning services) that also alleviate emotional distress (reducing the feeling of helplessness or being alone). Where specific coping efforts occur consistently across a variety of situations or circumstances, it is possible to view it as having trait-like qualities, or coping styles.

Many health care visionaries see human behavior as the next frontier and best hope of reducing health care costs. In the past several decades numerous studies have shown how "low-tech" and low-cost interventions may have potential benefit. For example, a cognitive coping activity as simple as disclosure concerning meaningful events appears to be health protective. Students writing their thoughts and feelings about upsetting events show reduction in health care visits compared to do those who did not (Pennebaker & Beall, 1986) and better immune system functioning (Pennebaker, Kiecolt-Glaser, & Glaser, 1988). Use of positive emotion words and moderate (but not high and low rates) of negative emotion words and causal and insight words in essays have been associated with indexes of better health (Pennebaker, Mayne, & Francis, 1997). It is now well-established that even moderate physical activity or exercise as behavioral coping confers widespread benefit, reducing depression, cardiovascular disease risk, and possibly even cancer incidence (Phillips, Kiernan, & King, 2000). Throughout the following discussions, the concept of stress and coping will permeate the different theories and models that have been developed in behavioral medicine–health psychology.

Coping With Chronic Illness

In the past century many of the infectious diseases that contributed to high infant mortality and low life expectancy have either become treatable or preventable for medical advances. This in turn has created a situation where diseases that develop over time, such as heart disease, diabetes, hypertension, arthritis, and cancer, emerge as chronic illnesses afflicting increasingly large segments of the population as it ages. Although many of these diseases are potentially life-threatening, the greater challenge often lies in adjusting to the condition. Initially following a diagnosis, there is a natural sense of loss of body invulnerability and need to reconcile to some limitation or loss of functioning. The rate at which this adjustment occurs may vary as a function of the suddenness of the disease.

Serious Illness as Crisis

The diagnosis of chronic illness has been described as a personal crisis for the individual. The initial diagnosis of serious illness will elicit a series of psychological events (Shontz, 1975). These include a state of shock in which bewilderment, stunned disbelief, and detachment occur as the individual struggles to function in an automaton-like fashion. This is followed by what Shontz has termed an encounter reaction, where the patient is confronted with overwhelming, confusing feelings of loss, grief, hopelessness, helplessness, and despair. Finally, there is retreat, where the patient begins to address the diagnosis initially by denial and protective self-withdrawal.

Coping with a diagnosis of serious, life-threatening, or life-altering health has been also regarded as a crisis by Moos and Schaefer (1984), requiring multiple adjustments and changes. These include role and identity changes, altered future expectancies, changes in social support, and even physical location (e.g., transfer to an out of town specialty hospital). Given the unpredictable nature of most serious illness diagnoses, there is no opportunity for preparatory coping, and there is often no previous experience dealing with this circumstance. Moreover, information concerning its causes and implications may still be indeterminate, yet a difficult decision may be immediately required—for example, exploratory surgery to determine tumor infiltration and metastasis, where mutilation may be an uncertain consequence).

If death and dying are a real possibility, initial confrontation with these prospects may elevate fear to a level where the patient is unable to consider anything but the danger itself. Chronic hyperarousal in turn may contribute to psychosomatic symptoms that become confused with the disease process. Whereas a cure may be the chief objective for nonterminal illnesses, comfort and palliation–psychosocial care are the preeminent concerns of practitioners for irreversible degenerative processes. The rate at which information is introduced concerning the illness and its course will vary according to the tolerance of the individual. "It is just as wrong to tell people too much, too soon, as it is to tell them too little, too late" (Parkes, 1997, p. 93). Stressful medical procedures may elicit efforts to avoid threat cues or conversely a need for information to provide some predictability and order to the anticipated unpleasantness. It should be noted that the form coping efforts may take can vary according to the phase of the illness:

"A medical problem consists of a sequence of changing episodes, and every episode consists of an unfolding series of differentiable experiences" (Parkes, 1997, p. 96). For example, individuals may use both emotion-focused and problem-focused coping in dealing with different aspects or phases of an illness.

Coping should be viewed as a process, involving first cognitive appraisal, which involves consideration and identification of the adaptive tasks or challenges that must be anticipated. These may involve pain and incapacitation, being hospitalized and undergoing stressful medical diagnostic procedures, and relating to a stranger—health care professional to which the patient's life may be entrusted. Concurrent with this, the patient must attempt to maintain an emotional equilibrium, sustaining some sense of control and efficacy, maintain relationships with family and other supports, and develop contingencies for various future scenarios that will unfold only over the course of the illness.

The nature of coping includes the initial appraisal phase involving reacting to the diagnosis and attempting to formulate initial plans and expectancies that may provide some sense of control or manageability. This may require efforts to redefine the illness to keep it from seeming overwhelming, which may involve using denial or avoidance strategies. As the appraisal process unfolds, problem-focused coping will take place. This will involve information gathering, recruitment of support, acquisition of initial illness management skills, and identification of opportunities to maintain a positive sense of self through fulfilling task accomplishment. Emotion-focused coping will involve activity to counter despair and generate a sense of hope, abreaction of destructive negative feelings, and efforts to work through the grief process leading to some acceptance of the illness. Based on their own analysis of individuals facing threat and traumas, Taylor and his associates have argued that coping should involve cognitive–emotional activity to gain a sense of meaning, mastery, and opportunities for self-enhancement (Taylor, Lichtman, & Wood, 1984).

Chronic Phase Adjustment

Following this initial crisis phase, the patient is confronted with a number of the secondary demands, including adjusting to the symptoms and restrictions produced by the illness, dealing with any special treatment required, and maintaining continuity in relationships with health care providers. Chronic diseases have been conceptualized as varying along a number of dimensions: controllability, predictability, and severity (Stanton, Collins, & Sworowski, 2000). Although multiple sclerosis may be often less severe in terms of lethality than heart attack, it may be less controllable or predictable given its waxing and waning course. Diabetes may involve long-term, insidious decline across multiple organ systems, but most cases are more predictable, controllable, and less immediately lethal than cancer or AIDs.

As the disease enters the chronic phase, where there is some stability to the condition, then attention shifts to maximizing patient quality of life, to the extent permitted by the condition. This will include consideration of such aspects as physical functioning, role, emotional and social functioning, general sense of well-being, stamina–fatiguability, presence–absence of pain, and presence–absence of emotional symptoms such as depression. It should be noted that although it would seem natural for comparisons to be made with patients' premorbid level of functioning–adjustment, patients may in fact shift their comparisons to how they are doing relative to other similarly afflicted individuals (Stanton et al., 2000). Not surprisingly, depression and anxiety are commonplace complaints, affecting nearly half of cancer patients, according to one meta-study (van't Spijker, Trijsburg, & Duivenvoorden, 1997). However, most myocardial infarction patients experience no persisting psychosocial decline (Ell & Dunkel-Schetter, 1994), and diabetic children by a year return to their prediagnosis level of adjustment (Cox & Gonder-Frederick, 1992). It would appear that although chronic conditions are associated with depression and anxiety symptoms, these generally are not of the magnitude of psychiatric patients (Cassileth et al., 1984), and mental health is the aspect of psychosocial functioning least affected by a chronic illness (Stewart et al., 1989).

In general, avoidant and emotion-focused coping appears most suited as a strategy for dealing with the overwhelming initial impact of a diagnosis or manifestation of an illness. Long-term, approach–problem-focused coping is more adaptive. In particular, avoidant tendencies are associated with poorer adherence to medical recommendations (Maes, Leventhal, & DeRidder, 1996), whereas problem-focused strategies may improve functional adjustment, providing the disease state does not disrupt such efforts to gain a sense of predictability and controllability. For chronic illnesses, Chesney and Folkman (1994) have introduced the Coping Effectiveness Training Program, which examines the way illness-related stressors are appraised and the different strategies that can be used to deal with them. A distinction is made between problem-focused and emotion-focused techniques. When stressors are viewed as uncontrollable, emotion-focused techniques may be most helpful, whereas problem-focused efforts will be more suitable to potentially controllable aspects of the illness.

DISEASE, BEHAVIOR, AND ILLNESS REPRESENTATIONS

Terms commonly used in behavioral medicine–health psychology include health behaviors (e.g., exercise, diet), illness behavior, and sick role behavior (Kasl & Cobb, 1966). Matarazzo (1984) importantly focused attention on "behavioral pathogens," or health-impairing habits, such as excessive alcohol consumption, smoking, and overeating. Conversely, there are "behavioral immunogens," behaviors that protect against illness, such as a screening evaluations.

Many theories have addressed how these behaviors develop and occur typically from a rational standpoint applicable to broad population groups (e.g., Ajzen, 1985, 1988; Becker & Rosenstock, 1987; Rogers 1975, 1983, 1985; Rosenstock, 1966; Schwarzer, 1992). Leventhal and associates in contrast have considered idiosyncratic or lay convictions about illness and behavior, which may involve irrational thoughts and actions distorted by emotion, unique past experiences, and learning histories more likely involved with personality pattern disorders (Leventhal & Crouch, 1997; Leventhal, Leventhal, & Cameron, 2000). In their view illnesses can all be represented in terms of the following characteristics that define its content: (a) its identity, the label or diagnosis given to the illness (by the individual or expert), and its symptom manifestations; (b) its perceived cause, biological, genetic, environmental, or psychosocial; (c) its time line, the length for an illness to run its course; (d) consequences—for example, death, pain, disability, emotional or material deprivation; and (e) its curability or controllability and whether it can be cured or effectively managed (and by whom). Illness cognitions provide the basis for understanding the particular illness self-regulation each individual engages in when afflicted or anticipating affliction.

An illness representation possesses a bilevel structure, both an abstract and concrete form. Often it is the concrete level that is the most important determinant of illness management behavior. For example, even though there are highly objective devices for measuring blood-sugar levels (abstract knowledge), many individuals with diabetes rely on subjective bodily cues (concrete information) to determine their insulin usage, even though this is less accurate (Gonder-Frederick & Cox, 1991). Meyer, Leventhal, and Gutmann (1985) observed that although 80% of hypertensive patients recognized that patients cannot accurately predict their blood pressure elevations, fully 90% subsequently assert they could tell when their blood pressure was elevated. Cues relied on were typically inaccurate manifestations of chronic elevations in diastolic pressure levels (increased heart rate or palpitations, feeling flushed, or having headache).

Other aspects of illness representations may be largely implicit or outside ordinary awareness—in other words, perceptual memories of illnesses (e.g., fragmentary childhood recollections of a family member's suffering) that are "matched" to current sensory experiences attributed to a disease process. These are what may influence momentary appraisals of health status and treatment efficacy and the experience of emotional states associated with health threats. Thus, patients in interviews may readily converse about the abstract, informational aspects of their illness but may have greater difficulty accessing their personal schemas and defensive processes associated with the concrete, emotional threat management.

The first stage of developing an illness representation involves interpretation of symptoms once recognized or perceived. Most commonly, social messages, consensual inferences concerning the significance of a symptom will govern its interpretation, although an individual's past history or idiosyncratic views may also play a role. In addition to a cognitive representation that is formed, there will be an emotional component—for example, fear, anxiety, alarm, panic—which may be an important determinant of the next stage in illness-regulation, that of threat management, or coping with the illness. Individuals must obtain information about their condition and determine how best to respond to it so that it may be alleviated. This requires analytical information processing, formation of numerous expectancies, and decision making, fundamental cognitive activities. At the same time, there is the simultaneous issue of addressing and regulating the emotions aroused by threat appraisals. Basically, this can involve approach or avoidance behaviors. Where an illness is chronic or recurring, the symptoms or illness manifestations are repeated over time. When illnesses recur, the earlier episodes of the illness may produce certain schemas or prototypical experiences and behavioral coping responses (or lack thereof) that will be reactivated.

PSYCHOSOCIAL SUPPORTS, RESOURCES, AND DISEASE

Obviously not everyone who copes poorly or who possesses characterologically related risk factors develops disease. In addition to genetic vulnerabilities to disease, stress and the negative impact of illness can be reduced by social supports. This may involve simply the availability of health care insurance, as well as a loving spouse or family to bolster morale or take care of needs–responsibilities that the patient is unable to do for him- or herself. Conversely, a lack of social support, or isolation and loneliness, and lack of resources (such as adequate funds for medications for doctor visits or follow-up) can represent ominous factors likely to undermine a positive illness outcome.

Wills and Filer Fegan (2000) noted that support has structural or quantitative aspects (the number of social contacts) and functional aspects, which relate to the quality of those supports. It is interesting that these two aspects of support are relatively independent of each other yet each are related to health variables. Specific types of support include emotional support (contact that provides the opportunity to confide, ventilate, or receive esteem-reassurance), instrumental support (material resources or actions solving practical problems—e.g., monetary, logistical assistance), informational support (advice, direction, explanation, feedback), and companionship support (sense of belonging to a family unit or reference group that provides shared contact during various activities; Wills, 1985).

Ways in which support might moderate the impact of illness include a general calming effect of being around other people, given humans' strong affilliative needs, especially when feeling threatened. A second mechanism would be the immune system, where functioning would be improved via reduction in anxiety or depression. Third, the presence of social support also may facilitate reduction of threat appraisal, leading to reductions in anxiety and depression. Fourth, support could buffer individuals from stressors, benefiting heath by promoting lower physiological reactivity. Fifth, support may reduce harmful health behaviors, such as continued smoking, drinking, or overeating. Sixth, the presence of others and material resources conversely makes healthy behaviors more likely, such as availing oneself of illness screening opportunities. Seventh, greater social support may facilitate coping by providing more models of different coping styles, advice concerning what to do, and reassurance when needed. In highlighting the importance of support, Wills and Filer Fegan (2000) noted "the effect sizes found for social support measures are sometimes comparable to effects found for medical risk factors" (p. 227).

The source of social support may be important. Family may serve best by providing emotional support, whereas the informational component best comes from medical experts (Dakof & Taylor, 1990; Rose, 1990). With cancer patients, an experimental study involving a program of group emotional support was predictive of survival time over a 10-year span (Spiegel, Bloom, Kraemer, & Gotheil, 1989). A methodologically comparable study of melanoma patients (Fawzy, Cousins, et al., 1990; Fawzy, Fawzy, et al., 1993) involving disease education and instruction in coping techniques resulted in improved immune system functioning and survival time over 6 years. Specific informational support has also been associated with increased treatment compliance and survival time (Helgeson, Cohen, Schulz, & Yasko, 1999; Richardson, Shelton, Krailo, & Levine, 1990). Hanson, Henggeler, and Burghen (1987) demonstrated that parental support enhanced adolescents' adherence to their treatment regimen and, in turn, metabolic control of their disease. An important meta-analysis of support—immune system functioning indicates a positive relationship between the two factors (Uchino, Cacioppo, & Keicolt-Glaser, 1996).

Empirical demonstrations of the benefit of support to health are abundant. Blazer (1982) in his investigation of elderly patients showed a 2.5-fold greater risk of mortality for men with low social support. Falk, Hanson, Iscacsson, and Ostergren (1992) also found that structural and functional aspects of support served to buffer job stress in their study population of males and reduced mortality rates. Rosengren, Orth-Gomer, Wendel, and Wilhelmsen (1993) also found a strong relationship between social support and subsequent mortality rate in men. This same research group found that degree of emotional support and social integration indexes were predictive of lower incident heart disease at 6 years follow-up. Recovery from illness is also enhanced by support. Williams et al. (1992) found that unmarried cardiac patients or those without a confidant had a much lower survival rate (50% versus 82%) after 9 years. A similar relationship with cardiac patients is also described by Berkman, Leo-Summers, and Horwitz (1992). Recovery or survival time for cancer has also been linked to support, defined by the presence of a marital partner (Neale, Tilley, & Vernon, 1986). Social network size also has been associated with enhanced survival following cancer (Funch & Marshall, 1983; Reynolds & Kaplan, 1990), as has social participation (Hislop et al., 1987) and social integration (Ell, Nishimoto, Mediansky, Mantell, & Hamovitch, 1992).

Support and resources in general may play a differential role depending on the disease process or illness context. They may also have a differential influence on the particular type of stress confronting the individual. This volume examines the implications of personality types as they bear on the ability to recruit or use these different aspects of social support in coping with illness.

ADHERENCE TO TREATMENT REGIMENS

If medical interventions are to be successful, long-range benefit largely depends on patient compliance–adherence with the treatment regimen. This low-tech aspect of medicine is extremely important to cost containment–health care economics. Despite this, data on long-range adherence is remarkably poor. Especially where patients feel well, there is a tendency for them to ignore health behaviors that will maintain their status, especially if it means sacrifice or inconvenience. One study (Cramer, Scheyer, & Mattson, 1990) estimated that 50% to 90% of patients with chronic illness failed to take their medications as prescribed. Even when symptomatic, such as during an asthma attack, use of vital treatments such as an inhaler is poor (Dekker, Kapein, Van der Waart, & Gill, 1992). Even for individuals given the "gift of life," heart transplantation, the rate of noncompliance increases dramatically by 2 to 3 years following surgery (Dew, Roth, Thompson, Kormos, & Griffith, 1996).

Compliance can be viewed from three different perspectives. Already discussed is the medical model, where a focus on noncompliance has been found unproductive because it views what people do not do rather than the necessary actions to facilitate adherence. This one-sided view fails to take into account possible failures of health care providers to communicate clearly to patients what is expected and to verify with appropriate follow-up that this information has been presented clearly. The second view, a behavioral perspective, emphasizes what people need to do to comply with their treatment regimen. It has been pointed out, however, that this orientation is limited in that it focuses on immediate antecedents and consequences, which during intervention are effective in eliciting high rates of compliance in contrast to posttreatment experience where previous behavior patterns reemerge. There is a lack of attention to what motivates long-range, goal directed behaviors. This is where the third view involving control theory and effectance is important (Rosen, Terry, & Leventhal, 1982). The individual as a proactive agent takes into account cognitive and motivational processes largely ignored by the medical model and behavior therapy paradigms.

An important distinction in compliance is between features of the disease and characteristics of the treatment regimen. It has been suggested that there is little relationship between aspects of disease and long-range compliance but that variation in the treatment regimen, especially complexity, is associated with different rates of compliance (e.g., a higher rate with less demanding or less complex programs). It is also clear that different compliance behaviors may depend on different processes. The relationship between the presence and absence of symptoms is an important consideration, as are the relationships between different illnesses and different symptoms. Educational factors may influence an individual's entry into the health care system but have little impact on eventual compliance. Purely behaviorist approaches view compliance or noncompliance as skill deficiencies to be remediated or new behaviors to be learned. Cognitive behavioral models covering the health belief model focus on a patient's concern about susceptibility to illness, the severity of the threat, considerations about the effectiveness, and potential harms and benefits of possible strategies.

Many investigators of treatment adherence in health care have embraced the notion of control systems and self-management, which emphasizes the relationship between personal representations of threats to one's health and those actions deemed necessary to reduce or control such dangers (Leventhal, Zimmerman, & Gutman, 1984). The particular representation of illness or health problem (e.g., the risk of serious illness stemming from poor health behaviors such as smoking or overeating) is often multidetermined from information sources such as the media, friends and family, as well as the patient and health practitioner. These in turn are further modified by patient defensive processes. The concept of effectance pertains to individuals' self-esteem convictions that they can manage to their own actions and emotions and constructively modify environmental influences (Rosen, Terry,

& Leventhal, 1982). Such individuals regard compliance or adherence as a manageable problem, whereas individuals with little effectance may feel overwhelmed by the prospects of participating in their medical care.

Communication models (Leventhal et al., 1984; Ley, 1997; 1989) examine the relationship of information provided to patient and attitude change as that may influence adherence or risk reduction. Communication involves different phases, beginning with generating the message, receiving the message, comprehending, retaining, and accepting–incorporating the message so that it is translated into action. Each phase represents potential points of intervention for the behavioral medicine practitioner. Examining these elements has led to the interesting observation that patients' noncompliance may be simply a provider failure to effectively convey a message, either at all or by giving confusing or conflicting information. How the information is assembled and the timing and order of presentation will determine how well information is received, comprehended, and recalled. For example, a threatening diagnosis may distract patients from details concerning their participation in treatment, because they may be imagining horrific scenarios of their illness while their physician is dispensing compliance instructions.

It is important to consider compliance–adherence as a process, because it involves behavior change, especially where habit and lifestyle change is involved. Behavior change involved in altering well-entrenched appetitive–addictive behavior patterns such as overeating, smoking, drinking, or overly sedentary lifestyle represents perhaps the greatest challenge for patient and practitioner alike. One of the most attractive process models of behavior change has been termed the transtheoretical stages of change model (Prochaska & DiClemente, 1984). Five stages are hypothesized: (a) precontemplation, idle or not serious consideration to change; (b) contemplation, or serious, reasoned thoughts about change; (c) preparation, or activity in anticipation of behavior change; (d) action directed at change; and (e) maintenance (of change). It is assumed that individuals more or less accomplish change by moving sequentially through the stages in order, not uncommonly moving back and forth between several stages before achieving more stable progression. Some consider that to enter a given stage assumes earlier exposure to the preceding one. An alternative view emphasizes states of change, which implies that an individual may move from any given state to any other one (Sutton, 1997). The importance of the concept is that interventions need to be matched to the particular stage an individual is in or it is less likely to be successful.

The stages of change model also specifies different interventions for change associated with the stages. These might include "consciousness raising" activities—in other words, increasing one's general knowledge about a health problem, self-evaluation about threats to one's health and what to do about it, counterconditioning measures or substitution of positive for negative health behaviors, and reinforcement or seeking someone to help maintain behavior change. Some studies have attempted to investigate stage-matched interventions against standard behavioral packages and have not demonstrated greater benefit for the former over the latter (Prochaska, DiClemente, Velicer, & Rossi, 1993; Velcier et al., 1993). Nonetheless, as a theory it provides a powerful tool for conceptualizing or analyzing where a patient may be in his or her struggle to manage an illness. For example, an acutely ill person hospitalized for a prolonged period of time may effect detoxification from alcohol and enjoy a period of abstinence that may be maintained following discharge. This state of change may not have been accompanied by contemplation, leaving the individual vulnerable to influences for relapse that might otherwise have been considered and dealt with by some prophylactic attitude or behavior change (e.g., avoiding bars and old friendships).

In the medical context the patient–physician relationship is the starting point for adherence to treatment recommendations. Ley (1989) emphasized medically recommended behaviors performed by patients were the result of satisfaction with the consultation process with the physician, patients' understanding of the information provided, and their ability to recall it. Anxiety; general knowledge of medical facts; the personal salience of the information; and message simplification, specificity, and redundancy were important determinants of information comprehension and retention.

Physician variables may influence the determination of a diagnosis, the treatment recommendations, and patient acceptance of their views. Physicians may vary greatly as to the role purely biological factors or psychosocial influences may play in explaining a symptom such as persistent fatigue (e.g., anemia, mononucleosis, or depression). Variability in the perception of an illnesses' base rate in certain populations (e.g., HIV) can influence initial medical hypotheses concerning medical work-up strategies. Physicians' stereotypical views of a patient can effect their sensitivity to the potential seriousness of a disease and whether treatment will be effective (Weinman, 1987). The congruence between physician knowledge, views, and beliefs and that of the patient is seen as an important predictor of successful consultation outcome (Pendelton, Schofield, Tate, & Havelock, 1984; Tuckett, Boultron, Olson, & Williams, 1985).

The extent of patient misunderstanding of diseases and the impact of this misunderstanding on treatment adherence is remarkable. For example, in a 1979 study Roth found that 50% of patients rated lung cancer caused by smoking as having a good prognosis, and 30% believed that hypertension could be cured rather than controlled by treatment. Even more intriguing is how some of their convictions come about. Although elevations in resting blood pressure are generally undetectable except by direct external monitoring, the physician's routine review of systems for a hypertensive patient may subtly create the impression that there are symptomatic indicators of hypertension (e.g., such as when feeling flushed, experiencing a headache or muscular tension). Meyer et al. (1985) found that over 6 months the proportion of patients who believed symptoms were reliable indicators of blood pressure changes increased from 71% to more than 90%, based on subtle inferences from the practitioners' questions about their state of health. In addition, 61% of newly diagnosed patients quit treatment after 6 months if they entertained the uncorrected belief that they could monitor their blood pressure by symptoms. Only 28% of this study's patients viewed their hypertension as chronic, compared to 40% who perceived it as an acute condition and who were much more likely to drop out of treatment.

PROTOTYPICAL MEDICAL CONDITIONS

In this section and the chapters to come, consideration will be given to the impact of certain illustrative medical diseases on the different personality disorders and, in turn, their influence on the medical and behavioral treatment of these illnesses. It is obviously impossible to consider potential behavioral medicine applications to all medical conditions, but it is hoped that the topics covered will provide practitioners with a framework for better understanding personality–illness interactions and their importance to illness management. Acute, transient, and resolvable diseases such as the flu will not be considered, because they have little persisting impact on the patient or the health care setting. Some of the conditions that are considered include the challenge of living with chronic or progressive conditions that are not potentially life-threatening—though they may shorten the life span because of secondary complications. Diabetes, chronic pain, and certain neurological conditions exemplify this type of illness. The following is a brief discussion of those exemplar conditions and the universal challenges they impose on practitioners and patients, irrespective of their personality characteristics. It is important to have a sense of the general base rate impact of illness before attempting to understand the more specific and unique influences of distinct personality types in relation to these different health problems and their management.

Somatoform, Stress-Related Conditions: Headache, Diseases of the Digestive System

Somatoform syndromes are quite similar to their medical counterparts in that there is a preoccupation with physical dysfunction or discomfort, the only difference being that there is either no medical basis or insufficient physical causation for the symptom. Somatoform disorders include somatization reactions, different symptom complaints in at least four organ systems or body areas. Hypochondriasis refers to a heightened state of anxiety over ill health that is unjustified, or anticipation of some illness, or misinterpretation of some bodily sensation or symptoms. Somatoform pain disorders can involve some organic component that is nonetheless insufficient to explain the severity of the patient's symptom complaints and distress. Typically with all these conditions, there is some benefit to the individual. This can include avoidance of responsibility or escape from condemnation or failure to meet others' expectations, or conversely, procurement of attention and nurturance. Physical symptoms also can inhibit unwanted behavior (e.g., acting on forbidden sexual impulses). They can also control others' behavior, especially expressions of anger or disapproval that are inhibited with those that are ill. Somatoform symptoms can also serve to obliquely express frustration, discharging feelings of hostility indirectly without incurring punishment. An important consideration for all therapists is that real medical conditions can coexist or develop in patients also presenting with a somatoform condition. It is thus imperative that the physical complaints be seriously considered from a medical standpoint to ensure that genuine conditions do not go undetected.

Specific stress-related conditions include headache, among the most common of ailments that is typically benign in nature. The majority of headache diagnoses are migraine, tension, or tension–migraine combinations. Chronic headaches can be a substantial source of suffering, even driving some individuals to suicide. It is a major source of work days lost (Ellertsen, 1997). Although chronic headache pain is rarely a result of a tumor, vascular disease, or other medical causes, the seriousness of these conditions always mandates careful medical work-up before any treatment is selected. Once an underlying medical condition has been ruled out, psychological–behavioral medicine treatments can be helpful. In the case of tension headaches, it is assumed that sustained muscle contraction is typically the source of pain. Electromyography-monitored-biofeedback (EMG) or progressive muscle relaxation therapy can thus be helpful. Migraine headaches are considered vascular in origin. Following sustained heightened sympathetic nervous system arousal, the rebound parasympathetic response is felt to cause painful engorgement of blood vessels. Clinicians have observed that unless intervention is successful at attenuating the sympathetic arousal phase, it is difficult to alter the course of the subsequent headache attack, except to treat it for pain and the frequently associated symptoms of nausea and vomiting. Although there has been considerable interest in "headache personalities," it has been difficult to sort out preexisting or predisposing personality characteristics from changes in one's adjustment as a result of the chronic headache pain (Ellertsen, 1992). Harper and Steger (1978) found that patient Minnesota Multiphasic Personality Inventory (MMPI; Dahlstrom, Welsh, & Dahlstrom, 1972) scale elevations were related to pain severity ratings but not actual EMG levels. Changes in MMPI profile with improvement in chronic headaches have also been reported (Ellertsen, Troland, & Klove, 1987)—in particular, diminished somatic distress, reduced tension, and increased energy and interpersonal functioning. Overall, depression, somatization, and anxiety are typical features of chronic headache syndromes, and recurring headache is a common occurrence in moderate anxiety.

Although hand temperature feedback has provided a model for migraine treatment, it is questionable whether "redirection" of blood flow from central to peripheral areas is the effective ingredient in treatment or whether increasing hand temperature is a way of monitoring generalized reduction in sympathetic arousal and normalization of autonomic lability. General relaxation techniques, EMG biofeedback, and hypnosis have all been found effective for migraine, tension, and tension–migraine conditions. Cognitive behavior therapy in combination with some form of relaxation therapy can also be powerful in identifying and modifying threats and stressors that are the precipitating factors for sympathetic arousal.

The role of stress in causing ulcers has remained somewhat controversial (Bennett & Carroll, 1997), although individual benefit from stress management approaches have been clinically observed in specific cases, especially in reducing relapse rate (Loof et al., 1987). Peptic ulcers consist of ulcerating lesions of the stomach or duodenum, experienced usually as epigastric pain several hours following meals, which is relieved by food. In a large study of more than 8,000 males, Medalie, Strange, Zyzanski, and Goldbourt (1992) found associations between duodenal ulcers and family problems, patient's internal agent of negative affect, lack of intimacy or social support, and smoking. Other prospective studies link life stress and prolongation of ulcer symptoms (Holtmann et al., 1992; Hui, Shiu, Lok, & Lam, 1992). Lower in the digestive system, an inflammation of the bowel may occur either in the form of Chron's disease or ulcerative colitis. Although early studies suggesting a relationship between psychological factors and these diseases have not been supported, evidence indicates that stress can exacerbate these conditions once they have developed (Bennett, 1997). Some intervention studies also suggest that psychologically based interventions can reduce symptom frequency and impact of the illness on adjustment (Milne, Joachim, & Niedhart, 1986; Shaw & Erlich, 1987).

Another form of digestive disease, irritable bowel syndrome, is characterized by the disturbance in large bowel functioning—in other words, diarrhea or constipation and abdominal pain. Most patients suffering from this condition do not seek medical intervention. However, irritable bowel has been associated with individual stress levels, negative life events, and reduced coping (Bennett, 1997). In turn, stress management techniques have been used to reduce symptoms (Bennett & Wilkinson, 1985).

Pain Management

Pain is a complicated, multidetermined experience consisting of a number of components, temporal (acute–chronic), categorical (neuropathic, somatic, psychogenic), and multaxial (location, body organ–system involved, etiology). Pain is one of the most common symptoms involving care seeking, accounting for more than 70 million office visits per year (National Center for Health Statistics, 1986), imposing an estimated per annum cost of about $65 billion (Bonica, 1986). It has been estimated that there may be 30 million individuals with chronic or recurring back pain and 37 million who experience arthritic pain.

The neurobiological determinants of nocioception, neural representation, and transmission of pain signals provide a basis for effective analgesic interventions. The specialist in behavior medicine in some ways is faced with greater complexity in the psychological aspects of pain. Melzack and Casey (1968) have proposed motivational–affective, cognitive–evaluative, and sensory–discriminative components as the three primary determinants of subjective pain experience or perception of nociceptive stimulation. Psychogenic perspectives have included the "pain-prone" personality (Blumer & Heilbronn, 1981; Engel, 1959), which has been critiqued by Turk and Salovey (1984), and more recently, a model proposed by Beutler, Engle, Oro'-Beutler, Daldrup, and Meredith (1986), where inability to express anger or control intense emotions is considered to predispose an individual to greater chronic pain intensified by the negative affect experienced.

Various medical conditions may produce persisting pain, chronic physical discomfort in the absence of disease progression (such as cancer). Arthritis and residual pain from injury to the back are among the most common causes, although even somewhat controversial conditions such as fibromyalgia (diffuse aching and stiffness of the muscles and connective tissues) may be represented in contemporary pain programs.

A primary distinction is made between *acute* and *chronic* pain, the latter involving persistent pain of continuous or frequent intermittent duration following resolution of the injury. In many instances, such as with back pain, there is no prospect of pain alleviation, and the patient is faced with the unpalatable prospect of "living with it." Typically, this forces an uncomfortable involvement with the medical community and places unusual demands on the individual's emotional resilience and commitment tolerance from family. A second critical distinction is between the subjective experience of pain, which is not directly observable, and its behavioral manifestations, which Fordyce (1976) termed pain behavior. This can involve verbal and nonverbal expressions of pain (vocalizations, screams, groans, grimaces) and also motor responses (restricted movement, limping, protective actions).

Although pain behavior may correspond with perceived pain initially following injury, over time pain behavior becomes governed by the responses it elicits based on operant learning—for example, sympathy and caretaking from others generated by the universally communicative effect of pain displays. Respondent learning also plays a role because aversive conditioning is obviously involved when events or activities exacerbate the pain condition, causing avoidance behavior motivated by the anxiety over anticipation of pain (Linton, 1985). Fear of pain that develops during the acute phase will generalize to the chronic state and maintain avoidance of even pleasurable activities such as sex if they once caused severe discomfort. In addition, anticipation of pain can produce muscle tension arising from anxiety-generated sympathetic nervous system activity (Flor, Birbaumer, & Turk 1990), and this can exacerbate pain in an individual predisposed to it by injury. As avoidance behavior increases, self-protective movements persist and deconditioning of muscles involved in normal movement may occur. In time, "the physical abnormalities often observed in chronic pain (such as distorted gait, decreased range of motion, muscular fatigue) may thus actually be secondary to changes initiated in behavior through learning" (Turk, 2000, p. 121).

Illness representations about pain are critical determinants of the meaning and response to pain. Pain viewed as an indicator of tissue damage will elicit more alarm, suffering, and behavioral compensation than if it is perceived as the consequence of a stable physical problem with some prospect of improvement (Spiegel & Bloom, 1983). Cognitive expectations exert powerful influence over pain and disability, often greater than the actual disease severity (Slater, Hall, Atkinson, & Garfin, 1991). Catastrophizing or alarmist negative anticipations of pain has been shown to be a strong predictor of medication use following surgery (Butler, Damarion, Beaulieu, Schwebel, & Thorn, 1989) and of pain and disability manifestations compared to disease-rated impairment (Flor & Turk, 1988). Negative appraisals of the ability to control pain is an important determinant of reductions in activity level, lowered morale, and hypersensitivity to physical sensations interpreted as pain (Turk & Rudy, 1988).

Pennebaker, Gonder-Frederick, Cox, and Hoover (1985) have noted that the memories and meanings attached to original pain experiences become stable cognitive structures that are difficult to modify. Where these convictions generate feelings of helplessness and inability to function when in pain, they must be addressed and altered if there is to be successful rehabilitation. Conversely, positive expectations, such as those that accompany high self-efficacy, benefit pain tolerance (Bandura, O'Leary, Taylor, Gauthier, & Gossard, 1987), psychological functioning, and disability level

(Lorig, Chastain, Ung, Shoor, & Holman, 1989). It has been suggested (Cioffi, 1991) that greater self-efficacy may reduce arousal level and anticipatory anxiety (thereby in fact reducing pain-producing muscular tension), that it may facilitate self-distracting techniques or even simple dismissal of pain signals during goal-directed behavior, or that it may lead to reinterpretation of the meaning of pain. When rehabilitation is successful, there is typically a greater increase in activity level, improvement in role and social functions, and sense of ability to cope with pain compared to any changes in the actual pain level itself.

Psychological interventions for chronic pain typically involve what has been termed remoralization, the introduction of hope and incentive in managing pain. Following this may be a remediation phase involving learning new ways to cope with the problem. Turk (2000) has distinguished between overt coping strategies such as rest or use of medication and self-relaxation techniques. Covert coping might involve self-distraction from pain, self-reassurance that the pain will diminish, and other problem-solving or information-seeking efforts. Given the importance of cognitive variables in pain perception and control, it is not surprising that a cognitive–behavioral model of pain control would emerge as the dominant approach. This involves careful analysis of illness representations and the coping responses associated with them, which produce either adaptive or maladaptive responses to their pain and injury.

Irrespective of the specific philosophy of an organized pain program, all view the patient role as an active and effective one in which he or she collaborates with health care professionals and gains increased control over the interfering effects of his or her discomforts. Goal-setting emphasizes management of pain with increased activity rather than pain-free expectations, so that the secondary effects of chronic pain (loss of favored activities and reinforcements) are reduced and the depressogenic effects minimized. Education concerning pain, and relationships between pain and mood state, and safe and unsafe activities increase the patient's awareness of how pain may be exacerbated or minimized. Biofeedback may be directed at the specific sites for nociceptive input or may serve to more generally influence relaxation and the psychophysiological arousal that can direct the patient's attention to pain signals and amplify them. For this reason, techniques that serve to distract (ideally activities or stimuli that are inherently rewarding or interest-generating) are frequently used. Hypnosis is a special method for focused attention or distraction from pain, which either can be eliminated or modified in terms of its subjective experience. Cognitive–behavioral strategies (Meichenbaum, 1997) are used to address dysfunctional aspects of thinking—for example, catastrophizing in anticipation of pain when trying new activities addressing the demoralizing effects of chronic pain. Specific behavioral approaches focus on the pain behavior and those things that either reinforce or extinguish it. Pain behavior can include maladaptive activity–rest cycles, pain-inducing postural states, and excessive inactivity or rest. Countering this are graded tasks that increase exercise and work tolerance, and social activities that facilitate extinction of maladaptive pain behavior and reinforcement of wellness behavior. Finally, rehabilitation will conclude with application of treatment gains to the individual's daily life and routines.

Diabetes

Of all the chronic diseases, diabetes ranks first for a lifetime of health care costs (Mokdad et al., 2000). In a national periodical (*Newsweek*, Sept. 4, 2000), it was estimated the average lifetime cost of the disease is $10,000 to $12,000 per year per individual. Retinopathy, even blindness, gangrene infection leading to amputation, renal failure, neuropathy, erectile impotence, and central nervous system compromise secondary to small blood vessel disease are among the long-term complications of diabetes. In the first year of the new millenium, the Center for Disease Control reported a 40% incidence increase of diabetes in people over 40 and, more alarmingly, a 70% rise among 30-year-olds. For the population 18 and over the increase in incidence from 1990 to 1998 was 33%, with the prevalence highly correlated with obesity (Mokdad et al., 2000).

Because blood sugar monitoring and management require the constant daily attention and commitment of the afflicted individual, the opportunities for noncompliance and the consequences are high. Many normal temptations such as sweets, cigarettes, and alcohol can exact severe costs on diabetic individuals, who must in turn learn greater restraint and self-control. For the juvenile this can represent an insurmountable obstacle, given the adolescent's need to conform to the peer group. Stress and its hormonal and metabolic effects can also greatly alter blood-sugar levels.

Behavioral medicine interventions for diabetic individuals include weight management and diet control, exercise, stress management, alcohol and smoking cessation, and general education concerning the disease process. The importance of health-promoting behaviors is critical for diabetic individuals, who may also suffer from self-esteem issues and mood disturbances secondary to the psychological demands their condition may impose, which include chronic requirements for self-discipline, denial, self-monitoring, and anticipatory behavior, burdens borne better by some personality types than others. Current tertiary treatment interventions include medication, injections of insulin, medications to increase natural insulin production or block or slow carbohydrate production. Use of these requires determination of blood glucose levels through periodic blood testing. For some, diabetes can be managed solely by dietary changes and weight control–exercise programs that naturally modulate carbohydrate intake and blood-sugar levels. Because the consequences of diabetes are not immediate, resolve is difficult to develop. Even for patients who have witnessed family members lose limbs and go blind, it is surprising that many have adopted fatalistic orientations to the long-term negative consequences, out of ignorance or to rationalize continuation of the immediate rewards of addictive–appetitive behavior patterns.

Neurological Diseases: Epilepsy, Multiple Sclerosis, Parkinson's Disease

Epilepsy is caused by a variety of conditions, inherited and acquired, and it can take many forms that are both treatable and in some cases relatively intractable (Scambler, 1997). It has been estimated that 1 in 40 people will experience two or more seizures in their life not resulting from high fever, and 1 in 200 will have chronic seizures (Duncan, 1991). The diagnosis of epilepsy itself can be devastating and have more negative impact than the condition itself (Scambler & Hopkins, 1986). The unpredictability of the attacks can be particularly demoralizing, especially when they occur in public, and the inconvenience of losing driving privileges is especially stressful. Occupational restrictions and job discrimination are an additional burden faced by these individuals. Obviously because seizure threshold is sensitive to fatigue, stress, and many chemical substances, including alcohol, these health behavior–psychosocial influences can also play a key role in precipitating episodes or ameliorating their frequency.

If epilepsy is poorly controlled, seizures can cause progressive cognitive dysfunction and personality change. Lifestyle can be severely altered by driving restriction, travel limitations, and physical exertion restriction. Some cases can be readily controlled with medication, provided the patient is compliant. The type of seizure can range from a potentially life threatening grand mal convulsion to petit mal seizures, and to complex partial seizures that may cause hallucinatory experiences or bizarre behavior episodes.

Despite medication that pharmacologically reduces the seizure threshold, stress and fatigue can alter it as well. Presumably, if the condition is well-controlled, behavioral medicine intervention is not required. Providing the seizure condition is not neurologically intractable (in extreme cases, requiring surgical intervention), increased seizure frequency can represent a need for medication adjustment, noncompliance (simply not taking the medication), or emotional–physical changes in the individual.

Multiple sclerosis is an inflammation of the central nervous system that disrupts transmission of nerve impulses, causing loss of or altered sensation, paraesthesias, ataxia, vulnerability to fatigue, visual impairment, cognitive changes, and even sexual dysfunction. It is an insidious, typically cyclical disease initially presenting with a perplexing array of symptoms difficult to diagnose. Often progressive in nature, it can fluctuate. By its very nature it can have enormous impact on all aspects of a person's individual, social, vocational, and family functioning. Depression can be a precursor or consequence of the condition. Most patients experience considerable anxiety or demoralization during and in between acute exacerbations, given the high uncertainty associated with the disease course. Demyelination in certain common sites (e.g., frontal lobes) may cause personality change including euphoria–emotional lability, impulsivity, or apathy. Numerous psychiatric organic mood disorder conditions may develop, including major depression and bipolar disorder. Bipolar disorder appears to be higher in patients with multiple sclerosis (Dupont, 1997). It is not uncommon for individuals exhibiting many of the symptoms of multiple sclerosis to be misdiagnosed with conversion hysteria or a somatoform disorder.

As would be expected, this insidious neurological condition can have profound effects on an individual's self-concept and view of the future. Therapies directed at these psychosocial issues can aid the patient in coping better with his or her condition and its vicissitudes. Family therapy can be critical in educating those around the multiple sclerosis patient on how best to adapt to his or her illness. Fluctuations in the disease course, dependency issues, lifestyle choices and changes, and marital stability can all intensify the misery of those afflicted—or, conversely, they can help to alleviate it.

Parkinson's disease is an insidious, inexorably progressive disease initially presenting with a perplexing array of symptoms difficult to diagnose. Most patients experience considerable anxiety or demoralization during and in between acute exacerbations, given the high uncertainty associated with the disease course. Like multiple sclerosis, Parkinson's disease is generally a progressive condition, although not immediately life-threatening. Its major features are tremor, slowed movement, muscular rigidity, and difficulties of initiation and execution. Its incidence is approximately 1 in 1,000, with typical onset in the 60s (Jahanshahi, 1997), although there are notable exceptions (e.g., Michael J. Fox). The rate of the disease course can be quite variable. Although not always present in its early phases, cognitive impairment may be present, especially for executive cognitive functions and working memory (Cummings, 1988). Affective flattening, in particular masked facies, is a feature of this disease. Disease-related alteration in brain monoamines may cause depression.

Depletion of striatal dopamine is the cause of the condition, and dopamine replacement therapy is the primary treatment. However, in advanced conditions high-dose treatment can produce psychotic side effects, including confusion and hallucinations. Cognitive impairment or dementia can be an associated feature of the condition (Cummings, 1988), as can be depression, which is a more common feature, affecting between 30% and 50% of those diagnosed with the disease (Cummings, 1992). Although pharmacotherapy is obviously the first line of treatment, individual counseling or family therapy can be helpful in enabling such patients to adjust to the self-image, self-esteem, and self-limiting aspects of the illness, as well as the dependency and control issues generated by the condition.

Cardiac Disease

Evidence for the role of psychological factors in the development of heart disease is mounting. Williams et al. (2000), in a study of nearly 13,000 African American males and females, linked trait high anger to a threefold increase in rate of sudden cardiac death, even after controlling for smoking, diabetes, or obesity. In a 10-year prospective study, hostility in African Americans was linked to coronary artery calcification, a precursor to atherosclerosis. Stress reduction and modification of hostile–aggressive, competitive behavior patterns can diminish the risk of recurrent myocardial infarction, as will treatment of resisting depression. In a large-scale study (Friedman et al., 1986) modifying Type A pattern and hostility, which used various interventions including lifestyle change and cognitive behavioral techniques, total cardiovascular mortality and morbidity diminished by 50%, especially for those individuals exhibiting the greatest reduction in Type A behavior.

Mental stress has been shown to be as powerful a precipitant of myocardial ischemia as overexertion. Poor coping, poor psychosocial support, and high personal stress have been linked to survival after cardiac transplant (Chacko, Harper, Gotto, & Young, 1996), and depression conferred a threefold risk of later death irrespective of heart attack severity (Frasure-Smith, Lesperance, Juneau, Talajic, & Bourassa, 1999), although social support moderated this influence (Frazure-Smith et al., 2000).

Obviously the first line of defense against heart disease is prevention. This involves altering unhealthy lifestyle habits such as smoking, unhealthy diet, excessive drinking, and overly sedentary lifestyle and detecting and controlling blood pressure, generally through medication. These are obvious interventions, readily detectable by any primary care physician, but getting the patient to comply, as noted earlier, is quite another matter.

It is not surprising, given asymptomatic patients' comparative indifference to risk factors and early prevention efforts, that behavioral "preventive" interventions are rarely introduced except after some cardiac event, where fortunately they still remain quite applicable. Although the role of psychological interventions in significantly modifying blood pressure (e.g., Johnston et al., 1993) has been subject to challenge (Shapiro, 2000), it has been linked to reduction in cholesterol (Gill, Price, & Friedman, 1985) and angina (Bundy, Carroll, Wallace, & Nagle, 1998; Gallacher, Hopkinson, Bennett, Burr, & Elwood, 1997).

The culmination of heart disease, a myocardial infarction, represents perhaps one of the most threatening and overwhelming health-related experiences an individual can have. By its nature, the sudden onset, the pain and life-threatening character can produce a high level of residual fear. As summarized by Bennett and Carroll (1997), up to 74% of patients experience persistent worry a year following their first heart attack, and 58% encounter friends or family who were protective of them not on the basis of symptom severity but rather because of their anxiety (Wiklund, Sanne, Vedin, & Wilhelmsson, 1984). While in the hospital, between 40 and 50% of heart attack patients described moderate to severe levels of anxiety. This is maintained in perhaps a third of patients 3 to 6 months after discharge, down to approximately a fifth at one-year follow-up. Depression may be present between 20 and 30% of patients, rising slightly even after the acute phase. It may confer an eightfold risk of death among males 18 months following myocardial infarction. This distress is not incidental to heart attack; measures of depression have been associated with poor psychosocial outcome. Although between 75 and 90% of postmyocardial infarction patients return to work, depression reduces this likelihood and is also associated with lower expectations of productivity. Return to sexual activities and work are considered strong indicators of recovery. By one year after heart attack, typically about 80% of patients return to their baseline level of sexual functioning (Stem, Pascale, & McLoone, 1976). Somatic complaints such as pain, fatigue, and shortness of breath were related to reductions in sexual activity, whereas anxiety and depression were not. A prominent behavioral predictor of recurrence of heart attack is resumption of smoking, up to 50% after the acute phase (Schwartz, 1987). Only about one third of patients have achieved complete cessation at one-year follow-up. In addition, maintenance of abstinence depended on the belief that smoking is detrimental to the heart. Although perhaps a majority of myocardial infarction patients attribute their attack to some life stress, it is not clear how many actively modify their psychosocial environment or lifestyle to protect against this in the future.

Psychological treatment of myocardial infarction patients or individuals with significant coronary artery disease is directed primarily at minimizing further deterioration or reversing it and attempting to resume normal life activities by working around or overcoming the interfering effects of heart disease. Some of the most common obstacles include angina, chest and left arm pain stemming from restricted blood supply to the heart muscle. Knowledge that angina may be a precursor to heart attack or stroke can be understandably threatening to patients, who may react by being overprotective. Widespread knowledge of the significance of chest pain in turn can have a debilitating effect on individuals experiencing atypical chest pain, angina-like symptoms without heart disease (Lavey & Winkle, 1984).

Although arguments have been made for aggressive psychological treatment of postmyocardial infarction patients, the time-consuming nature and expense of these approaches have discouraged their routine use. When such treatments should be offered is an important consideration. During hospitalization or shortly thereafter would intuitively seem to be the appropriate time, but often distress will appear later when the impact of the heart attack becomes more apparent as patients attempt to normalize themselves in the context of worried family members and workplace associates who may undermine early confidence about their recovery.

Cancer

As the second leading cause of death, only exceeded by heart disease, cancer exacts a unique toll in human fear and suffering. Cancers vary greatly in their prevalence and mortality. In the United States, 1.4 million people are diagnosed with cancer each year and one person dies of the disease every 90 seconds (Parker, Tong, Bolden, & Wingo, 1997). Sex differences are important; for males 32% of cancers are of the prostate, whereas for females a similar number contract breast cancer. Approximately the same number of males and females develop colonorectal cancer. It is believed that up to 85% of cancer incidence and premature death can be significantly reduced by simple behavior change (Ogden, 2000). For example, smoking has been identified as a source of 30% of all cancer deaths, not just lung but also cancer of the larynx, head, neck, esophagus, bladder, kidney, pancreas, and stomach. Recent research has related hormonal–immune systems to psychological stress (Andersen, Kiecolt-Glaser & Glaser, 1994) and behavioral factors such as poor nutrition and drug abuse to treatment outcome (Uchino et al., 1996). Prevention of cancer can also be significantly increased with diet modification, typically involving reductions in fat intake and corresponding increases in complex carbohydrates and fiber with weight reduction. In light complexioned individuals, reduction in exposure to the sun, use of the appropriate screening agents, and careful inspection of the body for suspicious growths can significantly diminish the incidence of melanoma. Careful observation of bowel habits and self-examination of the breast for suspicious lumps can promote early detection of quite treatable forms of cancer. Finally, noncompliance with cancer treatment as a result of discouragement because of side effects can also undermine survival.

Perhaps no disease engenders greater fear than this disease, which is believed to be synonymous with terminal illness. To be diagnosed with cancer implies potentially mutilating surgery, debilitating and painful chemotherapy or radiation treatments, and uncertainty about recurrence the rest of one's life. Psychologically it is a defining event signifying one's mortality and potential damnation to future suffering and painful death.

Once diagnosed, treatment is generally in the hands of experts and the patient is cast in a passive, uncertain role. The only "control" over the most unfavorable permutations of this disease is early detection, either initial or subsequent recurrence, or risk reduction in the form of avoidance of toxins—of which tobacco is the most prominent—and dietary changes to exploit cancer-enhancing or cancer-protective elements in many common foods. Cancer is probably first suspected in visits to primary care providers, and only detected in later referrals to oncologists specializing in its different forms. It is not automatic that patients immediately follow-up with such referral recommendations.

Given that early detection is critical to successful treatment, health beliefs and illness representations are significant factors for disease detection and management. Anderson, Cacioppo, and Roberts (1995) have conceptualized appraisal delay as involving delay in appreciation of the significance of symptoms first detected. This is the most important and psychologically determined interval before care-seeking, which accounted for 80% of the delay in seeking medical investigation for gynecological cancer and 60% for breast cancer. The complexity of the symptom and its similarity to more benign states is also an obvious factor influencing delays. Illness delay refers to the decision to make an appointment, and is followed by scheduling delays and treatment delay, both of which can jointly be influenced by patient behavior and also physician availability. Coping style also plays a role in that use of avoidant coping strategies have been associated with slowness to identify breast lump mass as worthy of attention (Styra, Sakinofsky, Mahoney, Colapinto, & Currie, 1993). The sheer threat of cancer identification represents a strong aversive influence to undergoing early screening (Lerman et al., 1991, 1996).

There is some evidence, however, that altering physician communication style to be more congruent with patient coping tendency may improve the interaction process (Steptoe, Sutcliff, Allen, & Coombes, 1991); a more hopeful mode of communicating also can reduce patient apprehension (Sardell & Trierweiler, 1993). Psychological interventions can alleviate the stress associated with diagnosis and treatment, as reviewed by Spiegel (1996). It appears these benefits are even detectable at the level of immune system functioning (Fawzy et al., 1990a, 1990b) and can be delivered in relatively brief time periods (Anderson, 1992).

Unlike such treatments for heart disease as bypass surgery, which can be quite successful after a brief period of significant debilitation, monitoring and behavior change, cancer treatment may require not only mutilating tissue removal but radiation therapy or chemotherapy, each of which can have harmful effects on other body organs, including the central nervous system. The protracted intervention with cancer and many side effects of treatments place additional demands for coping on the patient. The choice of cancer treatment and the risks and benefits of each is a common area where patients perhaps play a greater role in medical decision making than in other illnesses. In particular, the fear of recurrence forever remains a dread in the background of cancer survivor lives, affecting their outlook and those of other family members. Less obvious negative consequences of cancer survivorship include difficulties obtaining health and life insurance benefits and even employment discrimination. If the cancer does recur, this can be even more emotionally devastating than the impact of the initial diagnosis.

CONCLUSION

As illustrated in this chapter, researchers in behavioral medicine/health psychology have been fruitful in developing theories and demonstrating relationships between psychological factors and disease states and their treatment. It is hoped that this overview of their contributions will provide clinicians dealing with medically ill patients an expanded perspective from which to consider the stresses and challenges they and their patients face. For those patients with chronic adjustment disturbances, greater difficulty in dealing with an illness and its treatment, which may take on special meaning because of their disorder, can certainly be anticipated. The remainder of this volume will be devoted to a systematic review of the personality disorders, the phenomenology of each as it may be affected by physical illness, and the implications of these disorders for behavioral/medical treatment of physical illnesses.

2

SCHIZOID PERSONALITY

Schizoid personality disorder, categorized as a Cluster A disorder, is described by the *DSM–IV* as "a pervasive pattern of detachment from social relationships and a restricted range of expression of emotions in interpersonal setting, beginning by early adulthood and present in a variety of contexts. . . . " (American Psychiatric Association, 1994, p. 638). These symptoms must include at least four defining characteristics, which are not restricted to episodes of an Axis I condition, such as mood disorder with psychotic features, schizophrenia, pervasive developmental disorder, or the consequence of a medical condition: (a) no interest in close relationships, including being part of a family; (b) exclusive preference for solitary activities; (c) little or no interest in sexual contact; (d) anhedonia, experiences pleasure in almost no activities; (e) few or no close friends or confidants apart from immediate family; (f) indifferent to positive or negative feedback from others; and (g) emotionally cold, detached, flat in affective expression.

From the theoretical perspective adopted in this volume, the schizoid individual is most commonly recognized by his or her social aloofness, indifference, or unresponsiveness to social stimuli and by a generally apathetic adjustment. In terms of the polarity model, the schizoid patient is deficient in his or her capacity to experience either pleasure or pain, and because of this, the individual is strongly passive in his or her interactions with the world. Although not overly cathected to themselves, as in the case of the narcissistic individuals, schizoid individuals have little inherent interest in the affairs of others, especially how others might regard them.

CLINICAL DOMAIN FEATURES

Considering the clinical domains, schizoid personalities on the behavioral level in their functioning are from an expressive standpoint, lacking in spontaneity, animation, and emotionally in their interpersonal demeanor. In effect, they are flat, as schizophrenic individuals may appear, but lacking in the thought disturbance and in bizarre behavior that is evident with that condition. Their speech may be monotonic, lacking in appropriate prosody, and deficient in any appreciation of the emotional aspects of communication. They may appear aloof, disengaged, or "out of sync" with the interaction taking place around them. Their repertoire of social behavior is likely to be limited, perhaps even stereotyped to the observer. Unlike individuals with avoidant personality, they are not fearful of rejection but rather indifferent to it. Thus, if pressed socially, schizoid individuals may retreat into themselves rather than exhibit frantic efforts to escape from the social environment. Only if chronically confronted with persistent, inescapable social demands might they show decompensation into more disorganized behavior resembling that of a schizophreniform condition.

Examination of the schizoid personality type on a phenomenological level will reveal such an individual's thinking and ideation as deficient in social interests and concerns, and in that, a lack of normal coherence that would typify normal communication that is characterized by social involvement. This may give their thoughts a disconnected and vague character that others find difficult to track. Whereas avoidant individuals are often sensitive to social nuances, especially those that signify criticism or rebuff, the individual with schizoid personality may seem impervious to such considerations.

Individuals with schizoid personalities are indifferent to social stimuli, such as praise or criticism, and their disinterest in social phenomena may also make them appear in their interactions with others highly self-absorbed, even aloof or conceited. In fact, this reflects a structural deficiency, a lack of sense of self and self-awareness, an absence of introspection about their significance or impact on others, that can be mistaken for arrogance and even cruelty in instances where sympathy and emotional response would be expected in those contexts where others are suffering.

On a structural–internal level individuals with schizoid personalities have undifferentiated representations of past experiences, needs, impulses, and conflicts that characterize normal intrapsychic life. Their discussion and recall of personal experiences are often impersonal and emotionally removed. In Millon's view, individuals with schizoid personalities demonstrate unconscious activity that is quite meager and uncomplicated. On a biophysical level they are relatively untroubled by intense emotions, are unreactive to interpersonal relationships, and are difficult to arouse and activate. As such they hardly feel the impact of events and have little reason to devise complicated intrapsychic defenses and strategies. Millon has characterized the inner world of individuals with schizoid personalities as barren and demonstrated by an undifferentiated morphologic organization in which there is little active conflict or pressure to interact with the external world to meet its demands.

SCHIZOID PERSONALITY SUBTYPES

Millon (1999) further described four different schizoid subtypes to characterize the dominant prototypal features of the schizoid condition. Individuals with schizoid personalities with compulsive traits may have basic constitutional deficiencies in their ability to experience emotion. Their compulsive features may generate a monotonous routine sufficient to maintain employment and capacity to engage in formalized, uninvolved social interaction, but they will be notably lacking in emotional responsiveness or enthusiasm for virtually anything, even for those things they may profess an interest in. Another form of adjustment in the schizoid depressive traits will be characterized by the lack of energy and inertia inherent in their behavior. There may be some capacity for emotional responsiveness, however muted, but the range of activity of these individuals makes it unlikely that there will be many opportunities for affective experiences. In the individual with schizoid personality with avoidant features, social remoteness and behavior directed at avoiding social contact are the dominant features to the subtype's adjustments. The most severe prototype variant, the schizoid personality with schizotypal features, is represented by those individuals who appear to be eccentric, with idiosyncratic modes of thinking and behaving as a result of their not knowing who they are or being able to differentiate between self and other.

Perpetuating Features

As with other personality disorders, individuals with schizoid characteristics exhibit specific pathogenic behavior patterns and personality features that contribute to a self-perpetuation process wherein these characteristics maintain and intensify the individual's maladjustment. Their somewhat bland nature and unresponsiveness to the feelings and interactive nuances of others minimize the opportunities for relationships and experiences that might provide pleasures and differentiated experiences foreign to their bland existence. Their preference for self-isolation thus prevents enlivening events or corrective emotional experiences that might alter the polarity imbalance characteristic of their adjustment, especially deficiencies in the experience of pleasure and pain.

Because of the asocial nature of the individual with schizoid personality, psychological interventions are quite difficult, given that most techniques require some degree of interpersonal engagement. For example, behavioral techniques may be of limited utility given these individuals' deficiencies on the pleasure–pain dimensions. Interpersonal or intrapsychic approaches may have little effectiveness for an individual lacking in social needs or who is devoid of conflicts for which introspective tendencies have been developed. Cognitive approaches may be less threatening in that they can be applied in an impersonal fashion to provide a basis for examining beliefs and assumptions that self-isolation is preferable to social exposure, which is inherently unrewarding. Medications that increase schizoid individuals' energy levels and reduce their apathy can be helpful in enhancing their initiative for interaction, but only provided it does not expose them to experiences that would overwhelm their limited adjustment capacities with excessive stimulation.

Potentiated pairing of behaviorally oriented social skills training (in concrete situations anticipated for the patient) with cognitive–behavioral-focused discussions on interaction sequences and their impact on others, would be common treatment areas to target. In the case of the schizoid patient with depressive features, the initial thrust of treatment would be a raising of the individual's activity level, both cognitive and behavioral. This would be a necessary precondition, most likely achieved with pharmacotherapy before cognitive behavioral therapies could be applied synergistically. Individuals with schizoid personalities with prominent avoidant tendencies may initially have to be engaged in an uncritical, nonrejecting fashion, or their medical treatment may be the casualty if they withdraw from treatment to avoid the pain of interpersonal rejection.

INTERPERSONAL ASPECTS OF SCHIZOID PATIENTS IN THE HEALTH CARE SETTING

Depending on the medical context, schizoid personality characteristics may not be readily evident, unless these individuals are engaged in prolonged interaction when a condition dictates that a working relationship must be established. For routine health care visits, they may be refreshing to the primary care physician given their passive, undemanding mode of interaction and placid response to the physician's physical examination and brief verbal interaction. Routine preventive contact is likely only to be at the physician's initiative or from some instigation of a family member, because individuals with schizoid personalities will have little interest in their physical well-being under ordinary circumstances.

In addition to temporary and minimally disruptive conditions such as the flu, broken bones, or minor accidents, patients with schizoid personalities may be faced with chronic and potentially life-threatening conditions, such as multiple sclerosis, diabetes, renal failure, heart disease, emphysema, pulmonary fibrosis, or liver cirrhosis. It is in these latter instances that these personality types may become both perplexing and frustrating, because they can be difficult patients to care for, given their particular constellation of features.

For these individuals, persisting health problems that require attention can create inherent interpersonal stress by forcing unwanted interaction in the form of visits to the physician and contact with nurses and other health care providers. This patient–physician interaction can be demanding and stressful to these individuals, who have a natural aversion to social contact. This can also set in motion unintentional yet predictable scenarios difficult for the schizoid patient and his or her medical caretakers alike. Apart from trying to select the best match between intervention and individual, the health care provider conversely must exercise special care not to become exasperated with these patients, especially those with the schizoid–avoidant subtype, who may eschew interpersonal confrontation or demands.

Unless they are inherently affluent or talented enough to hold down a high paying job or one with unusual insurance benefits, most patients facing protracted illness must rely on their interpersonal connections and committed relationships to provide some form of material or moral assistance, especially during chronic, long-term illness. This may take the from of worry-easing activity such as feeding pets and watering plants while one is away for a prolonged hospital stay, active nursing care during at-home recuperation, and even fundraising for special treatments beyond the patient's resources. When specialty medical care forces relocation to obtain those services, then well-integrated programs (e.g., transplantation, cancer centers) often provide institutionally created supports in the form of groups of common sufferers, educationally oriented meetings, and the like. Other resources, such as hospital patient services departments, provide social work support to find lodging, financial aid, and transportation aid, all essential to securing needed medical care and transitions between inpatient and outpatient status.

Unlike other patients, who need and benefit from such services, social support for the schizoid patient can represent a stressor, if it comes in the form of increased social contact, that is sufficiently intense to be disruptive or anxiety-provoking to them, given their reclusive nature. As noted previously, assessment of the impact of group-oriented ancillary interventions may be important to determine if they retain their effectiveness with such individuals or might even be harmful in some way. In the latter instance, reduced social contacts may offer an alternative method for transmitting important information and "supporting" the schizoid patient's assumed lesser need for interpersonal support relative to material and instrumental assistance.

Schizoid patients' characteristics will make them difficult to involve in the treatment of their illness and health maintenance objectives. An understanding of their nature will not necessarily translate into behavior change increasing their capacity for self-management, but it can guide more realistic goal-setting for patient participation, reducing the risk they may disengage altogether from care planned on their behalf, if treatment expectations are too demanding and stressful.

Preventive Intervention, Lifestyle Choices

For all individuals, illness-preventive habit change involving smoking cessation, diet control for obesity, and abstinence from alcohol consumption can be extremely challenging tasks, difficult to achieve and maintain, especially if individuals are well or have recovered from some illness for which lifestyle change is indicated. Patients with schizoid personalities are by definition weak on the pleasure–pain polarities and are passive in their mode of action. Affective arousal, typically a motivator for change, is thus likely to be minimal, as will be any propensity for initiative to modify one's circumstances. Self-absorbed, morphologically undifferentiated, and poorly organized in their cognitive functioning, they are ill-equipped to engage in purposeful, particularly, *proactive* behavior patterns necessary to effect change in health behavior patterns.

Exasperation or pressure from the health care provider would be a natural response, given the seeming indifference of these individuals to messages that might have threat–motivating value to others. However, this is likely to be ineffective, and if it becomes intense and uncomfortable, the result may be the schizoid patient will drop out of contact, at least until the next emergency. If there is a significant other or family member involved, this may be the best medium of influence.

Stages of Change

From the perspective of the transtheoretical change model (Prochaska & DiClemente, 1982, 1984), the schizoid patient would be likely arrested at a precognitive level. Only if there were some immediate and concrete influence would alteration of a behavior pattern be likely, such as if there was some active disease process in effect suppressing the appetitive behavior pattern by "punishing" any consumatory behavior (e.g., exacerbation of pain from pancreatitis caused by continued drinking). Otherwise, the implications of messages from health care providers to adopt healthy behavior patterns would not enter their realm of concerns or preoccupations, which are minimal given their impoverished inner world. Certainly, schizoid patients' capacity for contemplative thought concerning long-range health issues would be deficient because of their undifferentiated morphological organization. This would leave them lacking in the capacity to develop realistic behavioral intentions, the precursor to action. For the health care provider, it would then be important to recognize these limitations in such individuals and that it would be unrealistic to expect them to be able to accomplish much at these levels, without active assistance from an "altar ego."

These patients would be also ill-equipped, given their inherently passive orientation to adaptive demands confronting them, to the later stages of preparation for change. The practitioner most likely will need to take over and negotiate with the patient a manageable set of intentions before and during the action phase. This stage will likewise require outside orchestration given the schizoid patient's passive, internally preoccupied mode of functioning that would make implementation and execution of a plan and persistent, goal-oriented behavior improbable.

These considerations would also apply to maintaining change, the final stage. Schizoid patients will be deficient in their capacity to generate a determination to act for change and in their probable skill to produce the behavior change itself. In those instances where personality factors are ignored, these individuals are at risk for pejoratively being labeled as "uncooperative," "noncompliant," "resistant," or "in denial," characterizations that in fact simply reflect a lack of appreciation of such patients' personological deficiencies.

Utility of Preventive Interventions

Many "package" primary prevention intervention programs have been developed for a variety of health-risk reduction. Most are well-thought out and implemented, and rely on social normative influences to generate and maintain change. However, they require a participant who can at least become interested and motivated to participate in the risk-reduction actions outlined. If they were to participate in behavior modification programs for smoking cessation and diet modification, or even AA-oriented groups for alcohol sobriety, schizoid patients would be stressed and distracted by the intensity of the social exposure. This would diminish their limited motivation to absorb and incorporate the otherwise helpful techniques to effect behavior change or positive influences of peer group influences. Individuals with schizoid personalities may require a personalized approach involving considerable work establishing a comfortable relationship with the primary health care provider or his or her representative (e.g., a trained, empathic, and patient nurse), who can assess the patient's capacity to process and follow even simplified, concrete medical directives. The intervention should exploit existing behavior patterns of these patients or be made a highly redundant activity requiring minimal forethought. If at all possible, an involved outsider (e.g., family member) should be available to perform the monitoring, reminding, and directing functions that may be lacking in these patients. Although these suggestions are universally applicable and effective with any type of patient, with the schizoid individual they may be the only realistic means of achieving some degree of risk reduction.

Secondary and Tertiary Care of Acute and Chronic Illness

Once a condition is diagnosed and requires treatment, health care consists of secondary or tertiary care. Help-seeking is the first step in patients getting attention for a particular symptom, and the earlier it occurs, presumably the more likely is a cure for many conditions, such as cancer, coronary artery disease, and the like. Unless schizoid patients are aware of some disease susceptibility by virtue of family history or occupational risk or is under stress and experiencing psychosomatic symptoms, they would be less likely to be in tune with symptoms and their health and respond to any disturbance by seeking early intervention. By virtue of their idiosyncratic thinking, they may interpret their symptoms in an unusual fashion that permits them to maintain their aloof, detached orientation to most things. Accordingly, their illness representations may require careful examination. It may be erroneous to assume they in fact are aware of certain "obvious" behavior–disease relationships. Leventhal et al. (1984) have emphasized that structural comprehension is knowledge in which the abstract aspects of the disease are carefully interconnected to concrete events experienced by the patient, such that appropriate patient responses may occur. In the case of schizoid individuals, their inner world may be so amorphous and poorly connected to outside events that ordinary communications concerning symptom disease issues will be lost on them.

Being socially isolated, they are also deprived of the interactive, educative process that takes place discussing health, symptoms, and illness concerns with peers and others. Whether social contacts model or stimulate effective or erroneous thinking about disease, their input nonetheless is a stimulus to cognitive activity about an illness. Appropriate practitioner understanding of the limitations of schizoid patients in this regard may lead to a different strategy or form of communication, more at the level these patients can appreciate. Where external monitoring of important body function changes (e.g., blood pressure, temperature) is critical to some intervention taking place, this may have to be overemphasized and repetitively concretized, concurrent with repetitive messages concerning symptom–disease relationships, to heighten awareness and sensitivity that may be lacking.

While accomplishing this initial objective, specific actions to be taken when some signal event occurs can be taught. Given that the schizoid patient also has a limited capacity to be engaged with external details, the practitioner would also be wise to develop a hierarchy or a list of priorities in the way of disease knowledge facts, to ensure the most important issues to the treatment regimen are learned and incorporated into the patient's part of the treatment plan. Common-sense assumptions based on normal judgment and concerns cannot be assumed, given these patients' tendencies to idiosyncratic, distracted modes of thought. Whereas individuals without schizoid personality characteristics may naturally make attributions concerning specific symptoms to give meaning to the disease process afflicting them, a poorly integrated schizoid patient may not even be engaging in such activity.

Coping With Illness

In assessing the coping style of an individual with schizoid personality, the practitioner should first evaluate what internal or external demands or stresses there are for the particular patient that either tax or exceed his or her adjustment capacities. A low-functioning schizoid patient who has few responsibilities (e.g., a janitor with no dependents and few expenses) has less need for adaptive skills than a single parent of several children with a mortgage and job to maintain. Problem-focused coping may thus be limited. The schizoid individual's emotional flatness and indifference to debilitating conditions may generate less emotional distress in coping with distressing affects and conflicts. At the same time, such a patient is unlikely to develop much of a sense of efficacy, because there has been little need for mastery and also his or her sense of self is less well-developed.

When schizoid patients are faced with an acute, debilitating, but time-limited illness, deficiencies in their coping capacity may have relatively little impact on management and resolution of the illness. However, if faced with a chronic serious illness, life-threatening or not, then a greater capacity for coping and sense of self-efficacy may play an important role in long-term illness management and preservation of patient health. For the practitioner, this may mean considerable investment in developing in these patients an awareness of emotions and practical problems associated with fluctuations in health. Problem-focused coping should be emphasized as emotion-coping could be threatening or more difficult to address. They will need to be taught skills to deal with those problems in a way that will generalize to future illness-related health crises when they arise. Although the schizoid patient may be less affected than others by changes in his or her physician given indifference to relationship issues, continuity in the management strategy and understanding of the patient characteristic will be important.

Medical Compliance

Schizoid patients by their nature are ill-equipped to deal with demanding treatment regimens, hastily conveyed compliance instructions, and the responsibility for self-monitoring and changing their habits, especially without supervision. Because they are not interactive, simple lack of comprehension may escape notice by well-intended care providers until an acute medical crisis reveals some basic misunderstanding that could have been prevented easily. These patients are also less likely to be aware of or convey potentially important symptom complaint information to their care providers that might indicate a need for some modification in their treatment regimen. Difficult to detect compliance errors of omission may be prominent in this population, rather than more noticeable noncompliance excesses or errors of commission.

In dealing with schizoid patients, assessment of their understanding of their condition and how it should be treated is the first step in fostering compliance. Expanding on this knowledge, verifying adequate understanding, and tying it to as simple a treatment regimen as can be designed (e.g., closely tied to natural routines) is the next step. Follow-up monitoring of compliance efforts will be essential to long-term maintenance, including strategically used "booster" education and treatment reinforcement sessions, both of which are necessary to promote long-term treatment adherence. This should include careful debriefing to identify misunderstandings or other external barriers. Whenever possible, involvement of family or significant others to participate in treatment supervision is desirable.

IMPACT OF DISEASE STATES ON THE SCHIZOID PATIENT

Accurate diagnosis of an illness and its effective treatment requires some degree of self-awareness and ability to communicate, typically limitations of the schizoid personality. The manner and degree to which this personality type may impact on the exemplar illnesses selected for review will now be considered.

Somatoform, Stress-Related Conditions: Headache, Diseases of the Digestive System

Somatoform disorders, although comparatively infrequent in schizoid personalities, may take the form of fatigability, weariness, or exhaustion that in fact reflects the absence of positive, pleasurable experiences in the lives of these individuals. Their feelings of emptiness may give rise to a vague malaise represented by shifting somatic complaints that at some level may serve to reassure them of their corporeal existence, despite their ill-defined sense of self.

Effective behavioral medicine treatment of all of these conditions have in common a requirement that patients be motivated to practice relaxation exercises, acquire self-monitoring abilities, and learn to generalize stress reduction to real-life situations. It seems doubtful that the schizoid patient has the requisite level of intrinsic motivation, self-discipline, and capacity for differentiating subtle nuances in personal body state changes and situational stress-producing influences given the basic deficiencies in self-awareness and connectedness with the external world of this personality type. To the extent that there are personological limitations of this kind, then the procedures may be correspondingly limited in benefit. The challenge for the clinician in these instances will be adequately concretizing a patient's treatment experiences so they can be linked with long-standing routines and are perceived as meaningful and beneficial from the schizoid individual's unique or idiosyncratic perspective.

Pain Management

Given that chronic pain has complex psychobiological determinants, the physician assessing the schizoid patient presenting with chronic pain may be faced with a difficult task in eliciting information about the experiential, psychological impact on the individual. Such feedback will be crucial in guiding the health care team concerning the effectiveness of the different multidisciplinary interventions that make up effective treatment for this multifaceted condition.

Education concerning the difference between acute pain, which signals tissue damage and danger to the organism, and chronic pain, which does not represent further injury, the danger of deconditioning and long-term analgesic use may have to be concretely personalized and reiterated in various contexts to ensure structural communication of these fundamental messages. The schizoid personality's passive, self-absorbed orientation would also seem poorly suited to the group- and milieu-based treatment programs that may produce added social stress to their physical misery. Poor self-awareness may hinder training in self-management pain control, use of distraction techniques, and self-monitoring of activity levels and pain experience over time. This is not to argue that schizoid personalities should not be considered for chronic pain treatment, but that there may need to be assessment of their capacity to participate in intense, socially based programs and reasonable goal setting. Mistaking characterologically determined deficiencies in readily acquiring effective self-management pain control techniques as poor motivation or noncompliance would be unfair to those suffering and in need of help. Use of an individualized approach involving more one-to-one interaction rather than group management could produce modest gains in reducing medication use and increasing functional activity levels.

Schizoid patients, because they are affectively bland, may be perceived as depressed when their flat affect is mistaken for dysphoria. Neurovegetative manifestations of depression may be difficult to distinguish, given the natural effect of pain in disrupting sleep and appetite, which may also be altered by medications given to alleviate discomfort. Some schizoid personalities, particularly those of limited native endowment, may, in addition to their limited capacity for emotional response, be deficient in their capacity to recognize subtle variations in feeling states, particularly anxiety or tension, that may be important to pain exacerbation and that might be alleviated by strategically timed relaxation exercises. They may also require extra help in understanding relationships between pain and mood states and pain and activity levels, especially when there may be delayed effects between the physical discomfort and these precursor events.

Assessment of the schizoid patient's capacity for self-visualization in relaxation exercises may be important, and some training or sensitization in interoceptive awareness could be necessary for these individuals to gain benefit from these techniques. The selection of a preferential technique—for example, fantasy imagery, autogenic self-instruction, or progressive muscle relaxation may have to be more closely supervised as well. Likewise, their perception of the effectiveness of pain medications, their appreciation of habituation–addiction issues, requires self-awareness that may have to be developed in these individuals, who may entertain private and idiosyncratic attributions to different treatment interventions.

Many successful operant pain programs rely on social reinforcement from staff to change pain behavior and motivate increased activity levels. The belief that interpersonal attention is a "reinforcer" may represent an erroneous assumption for certain personality types, the schizoid personality in particular. Awareness of the pain patient's premorbid coping style may reveal that they have *always* been self-isolating and absorbed, whereas in other patients such behavior patterns would represent the effect of chronic pain on their adjustment and thus constitute a target for improvement. In the case of the schizoid pain patient, escape from social contexts to isolation and private contemplation following participation in difficult reconditioning physical therapy exercises might represent the most effective reward for changed pain behavior.

Outpatient treatment that involves multiple appointments, organization–coordination of care based on multiple social contacts, and phone call interaction with different individuals may expose social skills deficiencies in schizoid pain patients. They in turn may be typed as unmotivated or noncompliant when they are in fact "incompetent" yet earnest in their hope for pain relief. In these instances, involvement of a family member or significant other, or designated member of the health care team, if there is one, in the role of a clinical coordinator and interpreter of the nuances of the health care system may offer some hope of at least partial treatment successes. As with other conditions requiring long-term adaptation and lifestyle change, the schizoid personality's passivity and social unresponsiveness may also be experienced at the least as unrewarding to work with for professionals in helping roles. For families, there may be covert anger and resentment over all the collateral adjustments and sacrifices they may have to make, while simultaneously providing the initiative that these patients may lack. Especially in these instances, it will be important for the care providers to recognize one another and particularly those helpers in the schizoid patient's presumably limited social support network for their efforts.

Diabetes

In many medical settings, once diabetes is identified, the patient is given cursory recommendations or reading materials and is perhaps shunted off to some education program. Schizoid personalities as a group would be more likely not to attend such activities (because group exposure or social commitments would be aversive), or they would incorporate and use the information imparted in this fashion less effectively. Such patients then could be identified as noncompliers who show poor blood glucose regulation on routine follow-up visits or who require recurring hospitalizations for diabetic crises.

Because diabetes represents a life-long struggle for patients, initial diagnosis and treatment require many fundamental adjustments. From the stages of change perspective, schizoid patients' undifferentiated inner world make it likely that there has been little or no precontemplation and that they may require assistance with any contemplative activity necessary to the planning stage for concrete action. Schizoid patients initially may be noncommittal or minimally communicative with strangers, but early in the illness idiosyncratic illness representations may develop, especially if disruptive social anxiety is present. Any distorted thinking needs to be identified and addressed, along with any deficiencies in health care beliefs that need to be engendered. If the schizoid patient's capacity to engage in this completion process is deficient, then involvement of some family member in this phase may be strategic, because they can help model this process or at least perform it for those patients who cannot do it for themselves. Likewise, their presence in the planning phase may be crucial, because details for medical treatment and maintenance are introduced at this time. Information to be imparted will include the nature of symptoms that signal blood glucose imbalance, the measures necessary to correct for this, and how they are to be implemented with specific treatments (e.g., injections, oral medications, dietary actions such as eating a particular food).

The schizoid patient's capacity to participate in these first three stages should give the clinician a sense of his or her ability to take responsibility for the action and maintenance phases of treatment, which is where the real work for the patient takes place. Success in the previous stages can provide motivational and behavioral foundations that can sustain the difficult behavior change; difficulties can alert the practitioner to potential problems that may occur in these later stages. In general, given the makeup of schizoid personalities, their detached, self-absorbed nature may make it difficult to engage them in treatment and keep them involved in learning and change processes.

Neurological Diseases: Epilepsy, Multiple Sclerosis, Parkinson's Disease

With the schizoid personality suffering from epilepsy, the most likely problem area would be awareness-related problems, medication compliance, and self-monitoring for situationally induced emotional tension and physical fatigue. Instruction concerning negative medication side effects would be important, as well as establishment of routine follow-up visits for drug blood levels to ensure that the patient is protected from unforeseen fluctuations in seizure threshold.

With multiple sclerosis the schizoid patient's cognitive impairments associated with the sensory and motor symptoms may differentially impact his or her limited capacity to deal with external stressors. Neuropsychological assessment may be important to evaluate for these deficits, so they are not confused with the schizoid personality's "normal" amorphous presentation.

In the instance of Parkinson's disease, it might be assumed that individuals with poorly differentiated psychiatric makeup, as in the schizoid disorders, might manifest some difficulty with their thinking that is a result of their personality-related idiosyncratic thinking rather than a feature of their neurological condition. A history from family members concerning the premorbid adjustment and characteristic modes of thought may be important, especially where use of major tranquilizers may be entertained. Because attacks of bradykinesia or freezing can be potentially hazardous (e.g., when driving), self-awareness and vigilance concerning timing of medication doses may be critical to effective functioning and personal safety. Patients who are comparatively disengaged concerning their illness may be at greater risk for dose-related neurological mishaps, so that they require greater watching and assistance in actively tracking their illness.

Cardiac Disease

The two main barriers to effective treatment of cardiovascular diseases are detection and compliance with medication regimens. If the schizoid patient has compulsive features, there may be a greater likelihood that compliance regimens (e.g., taking a beta blocker twice daily, even measuring blood pressure at fixed intervals) can be incorporated into their fixed, unchanging daily routines. Otherwise, their indifference to the external world and general social withdrawal may reduce their accessibility to detection–prevention campaigns or their likelihood to seek follow-up if their conditions are identified in routine well-patient visits. Some patients can be threatened or shamed into following treatment regimens through the interpersonal influence of their physician; schizoid personalities may be relatively impervious to such approaches. Regular follow-up and involvement of a family member with continuous or daily contact may provide the most reliable means of addressing these characteristics.

Behaviorally oriented intervention packages that rely on group influence may be inherently aversive to the schizoid patient, for whom more frequent personal contact with his or her primary care provider or allied health professional may be more effective. In particular, involvement of a trusted family member may be differentially important with these patients in facilitating and maintaining any change.

During the illness–crisis phase (e.g., when heart attack occurs or bypass surgery is needed), these patients may respond in a passive, bland fashion that initially may appear refreshingly "stoic" to the cardiologist or cardiovascular surgeon with a busy schedule, compared to more anxious, demanding types. Although these patients will attract little attention, this may be the best time to focus on their capacity to develop internalized representations and identify any idiosyncratic thinking in response to the threat they face. Because their family members may be agitated and distressed at such times, and the acute care inpatient medical environment is likely to be so busy that these patients will have ample opportunity to generate the interpersonal distance and emotional disengagement their temperament requires, at the expense of the patients' communication process with their physicians. At such critical times the presence of an interested, patient, and interpersonally gentle health care provider (nurse, psychologist, social worker) may be needed to create a communication interface between these patients and their health care team.

Because heart attack or coronary artery blockage represent attention-getting, life-threatening events confronting the patient with his or her mortality, more affect may be present at these times to potentially bind to newly developed health schemas or illness representations, to which compliance intentions and future health behavior planning might be linked. For example, this would represent a more meaningful context in which to sensitize the schizoid patient to certain important symptoms to communicate to the physician or nurse, either a side effect of medication monitored for or signal or some change in physical status, such as lower extremity swelling or shortness of breath on mild exertion, which could represent congestive heart failure.

Given that these conditions can impose significant change in one's activity level, the loss of a sense of health and vitality can cause despair and demoralization. Schizoid personalities do encounter existential-like crises in which their inner sense of emptiness and meaningless can cause anxiety or depression, and these occasions, if recognized, can represent relationship-building opportunities, where the practitioner or his or her associate (e.g., nurse) can become a more salient influence in such an individual's life. In addition, pharmacotherapy may need to be considered given the harmful influence of affective disturbance on the fragile cardiac status.

Cancer

Because education, vigilance, and self-awareness are essential to early cancer detection, it would be expected that schizoid personalities would lack these qualities as patients. Their weakness on the pleasure–pain dimension, passive orientation, and undifferentiated self would all tend to reduce the "healthy" influence of fear associated with the disease, its personal meaning to the self, and its motivating influence in the instigation and sustaining of behavior change. Once a diagnosis is made, there is often initial decision making required concerning various treatment options. Schizoid personalities' poorly differentiated psychic structures and their passive, disengaged approach may represent a source of frustration to the earnest practitioner intent on extracting the most informed choice from these patients, who may seem unaware or seemingly disinterested in the serious consequences of this decision-making process.

To the extent that active participation in treatment and monitoring of health care management can also reduce inadvertent treatment errors in all patients, the schizoid patient's passivity and lack of assertive skills place them at somewhat greater risk of unintended mishaps. Grief or a sense of loss is a common response following diagnosis of cancer, but again the schizoid personality's makeup may produce a muted reaction. Even though these individuals present as affectively bland, anxiety, depression, and hopelessness may be common features of these cancer patients, as they are with other personality types. Recognizing these conditions in emotionally flat and constricted individuals may require more sensitivity and relationship building for the medically oriented practitioner, who otherwise might treat the absence of visible distress as commendable stoicism.

As treatment proceeds, a lack of understanding of the side effects of cancer-fighting drugs and special combination treatments increases the likelihood of unintentional or intentional patient modification of the treatment regimen and consequent reduction of its effectiveness. Symptom monitoring and reporting may be essential to regulating medications, and it cannot be assumed that all patients will communicate important complaint information in support of this process. The schizoid patient's characteristics would make him or her less likely to report such details, if such an individual were even to recognize any.

Although a schizoid personality's detached nature may potentially diminish the impact of many aspects of the treatment process, which must be then checked for or bolstered, other behavioral medicine interventions may need to be considered for their utility or benefit on a case-by-case basis. For example, cancer support groups could prove stressful to an individual who might find those environments too interpersonally intense. Extensive emotion-awareness exploration assumes there is affect bottled up rather than missing, and concern about enhancing self-confidence in individuals who are disengaged with themselves may represent misplaced effort.

CONCLUSION

A lack of interpersonal skills and minimal interest in relationships will characterize patients with schizoid personalities. Their minimal social contacts and poor differentiation of experience, combined with the inability to efficiently integrate relationship events into a coherent personal history, will contribute to the predicted deficiencies in health behavior observed in Figure 2.1. Coping with health threats will be unfocused and ineffective, and the social isolation of these individuals will promote a low likelihood of early disease detection or proactive help-seeking even when conditions are identified. Disease diagnosis and management of existing conditions will probably be delayed. Illness representations will tend to be idiosyncratic, contributing to inconsistent adherence to proposed treatment regimens, although lack of understanding or disinterest will not be active or interpersonally based. Schizoid patients' self-isolating behavior will keep relationships distant and only vaguely interconnected unless there is a committed interested party (e.g., family member) to counter these effects, especially where illness requires active interaction between patient and provider. Whatever secondary gain behavior may occur would likely involve negative reinforcement—in other words, avoidance behavior to reduce aversive social

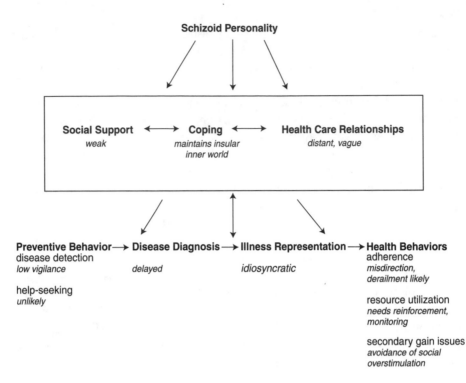

Figure 2.1. Schizoid personality.

involvements—if even well-intended as interventions. Knowledge of the characteristics of these patients will aid health providers in selecting appropriate resources and matching suitable interventions in their care management, but continued effort to maintain a comfortable engagement with these individuals will be necessary to keep them from drifting away from the care setting.

3

PARANOID PERSONALITY

The *DSM–IV* (American Psychiatric Association, 1994) describes the paranoid personality disorder, a Cluster A disturbance, as a "pervasive distrust in suspiciousness of others such that their motives are interpreted as malevolent, beginning by early adulthood and present a variety of contexts" (p. 634) These would include (a) unjustified suspicions of being harmed, exploited, or deceived; (b) unwarranted doubts concerning the loyalty and fidelity of friends or trusted associates; (c) unwillingness to confide in others because of fear that disclosures will be used against them; (d) perceived threats and derogation in innocuous events or communications; (e) a grudging, unforgiving orientation toward perceived attacks and injuries; (f) misperception of attacks on reputation to which there is a hostile, counter-attacking response; and (g) unjustified doubts–suspicions about one's partner's sexual fidelity. In addition, these symptoms must not be confined only to episodes of a psychotic–schizophrenic mood disorder.

The individual with paranoid personality is preoccupied with matters of adequacy, power, and prestige. They experience a general and unjustified suspiciousness, hypersensitivity to hostility and deception, and a self-isolating, constricted emotional life. The success of others relative to paranoid individuals' efforts is attributed not to the greater ability of competitors but rather malevolent forces preventing them from similar success. These rigid schemas are tightly maintained. Paranoid individuals will select isolated experience as "data" supportive of their convictions, discarding contradictory events or experiences. Their extensive use of projection of feelings of envy, resentment, and anger maintains their views of others as harboring ill-will toward them.

Paranoid personalities also tend to view themselves as superior to others and are often aggrieved about the efforts of conspiracies and enemies that deny them due recognition. With their considerable social isolation there is little opportunity for challenge of their inflated self-esteem or grandiose fantasies. They are among the most rigid of the disorders given their inflexible, extremely limited capacities for coping. Because their frame of reference is so centered around their unrealistically heightened self-regard, their social perceptions are necessarily distorted to conform with their expectations and feelings.

From the evolutionary perspective of the three core polarities, Millon has characterized paranoid personalities as manifesting *blocks* between each of the polar extremes of pleasure–pain, passive–active, and self–other. These produce adaptive rigidity such that they effectively preclude functioning in a manner that would create new experiences or alternative perspectives. Although paranoid individuals can be classified in terms of the variants combined with other personality styles, all share in common a fear of dependency because of the vulnerability inherent in that state and because of their inability to trust or experience weakness or to rely on others. Any threat to their autonomy or independence, especially by anyone considered more powerful than they, would be intolerable. It is the pervasive suspiciousness and mistrust that defines the paranoid adjustment. When their inflated expectations of themselves are not borne out, as would typically be the case with individuals who do not share this personality type, there is no corrective self-reflection and modification of self-image, but rather a confirmation of assumed hostile influences. Through constricted, narrow scanning and selective perception, extensive delusional systems can develop that have an internal consistency and reality to the individual with paranoid personality that defies reasonable construals of external events. Provided there are no challenges or violations to these false realities, the paranoid individual may enjoy psychological "comfort," free of apprehension or disappointment, given that any inadequacies or failures are considered a result of external causation. This state may not last if any adaptive failures result in some deprivation or direct attack on the person's (elevated) sense of competency. At such times such individuals may act out in protest and anger, seeking retribution for perceived injuries.

CLINICAL DOMAIN FEATURES

From a functional behavioral standpoint, the individual with paranoid personality carefully guards his or her emotions and maintains a vigilant state of awareness of potential attack, hostility, and betrayal. To others these individuals may appear to be carefully scanning or fixing on external environmental features they may regard as dangerous or harmful. Their gaze reflects an intensity of focus, and their body language may convey a rigidity (as if to fend off attack) or uneasy defensive activation in anticipation of confrontation. Their interpersonal behavior may be contentious and challenging, aversive, and even threatening, reflecting their sense of mistreatment and malevolence from others, which ranges from simple instances of being overlooked to being cheated or plotted against. Their recall for wrongs and injustices is indelible, as is their capacity to construe hostility and harmfulness from what others are doing "to them." When threatened to a point at which their defenses are exceeded, they may counterattack in tirades and invectives, or worse, physical forms of protest or retaliation.

The phenomenology of paranoid personalities is characterized first by a pervasive suspiciousness, which even extends to nuclear family members, close friends, and spouses, irrespective of their history and demonstrations of fidelity and trust. Given their anticipation of betrayal, individuals with paranoid personalities will selectively perceive interpersonal nuances as confirmations that others are intending, plotting, or conspiring to bring harm against them. Reassurances may be perceived as deceptions, efforts to disarm and inhibit counterattack. Because they operate in a social vacuum and view any external influence as a threat to their autonomy, the fears and fantasies of paranoid personality individuals become their reality because they have effectively blocked off any corrective information that nonparanoid individuals rely on to accurately direct their interpersonal behavior.

A paranoid individual's self-image is typically one of superiority or omnipotence, bound to a sense of prideful independence. The converse is unthinkable and intolerable, because in the eyes of a paranoid individual, to be dependent is to be weak, reliant on others, and subject to their influence. In effect, to the individual with paranoid personality, it involves sacrificing one's sense of self, giving up all control, and leaving oneself at the mercy of others, who are assumed to be the enemy. From this perspective there is no plausible argument for the paranoid personality changing, because that would only involve giving up (one's self) and incurring disadvantage (vulnerability) without meaningful gain. Supporting this view is the elevated sense of capability that they can manage and succeed on their own and that relationships are generally of little benefit.

The internal representations of experience and object representations of paranoid personalities invariably reflect their own early history of being mistreated, dominated, and betrayed by those prototypal figures of their early life—for example, punishing or sadistic parent figures or primary caretakers. These prototypical "objects" are immutable and their influence pervasive. Their malevolent nature and untrustworthy character are projected onto all others these individuals may encounter, irrespective of the others' actions and words. No amount of contradictory decent, kind, or caring behavior can persuade the paranoid individual otherwise, given their intractable schemas concerning their basic experience and view of relationships.

Intrapsychically, the primary psychological defense mechanism used by individuals with paranoid personalities is that of projection. Their anger, covetousness, and ill-will borne of envy, frustration, and disappointment is attributed to others who are thus viewed as threatening or malicious. Through projection, their weaknesses and fallibilities are externalized to others, who are thereby diminished in their stature and capacity to do harm. By doing this they can remain "superior" over antagnoists who are to blame for any misfortune or lack of accomplishment on their part. In constructing this position, the individual with paranoid personality achieves a consistency in sustaining a sense of persecution and righteous indignation for the unfairness he or she must face. Above all, the morphological organization of the paranoid individual is predominated by an inflexibility and rigidity that effectively prevents corrective experiences that individuals with other disorders can encounter.

On a biophysical level, paranoid personalities appear to be emotionally constricted, cold, distant, and aloof, yet easily offended, temperamentally sensitive, and overreactive to minor slights. Whether predisposed biologically or as a result of early learning experiences, these individuals appear lacking in a capacity for empathy or tenderness, feeling states that are viewed by such individuals as weaknesses. A stern and unyielding disposition emphasizing discipline and control may reflect the "contained" anger and resentment experienced by the paranoid individual in his or her compensated state. Overt outbursts of hostility invariably represent a response to perceived serious threat, which may reduce apprehension over loss of control or domination or serve to repudiate or retaliate for past or current injustices.

PARANOID PERSONALITY SUBTYPES

Some commonly observed variants of the paranoid disorder include first the paranoid personality with narcissistic features. These individuals are more disturbed from a structural standpoint than the narcissistic personality. Their sense of superiority and arrogance is so excessive that they are destined to experience humiliation when reality intrudes. Management of this type of paranoid variant is likely to be especially challenging given the extreme sensitivity to injury and fragile pride inherent in this adjustment and their likely intolerance of a patient role, which implies subservience to or reliance on another, even with a professional expert. An impersonal and professional manner conveying regard and sympathy for their distress over feeling persecuted is important to gain respect of these patients, whose inner superiority will otherwise cause them to treat the provider as a subordinate rather than an expert.

Paranoid patients with sadistic traits are consumed by envy of others, a need for power, and a desire to intimidate and dominate. They are especially vindictive and ruthless in seeking revenge for perceived wrongs. The need to mistreat or abuse others is assumed to stem from early sadistic treatment of these individuals by parent figures. Although these create schemas and prototype models for how to interact, dominate, or be dominated, the counterhostility and defeats encountered by behaving in such a fashion only intensifies their withdrawal and view of the world as antagonistic. This paranoid type is unlikely to be encountered unless situational demands (e.g., legal directectives) force such contact, such as treatment for illness. This may provide some leverage where intervention strategies can emphasize the self-preserving value of adopting less tyrannical, challenging, or threatening behavior as a means of maintaining their autonomy, especially if it is in fact threatened by illness. The practitioner must be careful not to get into power struggles or convey a condemning, judgmental attitude. Rather, a task-oriented approach may be more successful in that it depersonalizes the potentially threatening relationship component of treatment. This will have to be combined with firmness and steadfastness in pursuing objectives, which may be resisted or devalued by the patient. In this fashion a superficial alliance can be established in which the therapist can teach assertive rather than aggressive behavior that may in fact reduce counterhostility from others and be perceived as a useful tool for self-preservation.

Paranoid personalities with obsessive–compulsive traits are preoccupied with rules and standards, but unlike obsessive–compulsive individuals, they are unconcerned about gaining approval of others. In willfully pursuing their agendas, they will court antagonism in their rigid application of perfectionism. Their sense of autonomy and superiority come from adhering to and insisting on compliance, failure of which justifies hostile and vindictive responses. Perceiving themselves as a cut above and more virtuous than others, they will project their vaguely appreciated, self-despised shortcomings and vulnerabilities onto others, who are in turn vilified for them. Given their compulsive features, individuals with these characteristics will be preoccupied with fears of punishment or retailiation for their hostile feelings and wishes toward others. These concerns become the basis for delusional preoccupations of persecution based on others' envy and resentment of their superiority and their insistence on a higher standard. Their compulsiveness also allows, however, for focused, effective, goal-oriented behavior in areas where their paranoid fears do not impinge. Thus, these individuals may exhibit encapsulated areas of dysfunction that may emerge only when specific issues are activated, and at other times they may be able to function with reasonable normality. A supportive, reassuring orientation may help create a climate in which their presumptive fears of persecution can be allayed, such as through a combination of behavioral desensitization and cognitive approaches, as well as medication if anxiety is too intense or ideation too psychotic. After initial intense anxieties are reduced related to delusional beliefs, their assumptions that personal shortcomings in relation to their excessively rigid standards will result in failure or humiliation can be addressed. Some vestiges of approval-seeking needs may produce accommodating responses to therapeutic strategies. However, it is likely they will be incompletely incorporated into their behavior patterns, necessitating patience and frequent reintroduction of brief, specific goals to further concretize them.

Negativistic (passive–aggressive) features combined with the paranoid organization will produce a variant characterized by a chronically vociferous, discontented, complaining, contentious style in which anger is expressed indirectly against assumed injustices and irrational resentments stemming from the individual's profound vulnerability. Exploration of the situational determinants in a focused, directed manner may be all that is feasible, addressing the irrational assumptions only insofar as they pertain to the immediate specific pressures impinging on them. If even minor behavior change is able to alleviate in part the perceived external threats, some reduction in defensiveness may occur, permitting resolution of treatment impasses and interpersonal crises with authority figures.

Finally, a paranoid pattern may be combined with avoidant traits. Predictably, this will produce a particularly withdrawal-prone individual, anxious and hypervigilant to any sign of disapproval or rejection, conflicted over competing needs for autonomy–control and acceptance–approval. These types of individuals are extraordinarily sensitized to any behavior or influence that might resemble such a threat and prone to irrational beliefs and delusions that are unlikely to be modified, given their inaccessibility to others. Such pervasive concerns may crowd out any opportunities for development of grandiose compensatory fantasies that can bring comfort to other paranoid variants during periods of withdrawal. Management strategies should emphasize positive interpersonal encounters that counter schemas of rejection and harm and promote a greater tolerance for social contact. Pharmacotherapy may be helpful in reducing the chronic high fear that may otherwise overwhelm these individuals.

Perpetuating Features

The inherent rigidity and enclosed nature of the paranoid adjustment pattern virtually ensures continuation of the core adaptation, with little hope of correction or amelioration. If anything, the condition is destined to worsen with the natural vicissitudes and challenges of life that the paranoid personality is precluded from managing effectively. Their aversion to intimacy or reliance on others guarantees that external influences and opportunities for social reality testing are effectively prevented. Determined to "go it alone," individuals with paranoid personalities have learned to reject empathy and kindness, given or received, which heightens the likelihood that others will in time distance from them and act in a restrained or guarded manner in response to such treatment. However, this will only be perceived as evidence that others harbor ill feeling toward them.

Further contributing to maintenance of the paranoid state are those occasions where these individuals vent their built up hostility, typically when their vulnerability is exposed or they are overwhelmed with a sense of envy or unfairness. Because of their private conceptions and sensitivities, the precipitants may be seemingly trivial or hidden to the outside observer, who nonetheless will be predictably taken aback or antagonized by the reaction. A sense of righteous indignation over perceived mistreatments will prime the paranoid individual to respond to anticipated threats with a combative, retaliatory orientation that far exceeds the objective nature of any provocation. Subsequent guarded or hostile, controlling behavior from others becomes increasingly more likely and more intense, further crystallizing the paranoid personality's view of a hostile world.

Finally, paranoid personalities exhibit a propensity to rewrite history to fit their narrow, inflexible construals of the world. This includes their perception of how they have been treated, are being treated, and will be treated by others. This orientation effectively prevents relationships from having any potential value except as they may serve to facilitate interpersonal control, domination, or protection. Over time, as the inherent deficiencies in this adjustment pattern interferes with gaining success and the respect of others, the paranoid personality's reworking of such failures must necessarily become more extreme and disconnected from reality. The attribution of negative personal characteristics to others makes them unattractive, even worthy of contempt. But as the world around them is devalued, this will paradoxically reduce the potency of previously identified causes of failures. In turn paranoid personalities must search for more powerful, unseen forces in play that prevent their efforts to succeed. In this way a psychotic delusional belief system can be created, increasing the likelihood of psychotic acting out or full-blown emotional decompensation.

The particular therapeutic modality for accomplishing change with the paranoid patient must take these considerations into account or court almost immediate failure. Establishing trust and confidence in the therapeutic relationship and increasing paranoid individuals' sense of competence in managing threats to their self-esteem are fundamental and critical objectives that must be considered irrespective of the particular theoretical orientation of the practitioner. Behavioral techniques, for example, cannot emphasize external contingencies, because control from outside is what paranoid personalities most fear. Emphasis on self-efficacy and effectiveness in controlling the environment will have greater appeal. Social skills training to interpret or consider interpersonal communications in a less threatening way can promote a less defensive or counterattacking response and can be helpful if the paranoid patient can come to feel that this will increase his or her effectiveness, without sacrificing his or her sense of self. Pharmacotherapy can be beneficial to address any anxiety or depression associated with defensive failures experienced by the paranoid individual. This may be especially needed to potentiate him or her taking chances in treatment by trying new behaviors. Antipsychotics of course are the last line of defense against full-blown decompensation. Given that these are external agents, they may be resisted initially in treatment, and judicious timing may be required if medications are to be accepted.

In managing all paranoid conditions, recognition that their sense of autonomy is a matter of psychological survival is the essential starting point of treatment. No matter how arrogant, intimidating, or obnoxious their presentation may be, the practitioner must retain a sense of patience combined with firmness and nonjudgmental authority to gain the respect of these individuals as preliminary to establishing a trusting relationship. Empathy must be carefully expressed to be perceived as both credible and sincere and not a message of pity conveying superiority. Confrontation of delusional systems likely will only result in greater distortion or defensive maneuvers, because they represent crucial aspects of their efforts to maintain their sense of self-esteem and autonomy. Although fundamental change in personality functioning may be unrealistic for most cases, the benefits of a less alienated and more productive life may still be attainable for many, in the hands of a skillful therapist.

INTERPERSONAL ASPECTS OF PARANOID PATIENTS IN THE HEALTH CARE SETTING

The paranoid patient to the medical practitioner would probably present as, at best, superficially polite but for the most part constricted, rather grim, and guarded interpersonally. Such patients may provide a concise and straightforward expression of symptoms, followed by questions concerning their significance, especially in relation to anything that might be "done" to them. Beyond well visits, when there is a condition to be evaluated, practitioners may find themselves confronted with questions that imply doubt about their judgment and even intentions, which bring interpersonal issues into play. Behind this behavior will be paranoid patients' suspicious orientation and assumption that, at best, others do not have their interests at heart, and at worst, others desire to bring harm to them. When their challenging, confrontive behavior elicits defensiveness, exasperation, or counter-expressions of anger, these understandable reactions only confirm those suspicions of ill will toward them.

Most practitioners, used to being idealized or held in high esteem by anxious, worried patients reliant on their skills and judgment, will take understandable offense at this behavior. Some may even sense these patients' implicit feelings of superiority, which will make their critical orientation even more aggravating. These patients of course will regard any consequent antipathy as ill will generated by envy, thereby confirming their initial mistrust. From a standpoint of polarity theory, the patient–physician encounter would be predictably threatening to these individuals because it represents an interpersonal encounter defined by a prominent role disparity in status and power. Illness creates an immediate context of vulnerability, loss of control, and dependence on others, the essence of what paranoid personalities strive to avoid at all costs.

Because of their hypervigilance, ingenuine efforts to be personable and put them at ease may only heighten these patients' suspiciousness. Even genuine expressions of interest may be rebuffed because of the paranoid individual's aversion to attachment and feelings of dependence. A formal, respectful, but distant relationship in which there is a factual, impersonal exchange of information may be the most effective interactive posture. This can be followed by an open, undefensive discussion of the diagnosis and treatment plan rationale and its pros and cons, emphasizing these patients' final authority over any medical decision making. Recognizing that they are dealing with a disturbed patient and some appreciation of the dynamics that motivates the patient's behavior and thinking can help the practitioner to maintain a professional orientation rather personalize the patient's trying manner.

The notion of psychosocial support, and the obvious implication of reliance on others, will be antithetical to true paranoid personalities, even if their illness and circumstances dictate such need. Given their self-isolating personality characteristics, it is also unlikely that they will have extensive social support in the first place. It can thus be anticipated that efforts to connect them with traditionally oriented support settings might be treated with mistrust and even frank opposition. Group-based offerings emphasizing a socioemotional approach would be especially intrusive and uncomfortable for them.

Although this aspect of the paranoid personality would seem to defeat intentions to provide needed assistance, paranoid patients' privately held sense of self-importance could lead them to regard others as instrumentalities of their needs. Supports could thus be offered as "services" or "resources" made available, to be provided in an impersonal and businesslike manner that promotes self-preservation and maintenance of autonomy while undergoing necessary treatment. This task-oriented approach would appeal to their rational side while minimizing any threatening interpersonal aspects to this ancillary medical care.

MEDICAL MANAGEMENT ISSUES

Physicians are trained to be authoritative, charged with restoring health and maintaining wellness of their patients. The mere designation of status of "patient" implies a loss of autonomy and abdication of control to some external authority, basically an intolerable state of affairs for anyone whose sense of security requires isolation and autonomy from others. The inherent conflicts thus posed by the patient–physician relationship and the aberrant behavior of these patients in response to them will permeate their overt and covert interactions with their health care providers.

Preventive Interventions, Lifestyle Choices

If it is determined that lifestyle and habit change are required to curb appetitive–addictive behaviors such as smoking, drinking, and overeating, it will be important for the paranoid patient not to experience this as an arbitrary infringement on his or her personal life and threat to autonomy. Presenting these individuals with perfunctory, authoritative medical recommendations without careful preparation and justification could stimulate paranoid patients to feel conspired against, to deny them the recognition and pleasure in life that are their due. Especially if initial communications are presented in a patronizing or condescending manner or if their initial questions or protests are rebuffed, these individuals will either become confrontative or withdraw into a guarded, defensive stance.

If their health risks are sufficient to justify forceful recommendations for drastic habit change, it may be worthwhile to invest some time familiarizing paranoid patients with these facts. Expressing interest and concern about their health can be linked to information concerning the functional impact a disease may have on limiting their capability for autonomous, independent functioning, particularly important issues for these patients. Once their attention is drawn to a potential health problem, some discussion of how this can be prevented can then be introduced, specifically the availability of programs to facilitate behavior change (where it seems needed). This approach leaves the ultimate decision making and sense of locus of control with the patient. If the patient's initial reaction is "no," it will not represent a repudiation of the practitioner as an authority figure but of considerations the patient has made at that time, subject to change on later reflection.

Suggesting a formal program to effect change also allows the patient the opportunity to insist he or she can do it on his or her own, without outside help. The prospect of group-based intervention as the other alternative, short of defiance of medical recommendations, could serve as an important mobilizing influence, if only a stimulus for these patients to begin to worry about their health.

Stages of Change

The preceding may represent activity at the contemplation stage of change, where there is some thinking that behavior, habits, and lifestyle have a bearing on future health and well-being, especially if there are significant risk factors and examples in the patient's life to draw on (e.g., an obese diabetic parent, suffering blindness, a stroke, or loss of limb, emphysema in a family member). If the paranoid patient can be brought to this stage without becoming overly suspicious and antagonistic toward the provider, this will represent a significant accomplishment. Engaging these individuals in open dialogue and patiently providing them the opportunity to question and challenge may be tedious for busy professionals, but it keeps these patients engaged and reduces the secrecy and suspicion that can fuel the development of private delusions potentially fatal to any change process.

It may be that there is some merging of the contemplation with planning phases, because mistrusting, suspicious individuals often want to ponder all the implications of possible hypothetical scenarios before committing to a course of action. The practitioner could thus find him- or herself "contemplating" with the patient all the different behavioral steps that would be the focus of attention during the planning phase, the only difference being that the patient would not be formally committed to a course of action. In effect, the patient would be investigating what will be important for entry to the action stage, while maintaining a posture of autonomy and freedom of choice. If the patient opts not to effect change at that time, a posture of respect and interest has nonetheless been established, which may later bear fruit, as the patient with paranoid personality has not been cornered into a position of defying the authority's wishes but merely postponing additional action or consideration of a matter that may not go away (e.g., health consequences).

If efforts are made to change habits and lifestyle routines, then maintenance-stage activity will at some point be undertaken. Again, an approach of information sharing (rather than patient–physician or teacher–student role relationships) may be helpful. Involving these patients as "analysts" in forecasting potential barriers to maintenance or influences of relapse can help them maintain their sense of autonomy and reduce any sense of potential vulnerability or dependency that a significant health problem can engender.

Utility, Cost–Benefit Considerations of Preventive Interventions

With paranoid patients negotiation may be necessary before they will commit to any change. They will need to feel their autonomy is secure and that what they are doing is by choice, if even dictated by health exigencies, but based on their decision rather than by imposition of an external will. Considerable effort then may be necessary to engage them in treatment. Even then care may have to be exercised that they maintain their sense of control and are not threatened interpersonally during their stressful efforts to curb impulses and acquire new habits, which may leave them feeling more vulnerable. Only if the perceived locus of control remains with them, and if there is a sense that their personal integrity is being maintained and not diminished, will there be a likelihood of success.

The cost–benefit implication of this is that initially, disproportionate effort may be involved in pretreatment activity, where there is no health benefit experienced. There is also a risk that premature, intrusive efforts to sell preventive measures would cause the paranoid patient to withdraw and develop private, irrational beliefs concerning the hidden purposes of medical intervention. This would risk their mistrust, resistance, or refusal concerning medical matters of immediate consequence in the future. Like the other patients with personality disorders, the paranoid patients will transform and "personalize" interaction with professional authorities in ways specific to their pathology. In the case of these individuals, however, their fear that others wish them harm, if sufficiently activated, may cause them to distort even objective, impersonal factual information and develop a fixed conviction that this is a guise to trick them into receiving unnecessary and even harmful medical attention. If well intended but clumsy efforts at preventive care leads to their refusing surgery or truly needed medical treatment for immediate and not future risks to their health, then the cost of such effort is far greater than prevention of some disease process in the distant future.

Secondary and Tertiary Care of Acute and Chronic Illness

The advent of a symptom, fever, pain, or dysfunction representative of an active disease process represents two threats to the paranoid personality rather than the one experienced by nonparanoid individuals. In addition to the medical condition itself and the danger it poses to all patients, for paranoid individuals there is the additional problem of being "compelled" to interact with others in a situation where they are in fact vulnerable and dependent. All of these factors represent genuine threats to their tenuous sense of autonomy. There is thus a risk that paranoid patients may delay seeking care in the earlier stages of the disease process out of anticipation of these concerns. If sufficiently threatened with pain or debilitation and if they seek help and treatment, they may also exit treatment at the earliest feasible moment, if they distort the intentions of their caretakers and nature of treatment to be harmful. A major objective of secondary–tertiary care with paranoid patients thus will be keeping them in treatment. For this reason it will be crucial to effective medical management of these individuals to regard their trust and confidence as critical ingredients in their care, because these elements may ultimately determine their participation in medical decision making and whether treatment takes place at all. Establishing trust or confidence cannot be done by a superficial display of charm; paranoid personalities are too aware of ingenuousness, which only may raise their ever-present suspicions that there is some hidden agenda.

Paranoid patients' suspicious cognitive style makes their illness representations especially prone to distortion. Whereas a depressive personality may take information concerning a disease process and form a belief that the worst possible scenario will occur in his or her case, there may still be a decent understanding of the medical details they have been provided. Individuals with paranoid personalities, however, are at risk for developing the concern or belief that the source of the information—in other words, their medical provider or others behind the scenes directing their health care—has ill intent toward them. They would thus question whether the information itself might be inaccurate to support development of some nefarious plan where unwarranted treatment is justified. If there is this degree of mistrust and doubt about basic disease information itself, this could lead to unreliable reporting of changes in the patients' condition that the physician relies on for making treatment decisions. When inaccuracies of this kind lead to worsening of their illness course, paranoid patients would see this as confirmation of a sinister plan for their demise, fueling a self-perpetuation process ending in a disastrous medical course.

The difficulty for providers is that all this can be going on outside their awareness, because paranoid patients in their more compensated, guarded state are not going to share their suspicions with the "enemy," because that would be giving away an assumed advantage. Routine caretaking behavior on the part of staff may be experienced as threatening, given these patients' discomfort with intimacy and any experience that might stimulate dependency needs and threaten their sense of autonomy. Once the health care provider or team recognizes that something is not right concerning the treatment course, considerable damage may have already occurred to the relationship (and/or the patients' medical condition) that in some instances may be insurmountable.

If paranoid patients in fact act overtly paranoid in a fashion disturbing to their providers, confronting their behavior as such will only antagonize them and strengthen their conviction that they may be in danger. Suggesting that they need to talk to a mental health practitioner at that point may have the same effect. Acknowledging their concerns (without validating them) but recognizing the distress it causes can encourage more open discussion and potential reduction of their mistrust, at least to the point that they will be able to consent to critical treatment. Maintaining an open, undefensive position, where no question or concern is too aberrant to be worthy of discussion, may offer the best strategy of remaining connected with them across illness episodes.

Coping With Illness

Physical illness represents a "threat from within," the paranoid patient's own body in effect representing the source of betrayal. However, given their propensity to project blame, these individuals may assign blame to some external source such as deliberate infection with an illness, especially if it is a communicable disease. Many assumed hereditary illnesses can be viewed as triggered by environmental events (e.g., Parkinson's disease triggered by environmental toxins deliberately administered to the patient). Even if there is an indisputably genetic cause, paranoid distortion can dismiss such explanation as part of the "conspiracy."

With paranoid personalities, their emotion-focused coping may be difficult to address given their underlying feelings of vulnerability and their fanatic need to remain separate. Dealing with this rather inaccessible aspect of their coping will most likely require formal treatment with a mental health expert, for two related reasons. One is that the feelings involved and vulnerability associated with such individuals are likely to be unrecognized and so fragile that a skilled professional will be required to assess if they can be addressed at all. Second, even if emotion-focused issues can be dealt with, it may be better to keep those separate from the medical treatment, with more impersonal information exchanges and problem-focused issues.

More important to coping with illness, however, is how the paranoid patient will regard efforts to care for his or her disease. This will be difficult for the practitioner to assess, considering that paranoid delusions are not typically shared publicly but are protected behind a veneer of guarded, superficially compensated behavior. In most instances the paranoid patient will not be identifiable until there is some outburst of anger–resentment that spills forth in frustration or some deviant belief or idea shared at a moment of decompensation. Diagnosis and treatment of physical illness may initially proceed unremarkably until some interpersonal event triggers an outburst. Typically, this will be represented by some event that is experienced as demeaning, patronizing, or undermining in some way. When this occurs a series of interpersonal events can predictably unfold that threatens to produce alienation potentially disruptive to treatment and ultimately the welfare of the patient. The paranoid individual's cold, accusatory personality and demeaning challenges can be particularly aversive and disarming, even to seasoned professionals, especially because attacks from these individuals can come quite unexpectedly, often in reaction to some event that places the professional at some disadvantage (e.g., some minor oversight in treatment). The humiliation of such assaults will stimulate in the care provider natural defensiveness or outrage, creating a climate of avoidance or covert animosity that may only confirm the paranoid individual's suspicions of underlying hostility masked by superficial role relationships. The challenge for those treating paranoid patients is not necessarily to gain their full confidence but to reduce their suspiciousness or keep any mistrust at a level that does not disrupt their care.

Medical Compliance

Compliance with his or her treatment regimen is the paranoid patient's best way for ensuring his or her maximum possible autonomy through restoration or preservation of health. This reality, however, is likely to be overshadowed by the paranoid personality's preoccupation with autonomy and aversion to any reliance on others. Paranoid personalities are beset with poorly recognized feelings of anger over past betrayals, issues that are transferred to current relationships. Paradoxically this can be especially likely with nurturing health care providers, whose behavior may produce some kindling of dependency needs so threatening to the paranoid personality. As a result of these influences, what should be a natural partnership between patient and physician for the paranoid patient becomes an adversarial relationship, often unbeknownst to the health care provider. This may become evident over time, but by then the relationship damage may be done.

If the illness is an acute one (e.g., appendicitis) with little probable need for follow-up, these dynamics will be situationally bound and likely pass with an uneventful recovery. It is with diseases with a chronic or cyclical course, requiring prolonged reliance on caretakers, that predictable difficulties will emerge. Where there is any inkling of possible paranoid processes taking place during the initial stages of diagnosis and treatment, special consideration should be given to the interaction process with these patients. Busy, brusque physicians who emanate a superiority or authority may be especially at risk for problematic relationships. Developing delusional beliefs in the health care setting can be reduced by establishing open channels of communication with the patient, which permits ready interchange of information, especially from patient to physician. Although obviously a good practice, departures from this standard are most probably the norm, which can be tolerated by nonparanoid patients, even if they may become anxious. For paranoid patients, even delays in replying to their inquiries can be alarming, signifying that something may be wrong or that some activity is going on that the physician must first hide before responding.

In the acute stages of an illness where diagnosis is underway, sharing information with the patient concerning diagnostic possibilities at a pace determined by his or her own inquiries and levels of concern will help him or her retain whatever sense of control the medical condition permits. At the least, such an individual will have a role in regulating the communication process if not his or her physical state, a sense that will be crucial to the later stages of illness management. If in a state of pain and reduced physical functioning, prompt communication concerning efforts to alleviate discomfort and restore physical functioning will reduce anxiety and such patients' sense of vulnerability. This should especially include explanation for protracted time periods where nothing seems to be happening (e.g., time required for diagnostic laboratory tests to be conducted). Careful explanation concerning the value of even innocuous medications or procedures and the cost–benefits associated with them will familiarize the paranoid patient with this process, so that when more serious procedures or treatments must be considered, they will not be construed as potentially alarming events to be regarded with suspicion or mistrust.

Interactions of this kind can be considered precontemplation activity that can facilitate accurate illness representations preparatory to introduction of requirements for behavior on the part of the patient, which initiates the contemplation stage. This stage will typically occur in acute disease states as the patient is getting better and routine aspects of care, such as administration of medication. Other requirements may involve observation for symptoms, tracking medication side effects, and obviously, keeping follow-up appointments, including those to other specialists.

Although these steps seem obvious, some explicit planning may be important. For example, if there are many medications to be taken at different times, acquiring a special pill dispenser, time alarm reminders, or calendars may be helpful. Interaction of this kind, particularly because it is innocuous and impersonal, can serve to establish a history of information exchange with individuals who typically insulate themselves from others. If these discussions are conducted in a nonpatronizing manner as information that may be helpful, they can help sensitize the patient to the arduous nature of long-term compliance. All too often these interactions take place only after there has been some lapse in self-care that potentially defines the patient as noncompliant. Better that they be regarded as inadequately prepared for the demands of self-monitoring at a time they are likely to be distracted by the difficulties of resuming normal functioning and multiple responsibilities. Preparing the patient that some lapse in self-care is natural, even inevitable during the action and maintenance phases, and that such events can be overcome by problem-solving discussion, will enable patients to constructively share their mistakes without fear of vindictive punishment. Interaction with patients with paranoid personality should thus primarily emphasize restoration of their health (i.e., their sense of control and autonomy). The more seamlessly this can be accomplished from an interactive standpoint, the greater the likelihood the practitioner can be categorized, if only guardedly, as an "ally" rather than an antagonist.

IMPACT OF DISEASE STATES ON THE PARANOID PATIENT

The demands of a medical condition requiring intervention will invariably be experienced as a threat to the fragile adaptive state of the individual with a paranoid personality structure. Dependency on others is unthinkable but an unavoidable reality when one is gravely ill. Treatment often implies acceptance of unwelcome events such as painful treatment (e.g., surgery) that increases one's vulnerability and loss of mastery. It can thus be anticipated that when in a patient role, individuals with paranoid personalities may attempt to defend their need to be autonomous at all costs, even at the expense of rational medical decision making, illness management, and their future health.

Somatoform, Stress-Related Conditions: Headaches, Diseases of the Digestive System

Because somatic conditions, especially stress-related conditions, can serve as defenses against exposure of inadequacies, care must be taken in identifying them as "nonmedical" or "stress-related" in nature. Many physicians will refer patients to behaviorists with the unhelpful pejorative that their symptom or pain "is in your head," suggesting psychogenic etiology. For paranoid patients this would completely violate their efforts to maintain a sense of superiority by attributing deficiencies to "acceptable" (medical) causes. If they act on the referral at all, it will be necessary to counter some of the negative implications of their seeking treatment. Emphasis that all symptoms are real and indeed are represented in the head where the central nervous system resides that governs all experience and perception can be a starting point. Conditions such as migraine and even panic attack may have a genetic predisposition, and honoring the symptom as a serious condition that can indeed impede normal functioning does not challenge the patient's defense against overt failure. Once these basic, defensible protections are established with the paranoid patient, then he or she can be encouraged to consider some techniques for limiting suffering, without implying that his or her condition will be completely eradicated. This, of course, represents the contemplative preparation stage for the behavioral intervention.

As with most stress-related conditions, some form of relaxation training is used. It should be recognized that even these seemingly innocuous techniques can be potentially threatening if relaxation leads to reduced vigilance and a sense of loss of control with intruding, disturbing thoughts and perceptions. Some relaxation techniques, such as progressive muscle relaxation, may be preferable (to imagery activities) because it involves greater focus and volitional control (in tensing muscles). Biofeedback also involves some greater focused attention, although it may be threatening to patients overly preoccupied with successfully meeting criteria. Where this occurs, reversing the instructional set to increase tension-based readings can counter performance anxiety and in addition demonstrate the importance of volitional (bidirectional) control to overall mastery.

Beyond managing conditioned emotional or physiological responses, gaining instrumental control over social behaviors through discussion and modeling of assertive behavior and other social skills techniques can be helpful. A neutral, analytical style of discussion of offensive or objectionable behavior and how it can be diplomatically countered (especially with more dominant individuals, such as a supervisor) can reduce feelings of vulnerability during efforts to identify stressors. Only if the patient shares emotional distress in describing the stress should there be any probing of actual feeling states, which otherwise might represent an intolerable humiliation.

Although behavioral interventions for these conditions are time-limited, with paranoid patients, whose social perceptions and skills may be severely distorted or skewed, keeping the relationship open could be highly desirable, if trust and confidence has sufficiently been established to permit such a relationship. Most psychosomatic symptoms represent a barometer of stresses going on in such individuals' lives. Emphasizing that consultation of briefer duration to address periodic flare-ups can build on the earlier interventions while promoting a sense of mastery and confidence that symptoms can be managed and recurrence need not be feared.

Pain Management

Although individuals with paranoid personalities have a fierce need to maintain a state of autonomy and self-reliance, which would seem to provide motivation for rapid rehabilitation, their guardedness can interfere with effective treatment. This will be especially likely if they are threatened by an overly caring or intimate approach, which can constrict the communication process and inhibit patient disclosures needed to gauge the success of treatment interventions such as physical therapy, conditioning to resume employment (work hardening), and administration of different pain medication combinations. Also important is the patient's sleep and activity level. If dealing with a patient who is guarded and reclusive, there may be insufficient information by which to assess his or her needs, such as supplemental use of an antidepressant or hypnotic to facilitate sleep and improved rest.

For the paranoid personality interpersonal closeness, support, and psychological exploration of feelings that typically occurs in the controlled social environments that constitute most pain treatment programs are antithetical to their adjustment efforts, which are directed at protecting a rigidly constructed, grandiose self-image compensatory for underlying feelings of vulnerability and inadequacy. Because isolation from contradictory sources of information is critical in maintaining this tenuous position, exposure to a milieu and group-based program would likely be highly threatening or overwhelming. An intact paranoid personality would resist or reject such care, but a fragile paranoid patient might decompensate into a psychotic state. Where insurance companies may be funding treatment and rehabilitation efforts following injury, and patient's disability benefits are tied to his or her cooperation, this can prove a difficult situation for these patients, whose interpersonal difficulties make them appear resistant. It thus behooves the health care provider to carefully assess the motivational *and* characterological influences operating in such instances.

Given their natural suspiciousness and mistrust, encouragement to ask questions and express doubt may help reveal the otherwise unspoken discomfort these patients will have with emotion-focused activity when the interventions are described and proposed to them. In our era of modern, packaged (and not individualized) health care, once a patient is placed in a treatment milieu, there can be subtle to overtly coercive pressure to participate, lest the program be sanctioned in some fashion for a patient's lack of involvement. If, however, the patient's vulnerabilities are recognized and a rational intervention alternative can be specified (e.g., privately journaling about illness-related experiences rather than exposing feelings in a group context), then decisions to excuse certain treatment components should be justifiable. Having the paranoid patient also participate in decision making of this kind also maintains some sense of control and a positive respect for his or her autonomy and personal needs. In addition, instituting a more impersonal problem-focused activity (e.g., how to appropriately assert oneself with dignity concerning a handicapped access issue rather than emotionally exploring "what it feels like" when barrier issues arise) may address the underlying emotion (fears of inadequacy and reliance on others) implicitly but effectively, without risking patient humiliation.

Diabetes

When diagnosed with diabetes, realistic information concerning the toll that this condition may exact (e.g., renal failure, blindness, stroke, heart disease, limb amputation) must be imparted, but it should be accompanied by emphasis on the successful measures that can be taken to counter these events, which need not be inevitable. If the paranoid patient's fierce need for autonomy can be tied to efforts to manage this insidious metabolic illness, then the provider will have accomplished a great deal when the diagnosis is first made. Because diabetes requires a lifelong struggle, the provider needs to be viewed as an ally dealing with an unfortunate condition beyond the patient and physician's control, which in most instances can be managed to permit a generally normal life with appropriate patient self-discipline. This will invariably involve dietary discretion, nonsmoking, and restricted alcohol consumption.

If obesity and smoking are habits of the paranoid patient diagnosed with diabetes, it may be worthwhile to allow some adjustment time, unless there is a compelling or imminent danger involved in delaying habit change. This may reduce the possibility of any power struggle with the practitioner, who must adopt a long-range view of illness management. To the extent possible it will be helpful to give the patient a sense of control as much as possible, so that he or she has choices and consequences to consider concerning illness management. If the patient has never been ill before, as is sometimes the case on initially discovering a blood sugar problem, then the changes involved, especially if they are overeaters, drinkers, and smokers, can truly be overwhelming. An overemphasis on disease management at this time and insistence on immediate compliance, especially from the identified purveyor of bad news, may be experienced as strong-arming the patient with paranoid personality features, who is already reeling from all the implications associated with this disease. Better to offer the information with an orientation of concern (but not intimacy) so the patient has some opportunity to absorb the bad news, which will require giving up former pleasures and subjugation to a treatment regimen. If the diagnosis (in the form of a negative message from the physician) and recommendations are too closely tied together and presented with a sense of urgency and pressure, then this may be experienced as a personalized invasion of the paranoid patient's autonomy, fatally contaminating the patient–physician relationship.

Given the hypervigilant style of individuals with paranoid personality, it is unlikely they will remain in a precontemplation stage once a threat to their well-being is identified. Because a chronic disease does represent a loss, there should be some opportunity for grieving and its stages, which can be an emotional concomitant of the contemplation phase. What may seem "denial" for paranoid patients may be projection, that the diagnosis is wrong and a trick to induce vulnerability. If the anger–protest phase seems muted, this could represent a withdrawal into a defensive, protective stance where irrational beliefs may incubate. These grief-resolving processes may be impossible to appreciate if the patient's paranoid nature is unknown to the practitioner, and even if his or her personality makeup is recognized, it may have to be inferred given their guarded nature. Unless the paranoid patient introduces any discussion bearing on these issues, he or she may be better left alone. Rather, combining the contemplation and planning phases and directing educational, information-based interaction concerning disease management will probably represent the best strategy. As soon as action can demonstrate to the patient that he or she can regain general control and manage the threat, the other concerns may diminish on their own.

If there is more than one goal, such as stopping overeating and smoking cessation, collaborative decision making should take place, where the more attainable objective is pursued first and mastery established over that behavior pattern before other change is addressed. As a lifelong condition, investment in an alliance with the patient for effective disease management is favored over a rush to effect the necessary changes at once. Some patients, in their anxiety to master their condition, may seek simultaneous pursuit of multiple objectives (dietary change and smoking cessation), and the practitioner may need to discourage what can be otherwise a frustrating, demoralizing failure experience at the onset of illness management efforts.

Neurological Diseases: Epilepsy, Multiple Schlerosis, Parkinson's Disease

Epilepsy, if not readily controlled by medication, can represent a demoralizing disease for the paranoid patient because it is unpredictable, triggered by many events, and renders the individual vulnerable and out of control during the episodes. Poorly controlled over time it can produce progressive cognitive deterioration. Epilepsy additionally reduces the paranoid individual's autonomy in a number of ways, not the least of which is restriction from driving and forced reliance on other forms of transportation. Restriction from using alcohol or other agents that can alter the seizure threshold and requirements to monitor sleep, exertion, and fatigue level may increase such individuals' sense of vulnerability and suspiciousness that there is a conspiracy to deprive them of their rightful pleasures. To be able to participate in many activities (e.g., swimming, hiking), those with epilepsy must have a knowledgeable, trusted companion, and such a companion may not be available to these individuals, given their insular social life that restricts close attachments. If such a neurological condition develops in paranoid patients, this will represent a significant blow to their self-image as entirely self-reliant, and any reduced competencies produced by the condition may invite protective distortions of reality or compensatory delusions. Treating this condition should emphasize the likelihood of control and possibility of return to some degree of normalcy, provided the paranoid patients are properly educated about the condition and are medically compliant. Identifying sources of help as "services" available to the patient can deemphasize concerns about becoming indebted to others and therefore not autonomous.

Multiple sclerosis also represents a particularly threatening condition to a paranoid patient because its course can consist of a slow, insidious decline, with some waxing and waning, but little hope of actual reversal or cure. The sensory and motor impairments can certainly reduce competency in individuals of all occupations (e.g., blurred vision impeding an attorney's reading; muscle weakness and sensory loss ending an athlete's career). Because the causes of this condition are not fully known, there may be a temptation to find external etiologies that can even be perceived as directed against the individual. The unpredictable course and variable response to treatments (especially if there are other patients to compare oneself to) can also create suspicions with the physicians caring for the condition, who might be perceived as maliciously withholding treatments or favoring others with limited resources. Unless there is family or a trusted companion to assist with activities these individuals are no longer able to perform safely (e.g., cooking, driving), their aversion to reliance on others may also place them at greater risk for accidents.

Parkinson's disease involves similar consideration as multiple sclerosis, given that it is a progressive degenerative process with considerable variation in the trajectory of decline and possible compromise of cognitive functioning. Typically afflicting elderly individuals, it can produce a desperate reliance on medication to reduce the tremors and almost paralyzing bradykinesia or "freezing" episodes. The medications in turn can induce psychotic symptoms, hardly a desirable side effect for individuals vulnerable to distorted thinking. The dependence this condition causes can also psychologically intensify the biologically induced depression that is a common accompanying feature of the illness. Any sudden onset of suspicious or delusional thinking, accusatory behavior, or reclusive withdrawal should not necessarily be treated as a psychological exacerbation of preexisting character traits, but should be investigated for organic etiology, be it continued deterioration or drug toxicity effect. Newer classes of atypical antipsychotics can reduce some of these symptoms while permitting continued use of agents to address the movement disorder.

Cardiac Disease

Once the patient is stabilized following any acute event such as heart attack, then relationship building and cardiac education is in order if heart disease is a newly identified condition. Behavior change and long-term compliance is invariably a treatment requirement of occlusive artery disease. Paranoid patients may also be subject to postmyocardial infarction or bypass depressions but may not readily disclose their feeling states, or for that matter understand them. Accordingly, the burden is on the treating physician, cardiologist, or primary care provider to remain vigilant for symptoms of affective distress, which is both treatable and also a significant risk factor for poor outcome following myocardial infarction or bypass surgery. Antihypertensive and antiarrhythmic medicines should be carefully explained to these patients, especially their side effects, some of which can be mood changes, fatigue, and the like. Information that facilitates discrimination between genuine cardiac and anxiety-based symptoms will be important to reduce uncertainty and doubt about possible cardiac events and identify treatment opportunities for emotion-based symptoms (e.g., through pharmacotherapy, relaxation training).

Cardiac rehabilitation will doubtless be necessary, but interventions with paranoid individuals should be primarily task-oriented, directed at health restoration and away from emotion-exposing experiences. Monitoring that can show progress may help motivate effort and reward participation. Except where a poor prognosis is clear, a realistic but optimistic orientation about recovery should be conveyed but tied to health behavior change and adherence to new treatment regimens. Where noncompliance may occur with negative consequences (e.g., congestive heart failure or fluid retention secondary to dietary indiscretion), the predictability and reversibility of these event sequences should be emphasized, minimizing any disparaging interpersonal attributions, to avoid authority conflicts, parent–child or dominant–submission experiences, that would intensify the paranoid patient's sense of vulnerability and then mistrust.

Cancer

Cancer can be particularly difficult for the individual with paranoid personality, whose sense of integrity and safety is built on an illusion of superiority and invulnerability, supported by separateness from others and his or her private convictions or delusions of self-reliance. Cancer challenges all of these valued features of the paranoid individual's existence. To be effectively treated, a cancer patient is wholly dependent on the expertise of multiple diagnosticians and surgeons and internists specializing in oncology. For a single condition there may be multiple treatment alternatives, for which confidence and trust in the physician presenting the options is needed. Even when the most appropriate judgment is made concerning treatment, the outcome at best remains uncertain and without guarantee of success.

Acute treatment, once the course of treatment is determined, represents an abdication of control and autonomy and subjugation to an intervention protocol that may have powerful, debilitating side effects, in some instances justifying the old adage of the treatment being worse than the disease. There are uncertainties and potentially adverse events such as discovery of metastasis, recurrence, and collateral organ damage secondary to chemotherapy. All of these circumstances invite doubt, second-guessing, recrimination, and loss of confidence in decisions made. Because of this, a collaborative orientation and open sharing of responsibility is essential to maintaining the paranoid patient's confidence— or at least minimizing mistrust. Especially if central nervous system-toxic (CNS) medications are being used, more primitive, disruptive paranoid behaviors are likely to emerge as a feature of the patient's encepathalopathy.

The particular form that heightened paranoia might take is manifold. Distraught over developing cancer in the first place, a paranoid patient may become preoccupied with the notion of deliberate exposure to carcinogens. Recrimination and second-guessing over disappointing intervention efforts can be followed by feelings of mistrust. This can lead to accusations that the practitioner was deliberately sabotaging treatment to thwart the patient's recovery or hasten his or her demise out of envy or malice or as agents for others who have malicious plans. Once these ideas take hold, they can represent a malignant influence in their own right, interfering with rational medical decision making, causing premature termination of treatment, and seeking of "alternative" unproven treatment out-of-country or through unsanctioned forms of nonmedical care available to the truly desperate.

Efforts to counter such ideation might ordinarily involve increased displays of interest and emotional support. In the instance of these patients, however, this could lead to heightened suspiciousness, given that this would be experienced as an assault on their independence and self-reliance. Rather, to the extent that they would allow, use of major tranquilizers, those effective with delusional ideation, would be clearly indicated, especially considering there is not the luxury of prolonged counseling or therapy to modify such dysfunctional ideation. Nonetheless, some form of ongoing communication should be attempted as these other measures are pursued.

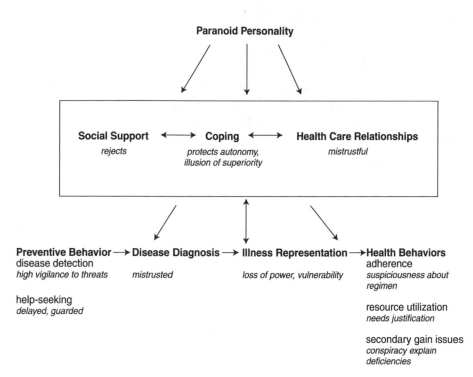

Figure 3.1. Paranoid personality.

CONCLUSION

Suspiciousness and mistrust will characterize the interpersonal orientation of the individual with paranoid personality. Except for circumscribed trusted relations, paranoid patients will likely be self-isolating and rejecting of support efforts to help, because of the unacceptability of a dependence on others. This will characterize their coping with health threats (diagrammed in Figure 3.1), which may be perceived as personal attacks to undermine their power and ascendancy. Preventive behavior will depend on whether they are sensitized to health threats, in which case vigilance will be high, although help-seeking may be delayed by their guardedness and concern that any weakness will be exploited. Diagnoses may even be mistrusted. Illness representations will be contaminated with fears, concerns about vulnerability, and loss of power and autonomy, contributing to mistrust about treatment regimens that may be challenged. Any use of health care resources will require careful justification about how this will protect or preserve rather than undermine the paranoid patient's ability to defend against threat and maintain his or her insular existence. If there is secondary gain from an illness that maintains physical symptoms, it would be that such symptoms explain why the paranoid patient has not been able to attain the lofty status accorded by their private fantasies of superiority that is envied by others. Given their guarded and secretive nature, recognition of paranoid personality characteristics in the health care setting will be difficult and may only occur after considerable conflict emerges during illness management. Use of a behavioral health care practitioner with expertise in this type of disorder may be critical to effective treatment of these individuals.

4

SCHIZOTYPAL PERSONALITY

Schizotypal personalities, the last of the Cluster A disorders, are characterized by marked social and interpersonal deficiencies, including a marked distaste and severely reduced capacity for close relationships, as well as eccentric behavior and peculiar thinking involving cognitive or perceptual distortions. These characteristics must be evident by early adulthood and manifested in five or more of the following features: (a) ideas (not delusions) of reference; (b) magical or odd thinking also expressed in deviant behavior; (c) unusual perceptual experiences, including bodily illusions; (d) odd speech and thought; (e) suspiciousness or paranoid ideation; (f) inappropriate, constricted affect; (g) odd, eccentric appearance and behavior; (h) absence of close friends except for immediate family; (i) unusually high social anxiety that does not extinguish with repeated exposure, often associated with paranoid fears. As with the other personality disorders, these characteristics must be present in the absence of an Axis I condition of schizophrenic and mood disorder.

Of all the personality pattern disorders, this is perhaps the most uncommon and most obviously "pathological" to the observer, when it can be seen in its full expression. Unusual thinking, perception, behavior, and often inappropriate affect are common features, but social impairment, a lack of interpersonal connectedness, is assumed to be at the root of much of these individuals' presentations. As with the avoidant and schizoid personality types, there is a lack of close interpersonal involvement, and with it, social knowledge that promotes good reality contact and awareness of appropriate behavior. Although resembling features of schizophrenia, the schizotypal personality represents a primitive but comparatively enduring set of personality features that do not necessarily represent a malignant, deteriorating adaptation such as in schizophrenia. There is presumably not an inherent disturbance in thinking necessarily reflecting fundamental neurocognitive abnormalities in executive cognitive function and working memory, as recently identified in the schizophrenic disorder (e.g., Green, 1996). The oddities of thought of individuals with schizotypal personality come from a loss of social contact and the corrective nature of such interactions on one's perceptions of the world as distinct from personal fantasies and interpretations of social events and their (limited) interaction experiences.

Millon's polarity model (Millon, 1999) views the schizotypal individual as lacking any basic position from which their adaptive efforts stem. On the contrary, they may easily shift or be deflected from a self or other orientation, from an active to a passive orientation, and they are weak in fundamental pleasure–pain preferences. Indeed, their oddity and vagueness derive from their lack of groundedness with a stable pattern of adaptive preferences. These weaknesses are structural in nature, whereas from a stylistic perspective, a particular schizotypal personality will gravitate toward either an avoidant or schizoid style of functioning, with the additional oddities and structural deficiencies of this condition.

Their emotional detachment and uninvolvedness contribute to significant depersonalization anxiety, a lack of a sense of coherent self, and a periodic fear of being "lost" or of disintegration of their fragile psychic structures. At extreme moments psychotic disorganization can occur in response to circumstances that confront schizotypal individuals with their fundamental deficiencies. Such episodes can be ushered in by social crises or rejections, often stemming from their inability to connect with others, and the risk that their idiosyncratic mode of thought and inability to appropriately modulate reciprocal social interaction results in their being typed and targeted for ridicule or increased alienation from the social milieu in which they are embedded, however tenuously. These experiences are likely cumulative in nature, reflecting a consistent failure at different developmental stages, to achieve certain levels of adaptation—for example, belonging to a group, dating, completing school, or seeking and holding down a job.

CLINICAL DOMAIN FEATURES

Perhaps the most striking interpersonal features of schizotypal patients are their visible eccentricities, their uncoordinated, odd interactive style reflecting little appreciation of the social and expressive nuances. Those who are more overtly expressive, in manner, speech, or dress, will stand out as different. Others who are more retiring may be less visible, particularly after having being singled out for derision or humiliation for their unusualness. The schizoid adaptation of this disorder may be less noticeable, because such individuals are more emotionally flat and uninvolved, but their speech and mannerisms when engaged may be equally peculiar to others. Reflecting their avoidant or schizoid tendencies, typically most schizotypal personalities will manifest reclusive, private behavior. This is a consequence of their inability to tolerate interpersonal closeness or to have positive social experiences. As a result, they may develop at the most peripheral social connections necessary to maintain their marginal adjustment. Their reclusive existence in turn promotes their odd private thoughts, fantasies, and magical thinking. What social accomplishments they may have attained may be short-lived (e.g., marriage, specific jobs), given their generally "vague" or negative impact on others, but also their amorphous lifestyle and lack of normal involvement in the basic pursuits of living.

Phenomenologically, schizotypal patients' mentation reflects their vague sense of self and fragmented view of the world. This naturally produces distorted perceptions and realities that impair their comprehension and empathic appreciation of relationships and social conventions. Their misinterpretations of social events may produce suspiciousness where none is warranted, or sometimes a sense of being appreciated or liked by another who may have paid limited attention to them but did not become "turned off." Because these individuals are faced with an amorphous, empty inner world, Millon (1999) has suggested that periodically they will engage in frantic efforts to experience something, to feel some coherence and sense of being real. For the most part, because of their structural defects in their self-image, schizotypal personalities generally feel chronically alienated and estranged, leaving them vulnerable to experiences of depersonalization and derealization. Their internal representation of object relations is disorganized and disconnected, consisting of unrelated, fragmented memories, need states, feelings, and impressions. Their lack of continuity in interests and strivings, and the organized experiences that come with them, give them little frame of reference by which to comprehend and catalog social experiences so they can consistently interact in an appropriate fashion.

On an intrapsychic level the schizotypal individual is particularly prone to use primitive forms of "undoing" defenses in coping with unpleasant feeling states, conflicts, or painful social experiences. In this way events that were unacceptable or intolerable are made to disappear. However effective in alleviating momentary discomforts, this mechanism only further alienates schizotypal personalities from whatever sense of history they may have about themselves and the world around them. Excessive use of undoing may intensify their sense of inner barrenness and of being lost, and contribute to severe episodes of depersonalization or derealization. It should not thus be surprising that the intrapsychic makeup of these individuals is characterized by fragmented personality structures that contribute to the disjointed thought and behavior that seems elicited by vague inner determinants rather than external social cues or well-formulated plans or intentions. Their inability to cope with ordinary interpersonal and life stresses given their deficient morphologic organization can contribute to disjointed but recurring experiences of anxiety, suspiciousness, or hostility that build up and can unpredictably burst forth, making the schizotypal patient seem even more strange or bizarre, and thus cause them to be avoided even more.

On a biophysical level, schizotypal individuals may evidence an emotionally flat and unresponsive demeanor, reflecting a phlegmatic temperament, lacking in a capacity for animated social responsiveness so important to meaningful interpersonal discourse. Alternatively, they may display avoidant features wherein they will appear socially apprehensive, uncomfortable, and easily alarmed and driven off by normal social demands.

PERPETUATING FEATURES

Given this amalgamation of characteristics, it is not difficult to see how schizotypal personalities seem destined to remain lost in another world, devoid of opportunities for corrective social experiences. Even more than the other disorders, the characteristics of this personality contribute to increasing alienation and defective social conduct, as the developmental demands for autonomous, effective functioning increase with age. Because of their fundamental structural deficiencies that prevent either effective modulation between the three core polarity positions or even maladaptive, inflexible positioning at fixed extremes, the schizotypal personality is more vulnerable to being buffeted and overwhelmed by life's demands. Given this natural history of their disorder, schizotypal individuals at critical developmental or life stress junctures may be vulnerable to micropsychotic episodes, in which their increasing sense of disequilibrium is discharged although overt manifestations of autistic-like primary process thoughts and actions, which nonetheless do not persist or manifest to such a degree as to constitute schizophreniform disorganization.

At other times schizotypal personalities may feel "dead" inside, because they have no continuity of experience and deficient capacities for attachment or empathic emotional involvement. In extreme states, they may act out with frenetic, bizarre activity in an effort to gain some self-definition they feel is so lacking, to overcome their fear of nonbeing. This is the common end state of either the schizoid or avoidant variant of schizotypal personality, the palpable lack of any sense of coherent self as a result of their progressive alienation from meaningful social life, both because of their inner deficiencies and because their strangeness frightens or repels others. Conversely, when circumstances force these individuals into overstimulating social milieus, they may become even more vague and distant, "zoning out" from what is threatening or pressuring, or again act out in unpredictable overt outbursts of disorganized, primary process behavior. In either instance, the fundamental deficiencies of schizotypal personalities' intrapsychic coping mechanisms predisposes them to drift off into more extreme forms of their condition, becoming increasingly inaccessible to any form of psychological intervention.

SCHIZOTYPAL PERSONALITY SUBTYPES

The schizotypal personality pattern has two basic subtypes, both eventuating in social isolation and disconnection from social learning experiences that might attenuate their deviant thinking and behavior. Those with schizoid features possess a passive-detached orientation to things social, they are uninterested, unstimulated, and thereby uninvolved in relationships and social matters. They prefer to remain involved in their self-absorbed preoccupations that are ungoverned by others' input or feedback. Schizotypal individuals with avoidant traits can be characterized as having an active–detached adaptive style, with social sensitivity and fear propelling the individual away from social encounters, intensifying their sense of remoteness even from themselves, given the importance of social interaction to self-definition and validation. Unlike the avoidant type, who feels cut off, rejected, or abandoned by others, the schizotypal personality with avoidant features extends this to self-rejection, resulting in loss of any internal frame of reference or anchor points by which one can grow and develop and construct an accurate social reality and mode of thinking.

Treatment of schizotypal patients must take into account their defective capacity to experience and be motivated by either pain or pleasure and by their detachment in relationships. Thus, stabilizing fluctuations in the pleasure–pain and self–other polarities is fundamental. Reducing social avoidance and isolation, one of the core perpetuating features of the condition, is another important goal. It is critical to establish a treatment relationship, without which none of the interventions discussed can take place. For most schizotypal individuals, their social world at best involves an overreliance or excessive dependence on a few social contacts—for example, parents or siblings, because these may come to suffice in meeting their weakened social needs. Very structured, supportive social skills training, observational learning, and modeling can help improve these individuals' superficial social functioning and correspondingly reduce their aversive experiences of repelling others who experience them as strange. Reviewing their social perceptions and reinterpreting them to correct for distorted cognitive schemas can gradually improve reality testing. Graded exposure to pleasurable experiences, regulating for intensity so that the schizotypal patient is not overwhelmed by overstimulation, can move them more into the pleasure–pain domain where they are inherently weak. Helping these individuals process new social encounters and experiences in a way that promotes a sense of self and continuity in their interpersonal history can provide an inner structure around which to organize these experiential and cognitive changes.

Because of these individuals' unusual, idiosyncratic mode of thought, therapists need to exercise caution in assuming how they are experienced or in what they are transmitting and how it is interpreted by the schizotypal patient, to ensure that it is reality-based. The patient–therapist interaction can also serve as a model for improved, more synchronous, dyadic interaction, by direct teaching of appropriate social behavior and increased awareness of social cues from others, that everyone relies on to gauge the impact of their behavior so that it can be modified or refined. Because their sense of self is so incomplete, an empathic focus on their shared personal experiences may be beneficial in reducing instances of derealization or depersonalization. Emphasis on positive self-attributes, especially distinctive accomplishments, can increase in the schizotypal patient's sense of self-worth and potentiate an interest in pursuing goals. Great care must be exercised by the therapist to not proceed at too rapid or enthusiastic a fashion, which could generate anxiety, withdrawal, or paranoia of the patient. Pharmacotherapy may be necessary to reduce anxiety or associated depression, and agents that have antipsychotic properties may also be required. Synergistic components of therapy include, first and foremost, a comfortable relationship with the therapist, opportunities and experiences of pleasurable events and activities, and medication to reduce the likelihood of disorganization or extreme avoidance reactions

INTERPERSONAL ASPECTS OF SCHIZOTYPAL PATIENTS IN THE HEALTH CARE SETTING

In the medical care setting the schizotypal patient should not be difficult to recognize, at least as being different, odd, or peculiar in his or her manner, thought, and action, compared to other patients. Many may be suspected of being schizophrenic, although benign in nature and not necessarily needing intervention. Like the schizoid patient, schizotypal patients may appear to be interpersonally remote, although some may show more animation and an other orientation with active coping, at least at times. However, their adaptive behavior and capacity for purposive, goal-oriented action in relation to their medical needs will be erratic and characterized by difficult-to-understand, idiosyncratic decisions and actions based on ideas and influences known only to those individuals.

For regular well visits and minor, nonchronic problems, schizotypal patients may be comparatively easy to manage, provided they do not develop unusual fixations that all or certain medications are harmful, or decide that some unproven fringe treatment is what they require. In those instances, the schizotypal patient will probably have self-selected out of mainstream medicine and will not present at typical medical care settings on a regular basis. However, if confronted with a significant health problem involving physical distress that motivates them to immediate help-seeking, then even some of these individuals will seek traditional care. Some may present with somatic manifestations of their disorder, complaining of vague symptoms that may represent depersonalization anxiety. Even symptoms of diagnostically straightforward medical conditions may be described in an unusual fashion, evoking some initial confusion in their primary care provider, until these patients' idiosyncrasies of speech and thought become more familiar to those treating them.

Unless there are sufficient family or financial supports existing before onset of their illness, it seems unlikely that schizotypal patients have the characteristics or capacities to mobilize social, logistical, or financial resources to bear on their illness course. Certainly it might be considered that *social* resources beneficial to other patients (e.g., psychosocial support or coping groups) could potentially be threatening or hurtful, and in turn, disorganizing to schizotypal patients, particularly if their peculiarities lead to public exposure and ridicule or rejection of their oddities.

Careful psychosocial assessment of these patients' basic needs should be made by a designated advocate, taking care not to introduce interpersonal stressors (e.g., too much or too intense social contact, too great intimacy, too frequent contact). It may also fall to this designated professional to problem-solve and procure the basic minimum resources necessary to support the patient's stay in the hospital and his or her adaptation to aftercare and long-term illness management. With this personality type certain supports and resources may have additive influences, but others may subtract from these patients' adjustment efforts.

MEDICAL MANAGEMENT ISSUES

Unlike other personality disorders discussed, where there are distinct interpersonal "agendas" that govern their adjustment patterns, it is the amorphous nature of individuals with schizotypal personality that may pose the greatest challenge to their health care providers. Communication leading to decision making and implementation of care may be experienced as haphazard and lacking in a shared understanding of the illness and treatment objectives. These difficulties may become apparent only after problems in care management materialize unexpectedly. At best these outcomes may be minimized but not prevented, by recognizing the interpersonal limitations of these individuals and how a practitioner can attempt to compensate for them.

Preventive Interventions, Lifestyle Choices

If lifestyle behaviors (e.g., smoking, drinking, overeating) serve to give schizotypal patients' some degree of personal definition beyond their confused and amorphous sense of self, then confrontive and critical communications about such unhealthy behaviors could be threatening and disorganizing to them, defeating the practitioner's intention to motivate behavior change. It is possible, however, that a somewhat formalized and highly structured relationship with a benign and supportive practitioner could help engage these individuals, giving them some substitute meaning, defined by intentions and guided efforts to develop more healthy behavior patterns. The challenge will be to fill their emptiness with something that appears tangible and real without introducing undue cognitive and interpersonal stress. This will require some careful assessment and individualized intervention planning. Simply plugging these individuals into some behaviorally oriented group dedicated to smoking cessation or weight reduction may be distracting and threatening, given all the interpersonal contact, especially if it results in subtle or obvious signals from others that the schizotypal patient is being experienced as "weird."

Stages of Change

It is probably safe to assume that schizotypal patients will be at a precontemplative level concerning any health care issue involving some demand for behavior change. Once initial medical recommendations are made for some action, then consideration of the contemplative activity in these patients will be both appropriate and quite important to prevent formation of idiosyncratic, peculiar interpretations and beliefs about the need for change, and how to accomplish it, that may derail them from appropriate activity. Indeed, it may be necessary throughout all phases of this change process to periodically ask such individuals to describe the thinking behind their behavior, especially as it departs from appropriate intentions and plans. The planning stage, for example, may need to involve structured, concrete presentations of a few rudimentary steps in behavior change, followed by a request for the patient to review his or her understanding of what was communicated and how he or she would personally operationalize what was discussed. A dialog concerning what would be appropriate and inappropriate examples of constructive behaviors, and the reasons for them, may help reveal any difficulties in the patient's thinking or perceptions.

Similarly, during the action phase, there is always the potential that some diversion, distraction, or unusual interpretation or formulation of what they are learning and doing could result in a digression from simple, effective intervention routines, disrupting or derailing the whole change process. Likewise, developing peculiar ideas and routines ultimately disruptive to relapse prevention during maintenance of realized change must be assessed, because these individuals will lack the capacity to be self-sustaining in pursuit of a direct course of action. This will be especially true where it involves giving up a former pleasure, especially one that may have involved physical as well as psychological addiction. In these individuals, higher order cognitive structures important to change maintenance, long-range risk perspectives, self-image modifications, and stable intention patterns cannot be expected, given the defective nature of their basic psychic mechanisms.

Utility, Cost–Benefit Considerations of Preventive Interventions

Although it is conceivable some schizotypal patients who are not strongly addicted may adapt without undue difficulty to giving up gratifying but unhealthy habits, the assumption must be that most will be too distracted, unfocused, and disorganized to effect and sustain major habit change without considerable guidance and follow-up supervision. The more steps involved and the more complex the information, the greater the likelihood of some distortion or transformation of the message that may alter the intervention effectiveness. A family member or significant other who has daily contact with these patients would change the benefit–cost ratio considerably if such a person were part of the intervention. Someone cooking low-fat, low-cholesterol meals, supervising smoking cessation efforts on a daily basis, or monitoring consumptive patterns (food, alcohol), as examples, will make a far greater difference than peripheral efforts to instill intentions and stable attitude–thought patterns in individuals with basic, perhaps structural deficits in their ability to generate such psychological functions.

Secondary and Tertiary Care of Acute and Chronic Illness

Individuals with schizotypal personalities' amorphous nature and vague contact with both their outer and inner world are not characteristics conducive to sensitivity and vigilance concerning one's health. It would follow that these individuals may be poor at monitoring themselves for symptoms indicative of expression of a risk factor (e.g., change in bowel habit in an individual with a strong family history for colon cancer). Such individuals will thus be slow at disease detection and help-seeking, if only because they are lost inside themselves, stressed out, or distracted by too many environmental challenges. Once a disease is diagnosed, there may be natural consequences (increases in caretaking by others, if even only health care providers; alleviation of certain responsibilities), but the operant influence of these secondary gains may have much less potency than with other personality types. Because of the deficits of such individuals, health care providers may have to assume the primary burden of managing the illness. This will involve recognizing that schizotypal patients have little capacity to establish and maintain a focus, even when faced with serious illness— or especially because of it.

In one sense the disruptive effect of the illness may not be as great compared to other patients, given schizotypal patients' already fragmented, chaotic mode of functioning. However, there is also no basis for assuming that an illness will necessarily instill motivation and especially a capacity to function adaptively and consistently in support of efforts to treat the disease and restore health. This may prove burdensome and frustrating to those working with these individuals, but recognizing that these deficiencies are not resistance or antagonism to the efforts to care for them—but rather in a real sense part of these patients' illnesses—will, it is hoped, reduce the negative feelings felt and communicated to these individuals.

In this regard it could be predicted that the process of forming illness representations, if this occurs at all, will be erratic and fraught with high potential for distortion or transformation into idiosyncratic ideas and perceptions. Communications with the patient concerning the illness, its symptom expression, how it may best be managed, and the role the patient may play in supporting treatment efforts may have to be repeated with many concrete examples. Even then, these patients' lack of stable inner psychic structures may lead to their missing or not appreciating the significance of important details about the illness and its treatment. This may prove both vexing and perplexing to their treating providers, although these patients' difficulties are quite predictable considering their personality characteristics.

It is important for caregivers to consider to what extent a schizotypal patient can give truly informed consent to many treatment interventions or participate effectively in decision making, from a medical–legal standpoint. This might behoove the provider to carefully and concretely document the specific communications made to these patients, how their understanding was assessed, and what accounted for any failure to maintain an accurate illness representation and patient behavior appropriate to their understanding of their illness.

Coping With Illness

Fragmented perhaps may best describe what can be expected of schizotypal patients' coping efforts in dealing with acute or chronic illness. Their poorly organized, rather autistic cognitive style and deficient defensive structure leave them ill-equipped to deal with significant stressors, especially if pain and suffering are expected to be accompanied by performance of new behaviors and adaptive changes. It is conceivable that when acutely ill the physical illness may have some organizing influence, producing transient abatement in schizotypal patients' overt psychiatric disturbance (like schizophrenic patients). However, there is a difference between a brief reduction in problematic symptoms and persistent improvement in adaptive functioning.

The safest assumption is that not much can be expected of these patients. The hope would be the treatment regimen is sufficiently organized that little initiative and patient participation is required. If disorganized behavior occurs low-dose neuroleptics may be indicated, especially if suspiciousness or mistrust emerges during treatment. A small distortion in understanding left unattended can incubate into major deviations in ideation concerning illness representations that may be hidden from the provider. Careful sequential debriefing by staff concerning the patient's understanding of each procedure, test, or medication, at the time it is proposed, administered, and even after (e.g., if there are side effects to a medicine or other intervention) should be pursued. If this history of the manner in which care is provided is not established beginning with treatment, then a suspicious or unsettled schizotypal patient may only become more so if such inquiries begin in response to unusual or dysfunctional behavior on his or her part.

Efforts to establish rapport cannot be forced, but will occur naturally if the treating personnel are natural and respectful or accepting of the patient's odd thinking and behavior when it occurs, gently redirecting or clarifying when needed. Following the lead of the patient interpersonally, helping him or her to establish comfortable "distance," and uncritically tracking where he or she is going in his or her thinking will help reduce the natural tendency to feel ill at ease in a situation in which relationships and interpersonal demands have been imposed on them at a time when they may be physically miserable. In general, a tolerant, parental orientation may be appropriate. This represents an interpersonal stance designed to facilitate comfort in the patient and also create a "set" for the staff that is considerate. Given these patients' potential for disorganization, coping should be concrete and problem-focused rather than emotion-focused in nature.

Medical Compliance

Poor compliance in schizotypal patients will most likely be a result of their basic cognitive, emotional, and behavioral deficiencies in maintaining consistent reality contact, recognizing inherent risk and danger, and planning and carrying out action. Psychologically healthy individuals will make use of natural reactions of anticipatory guilt, shame, and external disapproval from others, as well as any frightening images of disease consequences to inhibit unhealthy urges or temptations. These inhibitory influences may be largely absent in schizotypal patients, or if initially incorporated, certainly cannot be regarded as enduring, given the misdirection these patients experience with the intrusion of idiosyncratic ideas, social perceptions, and behaviors.

If medical compliance is the first occasion a schizotypal patient may have in establishing a relationship with his or her specialist practitioner (e.g., cardiologist), it is a disservice to both if these patients' interpersonal limitations and medical management liabilities are not described along with their physical symptoms and medical findings by the referral source. Unfortunately, it is all too likely in this age of managed care and shifting primary care physicians with restricted access to specialists that information of such value to the compliance process will be left out. Indeed, to cast these socially deficient individuals into a foreign interpersonal arena where they are expected to manage stressful encounters with physicians whose bedside manner and concern about social nuances may also be wanting is inviting great difficulty at the start of any treatment process.

What the involved practitioner thus must rely on is some reliable external means by which to monitor and regulate these patients' behavior. Self-preservation motivation and intentions will naturally falter as a consequence of the deficient structural characteristics of the schizotypal patient. Expectations about self-care and self-management appropriate to normally functioning adults must be suspended for these individuals in favor of external, substitute methods of compliance. Invariably, this means selecting some suitable individual in the patient's life to direct and oversee any compliance efforts. If the treatment protocol is complicated or even potentially dangerous, it is not safe to assume that the past successes at participation in treatment of such individuals will predict consistent performance in the future.

Obviously, where family members are not available, this increases the monitoring burden on those who have laid out the treatment regimen to be followed. The assumption with these patients is that there will be potentially important, possibly even dangerous failures to adhere to assigned regimens if such patients are left to their own devices. In addition, schizotypal individuals may be miscast as "noncompliant patients" or unmotivated or obstructionistic by busy practitioners who then show criticism or scorn unwarranted for individuals who constitutionally are not capable of establishing stable intentions and action patterns under most circumstances.

IMPACT OF DISEASE STATES ON THE SCHIZOTYPAL PATIENT

Because of the fragmented, disconnected inner world of these individuals, their specific response to particular illnesses may be more difficult to forecast compared to other personality types. This may be especially true concerning their ideas about their illness and treatment and their illness representations, which may be shifting and ill-formed, consistent with their inner world. Even if a "normal" patient–physician relationship is precluded by their condition, it will be important for health providers of schizotypal patients to establish a reliable means of monitoring these patients' thinking and intentions to ensure reasonable continuity of care.

Somatoform Stress-Related Conditions: Headaches, Diseases of the Digestive System

Because treatment of any stress-induced disorder will require some form of behavioral intervention involving new learning, sequential execution of different behaviors, self-monitoring, and goal-setting, the physician must recognize that the schizotypal patient may be deficient in these characteristics. Even simple interventions may become derailed by internal or external events that may be difficult for the outsider to discern. Relaxation training, for example, could involve such relaxation of physical and cognitive processes that the schizotypal patient could become lost inside and require redirection when this is discovered. Behavioral interventions that involve homework assignments may be overly ambitious. This is not to say that these should not be tried, but only that this type of patient can be expected to be less compliant where initiative and social contact is involved. Rather than expecting internalization of what is learned from the behavioral program (which assumes a reasonably coherent sense of self and history of goal-organized behavior), a more realistic initial objective would be developing routine habit patterns that could be concretely, successively linked to compliance activities. By taking into account the limitations of the schizotypal patient, behaviorally oriented interventions with modest objectives can be individually tailored to each patient, based on his or her characteristics.

Pain Management

Given the typically reclusive or avoidant lifestyles schizotypal personalities pursue, this greater interpersonal dependency may require establishing new social involvements to ensure basic needs are met (e.g., assistance shopping) or pain relief is obtained. The schizotypal patient may thus be faced with approach–avoidance conflict situations: To maintain living and personal comforts, one must be exposed to potentially aversive social interactions, which may be perplexing and uncomfortable at the least, or traumatic if there is ridicule and rejection over the patient's peculiarities.

Unlike others who may benefit from the stimulation and structure of organized inpatient pain programs, schizotypal patients could experience the social bombardment associated with these interventions as overwhelming or intolerable. The emotional and cognitive tumult this would generate could threaten any potentially beneficial learning that might occur. The benefit from social learning and modeling influences of other patients would be limited for schizotypal patients, considering their imperviousness to such nuances. Indeed, a central goal of the pain treatment of such individuals would be comfortably increasing their activity levels, particularly social involvement.

It follows that if patients of this kind are recommended for pain treatment interventions, there should be careful consideration of what benefits they might gain and what might be any unintended stressors or disruptive influences of the program. If they are enrolled in such a packaged program because of a compelling need to increase physical activity, modifications or allowances in goal-setting should be entertained lest the intervention become too aversive and discouraging. In addition to determining the most effective use of analgesics for long-term pain control, administering minor or major psychotropic medications may be critical to manage anxiety or disruption in clarity of cognitive functioning generated by these interventions. Where these patients have been uprooted from their habitual routines by their condition, they may require assistance in finding substitute patterns of behavior. If not, then efforts to educate about safe levels of exertion, rest needed, and exercise routines to combat deconditioning may be ineffective with patients lacking old structures that gave order and meaning to some aspects of their existence.

An additional problem for conscientious practitioners seeking to do what is best for their patients is that it is unlikely these individuals can communicate their needs and aversions effectively, given their own deficiencies of self and social awareness. Rather, intensification of idiosyncratic thinking or behavior may signal stresses they might be experiencing. It would be hoped that these patients' medical caretakers would recognize any interpersonal peculiarities as not merely charming eccentricity but rather signs of potential personal suffering, and seek expert referral to a mental health professional better trained to appreciate such patients' needs and limitations. It is the more severe personality types such as these that gives one an appreciation of the awkwardness and even potential harmfulness of "packaged" intervention programs that insurance companies and regulatory agencies often now demand, presumably to get the most for the dollar, ignoring the possibility that more is not necessarily better.

Diabetes

Diabetes imposes a continual need for self-monitoring and control of food intake as well as estimation of what glucose intake is appropriate in relation to exertion. Awareness of internal bodily sensations may be required to judge when to test for blood-sugar levels or to take oral medication and insulin. Only some individuals, those with more severe conditions, may be fitted with insulin pumps, but even these require attention and maintenance. In addition, effective management of diabetes requires social skills, to know how to gracefully refuse desserts or request assistance if needed. The complexity, regularity, and diversity of these demands can tax any medical patient, but the schizotypal patient may be least equipped to meet these demands.

Medical monitoring and follow-up are especially important to track disease progression (e.g., watch for retinal damage), and this will require special relationship-building on the part of the primary care provider following these patients. In the unlikely event there are stable relationship partners involved in these patients' lives, this can help reach the goal of developing stable cross-situational dietary habits, blood-sugar regulation, and exertion management. Otherwise, imparting these habits will likely involve a continuous effort on the part of providers, given the propensity of these individuals to drift away from practical issues of daily living with which their concern and involvement is at best tenuous. The burden for accomplishing these objectives will fall primarily to others, because these patients' inherent limitations make it unreasonable to expect them to be responsible for their self-care.

Neurological Diseases: Epilepsy, Multiple Schlerosis, Parkinson's Disease

Any alteration of consciousness as may be represented by epilepsy would in theory have unpredictable effects on schizotypal patients. Absence episodes associated with petit mal seizures could certainly promote a sense of depersonalization often quite threatening to these individuals. Complex partial seizures can involve loss of consciousness during which time the patient may engage in seemingly organized activity about which he or she may have no later recall. Medication compliance can be a problem area, especially if some of the drugs have side effects undesirable to the patient.

The cyclical but chronic and degenerative nature of multiple sclerosis can present a challenge to schizotypal patients and their care providers.

Initially there are generally sensory and motor changes producing varying degrees of discomfort or disability. However, in some instances but more commonly with advanced multiple sclerosis, demylenization may occur in brain centers governing higher cognitive functioning involving learning, memory, and in particular, executive cognitive activity. Where this occurs, there can be additional personality change or dementia, with disinhibition or greater apathy as a feature. Although the consequences of poor self-management of the disease may be less severe than with epilepsy (where a seizure can be precipitated), fatigue and physical or psychological distress can aggravate the symptoms of sensory loss and motor dysfunction. There can also be considerable demoralization associated with the chronic deterioration in functional motor capacity, especially when the patient begins to become dependent on others to manage basic activities.

Parkinson's disease will place a similar burden on these patients, especially as their disease increasingly robs them of freedom of movement. As they may be rather reclusive and not self-disclosing, it may be difficult to determine the adequacy of care resources available to them. Peculiar self-isolating individuals in the later stages of life (when this disease most commonly strikes) are less likely to have spouses or families to rely on. Given their reclusive lifestyles, as their disease progresses and particularly if dementia becomes a component, their capacity to manage may be seriously compromised. In addition, the effect of L-dopa used to treat the movement disorder and muscular rigidity could precipitate hallucinations in these already vulnerable individuals. Effective medical management of schizotypal patients with Parkinson's disease requires careful analysis of their psychosocial and psychiatric features, considerations that may be missed in traditional neurological settings.

Cardiac Disease

Because acute care for schizotypal patients who have suffered heart attack or who have undergone surgery to correct occlusive artery disease is intense and supplied directly by the health care system, no universal predictions about their behavior can be made for this time period. When most everything is being done for them, care may be reliably provided unless these patients develop some idiosyncratic concern or confusion about their treatment and obstruct the acute care in some way. Because this is not a remote possibility, patients who present as eccentric and peculiar during hospital stays should be followed more closely to ensure that they have not developed strange ideas about their care that may surface later when it is assumed they will be ready to assume self-management of their treatment regimen.

In addition to the physical shock of severe angina or heart attack from coronary artery blockage, the emergent nature of the treatment process and its intensity will place relatively extreme interpersonal demands and stresses on them. Interactions with highly trained physicians concerned about organs rather than psychology, busy and at times brusque nurses, and an assortment of rehabilitation specialists may represent an accumulation of overwhelming experiences. Even if there are no serious mishaps during this time, seemingly innocuous interpersonal encounters may give rise to some strange notion about their treatment that will "incubate" and emerge later when supervision and monitoring is not available.

Exactly how, when, or even if these interpersonal stresses and external demands may specifically affect post–heart-attack, bypass, or stroke rehabilitation efforts is not predictable with high certainty. But what is known of the schizotypal personality is that under stress such individuals are at risk for disorganization and micropsychotic episodes involving behavioral outbursts, paranoid suspiciousness, or extreme withdrawal. Such reactions could be risky to their health—in other words, failing to take medications on schedule, renew prescriptions, or become convinced their heart condition is a fabrication and conspiracy that can be disproven by contraindicated activity such as excessively vigorous exercise.

Finally, schizotypal patients' disconcerting, odd behavior may have disruptive impact on the efforts of those trying to help them. Although some of their eccentricities may be endearing, others can be exasperating or even frightening. In either case, caretakers may come to dread and avoid interacting with them or even forget or be distracted from giving out important information. Where follow-up is especially needed, these may be the patients least enthusiastically pursued, because they will require greater interpersonal diplomacy, medical monitoring, education and reeducation, and supervisory effort from staff than most other patients to ensure treatment adherence. The importance of identifying these individuals and their needs, and overcoming these natural tendencies to avoid them, is thus quite great.

Cancer

For schizotypal patients, early detection and recognition of cancer symptoms would likely stem from accidental rather than purposeful activity, given their amorphous and shifting behavioral, cognitive, and emotional worlds. Some schizotypal patients may have developed obsessional preoccupations with developing cancer, despite medical reassurance to the contrary. Where there is higher risk from family history, periodic medical examinations at the most frequent intervals recommended may be needed to compensate for their lesser reliability in performing self-examination–detection compared with other patients.

The initial standard treatment interventions initiated by the oncology team might require little patient involvement or exposure of their peculiarities. An important exception to this could be difficulties obtaining consent for certain procedures, particularly if these individuals felt threatened (if only by the interpersonal impact of the treatment setting and their providers). Confusion or decision-making paralysis, or paranoid resistance, could forestall the treatment process at times critical for a favorable outcome. The time involved in restoring a decompensated patient when urgent decision making and care is pending could significantly alter the treatment outcome.

Treatment of cancer with disfiguring surgery, loss or limitation of functioning, or chemotherapy that can produce central nervous system toxicity will have to be monitored carefully as schizotypal patients' responses to these stresses may be quite unpredictable. Finally, although cancers are successfully treated into remission, there is always a lingering concern with recurrence. Once diagnosed, a person is forever changed, and at best can hope for the designation of "cancer survivor." The significance and particular meaning of this for the schizotypal patient could be important determinants of his or her future help-seeking behavior.

CONCLUSION

The amorphous nature of the schizotypal personality will pervade how they interact with the health care setting. Given their tendency to a reclusive existence lacking in social feedback, what relations they have will likely come from the initiative of others, through family ties or prescribed contact (directed by social agencies). What social support they enjoy will thus be, in essence, incidental to their own behavior. As illustrated in Figure 4.1, their efforts at coping will be fragmented and disorganized but generally unfocused on the health problem at hand, often more directed at the situational interpersonal demands the illness imposes on them. This will lead to rather haphazard relationships with the health care setting, which will bear the burden of ensuring relevant care activity take place. Disease detection in the schizotypal patient stemming from preventive efforts may be "accidental" in the sense that contact will at best be irregular and governed by the shifting, idiosyncratic preoccupations of these individuals. When a diagnosis is made, often in a delayed fashion, its impact may be lost on these personalities who cannot maintain the coherent sense of self needed to maintain a continuity of experience and sense of enduring threat or whose undoing defenses may neutralize their transient fear. Illness representations thus will likely be confused and changing, depending on the immediate symptoms

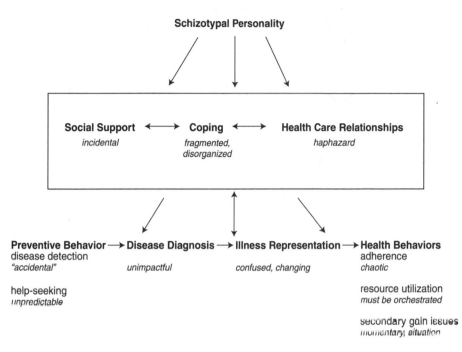

Figure 4.1. Schizotypal personality.

presenting, and this will contribute to erratic, unpredictable help-seeking activity. Application of health care resources will have to be orchestrated by the team, effective care depending on the maintenance of contact and minimization of distracting influences (external and internal to the schizotypal patient). Secondary gain from illness as such may well be difficult to define except by the momentary aversive situational influences from which the schizotypal patient may seek to escape. These individuals will not be difficult to identify in the health care setting, but managing them will be a challenge requiring external structure and monitoring to substitute for their inherent deficiencies in functioning.

5

HISTRIONIC PERSONALITY

Histrionic personality disorder, a *DSM–IV* Cluster B condition (American Psychiatric Association, 1994), is defined as "a pervasive pattern of the excessive emotionality and attention seeking behavior" (p. 657), manifest by early adulthood and in at least five or more ways: (a) discomfort when one is not the center of attention; (b) inappropriate seductiveness or provocative behavior characterizes most interactions; (c) rapidly fluctuating, superficial emotionality; (d) exploitation of physical appearance to attract attention; (e) speech characterized by impressionistic, exaggerated discourses lacking in specific detail; (f) manner of communication that is self-dramatic, theatrical, with exaggerated affectivity; (g) prominent suggestibility and vulnerability of the influence of others; and (h) assumption that relationships are more intimate than is the case.

Histrionic individuals have seemingly insatiable needs for relationships, especially for attention and affection. Whereas the dependent personality (chapter 10) is dominated by a polarity imbalance on the accommodation or passive pole, histrionic patients are at the active–modifying extreme. Histrionic personalities are as aggressive in their pursuit of attention and are perhaps less strongly desirous of caretaking and nurturance. The individual with histrionic personality will thus rather indiscriminately seek gratification of these needs, often forming brief-lived and superficial attachments easily ruptured by fluctuations in the other party's attentiveness. The dependent personality of course might exhibit similar behaviors, with the difference that he or she would likely stay in a given relationship rather than move on.

CLINICAL DOMAIN FEATURES

On the behavioral–interpersonal level, the histrionic personality above all displays a dramatic interpersonal style, one that is engaging, seductive, or enticing, that uses both language and nonverbal mannerisms that are exaggerated or theatrical in nature. All of this behavior is designed to serve an interpersonally attention-seeking function, in which others are actively solicited or manipulated into providing instrumental assistance when needed or more commonly affectional responses of reassurance and approval. When their ordinarily optimistic and conflict-avoiding needs are not met, histrionic individuals may then show negative volatility, vanity, aggressive flirtatiousness, even exhibitionistic acts or feigned distress, in an escalation of behavior designed to remain the center of attention.

On a phenomenological level, individuals with histrionic personality cognitively may exhibit little capacity for reflection, and especially, introspection. Rather, they may appear to be flighty and variable in their expressed beliefs and attitudes, which will vary depending on their success in attracting attention to themselves in a particular social milieu. This situation-dependent orientation will provide little continuity of experience. They will not incorporate the characteristics of others as will dependent personalities (discussed in chapter 10); rather, they may respond to other's interests superficially but only enough to allow them to refocus the interaction on themselves. A gregarious self-image helps support these individuals in their frequent shameless display of their seductive powers, physical attractiveness, and hedonistic orientation, which they may view as charm or interpersonal stimulation.

Structurally, histrionic personalities' internalized representations are likely a fleeting conglomeration of different social encounters typically encoded from a highly egocentric perspective. A lack of continuity or differentiation of the characteristics of past individuals may be apparent; rather, what the observer may see is a concrete blow by blow account of each interaction sequence, with much affective elaboration in terms of the impact of events on the histrionic patient.

On the intrapsychic level the most obvious characteristic of histrionic patients is their use of denial or *dissociative* mental operations, which can rewrite history to conform to a more favorable presentation of events, discarding negative and conflictual experiences and feelings in the process. This leaves them at a distinct adaptive disadvantage in that they are unaware and unable to access unpleasant events, conflicts, and experiences necessary to regulate future behavior, make accurate judgments, and refine their self-image in a realistic manner that facilitates interpersonal flexibility and emotional stability. They are thus vulnerable to repetitive mistakes, recurring bad choices in relationships, and stereotyped behavior patterns suitable at best only for circumscribed situations. Although actively involved in the interpersonal interplay, they are in fact reactive to and dependent on the responses of others to sustain their externally defined sense of self and disjointed morphological organization (Millon, 1999). When not so engaged and preoccupied, histrionic personalities may experience an alarming emptiness that can give rise to desperation and dramatic gestures—for example, suicide, that of course coerces attention and caretaking from others.

On a biological–temperamental level, the histrionic individual is naturally energetic and easily activated and highly reactive emotionally (autonomically) to events, especially of a social nature. Although such individuals may avoid conflict or confrontation and elicitation of negative feeling states, especially anger from others, they may be irritable and negative (often when making unexpected avoidance responses), although they will seek to justify their actions in a positive manner. These characteristics are presumably based on inherited tendencies in their fundamental biological makeup, which predispose development of these characteristics.

HISTRIONIC PERSONALITY SUBTYPES

As with other personality disorders there are various subtypes. Histrionic personalities with borderline features are typically emotionally labile, immature, and childlike in their behavior and prone to moodiness, demanding, clinging, and sexually provocative behavior. At moments of despair, dramatic and potentially serious self-destructive acts can occur in response to a loss of attention or nurturance. Chronic emotional turmoil in their lives and those in relationships with them characterizes their general social adjustment. Establishing a trusting relationship can be problematic given their tendency to anticipate disappointment or ingenuineness in relationships.

Histrionic patients with narcissistic features in contrast may appear more emotionally content, but in a self-absorbed, even smug manner, as long as there is sufficient regard and attendance to their persona. However, inattention, especially perceived mistreatment or disrespect, may elicit indignancy, irritation, or even rage and vindictive contempt against the transgressors. A lack of empathy and tendency to exploit others for satisfaction of immediate needs will be evident. Thrill-seeking, frenetic, even manic-like behavior patterns may reflect their high activity level and intolerance for boredom and frustration of sensation-seeking needs. Engagement in treatment will depend on careful attention to these individual's self-esteem and immediate preoccupations, provided this can be exchanged for some attention focused on their counterproductive behavior patterns and ongoing conflicts. In a sense, the therapist must engage in a quid pro quo therapy process, listening to interminable concrete descriptions of superficial social interactions in return for some psychotherapeutic dialogue about real life concerns and issues.

Another relatively common variant of the histrionic personality is one with prominent dependent and obsessive–compulsive features. These individuals seek attention primarily through displays of consideration, care-taking, and accommodation of others, anticipating their needs, showing regard and affection. In return for this, however, is the expectation of attention, approval, and recognition. Relative to other histrionic subtypes, their physical appearance is less important than tangible appreciation from those they are seeking to please. Whatever underlying hostility is experienced from frustration of these longings and efforts is likely to be repressed. Therapeutic interventions with these individuals will need to focus on increasing their sense of autonomy and self-reliance and reducing the dominance–submission patterns of their current and previous relationships.

Histrionic personalities can also manifest negativistic traits, which make them to the observer somewhat more impulsive, irritable, and subject to moody and erratic interpersonal behavior. Although they may exhibit an effusive, giddy euphoria evident in other personality types when receiving attention, they are also notably more pessimistic in their expectations of social interaction experiences. Although not intentionally conflict-seeking, they may be passively confrontive by being more negatively reactive than other forms of histrionic disorders. They may more readily express anger, complain of injury and hurt, and display a childlike, sulky demeanor. Dysphoria may be expressed in the form of lethargy, complaints of chronic fatigue, and brief-lived somatic complaints that fluctuate with their variable mood states. Therapeutic strategies would have to involve a firm but nonjudgmental and understanding orientation that emphasizes boundaries without challenging or repudiating the inevitable behavioral–expressive excesses that will occur. Special focus on these patients' negative expectations can be helpful so that their anticipated disappointments and frustrations are cognitively reworked rather than preemptively acted out.

Finally, histrionic traits can covary with antisocial personalities features such that there is a moral vacuum beneath the affable, engaging demeanor and social behavior of individuals presenting with this subtype, who are consumed with underlying resentments that motivate unreliable or devious, scheming behavior patterns. Such individuals are more readily viewed as being irresponsible, insincere, manipulative, and deceitful. Unlike the true sociopath, their manipulations may be directed at meeting ravenous need for attention, recognition, and caring from others rather than material gain. Establishing a therapeutic alliance and trusting relationship can be especially challenging, but will be critical to any hope of a successful intervention. Nonconfrontive, cognitive–reflective orientations that promote owning dishonest behaviors will be crucial to these individuals learning that they can earn trust from others rather than gaining it through ingenuous behavior. Brief, goal-oriented approaches are likely to produce a climate of success in using new behavior patterns rather than relying on their previous routine of deceitful maneuvers.

PERPETUATING FEATURES

The individual with histrionic personality is preoccupied with external appearances and especially the impact of his or her superficial characteristics—in particular, physical attractiveness—on others. Seductive behavior implying sexual arousal or interest is a strong motivating influence for members of both sexes, and this is a common feature of histrionic individuals' social behavior, although intimacy is not. Thus the histrionic individual may promise but not deliver many interpersonal benefits implied by his or her behavior and earn the pejorative descriptor of tease. Interactions may thus be initially intense and highly gratifying, but may end in frustration and accusation that individuals with histrionic personalities may not understand given their obliviousness to their impact on others.

If, as is often the case, these individuals are attractive, then the pattern can replay almost endlessly, the casualties being the disappointed, befuddled, and misled recipients of this quick but unreliable charm. As long as there is an audience, the histrionic personality may be undisturbed by the succession of superficial relationships, but eventually the supply may erode or a reputation established that results in a reduction in the attention and interest. It is at this time that such individuals may seek professional help, most likely for some physical ailment that reflects somatization of their emotional distress.

Although denial and repression are necessary and appropriate psychic defenses for many circumstances, the histrionic personality will use it excessively to block from awareness and reformulate upsetting or conflictual experiences that would provide them potentially corrective feedback that could interrupt vicious cycles in their interpersonal life. In addition, individuals with histrionic personalities may be too externally vigilant and embedded in their immediate social matrix to acquire, either through observational learning or reflection, more differentiated modes of interaction that might increase their social versatility. There is thus little opportunity for development of a self-image that is transsituational and enduring, rather than defined by the eyes of the beholder. Although histrionic personalities may enjoy great success during certain phases of life (e.g., adolescence, young adulthood), the burdens of age-defined adult challenges will eventually confront them with the one-dimensional nature of their adaptation and the terror of inner emptiness without adequate external distraction.

Treatment of histrionic patients must address their impulsivity, fickle social behavior, and overreactivity to events, especially those of a negative nature. Cognitive behavior therapy can help address their lack of reflection and tendency to dissociate when faced with conflict and stress. These behavior patterns prevent them from developing a true sense of continuity and from learning new adaptive behavior patterns or even vicariously participate in observational social learning. Provided these individuals have experienced sufficient adversity in meeting their needs to be motivated to engage in behavior change, focused problem-oriented psychotherapeutic–behavioral interventions may be feasible. Assertiveness training to substitute for seductive, attention-seeking activity can help reduce their conflict-avoiding tendencies. Relaxation training in turn can help decrease their arousal level, excitability, and tendency to somatize.

INTERPERSONAL ASPECTS OF HISTRIONIC PATIENTS IN THE HEALTH CARE SETTING

Histrionic patients' theatrical manner will represent both a source of entertainment and frustration to health care providers, given their dramatic, attention-seeking, and demanding nature when they seek care. When presenting for treatment, histrionic patients may exhibit a myriad of symptoms, sometimes initially difficult to distinguish from potentially serious illnesses. Over time these patients may gain a reputation for crying wolf and be regarded as "crocks" for their hypochondriacal, attention-seeking concerns. However, these individuals—like anyone else—can develop cancer, serious neurological conditions, and have heart attacks, and a serious consequence of their reputation is that they will not be taken seriously when they are in fact in need, and thus may suffer critical delays in caretaking.

For the sociable physician a histrionic patient can be an occasional elixir on a day of routine, unanimated patient visits, because they may be flattering, seductive, and pleasantly theatrical in their presentation of symptoms. However, over time continuity of care with them may seem disjointed because there may be erratic or no follow-up, alternating with urgent demands for appointments at unplanned intervals whenever their impulses are blunted or frustrated. To the busy, serious practitioner, these patients may become a source of irritation and resentment for the time they take up prattling about seemingly minute, superficial interactions in their life while the practitioner is struggling to maintain treatment-oriented interaction focused on pertinent diagnostic information. Given their frequently changing moods and interests, their care will be difficult to organize and manage, with the risk that if they are afflicted with a medical condition, their health may suffer accordingly. In addition, from a health care use standpoint, services may be misused, both over- and underused, at potentially considerable expense to the health care system.

Given histrionic patients' expertise in attracting attention to themselves, they typically should possess sufficient interpersonal skills to negotiate supports for themselves. Where they may have difficulty is translating that support into appropriate action concerning their disease management, given their lack of planning and organization. Their tendency to deny–repress or dissociate threats will also make it difficult for them to appreciate complicated aspects of their illness progression. Having been successful in garnering aid in the past, often at the spur of the moment, they may be overconfident about similar success when they are ill. However, the "supports" they may have enjoyed previously may have been superficial and fleeting, and also disinterested and unavailable for the serious nature of help required. A histrionic patient truly ill may lack the energy and entertaining vivaciousness necessary in superficial encounters with others who then may pursue more interesting and rewarding encounters. Given that these individuals will overoptimistically assume success in garnering needed aid, detailed clarification of the tangible nature of their claimed supports may be important to ensure their minimal needs are in fact capable of being met.

MEDICAL MANAGEMENT ISSUES

The consuming need of histrionic personalities for attention will assert themselves in the medical care setting, where interaction for them will be interpersonally centered, away from the serious focus of earnest health care providers on the "presenting problem." This can lead to disjointed, frustrating interactions, where different agendas play out in parallel, sometimes unbeknownst to either party. Recognition of the histrionic patient and his or her characteristics can reduce some of these difficulties, but not all of them.

Preventive Interventions, Lifestyle Choices

Although histrionic personalities perhaps have no special biological vulnerabilities to addictive substances, their attention-seeking and superficial lifestyles may place them in situations where exposure to tobacco, alcohol, and illegal drugs contributes to a greater likelihood of addiction than perhaps some other personality disorder subtypes. Moreover, unless these behavioral excesses are viewed as socially "unattractive," it is doubtful that these individuals would have much intrinsic motivation to attempt change. This is not to say that they would not transiently embrace some proposal for smoking cessation or reduction in alcohol consumption, but they are so "field dependent"—situationally determined and lacking in internalized controls—that carrying out any such intentions would be difficult without consistent external guidance.

Stages of Change

In response to demands or pressure for modification or cessation of appetitive or addictive and behavior patterns, it would be surprising if histrionic patients were at any stage other than the precognitive level, given that their behavior is so situationally determined—in other words, they are "now" persons. Although they may show immediate concern over warnings that they are at increased risk for some disease, their capacity to internalize any sense of alarm or concern and translate that into motivated, committed, goal-oriented behavior will be lacking. It may be necessary to find an interpersonal opportunity, either in the form of a group or an important relationship, to give meaning to the requirement for change. If dieting will make them more attractive or seductive, then there will be some motivation to alter their eating behavior. However, contemplation will likely be brief, sporadic, and easily interrupted by distractions and diversions. For this stage to be productive, an outsider may have to guide their train of thought, which will typically be fragmented and disjointed. Because histrionic patients are inherently unreflective, their productivity in this stage of change may be questionable. Some exploration of their capacity for thoughtful deliberation will at the least be indicative of their capacity to inhibit impulses and consider rather than react about things.

The preparation stage for histrionic patients may be therefore less grounded in the contemplative activity that has previously taken place. An actively involved mentor figure may be required to direct and guide efforts to prepare for change—in other words, identify barriers or change facilitators that will play a role. Group-based experiences may work best, given that they provide social stimulation and also competition for attention that is, it is hoped, contingent on performance of goal-oriented preparatory activity. The value of other group members modeling, reiterating, and reinforcing planning for change will be greater the more they are perceived as similar and attractive to the histrionic patient. It is especially important to identify substitute activities and behaviors incompatible with the appetitive or addictive actions, because these will need to be rehearsed and incorporated into the natural habits and routines of these individuals.

In the action phase these interpersonal influences will continue to be essential to elicit or model the behavior change for histrionic patients, who will probably be better at imitating observed social behavior rather than selecting and initiating new courses of action on their own. Although for a therapist this ordinarily would seem to be a less satisfactory mode of learning, this may represent the best way to address the limited capacity of these individuals to engage in, monitor, and modify purposeful behavior. Given their disjointed, fragmented representations of experience, it is unrealistic to expect that they will incorporate any changes into their self-image or will readily transfer what they have learned to other contexts. For example, although they may have rehearsed in group-settings techniques to curb impulses, in a real-life context they may become so distracted and caught up in the social moment that the notion of restraint will not even occur to them. In this respect, generalization of behavior change to real-life contexts may have to be carefully interwoven into existing routines to reduce the risk of relapse. This will be the primary focus of attention in the last, maintenance phase, where the behavior change is strengthened and the potential temptations for relapse are reduced by structured, planned activities. Ultimately, the histrionic patient may have to seek an entirely new social context, away from any preexisting negative influences to overeat, smoke, drink, or abuse drugs.

Utility, Cost–Benefit Considerations of Preventive Interventions

With any health-threatening lifestyle pattern involving self-restraint, the undisciplined nature of histrionic personalities and their impulsivity make them particularly susceptible to relapse or deflection from systematic efforts to adopt healthy behavior. As such, they are perhaps poor risks for first-time, entry-level interventions. If there is indication that the particular patient is showing seriously excessive behavior or early manifestation of a disease process accelerated by an unhealthy habit pattern, then great effort to initiate behavior change is indicated. Otherwise, involvement in an expensive program for a histrionic patient could represent a dubious investment.

A more realistic expectation would be that multiple, repetitive intervention efforts over time will be necessary, recognizing that relapse is a natural occurrence and that successful habit change may occur only after many unsuccessful efforts. Histrionic patients' capacity to absorb and follow through on complicated behavior change programs may be quite limited, especially if there are requirements for self-monitoring. Rather than extensive training in how to deal with situations involving resistance of temptation, investing effort and energy in situational management—in other words, removal from circumstances where temptation (and relapse) are likely—may be more effective.

Secondary and Tertiary Care of Acute and Chronic Illness

For diseases that are visible, the vanity and social consciousness of histrionic patients will be the motivating factor facilitating early illness detection. The threat of disfiguring breast or skin cancer or debilitating heart disease may strike sufficient fear in those patients at high risk for such conditions (especially those with a family member who has been diagnosed) to be more vigilant to early signs. Other less visible conditions, such as hypertension, will escape attention unless there is some manifestation through some other symptom (e.g., headache, dizziness).

When a condition is diagnosed, histrionic patients will incorporate it into their interpersonal style repertoire, which will involve dramatization, especially the interpersonal aspects of their experience with care providers. With family, friends, and even strangers, the symptoms associated with the condition, provided they are "fashionable" to display, will also serve attention-seeking functions. This dissociation from the underlying physiological process may represent a problem for the clinician who relies on symptoms to gauge disease progression, response to medications, and other aspects of the condition. The histrionic personality is also suggestible, and a review of disease-related symptoms may facilitate the conversion reaction process to which they are vulnerable. Even true manifestations of disease-related symptoms may become a model for later pseudosymptom episodes. When they are excessive with false alarms, wasting clinic visits, or exhausting family with caretaking demands (e.g., they complain of "fatigue" or "pain" but then show incongruous vitality or comfort when consequently attended to), the risk may be that something *real* will occur that is then disregarded with potentially adverse consequences. Although attention seeking may be the most likely secondary gain from symptom magnification (intensity, frequency, or both), avoidance of conflict, as well as unwanted responsibilities, will also be negative reinforcers for such illness behaviors.

Efforts to train histrionic patients to be independent or have self-mastery may be doomed to frustration or failure, if there is no recognition of their superficial interpersonal needs. Any intervention that serves to reduce contact and distance them from caretakers will run counter to their nature. Efforts or recommendations of this kind may therefore be ignored unless self-mastery serves to gain social attention rather than lose it. For example, it can be advantageous to have a patient "promise" to call in to report how he or she is doing when asymptomatic, at a fixed or scheduled time convenient to the clinician. This may help reduce erroneous symptom complaining and yet also serve to address the social demands that will be an inescapable, inherent part of the provider–patient relationship for this type of personality pattern.

A histrionic patient's interaction with physicians may be characterized by a supercilious presentation, where for every item of relevant information the practitioner will have to listen to and to acknowledge many lengthy details of some interpersonal interaction. This unfortunately will represent a quid pro quo, where meaningful information exchange can occur only when there is attention and acknowledgment to the social banter of the histrionic personality. Conveying annoyance for supercilious behavior in serious medical contexts may distract or upset these patients, who may respond by becoming more frantic or exaggerated in their presentation of symptoms to capture the attention of the practitioner. Warmly attending to the person (for a reasonable period of time) may satisfy the histrionic patient's need for interaction, paradoxically gaining the practitioner credibility for more serious discussion and transmission of important, authoritative medical knowledge.

Illness representations for the individual with histrionic personality will likely be emotionally charged and dramatic, serving to draw attention to him or her and perhaps in some respects "define" him or her in the illness-determined situational context. Simply providing accurate, objective information concerning a disease process for these individuals may not engender any degree of accurate understanding of the condition. Rather, this information may become transformed in some particular fashion peculiar to the patient. Accurate encoding may require review and clarification with the patient, who may even so not get it right initially, although the nature of the distortions can be potentially informative. The more concrete the illness representation information can be made and can be linked to the patient's specific experience and need for compliance behavior, the more likely there will be adherence to the treatment regimen. To the extent that a sequence of illness characteristics tied to compliance requirements can be identified, each linked to the other in stepwise fashion, the more coherent an understanding of the condition can be developed. Although for some individuals accurate knowledge about a disease process can constitute a reassuring sense of control, this may not be important for individuals with histrionic personality. Rather, what will be important will be how the information and behavioral expectations are linked to the patient's sense of relationship to the physician, which will determine its importance.

Coping With Illness

Unreflective, poorly organized, and flighty thinking and changeable, impulsive behavior represent potential impediments to coping with serious illnesses or other life crises. Although denial and distraction can serve as effective defenses against some stressors, this defense mechanism may be best suited for acute or brief-duration illnesses. It is more difficult to repress the implications of a serious long-term illness, one that has a degenerative, protracted course, especially where the disease affects physical attractiveness and capacity for socialization. When confronted with such a situation, these individuals may feel overwhelmed when undeniable levels of threat and stress emerge, leaving them paralyzed and helpless.

Because denial–repression involves not dealing with matters, there may develop a backlog of obvious problem- and emotion-focused coping matters in need of attention. Histrionic patients may have little idea about these issues that will affect them at various times they may not anticipate. The practitioner may have to introduce the issues and then model how both instrumental problem solving and emotion-focused coping can occur. Dealing with emotion-focused coping will be difficult for these patients when unpleasant feeling states are involved. It will be important to educate these individuals that negative emotions are natural responses to life's misfortunes. The idea of stages of grief, especially anger (often a frightening feeling state for these individuals), in relation to the loss of health, will represent an important concept and task to be negotiated. Especially where pain or prolonged loss of function is unanticipated, there can be great alarm and distress, involving poorly appreciated feelings of anger–resentment.

When confronted with serious illness, the histrionic patient may regress to a more primitive mode of functioning, which will involve more frenetic attention-seeking social contact in an effort to both distract him or her from the threat and reassure him or her that the world is still functioning in the same predictably erratic ways. When this fails, and there is a reduction in interpersonal activity, this will signify that such individuals are "defeated," at which time depression and uncharacteristic immobilization may occur. In their initial, frantic stage, some antianxiety agents may be needed to lessen extreme states; when depression–hopelessness emerges, antidepressant therapy will be indicated to mobilize them to a point of receptivity for even modeled coping.

Medical Compliance

Histrionic patients are temperamentally unsuited to develop and exercise self-management that might impose discipline over their spontaneity, impulsiveness, and need to participate in whatever indulging social milieu they may seek out. The distractibility of histrionic personalities and their state-dependent psychological frame of reference leaves them susceptible to marked departures from planned behavior when confronted with new situations. The dissociated, disjointed, state-dependent other-oriented manner of functioning of these individuals will make it genuinely difficult for them to maintain awareness of discriminative stimuli that may elicit unhealthy behavior patterns or changes in internal states that represent impulses consciously unacceptable to them. Recognizing anger and conflict in particular may be difficult given their aversion to experiencing unpleasant feeling states.

Difficulty in dealing with such challenges as abstaining from alcohol, smoking cessation, or diet modification should not necessarily be viewed as disease denial, resistance, or oppositional tendencies but rather as a consequence of characterologically determined deficiencies that must be taken into account in planning the compliance regimen of these individuals. Their state-dependent characteristics may enhance the efficacy of group-based programs in which a distinct milieu is established for reinforcing healthy behaviors. Particularly if there are social aspects to the group involvement that extend beyond the immediate experienced itself (e.g., a dieters brunch to reinforce the fashionability of eating low-calorie foods), then social contexts can become associated with new clusters of healthy behaviors. This approach may have more impact than classroom didactic instruction, where information is presented to be processed and stored and later translated into action. Histrionic patients may benefit less from an individualized, cognitively oriented intervention that depends on a capacity to internalize experience and generalize it across situations.

For those treatment regimens requiring medications that may have unpleasant side effects, histrionic patients may be vulnerable to compliance errors of omission—for example, "forgetting" to take medicines that may visibly diminish personal appearance, such as steroids that cause facial swelling. Medications that produce symptoms of nausea, fatigue, or alteration in mood and interpersonal vitality may also be aversive. Given their propensity to deny–repress unpleasant information, histrionic patients may even exhibit surprise and disappointment over such side effects, much to the puzzlement of those providers who carefully reviewed the cost–benefit effects with them. Because personal appearance and vivaciousness are more important issues to histrionic personalities than the concept of future health, "rational" justifications for medical interventions may have little impact. However frustrating this may be to the medical scientist bent on mastering a disease process, recognizing these unreasonable sensitivities and empathic discussion of them can facilitate relationship-building. A personalized discussion of the impact of a difficult treatment can create a relationship context and bond with the physician or nurse, potentiating more active monitoring of symptoms and more effective coping with unpleasant aspects of their long-term care.

IMPACT OF DISEASE STATES ON THE HISTRIONIC PATIENT

The presence of real illness in histrionic patients will likely place dual demands on their health care providers: alleviation of the physical illness and service of their patients' unfulfilled interpersonal needs. Given that the latter can be insatiable, this can be a demanding, even exhausting proposition if not carefully managed. Particularly where treatment gains are dependent on patient estimation of their sense of well-being, neglect of the personal needs of these patients may generate confusing pictures about treatment progress.

Somatoform, Stress-Related Conditions: Headache, Diseases of the Digestive System

Given that physical ailments socially compel displays of concern and sympathy, they present ideal attention-seeking mechanisms for individuals who require the solicitation of others to feel complete. Psychogenic pain may be common because it is an understandable but convenient source of preoccupation, and permits dramatic expressive displays that are sure to command the attention of others. Complaints of fatigue are less likely to gain attention but convenient to gain avoidance of conflict or unwanted responsibilities or demands on the histrionic personality. Tension- and anxiety-related conditions are common among histrionic personalities, given their preferential use of denial–repression as a defense and their discomfort with unpleasant feeling states. They are often subassertive and conflict-avoiding, as a result of which they may have difficulty saying "no" to others. This can lead to overcommitment at home or at work and a chronic sense of being burdened and overloaded.

Various behavioral therapies, including assertiveness training, relaxation exercises, and biofeedback, can address specific deficiencies in personal and interpersonal stress management. For those who exhibit some greater degree of insightfulness, cognitive therapy to identify self-perpetuating schemas may be appropriate. The goal is to enable the histrionic patient to recognize stresses, either external demands or self-imposed expectations, and intervene through self-management or appropriate interpersonal behavior before a chronic psychophysiological reaction develops.

Pain Management

Histrionic personalities' expressiveness and skill in communicating discomforts in a dramatic fashion can make it difficult to determine the degree to which pain is organic or psychologically determined. Anxiety and tension expressed through physical channels can genuinely aggravate physical pain. Chronic pain for histrionic patients represents a risk for inadvertent addiction given their propensity to use medication to provide relief when there are social stresses or losses in the social environment. Because complaints of pain initially command a rapid response on the part of nursing staff, those patients with the greatest social acumen will quickly learn what can generate desired attention and nurturance. When this social interaction cycle is reinforced and escalates with more and more requests for analgesics, this can be misconstrued as medication-seeking behavior and addiction, generating a negative response. This pattern can lead to destructive confrontations, because the histrionic patient may not have sufficient insight concerning his or her behavior to clarify his or her true needs, which involve feelings of loneliness as the source of help-seeking behavior. Any condition generating chronic pain that also imposes disfigurement and physical limitation can be a source of great social distress, particularly for a histrionic patient concerned with personal vanities. A reduction in physical mobility or more subdued interpersonal presentation may generate considerable erosion in a superficial social world reliant on seductive, engaging, and entertaining interchange.

Given histrionic individuals' social orientation, group-based chronic pain programs can be potentially helpful in that they provide information concerning the inevitable addiction potential of long-term analgesic use as a result of habituation and psychological dependence, without pejoratively characterizing patients and causing them to react defensively, often by intensifying their pain behavior or engaging in unhealthy activities that serve to justify their past pain behavior. Relaxation therapies and biofeedback may help identify specific muscle groups that may generate discomfort impeding the histrionic individual from remaining socially active. Use of mood elevators or anxiety-reducing medications may permit reduction of analgesic use without significant increase in discomfort. Increasing social activity also can potentiate distraction as an effective pain-reducing measure. This should be combined with reconditioning and hardening activities of rehabilitation programs, in which staff selectively reward well behavior and ignore pain behavior.

As these changes and new contingencies are established, it is critical to plan for aftercare and maintenance of these gains. It should be remembered that the histrionic patient is so situation-dependent that gains made in such special environments can disappear when replaced by pretreatment social contingencies. Involvement of family, appropriate workplace contact persons, and others who make up the patient's natural social environment to apprise them of these strategies and the role they can play will help contribute to more enduring benefit.

Diabetes

Preadult forms of diabetes, although typically more severe or brittle, at least provide the patient opportunities for parental management of the disease (e.g., blood-sugar testing, injections) that can establish habit patterns less easily disrupted by a histrionic individual's often rather fragmented, undisciplined existence. If diabetes develops in adult histrionic patients, their basic characteristics may divert them from developing stable overlearned routines that are relatively immune to situational, especially interpersonal, distractions. Timely monitoring of blood-sugar levels before the onset of cumulatively harmful symptomatic states may be difficult habits to establish, as would be the continuous evaluation of food types and glucose intake during meals, especially if dining out. It may be that for these patients, longer and more varied training may be required to potentiate greater generalization of knowledge of disease management applicable to their varied social environments. Where a social context can be introduced into such interventions, this may exploit or better suit the gregarious interpersonal orientation of this personality type.

The serious nature of extreme blood-sugar levels is certainly a potential weapon in the hands of an individual with strong needs for attention. Histrionic patients have been known to coerce attention or caretaking by instituting a diabetic crisis, especially if they feel a valued relationship is threatened. Their natural excitability could also cause genuine stress-related hormonal changes. Where there are unexpected crises of this kind, the practitioner may be tempted to consider this simply as willful noncompliance, justifying censure or disapproval. In turn the histrionic individual could react with frenetic activity to seek social reassurance, engaging in behavior (e.g., "partying") that undermines efforts to develop stable disease control routines.

Neurological Diseases: Epilepsy, Multiple Schlerosis, Parkinson's Disease

With histrionic patients, epilepsy is a condition particularly suitable for conversion reactions, the patient's true seizure serving as a model for psychogenic attacks. This may be quite unconscious, and for that reason difficult for the neurologist or medical practitioner to distinguish pseudo-seizures from genuine convulsions. Confusion stemming from such situations can lead to frequent changes or overdosing in anticonvulsants, with a risk of overmedication detrimental to the patient. Careful functional analysis of the patient's behavior and the eliciting circumstances (e.g., social isolation, presence of a particular family member or individual) can suggest the possibility of pseudoseizures. It is a condition conducive to considerable secondary gain (increased attention and caretaking from others, escape from conflict or responsibility). However, careful consideration also must be given to unrecognized interpersonal conflicts because stress can lower the seizure threshold and precipitate a genuine attack. Given that histrionic patients often have a poor appreciation of these difficulties, involvement of a family member or some informant familiar with the patient's psychosocial context can prove to be a crucial source of information. Even if it is not possible to confidently determine the true nature of each seizure, the psychological–interpersonal influences remain treatable aspects of this condition. It should also be considered that even for histrionic personalities, epilepsy can represent a major loss of social mobility and gratification of interpersonal needs, which can produce a depression that may be masked by the patient's character style.

Concerning multiple sclerosis, it is ironic that patients who present with vague symptoms of sensory loss or motor dysfunction are not uncommonly suspected of conversion reaction until later diagnosed with this unfortunate illness. Tests such as the Minnesota Multiphasic Personality Inventory (MMPI; Dalhlstrom et al., 1972) may show elevations on the Conversion Hysteria scale (Meyerink, Rietan, & Zelz, 1988) in patients later showing unequivocal manifestations of multiple sclerosis. Whether that particular elevation is a reflection of the individual's premorbid character structure or an incidental finding to the later multiple sclerosis diagnosis is unclear. However, true neurological symptoms do load on the Conversion Hysteria scale. As with any self-report personality measure, use of the instrument in isolation could lead to much confusion in patients with neurological disease, especially because true histrionic personalities are quite identifiable through their personal history and interpersonal presentation.

Histrionic patients afflicted with multiple sclerosis would be especially prone to functional elaboration of their basic neurological condition, creating confusion between psychogenetically determined disability and that stemming from the disease itself. Careful analysis of the psychosocial contingencies served by the symptom manifestation may be only partially helpful, because genuine symptoms of incapacitation will generate the same social response, which can potentiate conversion behavior. For these patients the disease management strategy should take into account both influences, even if they are not completely distinguishable. Although multiple sclerosis can lead to organic personality changes secondary to frontal demylinezation, producing exuberant, uninhibited, and impulsive behavior mimicking histrionic characteristics, misdiagnosis can be avoided by consulting those who have known the patients before the disease onset.

Parkinson's disease is a cruel illness for individuals who are vain and socially oriented, because it can be quite self-limiting and publicly embarrassing. Masked facies, an accompaniment of the movement disorder, can change the vivacious demeanor of histrionic patients. The presence of executive cognitive deficits can also reduce spontaneity and the social initiative prominent to the histrionic adjustment pattern. Depression is a not uncommon consequence of the neurochemical depletion underlying the disease. For individuals with limited psychological mindedness, the mood disturbance may not be readily evident and may be more manifest in sleep disturbance, uncharacteristic pessimism, and loss of interest in life.

Cardiac Disease

In the case of cardiovascular disease, individuals with histrionic personality conceivably could pose problems to the management of heart conditions through their excitable nature and tendency to somatize emotional distress. This could cause autonomic arousal detrimental to functioning of a compromised heart, a somatopsychic influence. Alternatively, the dramatic nature of heart attacks also affords these individuals an "audience" by which to orchestrate much attention-seeking behavior and secondary gain in the form of caretaking and escape–avoidance from conflict or unwanted responsibilities. Their suggestible nature also can contribute to conversion symptoms mimicking real heart disease (the patient's own experience serving as a model), which can generate confusion concerning important symptom reporting for medical disease regulation. It may be difficult to develop an interoceptive focus for the histrionic patient, whose dissociative modes of functioning, use of denial (of internal dissonance), and other-orientation would all represent impediments to developing internal self-monitoring of arousal levels leading to blood pressure changes. Relaxation training could help them to develop a means of reducing nonspecific generalized excitement and learn to create a state of calm.

Male histrionic patients who have relied on a high exertional activity level to meet their needs for attention and excitement may experience a significant depression from the loss heart attack may cause, in addition to anxiety over the uncertainty of recurrence. Alternatively, they could become more extreme in their use of denial and could jeopardize their recovery by engaging in inappropriate activity levels or lifestyle habits (e.g., dietary indiscretions, resumption of smoking, drinking excessively). Some may alternate between such extremes. More frequent monitoring of their condition and involvement of family members may be necessary to keep the cardiologist apprised of their treatment adherence and any continued risk behaviors. Stern communications by the physician may be pleasantly acknowledged by these patients, who may then be distracted by some new social context and with minimal awareness violate what they agreed not to do.

Some of these issues may best be addressed or circumvented by aggressive recruitment of these patients to hospital-based group rehabilitation programs, where peer involvement is a programmatic part of the change process. This will involve embedding cardiac care in a social context, where these patients can identify with others, learn observationally, and practice heart-healthy behaviors in a context where this will earn them the attention and recognition they seek. However, these efforts may produce only transient change if these patients return to situational lifestyle circumstances that contributed to their risk of cardiac disease in the first place. Individually imparted information may be less important than contemporaneous social environmental influences. Approaches that emphasize internalization of disease-specific information and illness representations by themselves thus may have limited impact on this type of personality.

Cancer

By virtue of their distractible nature, individuals with histrionic personalities are not suited to consider or heed health risk warnings or exhortations about early disease detection strategies. A good patient–physician relationship in which "visiting" takes place during routine appointments should encourage these individuals to keep routine appointments so that examinations and procedures appropriate to the patient's age, genetic, and other risk factors take place in a timely manner. A busy physician who conveys annoyance over histrionic behavior will only discourage the appropriate routine contact that would facilitate early disease detection.

If a favorable prognosis and uncomplicated cancer treatment course occurs, the histrionic patient's denial–repression-prone style may contribute to a comparatively pleasant, uneventful experience for the health care team. However, if there is unanticipated pain, loss of functioning, or physical disfigurement, there may be agitated surprise and dismay on the part of the histrionic patient. In these circumstances a sensitizing coping style may be more adaptive in preparing for adversity.

Disease management dependent on symptom reporting may be potentially problematic to the extent that histrionics patients' excitability, their propensity to use symptoms to serve interpersonal purposes, and their poor awareness of bodily states can hamper recognition of meaningful changes in their physical state. Especially when their social support is limited or erodes, histrionic patients may seek excessive contacts with their health care providers, who may become exasperated and rejecting, intensifying their patients' insecurity and counterproductive behavior. Recognizing this pattern and its negative impact on disease management can be countered by arranging for contact on a fixed basis that is reassuring to the patient but also comfortable for the practitioner's schedule.

Cancer coping or survivor groups can provide invaluable educational and emotional benefit, especially if there is limited genuine social support, given the superficial nature of histrionic patients' relationships and the risk they may erode when they become ill or less attractive. During interview intakes histrionic patients may describe a wide network of intimate relationships that may really reflect an unrealistically optimistic assumption of popularity and social holding power that will maintain under adverse circumstances. Especially during stressful and acute stages of illness, monitoring of hospital visitors may be important, as a sense of social abandonment will be particularly painful to these patients, contributing to anxiety or depression that can complicate the treatment course and even undermine the will to live. Early introduction of spiritual resources may also be beneficial for those histrionic patients with religious convictions, given their optimistic nature and natural disposition to take matters on faith.

CONCLUSION

The egocentric, attention-seeking nature of histrionic patients will make them highly visible and at times entertaining for providers in the health care setting. This may wear thin during periods of intense medical care as providers see how social supports are diverted to serve superficial

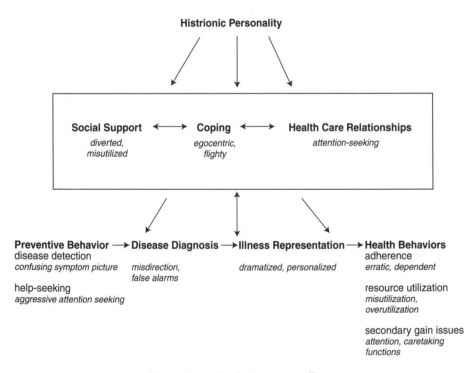

Figure 5.1. Histrionic personality.

interpersonal needs. The relationship between this personality and the health care it can engender is shown in Figure 5.1. When primary prevention disease detection or serious illness diagnosis is delayed, this may be a result of provider loss of sensitivity stemming from numerous false alarms and the frequently confusing array of complaints previously rendered to maintain interest and caretaking. Adherence to continuity of care and treatment regimens may be erratic given the flighty nature of these individuals and their reluctance to assume responsibility for self-care. Illness representations and symptom complaints will take on dramatized form, serving to capture an audience and support egocentric attention-seeking needs, the primary basis of secondary gain in these individuals. If the health care provider is tolerant and can meet some of these patients' interpersonal needs, however, these patients will remain "engaged" with their providers, unlike the Cluster A personality types that are at risk for dropping out except when confronted with acute care needs.

6

NARCISSISTIC PERSONALITY

Narcissistic personality disorder is considered a Cluster B disturbance. The *DSM–IV* (American Psychiatric Association, 1994) defines it as constituting a widespread pattern of grandiosity, in thought or action, insatiable need for admiration and insensitivity–lack of empathy for others, evident by early adulthood and demonstrated by five or more of the following characteristics: (a) inflated self-esteem and grandiose, exaggerated view of accomplishments and abilities; (b) preoccupation with imagined success, ability, attractiveness, and lovability; (c) conviction of being special or unique, capable of being appreciated only by remarkable high-status individuals or institutions; (d) insatiable need for admiration or adulation; (e) unjustified sense of entitlement, expectations of favorable treatment or of their needs being divined by others, with outrage when this does not occur; (f) exploitive of others, treats them as extensions of his or her own needs; (g) unempathic toward others, unable to identify with their perspectives; (h) consumed with a sense of envy or assumption that he or she is envied by others; and (i) arrogant and haughty interpersonal style or manner.

The narcissistic personality, like its Greek progenitor, is consumed with self-admiration and a sense of self-importance and specialness. Conversely, this enlarged self-regard is accompanied by a distinct vulnerability, a reliance on others for validation of their deeds and worth. This state reflects the ultimately fragile nature of the narcissistic personality's self-esteem, which developmentally has been unrealistically inflated by idealizing parent figures who supply undifferentiated approval and regard. Given that life invariably generates failures, unfavorable comparisons, and obstacles and frustrations in the course of even successful ventures, narcissistic individuals periodically encounter deflation in their self-esteem. Because of their egocentric nature and self-absorption, there is a fundamental lack of empathy or appreciation of others as distinct individuals with their own unique characteristics. Other individuals are frequently denigrated, especially when they represent obstacles to the narcissistic individual's objectives. Conversely, relationships that are useful may be overvalued until they inevitably become associated with some frustration or disappointment, and then are cruelly devalued. If faced with a succession of disappointments and failures the narcissistic personality may develop a chronic loss of confidence and persisting dysphoric mood, which may manifest in alternating episodes of despair and worthlessness or rage and vindictiveness toward the sources of frustration and defeat.

The polarity extremes of this personality type involve a strong emphasis on self rather than other. In contrast to the histrionic personality, the narcissistic individual's mode of functioning is predominantly passive–accommodating than active–modifying, because there is not the drive to extract from others attention and nurturance that provides their sense of self-definition. Rather, having been supplied with unconditional praise and admiration during early formative years, narcissistic personalities come to expect regard without having to exert any effort. A relative balance between pleasure and pain is seen on the enhancement–preservation polarity.

CLINICAL DOMAIN FEATURES

Considered in terms of the prototypal domains, the individual with narcissistic personality on the functional expressive level is frequently viewed as being arrogant, superior, insensitive to the feelings of others, and generally indifferent to social conventions and regulations that might constrain expressions of his or her needs. Under ordinary circumstances narcissists may convey self-satisfaction and a confidence that is inspiring or attractive to others at times, although on other occasions they may be viewed as pretentious, conceited, self-absorbed, or alternatively imperious, disdainful, unfeeling, cruel, and even vindictive. Interpersonal exploitiveness characterizes their social behavior, which is unempathic, self-centered, and typified by use of others as instrumentalities of their own needs states.

On a phenomenological level the narcissistic personality will be given to expansive modes of thought, especially involving exaggeration of personal accomplishments in the service of maintaining an inflated sense of self.

Realities are dismissed as unimportant details relative to the narcissistic individual's self-enhancing fantasies and unrealistic expectations. Structurally the narcissistic personality is defined by an inflated self-image, a sense of being unique and entitled to special privileges and favors irrespective of any actions or accomplishments that might justify such considerations. Their inner world may involve representations that are "contrived objects" (Millon, 1999), which are idealized to facilitate a sense of self-enhancement. Memories are reworked to serve a similar purpose of maintaining a sense of self-importance.

Intrapsychically narcissistic personalities will use rationalization and self-deception to maintain self-esteem and also to justify interpersonal exploitation or to shift accountability for personal failures or deficiencies. When their self-esteem is seriously threatened, then more primitive defenses such as projection may emerge, even delusional constructions. Also on a structural level the morphological elements that determine their coping and defenses are commonly inadequate to deal with disappointment, frustration, slights to self-esteem, and emotion–mood regulation. Normal responsibilities may become a source of personal offense, demeaning and mundane demands beneath what narcissists regard as their lofty station in life. When occasionally their defenses are overwhelmed, narcissistic personalities can show short-lived, severe decompensation even of a psychotic or delusional nature. In most instances they are sufficiently exploitive and skillful interpersonally in manipulation to avoid such crises. To the observer, they have an uncanny knack of "landing on their feet."

Biophysically narcissistic personalities will have a temperament that under ordinary circumstances is optimistic and unperturbed. This is because their expectation is one of success and admiration from others, based on a characteristic confidence that their superior qualities will produce a favorable outcome to their endeavors and that others will recognize their ascendance and pay them due homage. Only when there is humiliation will one see a combination of shame, deflation, or vindictive rage in response to their violated expectations.

NARCISSISTIC PERSONALITY SUBTYPES

Subtype variations of the narcissistic personality include antisocial personalities features. This involves a more "active" manifestation of core narcissistic traits, a stronger presentation of arrogance and personal sense of ascendancy, often seen in political tyrants, whose single-minded ruthlessness in advancing themselves is successful because of their insensitivity to social norms and lack of empathy for others frees them of the normal conscience-driven inhibitions. These individuals are also overrepresented among drug abuser and criminal populations, given their combination of self-indulgence, arrogance, and unscrupulous behavior patterns that push the limits of authority. A fearlessness and risk-taking orientation accompanies a skillful interpersonal style, involving charm, guile, and glib self-assurance, which is often attractive and compelling to others. Such individuals are not surprisingly quite difficult to treat, because they will attempt to dominate and manipulate their health care providers just as they do others in their life. Often a grudging cooperation is all that can be attained in the short run.

The narcissistic personality with histrionic traits is more consumed with self-aggrandizement through social conquest than gaining the attention of others. Although their self-centered and self-indulgent actions may be conventionally regarded as deceitful and exploitive, they are not motivated by malice, hostility, or sadistic satisfaction in seeing others hurt, but rather by a need to "prove" their prowess as charmers and seducers. Once relationship goals are consummated their partners are likely discarded for some other trophy, because there is no deep attachment or connection made, given these individuals' deficiencies in their capacity to bond and commit to relationships. Given their self-assurance and uninhibited confidence, such individuals can be quite successful at "sweeping off their feet" the targets of their amorous intent.

A final variation described by Millon (1999) is the narcissistic personality with avoidant and negativistic traits. These individuals are considered to manifest a narcissistic adaptation stemming not from early overindulgence and uncritical praise but rather from injuries and deprivations. In compensation for these injuries, fantasies of superiority and specialness will be developed. At the same time, there may be a hesitancy and fear to commit to situations that might risk rejection or disapproval. Negativistic features stem from early mistreatment that generates anticipation of disapproval from others, who are viewed as envious or jealous of these individuals' superior qualities and accomplishments.

PERPETUATING FEATURES

For the narcissistic personality the self-perpetuation processes derive from three fundamental defects in adjustment. The narcissistic individual's assumption of superiority creates no incentive to acquire skills that others pursue, efforts that would be considered demeaning. What would represent character building struggles are viewed as misfortunes reserved for others. Obviously when these attitudes are publicly displayed or conveyed, they will elicit antagonism from others or even exposure of unrealistic expectations and public humiliation. To avoid such dilemmas, these individuals may revert to a boastful but ineffectual existence where their claims of superiority are never put to the test. Naturally, over time in a competitive, adult world, increasing discrepancies may emerge between their assertions and actual accomplishments that may become painfully evident to all but them.

A pervasive sense of entitlement that justifies ignoring social constraints and conventions that regulate social behavior is another feature of the narcissistic adjustment. However, over time and across different situations, this behavior will eventually be challenged, exposing the underlying arrogance and conceit. Faced with such humiliation, the narcissistic personality may retreat into fantasy, where self-glorification can safely be maintained free of external contradiction. They may also retreat to social climates less competitive and more accepting but also of lower social standing, undermining any illusion of importance and high standing.

Finally, their lack of empathy precludes an appreciation of any of their shortcomings from another's perspective, which is critical to correcting social behavior or false pretenses. Rather, they are prone to devalue the views and opinions of others, especially when they are in disagreement with their own perspectives. This prevents any give-and-take social interaction and reciprocity that is crucial to building and maintaining relationships. The narcissistic personality thus will be comfortable only in situations in which they can unilaterally manage or control all social interchange and outcome. Unless they possess some talent, inherited name, or wealth, most narcissistic personalities will be unable to surround themselves with sycophants willing to reinforce their fantasies, and without an audience and support for their pathology, they may become increasingly isolated, deviant, perhaps even bizarre in their efforts to perpetuate their sense of importance.

Increasing the capacity of the individual with narcissistic personality to appreciate the perspectives of others is essential to rebalancing their skewed polarities. In addition, potentiating a more active-modifying adaptive style (rather than a passive, self-absorbed orientation) will help increase opportunities for constructive feedback and behavior change. On a more interpersonal level, social learning is needed to reduce their arrogance and inconsideration of others and also control manipulative or demeaning behavior. In therapy an orientation of acceptance of others and their inevitable shortcomings can create or model a climate where self-evaluation may be tolerated without fear of humiliation. This must be accomplished in the context of considerable mirroring of narcissistic individuals' assertions and beliefs, so that they do not feel too exposed or undermined.

INTERPERSONAL ASPECTS OF NARCISSISTIC PATIENTS IN THE MEDICAL CARE SETTING

The narcissistic patient typically presents an interpersonal challenge to primary health care providers, given their presumptuous, often arrogant manner that may offend even easygoing practitioners or infuriate those physicians invested in an authority role. Where contact is brief and goal-oriented, there may be minimal friction. However, if a prolonged or chronic illness is involved, then the likelihood of disruptive confrontation and alienation increases. The risk is that animosity created by such interpersonal behavior can greatly complicate treatment and use of care resources, sometimes even inadvertently affecting the health of the patient.

Physical illness likely will have a diminishing effect on narcissistic patients' grandiose aspirations or expectations. To the extent that a threatening diagnosis represents an assault on the individual with narcissistic personalities' sense of omnipotence, the health care provider may be cast in the role of bearer of bad tidings, and in turn may be singled out for punishment. A patient status implying vulnerability and dependence on others is unacceptable, and the narcissistic patient may attempt to transform this relationship by treating the health care provider as a servant whose duty it is to restore the health of the patient.

Because of their basic commitment to self-enhancement and self-aggrandizement, narcissistic individuals are not particularly inclined to seek treatment given their discomfort with relationships that cannot be dominated or controlled. Only if forced by circumstance (e.g., development of a physical illness requiring immediate attention) will they seek medical care. Narcissistic patients may also show an indifference to medical recommendations, which may be trivialized or mocked as a product of an overly worried caretaker whom the patient must humor. This orientation reflects the need to maintain a self-reassuring posture of importance and invulnerability, as when they were physically well. Efforts to diminish the provider's authority may include overfamiliar, subtly disrespectful, or even demanding dominant behavior. A professional task orientation of firm, no-nonsense limit-setting rather than righteous indignation may help facilitate a more respectful relationship.

There are occasions, however, when narcissistic personalities can become intensely hypochondriacal. When in a particularly vulnerable state after failure to achieve a goal or following public humiliation, they may be especially sensitive to physical maladies, and indeed in extreme instances can develop virtually delusional preoccupations about symptoms (e.g., migrating "bubbles" in the blood causing weakness that spreads to different parts of the body). Presumably these symptoms may symbolize their sense of diminishment and may also explain away failures that may be confronting them.

Where genuine fear is present, such as during a life-threatening illness where reliance on medical expertise is essential, a special relationship may emerge with the practitioner. The physician is cast in the role of a unique or exceptional caretaker whose lofty status is shared by the narcissistic patient. This idealizing transformation permits individuals with narcissistic personalities to maintain their sense of importance even if confronted with a garden-variety illness (e.g., an unspectacular case of cancer). This relationship may be seductive for the practitioner who feels valued and viewed as being "a cut above" his or her competitors. However, when the practitioner or the associate members of the health care team are disappointing, they will be devalued or mistreated as if they had somehow betrayed their patient.

Two kinds of relationships may be manifest with narcissistic patients and their supports when dealing with illness. For those established, stable relationships with family and close friends, the narcissistic patient may be quite presumptive, demanding, controlling, and bossy, acting in a fashion repellant to the outside observer—for example, nurse or other caretaker in the hospital. Presumably, the recipients of such treatment have largely come to tolerate this type of behavior and will remain responsive and helpful to these patients. Where there is insufficient support of this kind, either too few friends or relatives or where access to them is limited (the patient is hospitalized away from home in a specialty medical setting), then difficulties of an interpersonal nature may emerge. Narcissistic patients may fail to discriminate between new and old relationships, and regard new acquaintances as extensions of their own need states, mistreating them much as family and others who have tolerated their ways. The result is that they may alienate their newfound supports, causing narcissistic deflation, alarm, and panic or righteous indignation that those charged with meeting their needs were insufficient to carry out their wishes.

If narcissistic patients in a hospital setting behave in this manner, alienated staff may express covert resentment, such as by delayed responding to requests for pain medications. Any behavior interpretable as demeaning may be experienced as intolerable, particularly if the narcissistic individual is in a dependent and vulnerable position conferred by the patient role. What can ensue is an escalating sequence of alienating interactions that can distract both patient and staff from the inpatient treatment and discharge–aftercare plan.

Similar patterns may emerge in these patients' transactions with community resources. The presence of family members or trained staff (e.g., social workers) may be critical to the effective negotiation and mobilization of appropriate supports and resources. Once resources are mobilized, monitoring of their use by the patient may be necessary to ensure the supports are not mistreated or exploited (i.e., for other purposes for which they were designated, such as running personal errands).

MEDICAL MANAGEMENT ISSUES

Medical conditions to the narcissistic patient may represent a hidden threat to their elevated self-image or sense of invulnerability to the ordinary unpleasant vicissitudes of life. How they respond to this is likely to pose difficulties for their health care providers, especially if the sensitivities of patients with narcissistic personalities are not regarded appropriately.

Preventive Interventions, Lifestyle Choices

Medical recommendations to alter unhealthy lifestyle behaviors because of health risks may take on additional meanings to individuals with narcissistic personality. They may regard it as a personal affront that behavior on their part might require modification. This would represent imposition of a form of control over them that might threaten their sense of ascendancy, of being "above" others, not subject to the routine, mundane demands of life. To the extent that there would be messages that their health was at risk by continuation of lifestyle choices, this would also introduce a notion of vulnerability unacceptable to them. To not be able to drink, smoke, or eat as one pleases runs contrary to the expansive, self-indulgent nature of these individuals.

A further element may be the physiological and psychological needs these behaviors serve. Narcissistic personalities are poorly equipped to deal with frustration, boredom, or negative feeling states. They may address these with oral forms of coping—in other words, altering mood state by satisfying some basic appetitive urge, such as drinking or eating a favorite food. The tension reduction or comfort provided by these actions may restore the needed sense of inner satisfaction that is required by the narcissistic individual. This capacity for self-reassurance may overcome any momentary doubts created by a physician's expression of concern over their well-being. Once they have rationalized why this advice need not apply to them, lectures to the contrary by health care personnel can be haughtily dismissed as well-intended but inappropriate. More persistent or aggressive confrontation concerning their failure to respond to medical recommendations may result in angry indignation and devaluing rejection of the provider.

Stages of Change

The natural self-absorption of individuals with narcissistic personality would make it quite unlikely that they would be concerned about such ordinary matters as remote threats to their health. In this regard they would be very much arrested at the precognitive stage in relation to the issue of behavior change. This self-focus would also interfere with development of any contemplative considerations of lifestyle change, unless there were a valued family member suffering significantly from the consequences of some lifestyle choice (e.g., end-stage emphysema from smoking). In the case of obesity, vanity might propel some narcissistic personalities to consider weight control as an idea, although the notion of associating with other "fat people" might deter them from taking any concrete steps to enroll in a program except if it were particularly stylish or fashionable. As these individuals have little tolerance for being lectured to, they would seem to have little incentive to consider altering their lifestyle.

Similar considerations would apply to the preparation stage. The narcissistic patient would find it distasteful to be given a set of instructions to implement to change gratifying behavior patterns. Unless they were involved in an active partner role as an "expert" in the program (who could then proselytize to others their new-found skills or information), participation in this stage could be unpalatable, particularly if the patient were subjugated to a health care provider with less status than a medical physician (e.g., a dietitian). For narcissistic patients to be comfortably oriented to the action stage, they need to incorporate the intervention and its behavioral prescriptions as representing a special experience worthy of their participation. If actual self-denial is required, assistance in dealing with tensions stemming from frustrated impulses will be important. Especially if the intervention occurs in a group context, failure experiences in the presence of others would constitute an unacceptable humiliation and provoke angry program devaluation or hurt withdrawal. Communications emphasizing and praising their capacity to exercise self-discipline, if not conveyed in a condescending manner, could help narcissistic patients to adopt a "heroic" posture in overcoming these obstacles. Likewise, fostering patient identification with the maintenance aspects of the treatment intervention will be important to sustaining the behavior changes. Introduction of stress management techniques, coping skills training, and even judicious use of mild tranquilizers might benefit these individuals and save them from the risk of relapse.

In effecting health behavior changes where there is no acute illness serving as an incentive, an idealized relationship with the physician and appeals to make a "noble sacrifice" (for family, children) can facilitate a greater sense of cooperation or engagement by these patients. However, nothing would elicit a sense of antipathy and devaluation more rapidly than a loss of face and sense of being demeaned by the requirement to participate in some garden-variety intervention that "commonizes" the narcissistic patient. Conversely, a respectful but firm orientation, conveying a sense that such individuals are important can create a face-saving context in which narcissistic patients can gracefully concede that the practitioner has their best interests at heart, justifying their cooperation. This may require staff to exercise great patience in tolerating condescending treatment, over-familiarization, and demanding behavior in the course of engaging the patient in the planned medical intervention.

Utility, Cost–Benefit Considerations of Preventive Interventions

Intensive efforts at risk reduction with these patients probably do not represent a particularly cost-effective enterprise, given these individuals' disinterest in remote benefits that would require immediate sacrifice and demeaning activities such as attending behavior change groups with other ordinary people. Only if change were considered fashionable or if it constituted a visible expression of one's prosperity would such consideration hold any attraction for these individuals—for example, going to an exclusive spa for the rich and famous to lose weight. The stages of change model may be helpful in assessing the narcissistic patient's readiness to consider an intervention, before resources are committed to effecting behavior change–risk reduction. Initially, reading material describing the health threats and potential consequences can broach the idea. Suggestions for simple changes can assess patient motivation and that of their supports (e.g., a wife concerned about her husband's heart). In the instance of dietary change (e.g., lower salt and low cholesterol foods), providing substitute pleasures (giving the cooking spouse attractive heart healthy recipes to take the place of favorite unhealthy foods) will contribute to the greatest likelihood for change. The less disruptive the change, the more probable it can be sustained. If these measures are dismissed or ignored by the narcissistic patient, then the practitioner will have a better sense of the task at hand. Treating efforts at risk reduction as a process that is rarely instantaneous but that must evolve over time will more likely lead to success. Conversely, considering a failure to heed medical advice as an affront to one's authority will only invite defensiveness or irritation in the busy practitioner rather than the tolerant, good-natured but firm orientation that dealing with narcissistic individuals requires.

Where a substantial investment of time and effort is required of the patient, careful discussion of this in advance of some formal referral to another provider may be important. It is better to encounter verbal resistance and devaluation of a proposed group intervention (e.g., diabetic classes, smoking cessation), because this can lead to counterproposals to try an alternative patient-generated plan that will at least engage him or her in the preparation process. If the patient's plan subsequently fails, then there is a basis for gently pressing for a more formal, programmatic effort.

Secondary and Tertiary Care of Acute and Chronic Illness

Depending on the circumstances facing individuals with narcissistic personality, they may oscillate from feeling and acting omnipotent to being deflated and vulnerable to any threat and danger. These extreme states of mind can apply to situations in which there is diagnosis of some medical condition requiring secondary or tertiary care. If it directly impinges on their competence (e.g., arthritis diminishing the skills of a talented pianist), this can create a depression or other secondary psychological reaction that intensifies the discomfort or disability caused by the symptom. For example, where there is a failure to cure or successfully restore functioning needed to maintain fragile self-esteem, individuals in the "healing role" may be a target of disappointment, indignation, or rage over their ineffectualities. Paranoid accusations that the providers are somehow withholding deserved curative measures out of envy, competition, or jealousy are conceivable. What it likely is that narcissist patients whose comfort zones have been disrupted by an illness will thrash about for a period of time before they come to terms with the realities confronting them. Despite their difficulties in this phase, it is surprising how well these individuals can psychologically land on their feet and reestablish a new frame of reference that supports their entitled, egocentric orientation, wherein they reinvest in themselves in some other fashion that sustains their sense of uniqueness and self-importance.

Illness detection with the individual with narcissistic personality may be often delayed because of his or her external preoccupation with self-aggrandizing experiences that will cause him or her to ignore warning signals of a potentially ominous nature. For example, dizziness could be misattributed to excitement rather than the prodrome of a stroke. If there is no loss of efficacy or functioning, ignoring the symptom or even disease denial may represent the narcissistic patient's most likely adaptation. Disease detection could occur early if the symptom directly impinges on some valued attribute (e.g., a cancerous skin lesion that develops on a model). The shift to a different frame of reference, that of vulnerability, can occur dramatically. At those times narcissistic patients may become frantically sensitive to slight changes in their condition and panicked when there is no immediate medical care available. In their need for control, they may begin to independently manipulate their medications, creating problems where there were none. The challenge for the care provider will be to maintain a state of equanimity in the face of these patients' indifference to important matters and their alarmist, demanding behavior over trivial ones, combined with indignant, irate responses when their minor concerns are not taken seriously. However justified the practitioner's sense of outrage over these patients' behaviors, to respond in a way that makes the patient feel demeaned will only worsen the situation.

Concerning development of illness representations, narcissistic patients may experience difficulty in achieving a balanced view of their disease state, which may be exaggerated (and regarded as overly threatening) or excessively minimized. This will reflect their rigid need to maintain a sense of complete self-assurance. Alternatively, if their fragile sense of self is exposed and threatened, they may feel profoundly vulnerable. Including narcissistic patients as collaborators in their health care, provided they are held to a responsible role, may allow them to accurately incorporate much of the illness information, so that certain symptoms will trigger an appropriate response to seek physician intervention and others will be identified as illness-related changes that they can initially manage. In this way these patients can experience some sense of mastery or control crucial to minimizing their sense of vulnerability. Monitoring this process may be important, however, to ensure that these individuals cannot get carried away in their role and begin directing the physician's staff as their own or begin modifying their own medication regimen as if they had as much understanding concerning their treatment as their physicians.

Coping With Illness

The narcissistic personality may be particularly variable in his or her coping with illness. Where bravado and optimism can be adaptive, such individuals may show reasonable emotion-focused coping. Their ability to enlist others to ensure their needs get met may result in temporarily effective problem-focused activity. Where difficulties may emerge is when the two aspects of coping become simultaneously confounded with one another. That is, interpersonally abrasive problem-focused activity can lead to an interpersonal crisis requiring emotion-focused coping that competes with emotional issues pertaining to the disease. This in turn can derail needed planning or completion of practical, everyday activities. Illness and disease force an individual into a dependent role requiring reliance on others' good will. Narcissistic patients with physical power, wealth, or resources can seduce, coerce, or intimidate others into doing for them, irrespective of their feelings or inclinations. Patients who are unattractive or financially bereft do not generally succeed by acting in such a fashion. However, rather than behaving in an attentive, grateful manner, even these individuals can be demanding and arrogant, especially if physically in distress, as if there is an inherent right to be kept comfortable at all times. Remarkably, their forceful manner and sense of conviction that they are justified in their demands may even intimidate their physicians into medical decision making they might otherwise not consider. The potentially inflammatory and antagonistic nature of their behavior can result in either patient or physician "firing" the other and subsequent disruption of efficient health care use. It is most likely the subordinates that will take the brunt of the narcissistic patient's difficult interpersonal style. These same individuals in turn may behave deferentially to the physician authority, who then may not understand the resentment and antagonism experienced by the rest of the team. Where serious long-term illness is involved requiring many health care participants, communication among different team members and nursing staff shifts will be critical to establish continuity in the care of these patients as well as to establish the chain of command, which narcissistic patients may try to subvert.

Recognizing the inherent vulnerability of narcissistic personalities may soften health care professionals' reactions to their abrasive style. When humiliated by confrontation with greater authority, narcissistic patients may feel impelled to seek vindictive retribution. Maintaining a state of respectful formality, firm politeness, and professionalism offers the best means of maintaining a needed sense of some control in the relationship. Ignoring minor slights and overfamiliarities while expressing one's authority implicitly through displays of knowledge will serve to keep the interactive agenda task-oriented. Unreasonable and excessive requests or demands can be politely declined with appropriate justifications or deferred for consideration by the ultimate authority, the physician, if the interaction is with a subordinate caretaker. During those inevitable periods of aversive encounters with these patients, debriefing between staff may be helpful to ventilate frustrations and help support staff in maintaining a professional focus necessary to high-quality care.

Narcissistic patients' sense of investment in any treatment plan can be potentiated by giving them formal briefings concerning their condition and the treatment plan, and whenever appropriate and possible an opportunity to participate in decision making. Scheduled meeting times (at the convenience of staff, not the patient) can maintain both the sense of formality and regulated interactions. Maintaining staff morale may require learning self-reinforcement by the health care team as a substitute for patient gratitude, satisfaction from knowing that there was greater compliance, shorter lengths of stay, and lower care costs because of their professionalism. What will be challenging to the practitioner is adopting and maintaining an interpersonal style that commands appropriate mutual respect to maintain a task orientation focused on the patient's medical care needs.

Medical Compliance

For narcissistic individuals, illness and adherence to treatment regimens may represent a negation of grandiose fantasies of superiority and ascendance over others. Accordingly, such patients may resist their diagnoses. Effective long-term patient participation in illness management requires a stable self-concept and emotional state on which to introduce care routines. Unrecognized issues of loss may interfere with this. The phases of grief, denial, depression, anger, and reconciliation may need to be introduced to narcissistic patients, who may have little experience with such feelings. Given their deficient coping mechanisms, narcissistic patients are predisposed to rely on external agents such as mood-altering substances, hypnotics, or analgesics, to regulate emotional fluctuations they cannot manage on their own. Because these drugs may be used legitimately in the course of acute phases of the illness (e.g., to reduce anxiety, depression, pain, or facilitate sleep), their incidental or addictive effects in substituting for individual coping may also introduce complications that will surface in their long-term medical management.

An empathic orientation can help narcissistic patients retain some sense of uniqueness important to maintaining their fragile self-esteem while struggling with a patient role. An orientation of respect of the patient's need to be special, without catering to it, may facilitate a narcissistic identification with powerful physician figures and his or her treatment in an alliance against a biological enemy. In this context, discussion of the dangers of addiction, psychological dependence on medications, and the difficulty coping with fears and vulnerabilities can be prospectively introduced as general issues all patients face, so the narcissistic patient does not feel singled out and diminished. Careful presentation of treatment and adherence plans may provide narcissistic patients opportunities to view their illness as important, unique personal experiences worthy of recognition, consistent with their need for self-valuation. Such an approach also should appeal to their mastery needs, motivating efforts to overcome personal or situational barriers to adherence.

IMPACT OF DISEASE STATES ON THE NARCISSISTIC PATIENT

In addition to the natural impact of physical discomfort or disability imposed by illness, the narcissistic patient will suffer additional "injury" when confronted with altered role-relationships—in other words, they are the (subservient) patient to the (omnipotent) doctor. This will be inherently uncomfortable to them and a constant source of contention that will wear on the health care team. The challenge to the health care providers of these individuals will be to establish and maintain a therapeutic alliance that keeps the focus on disease treatment or eradication rather than matters of interpersonal control or ascendancy so important to the narcissistic individual.

Somatoform, Stress-Related Conditions: Headaches, Diseases of the Digestive System

Given their frequent disappointments and narcissistic injuries when their expectations are not met, individuals with this type of personality disorder may frequently be subject to situationally based tensions. This would be particularly likely in situations such as work environments where discrepancies between their pomposity and actual accomplishments are subject to public exposure. Narcissistic personalities may thus exhibit hypochondriacal apprehensions or somatoform conditions when they are feeling vulnerable, especially when they are shamed and humiliated. In addition to potentially providing an excuse for any failure, these conditions permit narcissistic individuals to provide self-administered caretaking and nurturance to themselves as a substitute for loss of regard and concern from others. Their physical complaints can also serve to intimidate or coerce concessions and accommodations from family or those close to them, who otherwise may be disgusted with them.

Behaviorally oriented treatments for dealing with general bodily stress require self-discipline, introspection, mundane practice, and a tolerant orientation toward oneself and others to work best. Many narcissistic personalities are far too impatient to tolerate such plebian approaches, and are disposed to quick alleviation of their symptoms through chemical agents. Where prescription tranquilizers are not readily available, they may self-medicate using alcohol, which itself is an effective short-term anxiety and tension reducer with dangerous long-term consequences.

Narcissist personalities are prone to experience poorly recognized feelings of rage toward others who may have, wittingly or unwittingly, injured them in some fashion. Inescapable situations that promote such experiences, such as workplace environments, can be extremely tension-producing for these patients, both for their feelings of anger–resentment toward others who are seen as devaluing them and also for their efforts to anticipate and avoid additional embarrassments. Simply having a patient of this type practice relaxation without any appreciation of the powerful dynamics of the characterological contribution to the tension-related illness may produce meager results. Cognitive–behavioral approaches may be quite useful in this regard. The emphasis on analysis rather than feeling can help reduce some of the intense emotionality these patients may have about narcissistic injuries, while providing reinterpretation of ego threats as challenges rather than dangers. Where depression is a component of these tension-related ailments, certainly medication to restore mood and energy level is justified. Anti-anxiety agents, such as benzodiazipines, may have to be used judiciously given the risk they could be overused, promoting addiction.

Pain Management

When confronted with chronic, unremitting pain, narcissistic patients are ill-equipped to deal with the restriction, constraint, self-discipline, and self-regulation required to effectively manage it. To the extent narcissistic patients need to be active and sensation-seeking in their pursuits, adjustment to chronic pain can be additionally difficult. The need for analgesics also presents a risk of overuse and habituation, leading to addiction, especially because these agents can easily serve to numb or ameliorate emotional pain associated with the loss of functioning and diminished sense of importance that may occur.

The injury and reduction in functioning as a result of chronic pain often brings with it a loss of contact with former nurturing contexts they may have created for themselves. As a consequence, this can threaten their basic sense of being, exerting psychological impact far beyond the natural distress people without this disorder experience over loss of function. All patients will grieve at not being able to ski, lift weights, or play tennis again, if those were favorite activities. However, in a psychologically healthy individual, there is the capacity to disengage from interests that can no longer be pursued and reinvest in other involvements more in keeping with the limitations imposed by the illness. Unlike with the narcissistic personality, this is only a matter of what one does rather than who one is. The narcissistic patient's identity is fragile and dependent on self-generated fantasies or validations from other admirers in his or her life. Dealing with chronic pain is not a conspicuous fight for survival like cancer that can engender some sense of heroic coping. Rather, coping with chronic pain represents endless adjustments to intractable discomfort, little private battles won and lost. Audiences to support these struggles tend to shrink and become increasingly disinterested over time, even within family where members may experience resentment for the burdens they have had to take on because of the illness.

Treatment of the chronic pain patient with narcissistic personality features can be made more manageable by allying with the narcissistic patient's efforts to transform his or her unenviable situation in some fashion as to remain superior, special, or unique in some way. Such individuals' admirers in this instance are the staff and other patients in the program, whose external praise and encouragement can represent those building blocks for a new sense of self, perhaps no less fragile but nevertheless adapted to the patient's new circumstance. Naturally, for this approach to work in a group context, the patient must value and respect the staff and their feedback. More so than with other patients, the presentation or packaging of the program must be such to make the participating narcissistic patients feel like they are involved in some fashionable and enviable process, at least relative to others not afforded such a program. Narcissistic personalities in fact will tend to idealize any activity in which they have an investment, provided this process is not sabotaged by others. Unfortunately, the arrogance and disregard for the feelings of other individuals with narcissistic personality often brings negative, devaluing reactions that may prevent this from occurring.

Many pain programs emphasize the distinction between what a person says and what he or she does. In the case of the individual with narcissistic personality, if his or her grandiose self-evaluations are too discrepant from observer assessments, resulting in humiliating confrontations, then this will create great dissonance and discomfort, and the treatment milieu may be devalued and rejected. A basic strategy of respect for the patient and careful attention and recognition to what these particular individuals say (about themselves) are critical to enlisting their support and cooperation. Once accorded that status, then staff so regarded may be listened to rather than dismissed, and their responses and feedback will represent influential experiences that potentiate positive coping.

Diabetes

Diabetes requires an orientation of constant vigilance, self-monitoring, and willingness to engage in self-denial (of foods and activities that would alter blood-sugar levels). Any individual who is frequently adrift with lofty fantasies or preoccupied maintaining a self-important posture with others is ill-suited to participate in the mundane, humbling tasks of self-discipline that diabetes requires. The presence of a family member, especially a spouse who does the cooking, can be invaluable in providing some limits to the narcissistic personality's tendency toward self-indulgent excess. However, the spouse may also bear the brunt of his or her narcissistic partner's frustration in the form of displacement of anger over such constraint. These patient's health care providers should also expect cavalier, dismissive behavior from these patients, who may treat their condition as their medical team's responsibility. Even if the narcissistic patient pays limited lip service to health care directives, small deviations from full compliance can have long-range consequences for related disease states linked to diabetes.

It may be that for these individuals, the best that can be hoped for is continuity in the patient–physician relationship and a reasonably effective if imperfect strategy for dealing with issues of treatment adherence. Simple emphasis on the importance of long-range compliance and the future risks of health problems if they are ignored may have little impact. The absence of any dramatic immediate consequences (e.g., to continued smoking for diabetic individuals) may result in the patient condescendingly humoring the physician as an alarmist. This interpersonally provocative behavior in the face of medical knowledge about their condition and long-range risks can be infuriating and test many dedicated professionals who might be tempted to write off such individuals as patients. The more burdensome routines required to control the condition (e.g., need for diet control, multiple daily injections and tests), the more likely deviations from optimal treatment is likely. To the extent that devices such as an insulin pump can reduce patient involvement, they may represent a highly cost-effective investment. Maintaining sufficient rapport so that the patient is appointment-compliant will be important, especially to ensure identification and treatment of early manifestations of related organ disease (e.g., retinal changes, renal dysfunction, peripheral neuropathy).

Neurological Diseases: Epilepsy, Multiple Schlerosis, Parkinson's Disease

The impact of epilepsy on the individual with narcissistic personality would most probably depend on the degree to which it is stable and controllable and the nature of the changes it would impose on the individual. A child or adult athlete who could no longer participate in a sport in which her or she excelled would obviously suffer critical loss of self-esteem. Inability to drive or perform hazardous work would also represent loss of prowess and mastery. This could induce a significant depression and regression or contribute to counterphobic behavior, testing illness-defined restrictions and limitations. For example, by engaging in those activities that challenge the medical condition (drinking and risking a seizure), narcissistic patients can "prove" to themselves and presumably others that their superiority is undiminished.

Multiple sclerosis is a condition that typically has a cyclical course, and can be particularly cruel to individuals who rely on physical coordination or prowess of some kind for their self-esteem. The subtle nature of the condition can make it difficult to diagnose, robbing the narcissistic individual even of a protective (e.g., medical) explanation for his or her diminished competence. As it progresses, multiple sclerosis can affect not only sensory and motor but also central nervous system functions, affecting initially the ability to perform complex skills, then even simple activities of daily living. Multiple sclerosis can also undermine the narcissistic patient's limited capacity for coping with emotional states through demyelinization of frontal brain pathways and structures important to regulation and control of impulses.

Parkinson's disease also represents a progressive neurological condition that gradually destroys a person's independence and capacity to function effectively. Tremors can produce notable, embarrassing motor conditions and even changes in ability to organize behavior and regulate emotion. It is a merciful disease only in the sense that it typically affects elderly individuals. In that respect the condition does not affect what might have been but nonetheless reduces an individual's capacity to manage and maintain a sense of mastery over his or her own being. Relying on medications and others for physical assistance can pose stresses, especially if these resources diminish over the individual's life span (e.g., death of a spouse). Narcissistic patients, through their interpersonal aversiveness, may be subject to greater attrition in their peripheral support base.

Cardiac Disease

For individuals with narcissistic personality, especially those whose identity is based on physical vitality (e.g., an athlete), heart disease will represent a core thereat to their sense of being as invulnerable or superior. Their response to heart attack or heart disease (eventuating in bypass or transplant) can vary from severe depression and giving up for a period of time following development of the condition and confrontation with its limitations to risk-taking counterphobic behavior, such as high-altitude skiing, mountain climbing, or deep sea scuba diving, clearly prohibited activities following bypass or transplant surgery.

Given the transcendent importance of sense of self to the narcissistic patient, "what it means" can be an essential question to pose following diagnosis of a heart condition, which inherently implies some significant alteration in lifestyle and habits, as well as self-image. Depression and emotional deflation are psychiatric consequences of heart disease that bode poorly for recovery or maintenance of a fragile physical condition. Illness denial may follow as a reaction, posing its own set of risks. An involved, comfortable working relationship with this type of patient will be required to ensure transmission of appropriate information concerning heart disease and its treatment requirements, leading to accurate illness representations appropriately tied to the patient's compliance role. Otherwise, the narcissistic patient's tendency to retreat into compensatory fantasizing may reassert itself, creating potentially dangerous distortions concerning treatment.

Narcissistic patients are unlikely to be inhibited in reporting symptoms of concern to them. Unless they are in active denial of their illness and engaged in counterphobic, overcompensating behavior, symptoms of a cardiac nature will produce excited and demanding behavior. Their sense of alarm may produce irresistible pressure for immediate symptom relief that competes with more prudent medical management. Education concerning predictable symptoms and the actions to take to deal with them can counter tendencies to respond with excessive behavior that itself could be problematic (e.g., overmedicating).

Participation in cardiac recovery programs can be beneficial to the extent that it gives the narcissistic patient some sense of control. However, those providing such services may find these patients prone to devalue those groups if they find them commonplace and if they are not treated as elite rather than ordinary. Especially because they can be obnoxious in their manner, there may be a temptation to put such individuals in their place in the group context. This impulse should be resisted, because it can lead to escalating efforts to produce acknowledgment of the patient's importance, diverting the treatment process to the detriment of the well-being of these patients.

Control of emotion and tension can be beneficial to blood pressure control and heart rate (where arrhythmias are a problem). Anger–rage in particular can be a feeling state common to narcissistic personalities when they are frustrated over unmet expectations and disappointed in others on whom they depend. Relaxation training may be useful but will need to be accompanied by a particular rationale (that it promotes self-mastery in the face of uncontrollable adverse events), because these individuals may temperamentally favor direct action and confrontation over responses emphasizing restraint and tension reduction through self-control rather than emotional–interpersonal catharsis.

Long-term maintenance of cardiac disease will require an empathic orientation from the cardiologist or internist, who will need to be willing to tolerate these patient's efforts to establish an intimate or overpersonalized relationship. A reassuring, understanding approach combined with a respectful but firm focus on important compliance behavior (e.g., following a heart-healthy diet, taking cardiac medications religiously, showing up for regularly scheduled follow-ups) can be helpful. Especially if the narcissistic patients' premorbid adjustment was an active one involving substantial accomplishment, these patients may tend to get caught up in their success fantasies and revert to overactive modes of functioning dangerous to their recovery or disruptive to future medical monitoring. Emphasizing their physical well-being as the basis on which their accomplishments and future successes are dependent can help maintain motivation focused on their cardiac condition while minimizing any feeling of being overly constricted or controlled. By creating linkage between their inner need states (the need to feel superior and important through success) and health behaviors as a necessity for realizing their aspirations, adherence to treatment requirements may be potentiated.

Cancer

Once cancer is diagnosed, treatment for the condition is shared with an expert oncologist and surgeon cast in omnipotent, lifesaving roles. When confronted with an immediate threat to their mortality, many narcissistic patients may manifest uncharacteristic vulnerability and dependence on their primary health providers, who previously may have been treated in a disdainful, scornful fashion. They may be initially apologetic and self-recriminating concerning how they have mistreated those on whom they now rely for survival. This form of behavior, however, is likely to be short-lived. Once distracted by the treatments and suffering associated with surgery and chemotherapy, they may revert to their premorbid or even more regressed mode of functioning. This can involve intolerance to pain and uncertainty, rage at subordinate hospital staff for delays in response to their requests for medication or information, and demanding or protesting behavior toward their physicians. The health care staff may feel held hostage and powerless to retaliate with rejection given such patients' dire states.

This experience will be understandably contrary to what most oncologists and surgeons have come to expect from patients and can serve to antagonize and polarize a relationship where hope and faith would ordinarily be a critical ingredient of the treatment. Further, where treatment may be initially successful, any antagonism stemming from such interactions can have an impact on the all important follow-up care, including timely return visits for detection of recurrence.

An alternative interpersonal scenario can involve a hopeful idealization of the care team, especially the physician, who may be deified as the all-knowing healer who will rescue the patient from death or disfigurement. This relationship can develop from the qualities of the physician as well as the patient. The physician and surgeon who is personable but maintains an authoritative mystique may facilitate this idealizing response by the narcissistic patient. Initially there may be considerable politeness to all members of the treatment team, given the aura of being under the care of someone so special (who in turn makes the patient special as well). However, this may break down as status roles become defined once treatment unfolds. At some point these patients may begin to show a lack of consideration to subordinate team members involved in their care. Patients may displace on to them whatever minor anxieties or frustrations they may experience during treatment, while maintaining an idealized view of the physician, who may be unaware of the interpersonal difficulties occurring with other team members. To the extent that aversive interactions in acute cases can have a significant impact on overall treatment (e.g., recognition–development of infection, early detection of side effects that will be dependent on the alertness of the on-hand staff), problems of this type with nonphysician staff are not trivial.

Although these events may be impossible to completely prevent, staff morale can be maintained by recognizing that the patient's personality characteristics are part of the illness management challenge. Providing recognition to those staff who are most tolerant of such difficulties and skilled in keeping the patient maximally focused on compliance with the treatment regimen can turn properly managed aversive interactions into care achievements. While rounding or meeting with these patients, including ancillary staff in the meetings to assign roles identified as important by the medical authority can create status for these individuals, as can a respectful orientation toward them.

If the illness takes an unexpected negative course, then generalized disillusionment may set in, and the health care team may be in for devaluation, even accusations of incompetence or malpractice. The more extreme reactions, however, may depend on the extent to which these patients may feel betrayed by unrealistic expectations, which may be self-generated by their own need to feel their case is special and will therefore yield an unusually favorable outcome. If an idealizing relationship is established, frequent contact with the patient may be necessary, to both support the positive transference that the patient has established and also to partially transform it into one where the patient is realistically informed concerning the illness course. If treatment is going well, contact with the medical authority understandably may be more infrequent and remote. However, this unwittingly could amplify expectations and idealizing fantasies that develop in this isolation, which will later backfire when they are unrealized. Maintaining periodic contact even during an uneventful phase of treatment will serve to reinforce an appropriate sense of guarded optimism. Realistic warnings that their condition could deteriorate can be accompanied by assurances that there are strategies for dealing with many such eventualities. In this way these patients can be engaged in treatment, where the process of sharing information can represent a form of control through intellectual mastery—understanding of the condition and illness course. This context also allows development of a shared suffering for dealing with treatment disappointments through the patient–physician partnership that has been forged to combat the dread disease.

Although there is no absolute guarantee this manner of dealing with these patients will prevent any recrimination or antagonism, it does create role relationships to which patients can return, in a face-saving fashion, following predictable outbursts at times of special stress, which in turn can be treated as understandable. Alternatively, if the narcissistic patient is left unmanaged to effect estrangement with all levels of the treatment team, there will be no basis for rapprochement at all. Support groups could be potentially helpful, although frequently the more so for family or relatives of narcissistic patients, who may find this form of intervention difficult to tolerate if it makes them feel ordinary. In addition, in their efforts to establish their superiority, they may attempt to dominate the group process with their pseudoexpertise, risking painful put-downs by the groups leaders or other patients who would naturally resent their arrogant behavior.

CONCLUSION

Narcissistic patients when well may be superficially gracious and charming, with a sense of importance and invulnerability. This will quickly change when confronted with illness and a patient role conferring subservience. Their need to be superior will drive them to undermine traditional medical authority roles and cast caretakers as servants, generating resentment and conflict, undermining the care process. As displayed in Figure 6.1, their use of supports is likely to be generated by entitled, demanding behavior. Preventive measures may be dismissed as beneath them, but diagnosis of disease, which may be delayed by overconfidence, may result in disbelief

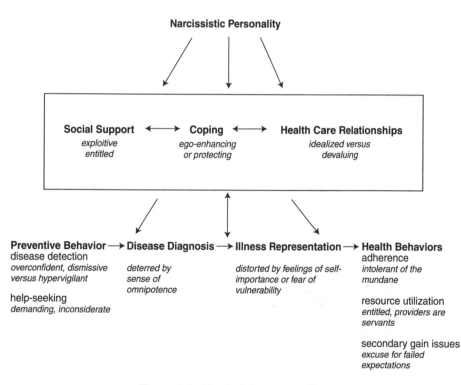

Figure 6.1. Narcissistic personality.

or, conversely, panic and deflation if perceived superiority is threatened. Their inflated but fragile self-esteem will doubtless contribute to distortions in their illness representations. Matters of treatment adherence will be complicated by narcissistic patients' tendency to devalue and reject demeaning self-management requirements. Their behavior may be especially abrasive when threatened and most vulnerable, and self-esteem issues for them may assume greater importance than critical care matters. Managing these patients with a combination of respect and authority to curb their excesses will determine the effectiveness of their treatment.

7

ANTISOCIAL PERSONALITY

The Cluster B disturbance, antisocial personality disorder, is defined in *DSM–IV* as "a pervasive pattern of disregard for and violation of the rights of others occurring since age 15 years" (American Psychiatric Association, 1994, p. 279). Manifest in this pattern must be any three of seven characteristics not explainable as a feature of an Axis I schizophrenic or manic episode in an individual 18 or older who previously evidenced a childhood conduct disorder: (a) repetitive legal infractions; (b) chronic deceitfulness and lying, conniving, exploitive behavior; (c) lack of foresight and planning; (d) irritability and combativeness, demonstrated by treatment fighting and assaultive behavior; (e) reckless disregard for the welfare and safety of others; (f) chronic irresponsibility, habitual failure to honor work and financial commitments; and (g) absence of remorse for wrongdoing, rationalization or projection of blame.

Although many of these characteristics are shared by the individual with narcissistic personality, the major difference is that narcissistic individuals customarily expect reward and recognition will be theirs without effort, whereas the antisocial personality assumes that nothing will be theirs unless they connive, scheme, cheat, or aggressively impose their will on others. Unlike the narcissistic individual, the antisocial individual is thus strongly at the active–modifying end of the second polarity. Both types are at the extreme end of the individuation–self versus nurturance–other pole. Each type also is stronger on pleasure enhancement than pain avoidance. Aversive

157

consequences thus have minimal effect, and do not build a sense of conscience or even anticipatory fear concerning future punishable transgressions.

CLINICAL DOMAIN FEATURES

On a behavioral level, the antisocial personality from a functional standpoint is expressively impulsive—that is, hasty in action; lacking in judgment, foresight, and sense of caution; and incapable of or unwilling to consider consequences in the face of temptation. There are also more refined antisocial personalities who have developed greater self-control in the form of a chameleon-like capacity to adapt to different situations, using charming and guile for personal self-aggrandizement at others' expense. Interpersonally the antisocial personality is strongly defined by an irresponsible attitude toward society. Individuals with antisocial personality are unreliable, uncommitted to any course of action not in their immediate or shortly realized self-interest.

Phenomenologically, antisocial personalities are characterized by deviant cognitive processes predominated by amoral or socially antagonistic values and perspectives that leave them contemptuous or chronically resentful and angry about social conventions and laws that would constrain their freedom of action. They harbor the view that life has short-changed them and that it is up to them to correct matters, the ends justifying virtually any means, no matter how hurtful to others.

Among less cognitively developed antisocial personalities, their lack of appreciation or understanding of social values may contribute to poorly thought out or impulsive behavior. Whereas normally socialized individuals may resist temptation on both a cognitive level ("this is wrong") and because of conditioned emotional inhibitions ("I will be punished if I do this"), antisocial personalities even on a cognitive level do not appreciate the probable negative consequences their actions will elicit. Their lack of self-insight also interferes with self-monitoring and correction of their behavior patterns, even when that would seem to be to their advantage. Deficits in empathy and the ability to adopt the perspectives of others also impede development of a social conscience based on anticipation of others' pain stemming from one's actions. Whereas most individuals, even those with other personality disorders, are deterred by social rules and sanctions from acting on their aggressive or selfish impulses, individuals with antisocial personality are unaware of or unconcerned about such matters. This egocentric orientation also intensifies these individuals' sense that their needs deserve fulfillment over any regard to the values and social constraints that regulate fair interpersonal behavior. These attitudes can be seen in antisocial personalities' facile but insincere justifications or rationalizations of their behavior. These may involve bland assertion of innocence and wrongful accusation or construal of injustices on which to legitimize aggrandizement as righting actions. Although lacking in any sense of morality, they may plea earlier mistreatment and victimization to elicit sympathy in others and thereby reduce sanctions for their behavior.

On a structural level antisocial personalities maintain a self-image frankly contrary to the characteristics valued by conventional individuals. Whereas loyalty, generosity, and straightforwardness are widely viewed virtues, antisocial personalities may gain satisfaction in seeing themselves as more devious, scheming, crafty, and exploitive than others. This provides a sense of freedom and autonomy from the constraints of group mores. Often they maintain a heightened sense of arrogance toward others that can provide justification for mistreating them. Individuals with antisocial personality feel a fierce independence that prevents them from relying on others when in true need, which would leave them exposed to humiliation or obligation. Such a vulnerable state may reenact early experiences of helplessness, pain, and rejection that these individuals are determined never to reexperience. The internalized object representations of relationships of individuals with antisocial personality at most may reflect fragmented recollections of dissolute, corrupting, degrading experiences and persons. These give rise to the need for revenge–retribution and contempt for values or conventions that failed to protect them from those debasing interpersonal experiences.

On a functional intrapsychic level, individuals with antisocial personality exhibit a lack of inhibitory or impulse-regulatory mechanisms, so they are typically acting out negative urges with little regard for their impact, guilt, or concern about consequences. Projection, especially of inner feelings of hostility onto others, can serve as justification for aggressive acts, on the grounds that they are defensive maneuvers designed to protect rather than aggrandize. Antisocial personalities can be said to have unruly internal organizing structures that ineffectively deal with impulses or past unpleasant events, preventing any profit from experience. Their here and now orientation reflects the immediacy of their needs, their missing sense of a meaningful past or future goals and expectations by which to plan and regulate action. Because there is a basic mistrust for others and negative anticipation of any future prospects that are left to chance, the antisocial personality is driven to hedonistically pursue immediate pleasures and gains lest the opportunity for any gratification be lost.

Finally, on a biophysical level the antisocial personality may be endowed with strong basic sensation-seeking characteristics, a need to generate or experience excitement, and a lack of responsiveness to punishment. When combined with a lack of empathy and altruism, the antisocial personality can be viewed as being refractory to experiences by which ordinary individuals are conditioned into their social values and constraints.

ANTISOCIAL PERSONALITY SUBTYPES

Individuals with antisocial personality with narcissistic features have especially strong feelings of entitlement. They behave in a self-aggrandizing fashion with contempt and disregard for the needs of others, but with disregard for general social conventions and the consequences of deviant and illegal behavior. They also are more impulsive than pure narcissistic personalities, and more easily offended and enraged by slights to self than other forms of antisocial personalities. Material possessions are coveted and sought after, but they are insufficient to right the balance sheet of earlier experienced deprivations and losses. Taking from others valued roles or possessions brings greater satisfaction than acquiring such things through hard work and honest effort, because it represents a righting of past wrongs for perceived unfairness (i.e., others are undeserving of what is envied). Relationships are particularly likely to be viewed and valued only as useful instrumentalities in securing power and possessions. Trophy wives or husbands may be prized for their beauty or success and the envy generated in others. If time or misfortune diminish their value, they may be discarded as no longer useful, without regard for past loyalty or devotion. Although single-minded in aggressive pursuit of their self-aggrandizing objectives, antisocial personalities with narcissistic features remain vulnerable to insecurity, remaining unfulfilled despite personal successes and gains achieved. This sense of dissatisfaction in turn can motivate insatiable strivings for power, possessions, and ruthless efforts to remove any impediments to such goal attainment.

For individuals with antisocial personality with sadistic traits, the pursuit of materialistic belongings is less important than power or ascendancy over others. Their objective is protection of personal stature and an impregnable position against slight or attack. In dealing with this variant of antisocial personality, it may be useful for the practitioner to "recognize" the prowess or significance of these persons. This can make them feel more comfortable and thus more able to accept the expertise of the health care provider without feeling threatened. Otherwise, they may try to contest their practitioner's authority or even attempt to dominate them, especially if they feel vulnerable from an illness that literally leaves them feeling weak and diminished.

A combination of antisocial personality and histrionic traits will produce a particularly impulsive, pleasure-seeking or risk-taking adaptation. Rather than being driven by a need for control, revenge, materialistic or reputation aggrandizement, antisocial personalities with histrionic features are driven by a lust for life that pushes the envelope of experience in pursuit of excitement, heedless of social convention or responsibilities that are discarded in favor of reckless behaviors. Conversely, such individuals are quite prone to feel bored, constrained, and fenced in by ordinary social conventions and role expectations (e.g., that of marital spouse or parent), which constrain them from a lifestyle that masks inner feelings of emptiness at the core of their psyche.

Individuals with antisocial personality with avoidant or schizoid features show an extreme aversion and antagonism toward society. Rather than responding with retaliation or attack, their tendency is to attempt escape. What characterizes them as antisocial personalities is their disregard of ordinary conventions, the needs and feeling of others, in pursuing their objectives. They may drift in seemingly passive fashion from one environment to another in a migrating, gypsy-like lifestyle. However, when escape is blocked, their needs for pleasure and tension reduction frustrated, or when they are disinhibited by drugs, they may act in an explosively violent fashion. Defects stemming from early experiences of abandonment, emptiness, and mistrust of primary relationships may be overrepresented in such populations, which may include prostitutes (male and female), alcoholics, panhandlers, and homeless individuals.

Finally, antisocial personalities with paranoid traits constitute the most ruthless and vengeful and the least psychologically accessible variant. They are deeply resentful and mistrustful of any signs of tenderness and warmth, which are regarded as nefarious ploys to gain advantage. Acts of brutality, coercion, and domination are used to ensure a sense of safety and exact retribution, objectives more primary than self-aggrandizement and sheer pursuit of pleasure. Such individuals typically are seen in the health care setting only if faced with debilitating illness or legal pressures that force treatment on them.

With all of these subtypes, the problem faced by providers is their relative lack of influence, or their impotence relative to the gain realized by the unrestrained manipulative behaviors of individual with antisocial personality. Transient treatment alliances can be undermined by the understandable abhorrence these individuals elicit in caretakers for their reprehensible, exploitive, asocial behavior. For these reasons, successful interventions are generally circumscribed and brief in nature. Once the situational dilemma is resolved, the antisocial personality will move on to other pursuits.

PERPETUATING FEATURES

The antisocial personality's orientation that one exploits–abuses or is exploited–abused will naturally repel or antagonize others, confirming the core conviction of these individuals that people cannot be relied on. These individuals will assert that only if one has the power to coerce can one be sure of getting affectional or physical needs met. Charm and guile are tools to achieve these ends, to manipulate loyalty and acquire influence, but only in the service of immediate need gratification. Because of this the antisocial personality's relationships may be relatively short-lived. Although these individuals may be successful in cycling through different environments exploiting others with the same repertoire of behavior, eventually they will incur the wrath of someone more powerful or will exceed the bounds of tolerable misconduct, and thus will incur punishment. In turn, this will further solidify their chronic resentment toward "society" and their conviction that they must go it alone.

Because much of their behavior may be driven by earlier mistreatments and harm brought on them by individuals in whom they may have placed trust at one time (e.g., parents or family members), the antisocial individual may feel a need to redress these grievances by punishing or mistreating others in turn. Such vindictive tendencies may motivate and justify taking from others through devious means rather than by honest exchange and effort. Their efforts to control and dominate and thereby ensure no possibility of future mistreatment is often reinforced in the short term, with immediate rewards and pleasures that perpetuate the eventually self-destructive behavior patterns. Ultimately the repetition of these actions will evoke angry retribution or rejection, which will reduce or eliminate their capacity or opportunity for continued self-aggrandizement. Antisocial personalities will thus lose what they had gained in their present environment and be forced to start over again in a new one. If their behavior is sufficiently deviant, then incarceration may be the consequence, with lack of access to immediate pleasures, an even worse, loss of freedom and autonomy.

Antisocial individuals' chronic anger toward authority and rejection of social conventions makes it unlikely that they will develop coping mechanisms for delaying gratification or tolerating frustration. Punishment or interference in the expression of their needs may only provide additional justification for further acting out in retaliation for the perceived unfairness of such constraints. Their excessive use of externalization of blame as a defense perpetuates a view of the world as being at best disappointing, frustrating, or unfair, and at worst as malicious or vindictive as they are. The result is that there is virtually no opportunity for corrective experiences by which they might learn new behavior patterns.

Because it may be essentially impossible to see through skilled antisocial patients or track all their devious maneuvers, it may be best for the provider to simply acknowledge their inherent disadvantage to deception and manipulation, while pointing out that such maneuvers are likely to be counterproductive in the long run. Where there is an opportunity to exert influence and build a relationship, the practitioner can consider the theoretically derived fundamental polarity imbalances of antisocial personalities. This leads to a focus on moving the antisocial patient's attention away from self-centered, exploitive, vengeful behavior to the needs of others as a way of promoting socially rewarding encounters, to reduce the likelihood of future self-perpetuating antagonistic interpersonal experiences. Because the health provider may uniquely possess some desired service or benefit for the antisocial personality, he or she is in a position to wield some influence, because the patient needs those services. As such, the health care provider can encourage the antisocial patient to curb impulsive acting out and instead attempt cooperative or at least reciprocating forms of behavior. To the extent that these influences can be brought to bear on the antisocial patient's experiential world, this may also reduce his or her anticipation of mistreatment and being harmed. The health care provider can also serve as an alter ego to the antisocial patient, offering him or her realistic appraisals and forecasts concerning the consequences that impulsive acting out may produce.

Given that the antisocial patient is likely to mistrust expressions or acts of goodwill or affection, efforts to persuade the antisocial personality that gentle, caring behavior is inherently desirable may only produce a loss of respect for the provider, given the patient's callous, cynical orientation. Decent behavior may be viewed as a weakness to be exploited. Rather, emphasizing the practical advantages of cooperative, prosocial behaviors, in terms of the patient's self-interest, is more likely to elicit changes in habitual behavior patterns. When there is direct benefit from such changes, then the antisocial patient may begin to view these new behaviors as "useful." Conversely, examining the amoral, illegal, or repugnant actions of the patient from an objective, nonjudgmental perspective may help the antisocial personality reflect on and appreciate the self-defeating consequences of the behavior and the advantage of more cooperative behavior as a means to the end.

INTERPERSONAL ASPECTS OF PATIENTS WITH ANTISOCIAL PERSONALITY IN THE HEALTH CARE SETTING

All health care providers have to make the initial assumption that the symptoms patients describe may be genuine reflections of disease processes requiring treatment. From that point, clinical observation of the patient's behavior and positive or negative medical tests provide clarification concerning the initial impressions, leading to the actual diagnosis. An antisocial personality who presents to the medical setting may be in genuine distress from real illness, but this individual introduces the additional possibility of prevarication, conscious manipulation, and exploitation of the health care system. Alternative motives include drug seeking in support of a habit or escape from unwanted responsibilities or legal entanglements and consequences for criminal activity (e.g., withholding a portion of illicit drug sales from the distributor). Compensation-seeking following accidents in the form of damages for alleged injuries or disability income payments can be other motives. In pursuing these covert aims, antisocial personalities can be quite ingratiating and charming, because they are skilled in interpersonal persuasion and manipulation. Although they may be impulsive and irresponsible in their interpersonal behavior, this may characterize the conduct of their relationships once they are in a position to exploit. The primary care provider will not likely see the true character of these individuals unless they are experiencing a chronic illness that forces long-term contact. In other instances, the contact will be irregular, serving the immediate impulses of the patient rather than any reasoned health management strategy.

Because they are acting on behalf of their own agendas and timetables, it is difficult to think in terms of their responsiveness to medical recommendations. If the medical guidelines are in keeping with the patient's agenda, then the guidelines will be acted on. If the patient is seeking other goals, such goals will be pursued in earnest and at most lip service will be given to the medical care recommendations, only so long as the provider is useful. What the health care provider must ultimately realize with this type of individual is that under ordinary circumstances, there is no realistic likelihood of establishing an ordinary patient–physician relationship. Rather, recognizing these patients' personality characteristics will help counter but not prevent all of the manipulation that occurs, while attempting to provide appropriately for any genuine medical needs. Under these circumstances, the patient may develop some respect for the clinician as impervious to manipulation, and thus seek other avenues for his or her nonmedical agendas.

The antisocial patient may vary in the kind and quality of psychosocial resources, largely dependent on his or her socioeconomic status and other personal qualities (e.g., intellect, physical attractiveness, and the type of variant he or she represents). What most antisocial personalities have in common is their manipulative and exploitive use of those resources to meet their ends. The provider should be wary that those ends will differ from those of other patients. The physician or social worker may find themselves enlisted as extensions of the antisocial personality's schemes and commitments that have been frustrated or interrupted by their illness. For example, exaggeration of financial needs would not be surprising. Minimizing their own resources to protect them from financial obligation or exaggeration of their assets to secure needed services (without any intention of assuming responsibility for them) would be possible scenarios. Individuals with antisocial personality may seek verification of illness to employers or others to support inflated assertions that they should be exempt from responsibilities or excused from past obligations on the basis of their condition.

Skillful interpersonal displays to elicit sympathy and outright fabrications about their circumstances (e.g., that there is a dependent family in need) would not be uncommon maneuvers. Careful verification of actual need should take place to ensure finite health care–patient assistance resources are not misused for other ends. Antisocial patients' illnesses will not cause them to suspend their normal mode of functioning, which is to be constantly on the lookout for opportunities to gain at others' expense. Indeed, an illness may represent an excellent context from which to operate. Hospitals with emergency rooms not infrequently find themselves visited by these patients, who are well aware of the coercive influence of adverse publicity or legal sanctions for failure to treat as a way of getting service.

MEDICAL MANAGEMENT ISSUES

With a patient possessing antisocial personality characteristics, the process of administering medical care likely will involve two distinct agendas. For the practitioner one obviously will be the "clinical pathway" laid out for treatment of various conditions, and the other will be the goals of the antisocial patient, to gain advantage wherever opportunity presents. This dynamic may be hidden beneath superficial charm of such individuals and not become evident until some ulterior motive surfaces well into the care process. Realistically, health care providers should not expect to "outsmart" these individuals, but only in reasonable time to recognize and curb their excesses before they become destructive.

Preventive Interventions, Lifestyle Choices

Given their deficient foresight, lack of impulse control, their dislike of social conventions, and their intolerance of boredom and propensity to seek out stimulation and excitement, individuals with antisocial personality are particularly prone to develop unhealthy appetitive–addictive lifestyle patterns. Apart from a lack of concern and respect for other's opinions, especially those in authority, individuals with antisocial personality may react to medical recommendations to curtail sexual promiscuity, smoking, alcohol use, or misuse of illicit substances with mistrust and defiance as unwarranted restriction of their freedom. In keeping with their anticipation that others are trying to harm or deprive them of their rightful due, this attitude represents a nearly insurmountable obstacle to motivating lifestyle change. An assumption may thus be made that most lifestyle choices or preventive interventions for individuals with this personality type will pertain to altering behavior that has somehow got them into trouble and that preserving their freedom and autonomy is the motivating influence for change, not some future state of physical wellness.

Stages of Change

The individual with antisocial personality, by virtue of his or her psychological makeup, will be at a precognitive stage concerning any issue of lifestyle change, unless he or she is facing legal sanctions or recurrent danger (e.g., physical harm from drug dealers seeking payment). Warnings that behavior places such individuals' future health at risk is likely to go unheeded, after perhaps polite acknowledgment of the message. Even if there is some particular incentive for cessation of a habit—for example, abstinence from alcohol or marijuana as a condition of probation—this is motivated only out of a wish to avoid certain punishment, not out of an intrinsic, mature appreciation of potential harm. The contemplation stage will thus need to focus on behavior change as an expression of immediate self-interest. In the case of individuals with antisocial personality, the focus needs to be more on the immediate consequences of alcohol use (e.g., incarceration) and the certainty of detection (e.g., mandatory drug screens as a condition of probation) of wrongdoing. These considerations are likely to be far more relevant than warnings of potential deterioration in brain functioning or liver or pancreas damage, which develop slowly and pose no imminent threat.

In this model the preparation phase would involve considering barriers to change, in particular temptations and probable motivational lapses resulting from the patient's lack of inner controls. Given the antisocial personality's dislike of authority or moralizing–controlling manners, an impersonal orientation on the part of the practitioner may elicit the least antagonism or resistance. The content of discussion could center around the patient predicting what he or she is most likely to do, given certain scenarios (e.g., if exposed to some drug user who might tempt relapse). The emphasis would be on the pragmatics of ensuring his or her freedom by not using and getting caught.

The action phase for individuals with antisocial personality will be a particularly challenging portion of the change process because the ultimate criteria will be *not doing* something—for example, not consuming alcohol or drugs. Other behavior that would potentiate the continuation of change into the maintenance stage, such as staying away from bad influences, cannot be monitored reliably through patient self-report. Involvement in relapse prevention programs and attendance verification requirements would offer some means of documenting superficial participation, but not change that is genuinely internalized. Family members could assist as verification agents, but hard-core antisocial personalities would not likely tolerate unwanted scrutiny or control any longer than their needs would dictate.

Utility, Cost–Benefit Considerations of Preventive Interventions

The preceding discussion should cast doubt on the cost–benefit ratio for this type of individual concerning preventive interventions. Those mechanisms necessary for restraint and self-control would have to be externally imposed with a realistic likelihood of detection and unwanted sanctions. This is not to say that warnings about health risks to antisocial personalities should not be given and repeated or that opportunities should be denied for risk-reduction interventions (e.g., obesity groups, smoking cessation programs) *if* such individuals demonstrate interest and initiative and commit the resources (financial, time, energy) to effect such change. However, to use heroic efforts at prevention with this type of individual ignores what is known about this condition.

Secondary and Tertiary Care of Acute and Chronic Illness

Given antisocial personalities' intolerance of being in a controlled, dependent, or beholden role, considerable mistrust and defensiveness may occasion receipt of a medically unfavorable forecast. If symptom relief can be obtained, or the immediate distress passes on its own, there may be delays in seeking additional care, reflecting both the dislike of reliance on others of individuals with antisocial personality and their disinclination or inability to plan ahead with a sense of caution and prudence. Their propensity to anticipate mistreatment during the stress of illness may elicit antagonistic, challenging behavior toward those who are attempting to help them. In reaction to discomfort over the dependent patient role, antisocial personalities may seek to restore some sense of control by behaving in a manipulative, contrary, or provocative fashion. In some instances this could take the form of threats not to follow medical procedures however potentially harmful that might be to them. If physical discomfort is involved, drug seeking may quickly develop because self-medication may be the antisocial personality's most familiar means of dealing with anxiety or distress. Individuals with antisocial personality may vary considerably in their behavior, depending on the circumstances. When feeling trapped they may behave as such, in a sullen, irritable, guarded manner that may court antagonism confirming their assumption that displays of weakness will be exploited, just as they would do with others. Alternatively, they could act charming or sympathy-eliciting; often this will signify they want something and are gearing up to use their interpersonal powers of persuasion.

Development of accurate illness representations, although an important goal for the physician and treatment management plan, may be a peripheral consideration to antisocial personalities. They may have little concern about how the illness develops, its course, and how it is best managed from the patient's standpoint and requirements for participation. Their primary interest will be in reducing their immediate discomforts and physical restrictions that curb their freedom of action. During interactions with the physicians and health care team, their appearance of listening to important information may disguise their scrutiny of the communicators' personalities and how to manipulate them. Even if these patients are able to accurately recite what they have been told and articulate reasonably accurate illness representations, this in no way will ensure effective use of that information. The goal of the individual with antisocial personality will be for others to do for them, because their true skill is in interpersonal management rather than self-management. As such their objectives and that of the health care system will be quite different, although theirs may be a hidden agenda, a natural, instinctive consequence of their makeup and not necessarily a premeditated consciously planned strategy.

Coping With Illness

"Coping" for the individual with antisocial personality involves primarily maintaining an advantage against others who are viewed either as weak and vulnerable to exploitation or who are regarded as capable and potentially dangerous. When confronted with serious physical illness, individuals with antisocial personality may be reluctant to seek needed support given their intolerance of dependency and good will from others. To rely on others would be a sign of weakness based on the assumption that others will take advantage of them just as they exploit any similar opportunity. In evaluating these patients' coping, there is little need to consider internalized conflict given their lack of conscience or internalized norms. Acting out is the predominant response to anxiety, tension, or need states.

An inherent advantage that antisocial patients may have is their basic conviction that they have the absolute right to what they can connive, so that manipulative behavior is justified, even when clearly at the expense of others. Because well-intended individuals with a conscience (e.g., those in helping professions) tend to assume others possess similar virtues, they are natural prey for antisocial patients who are ready to exploit this misconception for maximum gain. When confronted with difficulty—for example, being caught in their machinations—individuals with antisocial personality will externalize blame and justify their actions based on any number of extenuating circumstances. Often they may portray themselves as victims rather than perpetrators. For example, it is the unscrupulous physicians they have seen that caused them to become addicted, not their own appetite for mood-altering drugs.

Treatment requirements that involve significant restriction will be particularly threatening and difficult to tolerate for this individuals with this personality type. If imposed in an authoritarian fashion, those conditions may be particularly intolerable, generating rebellion even to the extent of potentially self-harmful actions (e.g., leaving the hospital against medical advice, risking infection or reinjury of the condition being treated). Judgmental, condemning reactions to irresponsible behavior of that kind will be answered by countercondemnation or escalating defiance.

Although antisocial personalities may respond to stresses in many unusual ways, certain strategies may help to counter some of their predictable reactions to loss of freedom and control and their sense of vulnerability. When confronted with serious illness, they may balk at the idea of a health-saving intervention, fearful of the period of increased vulnerability that will impose. If in acute physical distress, these individuals may press for some immediate reduction of discomfort, even surgery, without thoughtful consideration of any cost–benefits issues outlined in consent procedures. There may be little attention paid to posttreatment restrictions in activity or lifestyle routines, which then catch them by surprise, causing much protest and caretaker consternation. Discussing the dangers of impulsive decisions or inaction, emphasizing how the intervention and recovery procedure can be favorably structured, can introduce some sense of control. This should involve attention to the psychological state of the antisocial patient and consideration of elective short-term use of anxiety-reducing agents, as opposed to sedation through use of analgesics with addictive potential. Relaxation training could be helpful, although it may not provide immediate enough relief to be effective. If physical restraint is involved (e.g., traction, body immobilization), opportunities for external stimulation, including desired interpersonal contact, can lessen these patients' anxieties and improve their overall treatment course. Although antisocial personalities are disposed to mistrust efforts to help and expressions of good will, open recognition of their psychological discomforts and sincere discussion of the options available to them can reduce their inevitable sense of being imprisoned by their illness.

Medical Compliance

The goal in potentiating compliance with these individuals is to focus their attention on self-care acts that will serve their immediate needs—in other words, to restore their health, so that they can maintain their autonomy and escape the vulnerable, dependent role their illness may have placed them in. Where compliance involves maintaining wellness by reducing potential health risks, the matter is much more problematic. This involves a choice to give up some immediate pleasure in favor of a remote prospect of some future consequence. Such a proposition may elicit earlier negative schemas of deprivation and arbitrary denial of pleasures that was perhaps simply out of malice on the part of some parent figure. A judgmental or patronizing mode of communication will only further antagonize these patients. Providing objectified information in a neutral fashion to sensitize the patient to some health risk (e.g., high-cholesterol foods and the risk of a stroke) and all the restrictions and disabilities this would bring may represent the best means of introducing a prospective orientation unfamiliar to the antisocial patient.

Any sense of being controlled is likely to elicit deliberate misconduct, just to make the point that ultimately they have the power to facilitate or sabotage the treatment course. Individuals with antisocial personality may also sense their provider's need to successfully administer the best medical care and use it as a means to exert their own control and influence, however potentially harmful that might be to their own well-being. Minimizing conflicts over control will not produce perfect compliance, given these patients' deficient impulse control and inability to resist temptation. However, a frank, pragmatic orientation over time can establish credibility and some measure of trust with the provider, which can enhance more constructive, goal-oriented patient–physician health management.

IMPACT OF DISEASE STATES ON THE ANTISOCIAL PATIENT

Patients with antisocial personalities will have legitimate illnesses in need of care, and when acutely in distress they will seek help. Most have sufficient social skills to make favorable impressions, but as care becomes more involved and intimate, the likelihood of manipulative, exploitive behavior may emerge. At best, different goals and expectations may be required for this type of patient, who may not be able to tolerate demanding treatment regimens requiring discipline and extensive behavior change.

Somatoform, Stress-Related Conditions: Headache, Diseases of the Digestive System

When confronted with stress, interpersonal or psychological, antisocial personalities will exit the situation if they can or resolve the conflict, often with little regard for the rights and considerations of others. Only if they are captive, such as incarcerated or constrained by serious physical illness, might tension-related conditions be manifest. Techniques such as relaxation training are worthwhile to consider, because there is no risk of addiction compared with drugs that provide more immediate relief. However, the patient may not have sufficient patience or self-discipline to practice adequately to realize benefit. Their response in turn may be to seek relief elsewhere. In those circumstances, it will be necessary to consider the alternatives. If the patient is truly captive, with no possibility of escape, and his or her only recourse is a behavioral technique, then it may be important to couch its benefits as a self-control, self-mastery technique to appeal to the importance of autonomy, a means of freeing him or her from reliance on the health care setting and others.

Pain Management

Temporary debilitation from acute injury and pain, especially in the first occurrence, can be frightening to individuals with antisocial personality because it represents a threat to their need for autonomy. Anticipating mistreatment from outside sources, they are compromised by reduced mobility and pain that prevents protection from competing predatory influences. Dangerous self-protective measures could result from this sense of vulnerability (e.g., carrying and using a weapon). To the extent that some sense of autonomy can be restored through either psychosocial intervention or psychotropic medication for anxiety and depression, such risks to others or self can be lessened.

For an individual for whom autonomy and personal freedom are the driving influences in life, chronic pain represents a crisis, especially if accompanied by physical limitations. These needs might in theory motivate effective participation in programs designed to increase physical independence and self-reliance. However, unless there is a prospect of rapid and significant improvement, in reality the more reprehensible characteristics of the individual with antisocial personality may well undermine this opportunity, especially if there are delays in him or her receiving care. Even if extreme diplomacy is exercised in appealing to these patients' self-interests, the reality of inherent dependence on others for the near future may be an insurmountable prospect for them.

It is not unlikely that the dismay and anger of individuals with antisocial personalities over their circumstances will be projected against their health care providers, resulting in conflict, power struggles, and treatment failures. Given that their condition is unchanging, these patients will continue to need services, at least for some relief of their pain. Having no scruples or concern about social conventions, "doctor shopping" and manipulation of multiple pharmacies may become their mode of functioning to obtain analgesics that are habit-forming. These individuals will adapt their interpersonal presentations at clinics to suit their agendas and will exploit all their interpersonal charm or coercive skills to reach their ends, which in this instance may be to reduce their distress over being imprisoned in a partially broken and painful body.

Given their cynical orientation, there is little likelihood that empathic displays of concern and understanding of antisocial patients' suffering will have a positive motivational effect. More likely these patients would exploit their plight to support a drug habit or meet aims that have little to do with rehabilitation. The health care providers could become unwitting participants in such pursuits. Diligent history taking and an insistence on communication between medical facilities (through patient releases of information and records requests) eventually will reveal these hidden agendas. At that point these patients can be confronted with their history and given a choice of making some changes in their modes of functioning, with appropriate monitoring and supervision safeguards in place (e.g., drug screens for abuse situations).

Diabetes

Not infrequently this disease is brought on by behavioral excesses such as overeating and heavy alcohol use. Management of diabetes will thus involve patient self-control and denial of pleasure contrary to the basic nature of the individual with antisocial personality. Treatment will likely be a frustrating prospect, dealing with noncompliance in all areas, including appointment follow-up, diet, and drug use. Given their antipathy to control and mistrust of authority, great care must be taken to relate the disease and its management to the patient's self-interest and self-preservation. Focused and repetitive concrete presentations of the long-range consequences of the disease (e.g., blindness, limb amputation, renal failure) may be important to establish the need for self-regulation. Undue pressure and criticism early in the process may only antagonize these patients, alienating them from maintaining contact. A neutral, factual approach to this disease may not generate alarm or enthusiasm but it will help reduce inevitable relationship issues guaranteed to disrupt the care process.

Given that these patients are prone to irresponsible, unreliable behavior, the task of the health care provider is to minimize these tendencies over time, recognizing that diabetes is an insidious lifelong battle. Adopting a long-range perspective that the health care team is a resource that the patient must learn to use effectively in making basic decisions about his or her welfare can help reduce provider frustration and maintain a focus on patient responsibility. Over time this can promote development of an accurate illness representation based not just on general information about the disease process but on each patient's health behavior as it is concretely influenced by favorable or adverse medical events. Obviously any stable relationship supports (e.g., a spouse) will be invaluable as a source of monitoring and change (e.g., diet modification through different meal preparation).

The more stable the location and the greater the structure in the patient's life (e.g., a regular job and activity level), the greater the opportunity to integrate disease control methods into the patient's routines. Special emphasis must thus be given to situational supports and influences that can counter deficiencies in these patients' coping styles and adjustment patterns.

Neurological Diseases: Epilepsy, Multiple Schlerosis, Parkinson's Disease

Epilepsy for individuals with antisocial personality, if poorly controlled, would represent a weakness that would be difficult to accept, given their intense need for autonomy and fear of reliance on others. When feeling vulnerable, the individual with antisocial personality may tend to act out as a means of creating an illusion of control. Even if their seizures were ordinarily well-controlled with medication, this could be undermined by alcohol and drug abuse common to these individual. Seizure-induced organic personality changes could have an additional disinhibiting effect on already impulsive behavior patterns. If there are legal difficulties in these individual's lives, the provider should expect this condition will be used to mitigate or excuse any aberrant behavior.

Multiple sclerosis also represents a state of reduced control and unpredictability given its uncertain course. If confronted with neurological symptoms of motor weakness, sensory impairment, fatigue, and reduced physical prowess, this can be demoralizing to the individual with antisocial personality, and can precipitate self-sedation through alcohol or substance abuse that only complicates the care. Use of steroid medication during acute exacerbations of the illness may also induce psychiatric symptoms, including paranoia, irritability, and general exaggeration of personality characteristics.

As Parkinson's disease typically afflicts older individuals, this would be a time when the worst aspects of the antisocial personality typically have burned out. Cognitive slowing, tremors, and reduced mobility all represent diminishments that would require the individual with antisocial personality to rely on others for help and to experience humiliation at being viewed as different. In addition to the biologically determined depression caused by depletion of dopamine, a psychologically induced depression can develop. In addition, cognitive impairment and features of the subcortical dementia that often accompanies the disease can produce losses in judgment and inappropriate, even dangerous attempts to function "normally" (e.g., insisting on driving when motor control is too diminished to do so safely). The levodopa used to treat the disease also can create psychotic features and mental confusion that exaggerates aspects of antisocial personality characteristics.

Cardiac Disease

Provided the form of heart disease is not debilitating or physically limiting, individuals with antisocial personality will in all likelihood lack the future perspective and psychological makeup to develop enduring concern about their future well-being. Unless there is a crisis such as a heart attack, or recurring acute symptoms such as severe angina, there will be no stimulus for change, given their weakness on the pain polarity, which would be the core mechanism to generate enduring self-preservation concern. With severe heart disease that imposes physical limitations (e.g., shortness of breath, fatigue, and chest pain), antisocial patients may experience uncharacteristic depression and anxiety because they are "prisoners" of their own bodies. This may initially produce a frantic press to regain functioning or restore some sense of control. If improvement is not forthcoming and depression develops, resumption of self-destructive habits such as overeating, excessive drinking, smoking, and drug use may be a consequence of loss of resolve or an effort to restore some sense of control and freedom. Identification and treatment of such affective and psychological distress will be important to effective rehabilitation. If there is open heart surgery or an acute heart attack, rehabilitation activity at the earliest possible opportunity may facilitate a prospect for greater autonomy. Judicious use of pain medications may be worth considering to potentiate an increase in activity level and reduction in the sense of confinement. Consideration should be given to use of antidepressant and antianxiety agents to alleviate the emotional distress associated with acute debilitation, which can reduce the potential for later compensatory or counterphobic acting out.

Long-term maintenance of antisocial personality disorders is problematic given these individuals' fundamental deficiency in forming stable attachments and their characteristic mistrust of authority and caring orientations. This would suggest that the relationship the patient establishes with his or her physicians and other health caretakers, and the degree to which his or her acute care is comfortable or distressing, will determine the extent of influence and credibility the providers have in the postrecovery phase.

Cancer

Early detection of cancer through self-screening would appear unlikely with this population, given their impulsive nature and lack of foresight, especially if the cancer indicator is a subtle sign involving little physical discomfort or limitation. The likelihood of identifying cancer in its first stages would depend on such factors as whether physicals were required by the employer, if other medical conditions kept them in contact with their physician, or if a spouse or family member were concerned about some known familial health risk.

The prospect of terminal illness involving pain and suffering of the kind associated with cancer will be sufficient to get the attention of even an anti-social personality. Initially after the shock and fear associated with the diagnosis, understandable feelings of anger and bitterness will likely emerge. However, this "why me" sentiment for the individual with antisocial personality may generate acting out. Especially if the medical forecast is unfavorable, this could take the form of increasingly reckless hedonistic behavior, such as drug abuse, sexual promiscuity, and the like. Fear of pain, mutilation through surgery, and confinement could elicit mistrust and anger that would be projected onto the health care providers, who would be viewed as the enemy.

Encouraging forecasts accompanied by strong displays of caring and concern could be regarded with mistrust, promoting suspicion about treatment that has a high prospect of cure. Such patients' focus may be on the immediate debilitation, disfigurement, or loss of freedom caused by surgery or chemotherapy. Cynical views that the health care establishment's primary interest is not the patient but the fees generated by such services would reflect a projection of how antisocial personalities might exploit such situations for themselves.

Although the individual with antisocial personality might display primarily anger about the diagnosis, early consideration of medication for anxiety or depression could address feelings of despair and apprehension that may be unrecognized. This in turn could reduce any distracting emotional noise at a time of important medical decision making. A factually based approach concerning the disease process, as well as neutrally presented descriptions of the treatment events, including perhaps even visits to the treatment setting (if that would be reassuring) could promote some sense of control through predictability and information sharing. Family may be helpful, primarily to provide for some monitoring of patient behavior and accountability for self-management requirements. The value of support groups is less certain and may depend on the particular needs of the patient and what the other members can provide at that time. For individuals with antisocial personality, an interpersonal context is an opportunity for manipulation. Persistent, rewarding expressions of gratitude may well signal some hidden agenda is underway.

CONCLUSION

The antisocial patient is unlikely to interact with the health care system unless he or she is injured, ill, or abusing drugs and using the system as a source. Even then, these individuals will pursue an agenda centered around maintaining freedom of action and opportunity to exploit and take advantage of others. Given their hedonistic orientation and lack of foresight, abuse of substances remains a continual risk. These desires and intentions will be hidden beneath charm and a superficially cooperative orientation until their opportunities to exercise their guile and plans are constrained or thwarted, at which time more aggressive, coercive behavior may emerge if they do not exit the health care setting. There is little the provider can do to fundamentally change antisocial patients, but recognizing their behavior patterns can limit their self-serving maneuvers, and management strategies emphasizing their self-interest can promote more effective care. The provider must recognize that his or her "authority" as a healer may mean nothing to these patients unless it is translated into concrete gain from their perspective. If loss of freedom and constraint of action, especially subservience, which creates a sense of vulnerability, is the consequence of being ill, then power struggles and conflict or termination of care is likely. The dynamics are illustrated in Figure 7.1.

Grudging respect from an awareness that the provider is on to them may allow for some transmission of self-care skills that can promote restoration of health or reduction in vulnerability. Communication among health care

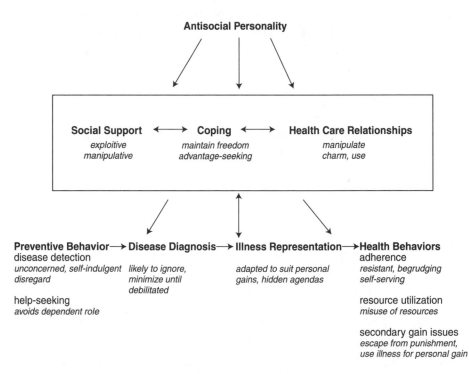

Figure 7.1. Antisocial personality.

team members will be crucial to recognizing devious schemes and manipulations, so that health care resources are not squandered or misused. Treatment strategies must have, to the extent possible, immediate concrete benefits, because promises of long-range wellness will not sustain fragile efforts to comply or cooperate that are motivated by acute distress.

8

BORDERLINE PERSONALITY

Borderline personality disorder, a *DSM–IV* Cluster B disturbance, is descriptively characterized by pervasively unstable affect, self-image, and interpersonal relationships, with prominent impulsivity present in multiple contexts, apparent by early adulthood (American Psychiatric Association, 1994). Five or more characteristics must be present to meet the threshold criteria for diagnosis: (a) preoccupation with and frantic precautionary activity to prevent real or feared abandonment; (b) recurrent unstable and intense relationships alternating in idealization and devaluation; (c) unstable sense of self and identity; (d) impulsive, potentially harmful behavior patterns demonstrated in two areas of functioning; (e) recurrent suicidality or self-mutilating activity; (f) chronic affective instability of brief duration (rarely for more than several days); (g) chronic feelings of emptiness; (h) ineffective modulation–control of anger, resulting in recurring displays of hostility and fighting; and (i) brief, stress-induced paranoia or dissociative symptomology.

Commonly an Axis I disorder is present with the borderline personality, such as agitated or retarded depression. Biologically oriented neuropsychiatrists such as Akiskal (1981, 1984) have proposed that borderline condition is a component of a spectrum disorder, a subaffective condition with a lifelong course and vulnerability to acute exacerbation of affective disorders. Virtually all views of the borderline condition incorporate a defective sense of self, aggravated or even caused by unstable mood swings. Some personality theorists place greater emphasis on defective ego development (e.g.,

Kernberg, 1975) as a precursor and contributor to the borderline personality's chronic affective instability, whereas Akiskal has argued that the unstable mood interfers with development of a sense of emotional history and continuity necessary to a stable self-image.

From the perspective of the core polarities that contribute to each personality pattern, what distinguishes the borderline condition is that all the elements are in conflict. That is, there are moderate degrees of enhancement and preservation needs, but these are chronically in flux, producing erratic emotional and behavioral outbursts reflecting this ambivalence. Likewise, the borderline personality is inclined on both active and passive forms of adjustment and is also intensely ambivalent and vacillating between self and other orientations—in other words, between individuation and nurturance. The result is that these individuals are extraordinarily insecure and vulnerable, especially to the experience of fear of abandonment. When their mercurial, rageful, attacking behavior drives others away, they may panic in response to the ensuing separation anxiety. At such times they may become acutely suicidal, feeling empty and bereft, with intense despair and some even a sense of personal annihilation. The negative consequences of a poorly formulated attempt at assertion may leave individuals with borderline personality feeling self-punitive and betrayed by their efforts to express their ravenous dependency needs. Self-mutilating acts may represent atonement for such behavior; individuals with borderline personalities may also engage in substance abuse to anesthetize themselves from their feelings of self-recrimination and despair.

CLINICAL DOMAIN FEATURES

On a functional behavioral level, individuals with borderline personalities are characteristically erratic in their display of emotions, which are impulsively expressed or poorly modulated in response to the events around them. This leaves others mystified, shocked, or repelled at the unpredictable nature of these individuals. Their behavior is also interpersonally inconsistent, even contradictory, because their neediness and dependence may be rapidly replaced by oppositional, defiant, and provocative actions that seemingly defeat their purpose. This is a reflection of their ambivalence and fears of intimacy, which become activated if their dependency and ingratiating behaviors are met. Even when they are not behaving explosively, they may display subtle, passive–aggressive maneuvers almost at the same time they are exhibiting affectionate, solicitous behavior.

Cognitively, borderline individuals' thinking may fluctuate rapidly, from trust to mistrust, high regard to contempt. Even more difficult for them is their fluctuating perception of relationships, colored by their desperate

dependency needs and competing fear of abandonment, which make relationships seem alternately ideal and then threatening and others as helpful
and caring and then malicious and insensitive. Feeding these fluctuating
patterns are the understandably perplexed reactions of their interactive
counterparts, whose confused responses may be interpreted as confirming
their unrealistic hopes or worst fears. Because they are so feeling-dominated,
situation-dependent, and reactive, individuals with borderline personalities
in a real sense are living in the moment. It is difficult for individuals with
borderline personalities to form consistent and stable plans, intentions,
perceptions, and attitudes that promote a sense of continuity and history
necessary to form a stable self-image. Their sense of self is fluid and often
dependent on the situation or moment they are experiencing and easily
shattered by upsetting events. Just as their perceptions of others are contradictory and characterized by splitting (all good or all bad), their conceptions
of self may be similarly construed, depending on their situational and emotional state. They thus lack the coherence and cohesion of a self-image
that can weather the vicissitudes of daily events, evening out frustration,
disappointment, and facilitating delay of gratification and impulse control.

Likewise, the internalized representations of individuals with borderline personalities are typically primitive, reflecting contradictory or inconsistent experiences, contaminated by unconscious conflicts and fears, especially
that they ultimately will be disappointed and abandoned, often because of
personal characteristics that are a source of self-loathing. Typically their
schemas are tightly organized into positive and negative dynamics, with
little appreciation or capacity to tolerate the shades of gray that characterize
normal psychological functioning. Earlier relationships, often prototypical
ones with parent figures, have shaped their images of interpersonal experiences as involving contradictory demands followed by rejection for efforts
at assertive, autonomous functioning, and also seductive enticement to
remain dependent at the cost of punishment and frustration. These early
traumatic and frustrating experiences create enormous resentments and apprehensions that are reactivated by later attractions and intimacies, causing
replays and fragmented efforts to work through previous relationship failures.

On an intrapsychic level the borderline personality's fragile, frequently
defective coping is predominated by use of primitive regression to earlier
developmental forms of behavior, often infantile rage attacks. Once hostility
is expressed, consequent guilt and recrimination may motivate expiatory
behavior in which residual hostile impulses are self-directed. This may be
represented in self-derogating and demeaning verbalizations and exaggera-
tions of inadequacy and pitifulness, which also serve to neutralize hostile
counterattack. In more severe cases, this may even involve self-punitive,
mutilative actions that others are powerless to negate. Splitting, as noted
earlier, is a term common to borderline states, reflecting discontinuous,

dichotic thinking and boundaries, from all good to all bad, love to hate. When experiencing excessive conflict, a complete breakdown in boundaries may develop, ushering in a psychotic decompensation.

Finally, from a biophysical perspective, individuals with borderline personalities may by temperament have an overreactive nervous system, wherein they are often overwhelmed by moods and impulses and governed by marked shifts from euphoria to depression and dejection, anger–rage, and debilitating anxiety. Ordinarily one adjustment will dominate and be replaced by divergent, extreme emotional reactions.

BORDERLINE PERSONALITY SUBTYPES

Individuals with borderline personalities carry features of all other personality disorders, with perhaps the exception of the schizoid and compulsive types. The determining characteristics of the individual with true borderline personality, however, is the persistence and enduring nature of affective instability and propensity for self-destructive behavior patterns and emotional decompensation. Although other personality types may evidence borderline-like behavior patterns when faced with acute stresses and losses, the core borderline disorder manifests structural deficiencies in the afflicted individuals' psychic organization and impulse control mechanisms, which create interpersonal instability even in the absence of stressors. For example, when relationships are going well, other personality patterns may be relatively quiescent, whereas for borderline personalities conflicts concerning intimacy and trust will continue to produce anxiety that stimulates relationship-eroding challenges.

Individuals with borderline personalities with a combination of dependent and avoidant features will be relatively meek, subassertive and acquiescing, overly compliant to the needs of those with whom they become attached. However, even when confronted with displays of contentment or satisfaction from their partners, their core insecurity and lack of trust provokes a hypersensitivity to imagined rebuff, a vulnerability to depression or alarm, or listless, helpless behavior that is perplexing to their partners. Interspersed with these displays may be episodes of explosive anger, outbursts or expressions of resentment over their self-imposed exploitation. These can leave their partners feeling initially guilty and confused, then later angry and resentful once these events are recognized as a common theme or pattern to the relationship. Like their dependent personality counterpart, these individuals have learned from early life to submit and acquiesce to parental figures on whom they were wholly dependent for their security needs. However, they may also have been betrayed by being disappointed or punished with rejection or disapproval by not having precisely done what was expected. This can create a sense of insecurity and mistrust that accompanies the basic dependent adaptation and behavior pattern and vulnerability to rage over the frustration from inconsistent outcomes and violations of basic interpersonal contracts. Especially because of their strong dependency traits, these individuals are particularly threatened by their feelings of hostility, which they recognize as a danger to maintaining those relationships that provide them within any sense of security and personal integrity. As a result, self-punitive behavior, an inward turning of anger, serves to both symbolically atone for such feelings and also to dramatize the distress experienced over their inner conflicts.

Perhaps the most visible borderline personalities are those individuals with prominent histrionic and antisocial personalities traits. These are the most dramatic, expressive, and manipulative of the borderline types. Although these individuals can behave in a seductive and exploitive fashion, their interpersonal history is likely to be erratic, reflecting their basically deficient coping and inability to sustain relationships, owing to their affective instability and inherent impulsiveness. Substance abuse to feed the need for external stimulation and excitement may be more likely with these individuals, who may medicate themselves as a substitute for psychological coping with strong feelings. Unlike their dependent–avoidant counterparts, these individuals need to be in control of or dominate relationships, given their more active orientation. Generally, they are not likely to seek a health care professional's assistance unless there is some external determinant (e.g., legal or financial difficulties) creating distress.

The borderline personality with negativistic traits is a subtype that may be difficult to initially differentiate from its primary counterpart, the negativistic personality disorder, until the more unstable, structurally defective personality features emerge. These individuals are characteristically complaining, envious, pessimistic, and chronically feeling cheated and shortchanged that others get a "better deal." Although dependent and longing for security, the core conflicts concerning intimacy and trust and their propensity for resentment, sullen, and contrary moods creates chronic ambivalence and resistance to longed-for attachments. A bitter, depressed, orientation reconciled to disappointment may oscillate with occasionally accusatory, blaming psychotic tirades, invariably followed by anxious or panicked remorsefulness in reaction to fears of abandonment.

Finally, perhaps the most self-destructive of the borderline personality variants are those individuals with prominent masochistic and depressive features. Self-mutilation is particularly common, reflecting a long-standing desire of hurting oneself out of a conviction that those abandonments one experienced were because one was "bad" and deserving of punishment and even self-hate. Suicidal ideation is never far from the surface with these individuals. Relationships are likely to be particularly short-lived, reflecting the extreme vacillation between feeble autonomy strivings and despair when alone and isolated. As with other borderlines personality types, there is an anger over needing others, who become resented for their reliance on them for their security and self-esteem. To defend against these negative feelings and the threat they pose (of abandonment), these individuals may become overly accommodating to the moods and feelings of others, but only at the expense of feeling cumulatively exploited and used for those sacrifices they have made. When able to tolerate relationships even in the short-term, the invariable discomfort with intimacy gives rise to intropunitive impulses rather than externalized blame and complaints.

In general, treatment of all the borderline variants is a long-term investment of time if fundamental personality changes are to be accomplished. Individuals with borderline personalities are capable of functioning in a socially appropriate and productive manner if they feel secure and are not threatened with relationship abandonment fears. Given their fragility and propensity to challenge relationships out of mistrust and insecurity, however, they are quite vulnerable to crises and decompensation. When this occurs, rapid but brief hospitalization and increased medication management may be necessary. Long hospital stays should be avoided because this will promote unhealthy dependencies and then problematic relationships with staff in that context, which will be destabilizing when discharge becomes necessary.

PERPETUATING FEATURES

Virtually all of the behavioral fluctuations of individuals with borderlines personalities, by virtue of their contradictory and unstable nature, have the effect of frustrating their attempts to secure love and stability. In their efforts to establish intimate, fulfilling relationships, they may initially behave in a dependent, self-sacrificing, and self-effacing manner intended to endear themselves and also elicit some reciprocal caretaking, but primarily to establish a bond protecting against abandonment. Yet it seems even when these tactics are successful, inner feelings of mistrust and anxiety will emerge, producing contradictory modes of coping that is confusing and misleading to their relationship partner. The perplexity and withdrawal that ensues in turn will alarm the borderline patient who is also frustrated over these self-inflicted disruptions. This frustration in turn will elicit hostile, confrontive, and demanding behavior that further pushes away the loved one, perpetuating the prophecy of abandonment and fear—conviction that relationships cannot be trusted.

The borderline personality's conflict and relationship ambivalence produces chronic feelings of apprehension and anger. In a more compensated state this anger may be confined to typically indirect, covert expression, perhaps in the form of exasperated pleading or displays of despair designed to elicit concern and nurturance. Depressive behavior, in the context of their efforts to manage their relationship, may serve to punish others for not meeting earlier needs. Displays of sulking, pitiful states will dramatize the harm the borderline personality has experienced at the hands of the loved one, who by implication should make some form of atonement or restitution. This behavior also serves to exempt these individuals from facing unwanted responsibilities, which then can be shifted onto their relationship partners.

Although their tensions may be reduced in this fashion, individuals with borderline personalities incur a cumulative price by wearying their love objects. Eventually their partners begin to pull away, causing an intensification of alarm straining the coping mechanisms of these fragile individuals. At some point their anger will become more intense, confrontive, and poorly modulated, threatening or causing dissolution of the relationship. During this time there may be brief intermissions in the display of rageful behavior, where the individual with borderline personality may show temporary restraint but also an insatiable need for reassurance and attention. Eventually when these fluctuating tactics and emotional excesses completely sabotage the relationship, either additional decompensation occurs or efforts are made to project their own failings onto their former loved ones, who now may be despised and condemned.

Although unable to modulate expressions of hostility, individuals with borderline personalities possess ample social skills to recognize the problematic impact of their antagonistic behavior on others on whom they are dependent. To reduce the likelihood of reciprocal hostility, their outbursts may be followed by correspondingly intense self-denigration and reproach to neutralize or defuse anticipated negative counter-response. By attacking themselves, it is hoped that they can preempt attack—rejection from those who they may have provoked. In doing so they unilaterally seek redemption by disarming their interactive partner, who may feel compelled to show mercy. Over time, however, this maneuver may prove to be ineffective, even destructive, as partners' hurt and resentments are prevented from expression, obviating any possibility of productive interchange that might clarify misunderstandings and restore good feeling.

The difficulty in changing borderline individuals' dysfunctional behavior patterns is related to their emotional intensity during their behavioral extremes. When enraged, they are hardly accessible to reason. When in their atonement mode, they are likely to overexaggerate any constructive negative feedback so that it reinforces an unhealthy sense of self that promotes their feelings of insecurity and instability. The task is then to aid borderline patients in controlling their anxiety or rage to levels where they can reflect on their feelings and respond nonreflexively in a moderate fashion less likely to produce problematic consequences and more likely to foster emotional growth.

Because of the nature of their perpetuating features, borderline personalities present special challenges to those treating these individuals. Foremost, enormous perseverance and patience is required to deal with the interpersonal instability, mistrust, and testing of the therapeutic relationship. No amount of skill can prevent some degree of interpersonal volatility on the part of these individuals, whose needs cannot conceivably or practically be met. Indeed, one of the core areas of growth and change for the borderline individual is dealing with these issues. The therapist or health care provider must be prepared to cope with alternative idealization and devaluation, without experiencing damaging counterhostility. Particularly vexing may be borderline patients' efforts to extend the relationship and personalize it outside of the professional context, for example by making phone calls at off hours, often on an escalating basis that may eventuate in coercive suicide threats and gestures. This blurring of boundaries can be particularly threatening for the therapeutic relationship, which may ultimately have to be terminated if some rules concerning the limits of the treatment cannot be established. In particular, careful delineation of the treatment expectations and objectives at the start of therapy is essential.

Because of the profound imbalance between dependence–independence–autonomy for the individual with borderline personality, a primary goal of fostering independent and more satisfactory interpersonal functioning must be specified and periodically reviewed. These individuals' propensity to regress into a helpless, dependent role may prove seductive for the health care provider to assume the role of problem-solver or savior, thereby defeating efforts to enhance any sense of self-sufficiency and esteem through successful negotiation of the patients' many crises. This will be difficult to avoid given the typically tumultuous nature of these individuals' personal relationships, which often turn into crises. Only a very structured approach accompanied by frequent reviews of the therapeutic contract and the patient–therapist relationship can combat these common difficulties.

INTERPERSONAL ASPECTS OF BORDERLINE PATIENTS IN THE HEALTH CARE SETTING

In the medical clinic context patients with borderline characteristics may initially present as quite varied. Some may appear to be relatively pleasant, engaging, and responsive. Others, however, may appear depressed, sullen, confused, even disorganized. Yet others may present as angry, demanding, drug-seeking, and manipulative. All of these presentations will represent different aspects or variant combinations of borderline personalities. The medical practitioner with a borderline patient may have to prepare for an emotional roller-coaster ride. To the extent that they are engaged by the patient in extended intimate encounters, there is a greater likelihood of enmeshment and emotional volatility even with primary care providers or specialists. Given their social skills, patients with borderline personalities may be difficult to recognize initially until their difficulties maintaining interpersonal boundaries emerge. They may be psychologically beguiling by their flattering overidentification and idealization with their health care providers, and even sexually seductive. Practitioners may be only vaguely aware of such interpersonal influences intensely experienced by such individuals, and may be surprised and overwhelmed when their patients abruptly change from an adoring, idealizing posture to an angry demeanor of a person feeling betrayed. Providers and their assistants will naturally respond with initial bewilderment, confusion, and then later anger over such outbursts.

Once the affective intensity of these patients diminish and they return to a more quiescent state, they may attempt to conduct interpersonal business as usual. They may act as if nothing happened, perhaps reflecting the commonplace nature of such outbursts from their perspective, or they may act anxiously contrite and self-denigrating, hoping to placate their practitioners on whom they are ultimately dependent. The health care providers who have been buffeted by these patients' erratic behaviors, however, may predictably change their demeanor to a more guarded, defensive, even angry posture, which will alarm the patients who are ultimately fearful of abandonment. This may elicit displays of distress and self-atonement, even self-punitive actions, in an effort to demonstrate penance and disarm or re-engage the sympathy of their designated caretakers. For experienced primary care practitioners or nonpsychiatric physicians, these events reflect the fragile boundaries of these individuals and the precarious nature of their relationships, which can make them so difficult to deal with.

Enmeshment characterizes much of the interpersonal relationships of individuals with borderline personalities. The natural relationship stresses imposed by illnesses can intensify the effects of this enmeshment, creating overpersonalized abandonment experiences for the borderline patients when their regular social supports are available. This can introduce relationship volatility ill-suited to a health crisis situation. At such times these patients may show regression in adaptive behavior and intensification of expressions of dependency. When expectations of caretaking are unmet, the borderline patient may react with disruptive rage and demoralization, adding emotional decompensation that may undermine treatment of the physical illness. Introducing new supports provided by the health care system will require that the providers are prepared to deal with individuals who are desperate and needy and primed to experience rejection.

When initially seeking care and establishing relationships borderline patients may make few initial demands out of instinctive appreciation of the damage their recent disruptive behavior may have caused them in other relationships. Once some of their needs begin to be met by their designated caretakers, they may begin to personalize these relationships, reducing their sense of any interpersonal boundaries. As this process unfolds they may then resume their tendencies to alternatively idealize and then devalue those in their life on whom they rely to meet their needs.

In an inpatient psychiatric setting this process can be seen as borderline patients reconstitute their defenses following the decompensation that brought them to the hospital. As they become more comfortable in the setting, their regular mode of functioning returns; where relationships become more volatile, splitting begins to occur with patients and staff, and there is a risk of deterioration in these patients' adjustment, which threatens their discharge in a restored, healthy state. This scenario predictably can and does occur in nonpsychiatric, medical inpatient environments, especially where there is a prolonged stay sufficient for the patient to begin to establish relationships with the staff. Reversing these processes is a challenge for skilled psychiatric staff; for medical personnel responsible for other acutely or chronically ill medical patients, this can be a demoralizing and overwhelming experience. Eventually there may be a call for outside help as the conflicts escalate, or the patient may be precipitously discharged, either because of unreasonable demands or because his or her physician is disgusted with the patient. In either case, the health of such individuals may be at risk, because these patients may retaliate by failing to take their medications, such as steroids to reduce brain swelling following neurosurgery, a crisis that in fact confronted the author during his internship training.

Experienced social workers or pastoral staff can be invaluable in recognizing these patients early in the process, so that they can intervene in the sense of alerting other staff to interpersonal boundary issues and serve as a conflict-diverting conduit for the patients' interpersonal demands and counterproductive staff responses. There is no guarantee that these patients may still not subvert this process in their need for interpersonal control, but it can minimize the potential for escalating conflict and serious compromise to patients' medical management.

MEDICAL MANAGEMENT ISSUES

From the foregoing discussion, it should be clear that managing the health of patients with borderline personalities, be it preventive measures of acute care, at best will be an "interesting" experience but not uncommonly chaotic and even traumatic. Early recognition of these individuals' inherent instabilities can reduce the relationship tumult that may be inevitable, improving overall health care use and outcomes.

Preventive Interventions, Lifestyle Choices

Individuals with borderline personalities, because of their unstable mood and reactive, impulsive, and contradictory thoughts and actions, are ill-equipped to modify consumptive behaviors such as smoking, drinking, and overeating. Being here-and-now individuals, with behavior highly state-dependent, implementation of strategies involving monitoring, behavior substitution, and delay of gratification may exceed their characterological or constitutional capacities for consistency and self-regulation and self-correction.

Stages of Change

Conceptually, this model invites consideration of change as an orderly process where individuals sequentially move from one phase to the next, gaining a cumulative sense of mastery in the course of acquiring some new healthy behavior pattern. In actuality, for any person there is considerable fluctuation between stages and uneven progress, even skipping certain phases. This will be most true for individuals with borderline personalities. The model is nonetheless valuable in specifying the different states of mind and action that characterize change in its different stages, which do tend to adhere to a certain order.

Precontemplative activity for the patient with borderline personality is likely to be shifting and reversing considerations and intentions, accompanied by much emotionality. For example, obesity in a borderline patient is no doubt shrouded with urges for self-gratification competing with feelings of self-loathing over body image distortions and guilt when overeating occurs. Social stigmata against fatness are ubiquitous enough not to require formal medical recommendations, and being overweight is a matter of some torment for any overeater. Stressors such as anticipated, imagined, or real losses may stimulate binges that in turn elicit self-punitive feelings hardly conducive to a stable self-image or coping that could support the difficult battle involving self-denial. These influences should be addressed during formal contemplative activity after medical recommendations are issued.

With other unhealthy behaviors such as drinking, smoking, or substance abuse, defensive processes against acknowledging and owning those behaviors may be more prominent. The extreme mood changes of borderline personalities and their fluctuations in their cognitive perspectives may make it difficult to establish and maintain a consistent focus on problematic behavior (that there is an addiction) and intentions (a need for change). In particular, fluctuations in interpersonal experiences producing abandonment fears and marked regression will have a disruptive influence.

The preparation stage will have to address any basic ambivalence to a formal proposal for change involving denial of appetitive urges and interpersonal commitment such as enrollment in groups. To the extent that multiple providers are involved, there may be efforts to forge alliances for support and advantage given the borderline patient's propensity for splitting. Potential barriers for change will need to be identified, especially problematic interpersonal influences (e.g., a boyfriend who abuses substances or still smokes), especially because these could represent fatal obstacles to change.

The action and maintenance stages may be characterized by much tumult as borderline patients struggle with primitive impulses and the meanings attached to their appetitive behavior patterns and the responses their efforts and lapses elicit in others. The borderline patient's tendency to perceive and resonate emotionally to events on an all-or-nothing basis may make it difficult to tolerate the inevitable impasses and failures experienced in making behavior change. Splitting in response to unexpected disapproval from inexperienced providers can precipitate abrupt termination of the intervention. Borderline personalities may also respond to expression of unwanted or shameful impulses with self-punitive acts. The real challenge for these two final stages will be developing some sense of continuity and history of more stable coping that resists those inevitable influences for relapse.

Efforts to follow a model of change such as this with borderline patients will doubtless prove frustrating for the behavioral medicine practitioner, particularly one who has not had extensive grounding in dealing with severe personality disorders concerning targeted behaviorally oriented change. It can be overwhelming and demoralizing when the patient with borderline personality shifts the focus from specific behavior change to affectively charged relationship issues dominated by transference issues. The practitioner should keep in mind that even for relatively healthy individuals, it can take many attempts to overcome addictions such as smoking and overeating before change is successful and enduring.

Utility, Cost–Benefit Considerations of Preventive Interventions

For a severe personality disorder such as the borderline type, the prospect of straightforward behavior change from appetitive–addictive behavior patterns to abstinent or healthy behaviors is highly unlikely. Certainly if there is an overwhelmingly motivating influence such as severe, life-threatening pneumonia to influence smoking cessation, then initial change may occur. However, as health is restored, individuals will revert to their old patterns, especially when their ordinary routines return, to which the unhealthy behaviors are associated. It will then be the history of successfully struggling with temptations and impulses after some failures of will, and the new coping techniques for preventing relapse, that make the difference in the long range. With borderline patients who are well and relatively asymptomatic, the cost of insisting on adoption of completely healthy behavior patterns will likely be unreasonably high in relation to the benefits obtained. However, for the overweight, diabetic individual with borderline personality, at high risk for heart attack, stroke, or renal failure, a persistent, intensive effort involving multiple attempts to effect long-range behavior change may be strongly indicated. The investment involves lifelong considerations about compliance, self-discipline, and self-mastery, essential characteristics for preservation of a person (and health cost dollars) whose biological vulnerabilities place him or her at risk for chronic, deteriorating illness. Especially because the borderline patient may tend to excesses and extreme behaviors, any strengthening of coping and self-controls that would attenuate such tendencies would be welcome and justified from a cost–benefit standpoint. This may come through multiple fits and starts in different interventions over time, which actually may have some cumulative long-range benefit.

Secondary and Tertiary Care of Acute and Chronic Illness

With borderline patients the tumult of normal functioning and chaotic interpersonal relationships may overshadow most other concerns, especially seemingly minor physical symptoms and ailments, unless their health becomes an issue tied in with their other conflicts. Even when persistent symptoms are present, they may escape attention if these patients are experiencing one of their many relationship crises or if they are engaged in some form of substance abuse in an effort at self-tranquilization, which distracts from, masks, or mimics the manifestation of real physical illness. Their disturbed self-image, which may play a role in dissociative episodes involving self-mutilation, also may contribute to being out of touch with physical symptomology, making them poor candidates for early illness detection dependent on personal awareness. Because of their unstable nature, they may enter and exit primary medical care practices rather erratically, making continuity of health care management difficult as well, so that when risk factors are known, they may not be systematically attended to at appropriate time intervals through failure to follow up.

Once a symptom reaches a threshold level where it cannot be ignored or produces significant debilitation, then it will predictably become interwoven with these patients' psychopathology. Because any physical ailment universally elicits concern and sympathy at least initially, it can represent a powerful influence to coerce support and tolerance from others. The natural emotional lability of borderline patients and their interpersonal excesses can now be attributed to their not feeling well or consequences of the illness. These individuals may feel disinhibited emotionally with such potential sanction and may act even more demandingly with family or other caretakers aware of their condition.

For borderline patients, the development of illness representations may be complicated by the many distortions that can take place, given their primitive, often primary process modes of functioning. Unless these patients are asked to recite their understanding of the disease, its course, typical management, and their role or responsibilities for self-care, it may be difficult to determine any private or idiosyncratic extra meanings they may have attached to their condition. For this disorder it is highly likely that interpersonal issues will exert a prominent influence. For some patients their condition may stimulate great alarm and fears of abandonment (as a burden to a weakly committed significant other or family member). For others, it may represent a virtual guarantee against rejection so long as the condition persists. Conversely, it could provide justification for breaking a commitment ("the relationship is aggravating my condition"; "if I have only so long to enjoy any quality of life, it will not be with that person") or for continued involvement in an aversive relationship ("who would want me now, the way my illness has made me?"). It would be unlikely that busy practitioners oriented only to rational illness management would be unaware of such dynamics, which are often hidden to the patients themselves. Recurrent thwarting of treatment plans and care-disrupting conflicts is likely to be the result.

Coping With Illness

Most individuals with borderline personalities are typically endowed with reasonably decent social skills; their undoing is their inability to sustain relationships, tolerate frustrations, and maintain a coherent, consistent course of action. Their history is one of moving from relationship to relationship. Provided they are sufficiently attractive and personable, they may be able to forestall serious, debilitating decompensations by moving on with some new interest. It is when they are trapped or constrained in relationships, by external circumstance or their own psychological dependence, that their real vulnerabilities may emerge. A serious, prolonged illness can provoke such a crisis by constraining these individuals in a number of ways. First, they are made more dependent on others for basic needs that they cannot provide for themselves: money (if they are unable to work), transportation, errands and other routine instrumental activities such as shopping (if they are bedridden), and other illness-specific activities such as filing insurance forms. All of these are examples of problem-focused coping or "taking care of business," which may be disrupted by acute illness episodes that keep them from performing these activities themselves. If these demands and consequences of their illness mount up, they will become serious stressors in addition to the burden of feeling physically bad. For most individuals they are relieved by the social support of family members, spouses, or agency help, where that form of assistance is mobilized by the health care system. Continuity of such aid is generally dependent on maintaining at least a formal, superficially cordial relationship with these help-givers. Given that erratic, capricious interpersonal behavior is the core feature of the borderline personality's typical adjustment, this may prove difficult.

Emotion-focused coping is another separable aspect of significant physical illness. Borderline patients are also poorly equipped in this area, given their chronic mood instability and the reverberations of their erratic interpersonal behavior on their emotions and chronic sense of insecurity. With the increased dependence posed by illness comes an intensification of feelings of vulnerability, and both pragmatic (i.e., instrumental requirements of living) and emotional issues are likely to be confounded. Especially for these individuals, with their difficulties maintaining boundaries, they may make emotional demands on individuals prepared only to provide instrumental support for problem-focused coping. When these caretakers predictably fail to meet those expectations, they may be faced with accusatory rage, hurt withdrawal, or both reactions in any order. Those providers designated to provide primarily emotional or moral support (e.g., pastoral services) may find themselves as under attack ("what good are you?") if they fail to solve some practical problem in keeping with the patient's desperate sense of urgency.

In addition to dealing poorly with the emotional and problem-focused aspects of the illness confronting them, borderline patients' chaotic interpersonal conduct will alienate others, further heightening their sense of vulnerability, undermining their efforts to manage the illness or recover from the effects of the interventions (e.g., surgery, chemotherapy). The medical condition may then become a secondary issue to the emotional crisis that can itself threaten treatment or recovery. Early detection of these patients' instabilities and involvement of personnel experienced in dealing with the complicated management issues their treatment will pose may minimize much grief and health care expense, both in dollar cost, wear and tear on the professionals involved, and the time diverted from their other patients.

Medical Compliance

Borderline patients' emotionality and reactivity to events, especially those of an interpersonal nature, leave them particularly prone to compliance problems. Their poor coping with impulses make them susceptible to appetitive or addictive behaviors, especially substance abuse, and their amorphous self-image provides a poor reference point by which to develop and link intentions and action strategies to a goal of self-enhancement. Medical illness may require complex compliance requirements involving self-denial, temptation control—suppression of impulses, and prospective social judgment to avert negative influences (e.g., old drinking partners, drug abusers). It is thus not surprising that borderline patients are high maintenance cases for chronic illnesses such as intractable pain, organ transplant, diabetes, and the like, where sustained compliance is a requirement.

Even where pain and some degree of debilitation may temporarily motivate compliance, the shifting emotional states of borderline patients and the probable state-dependent nature of their learning make it more likely that relapse behaviors may occur. When upset or overcome with cravings and impulses, self-preservation concerns may be sharply reduced, even in the face of life-threatening consequences (e.g., drinking when being treated for acute pancreatitis). Borderline patients' ambivalence about autonomy needs and fears of subordinating themselves in a dependent role may contribute to confusion about having to submit to the medical recommendations of some authority figure—for example, their physicians. When in an idealizing mode with the physicians or caretakers, they may embrace the treatment regimen, and it may seem a stable treatment course has been achieved. Then when there is some interpersonal slight or conflict, even the obviously beneficial features of treatment in the patient's self-interest may be angrily rejected along with the source. Although requirements to stop smoking, drinking, and to take medications with distressing side effects can be presented logically as required for treatment, it will be the manner in which the message is delivered that determines its impact and these patients' responses to it.

It follows from these considerations that medical compliance with borderline patients will tend to be at best an inherently unstable process, especially when relationship issues intrude. These patients will require close monitoring in a fashion that maintains a certain degree of psychological distance to provide a stable interpersonal boundary. It is when the health provider becomes unwittingly enmeshed as a result of the borderline patient's erratic efforts to establish intimacy (about which he or she is fundamentally ambivalent) that confusion in treatment develops. Especially where treatment is intensive and compliance critical to outcome, it may be important for the patient to establish a psychotherapeutic relationship separate from the medical treatment, to transfer some of the intensity that will develop in the medical setting to mental health professionals experienced in dealing with this serious form of psychopathology.

IMPACT OF DISEASE STATES ON THE BORDERLINE PATIENT

Illness, especially a serious one requiring numerous specialists and complicated treatment regimens, can be especially difficult to manage with the borderline patient, given the number of relationships involved and the opportunity for "splitting." In addition, the propensity for self-punitive behavior and suicidal impulses introduces a new element in their care, where there can be risk of active sabotage of care or misuse of powerful drugs to "punish" providers for their interpersonal sins. With such individuals, relationship management may be as important a part of their care as the medical management objective.

Somatoform, Stress-Related Conditions: Headache, Disease of the Digestive System

It should not be surprising that individuals with borderline personalities would be vulnerable to stress-related conditions, given their pervasive emotional lability. This would apply particularly to those with histrionic or avoidant–dependent features, where there are characterologically based inhibitions against natural expression of feelings, either through conflict-avoiding tendencies or fears of rejection. Given their incomplete, fragmented sense of self, deficient ego boundary and ambivalence concerning pleasure–pain and active–passive modes of functioning–coping, behaviorally oriented techniques involving relaxation training and use of interoceptive cues could prove problematic. Any therapy, even if structured but oriented toward identification of stressors, could be destabilizing if the patient's psychosomatic presentation represents a defense against incipient decompensation. Although relaxation training appears innocuous enough an intervention, the act of reclining, reducing external stimulation, and attempting to drift mentally as a means of letting go is not unlike the conditions of free association, and could promote surfacing of frightening thoughts or impulses that the patient's tension-based symptoms serve to defend against.

A certain amount of sizing up patients may thus be necessary even for what on the surface would appear to be focused, low-risk therapies. It is also in the nature of characterologically disturbed patients to experience even innocuous interventions uniquely in terms of their own dynamics and psychopathology. Any experienced behavior therapist has discovered the phenomena of transference irrespective of how behavioral their treatment may seem to be. Sensitivity is thus required to ensure that even these seemingly harmless approaches are experienced in the fashion intended, and are not transformed into more complex or confounded interpersonal events of a potentially aggravating or even iatrogenic nature.

The readiness for change model can be helpful in this regard. During even the first few visits, consideration of the patient's precontemplation state (in terms of addressing the psychosomatic condition) can provide useful clues about their capacity to focus on an intervention strategy. If in acute crisis, they may be too fragmented or disorganized to benefit, and may require medication to stabilize mood or address a low-grade thinking disturbance. Introducing contemplatively oriented discussion in the early pretreatment interview can help the therapist determine if addressing the physical symptom and any related emotional dynamic threatens to undermine tenuous defenses against disorganization. Likewise, careful scrutiny of the patient's participation in the planning phase and understanding of any resistances that emerge can guide the practitioner in determining what these patients can tolerate in the way of change and the potential consequences or costs to them of treatment outcome (e.g., unwanted independence). All the time, consideration of the practitioner–patient relationship will be required. Heavy-handed communications of disapproval that a patient has not carried out his or her homework assignment can be experienced as traumatic rejection to an abandonment-fearing borderline patient, whereas such messages with other individuals may be quite appropriate to motivate action.

Although behaviorally oriented, empirically based treatment packages have become the interventions of choice for psychosomatic conditions, their programmed or "cookbook" nature may be insufficient to deal with the complex clinical scenarios that can occur with borderline patients, even with seemingly circumscribed symptoms (e.g., tension headaches). As systematic and focused as behavior therapy treatment may be, it still requires a relationship with a patient and opportunities for transference phenomena, even if that is not part of the behavioral medicine lexicon.

Pain Management

Borderline patients' deficient coping skills, poor time sense, and intolerance for discomfort may make it particularly difficult for them to endure prolonged acute pain, especially if they are not prepared for it. Self-inflicted injury deriving from dissociative self-punitive episodes represents a different experience concerning the meaning and significance of the physical nociceptive signals. Where such behavior occurs, it can be assumed that the psychic pain generating such self-injurious activity is far greater than the consequent physical experience, which may represent some form of atonement or self-repudiation consistent with the state-dependent dynamic in operation. Where the physical pain derives from some disease process or injury exogenous to the personal dynamics of the individual with borderline personality, it may well exert the same sense of physical distress as in other personality types.

As with anyone, if there is explanation concerning the meaning of pain (e.g., that it is the result of successful surgery where healing and recovery can be expected), then it is more probable that it will be endured with greater patience and more positive expectations. Nonetheless, the borderline patient's tolerance of discomfort will typically be of shorter duration than other individuals. Even a charismatic physician whose initial pronouncements following surgery are glowingly accepted by these patients will be in for a rude surprise (e.g., devaluation and attack), if after a comparatively brief period of time his or her borderline patient is experiencing significant physical discomfort. The concern would be the extremes that borderline individual's emotional outbursts could take, such as physical injury or at least disruption of recovery (e.g., rupturing stitches getting out of bed to leave the hospital). This would be more likely if these patients' protests generated a rejection experience that induced subsequent emotional decompensation. For this reason, if the acute pain is not expected to extend for a period where significant habituation or addiction to narcotic pain medications is a risk, it may be best to aggressively medicate these individuals with analgesics and sedatives or mood stabilizing drugs, to maximize physical and emotional comfort, at least during the most important healing phase.

Where chronic pain is concerned, the long-range management of the borderline patient is of central concern. There are marked risks for addiction, misuse of medications (with greater suicide risk given their availability), and a particularly unstable form of chronic depression secondary to the prolonged physical restrictions and discomforts associated with persistent physical disability accompanied by pain. Those borderline patients with a particularly low tolerance for inactivity and unchanging physical environments will find this condition particularly intolerable, especially if their relationship partners have high activity levels and are disinclined to change their lifestyles. What may ensue is a pattern of excessive overdoing after a restlessness has built up or if there is a sense that a relationship partner may be losing interest and looking elsewhere for companionship. This will be predictably followed by an exacerbation of the pain, causing reduction in activities that ordinarily could be tolerated, and intensification of the patient's misery. This pattern is certainly not restricted to borderline types of patients, but they may resonate and react more strongly to these influences, so that their overdoing may be more extreme, reflecting their poor judgment. In turn, their response to the cost of such excess may be extreme distress, demoralization, and despair, even to the point of serious suicide attempt.

Considering that pain behaviors and secondary gain are invariant features of the chronic pain syndrome, some form of psychological–psychiatric care oriented to chronic pain management should be mandatory for borderline patients, given the regression and conflicts their condition will produce. In addition to the importance of early use of appropriate medications for anxiety–depression or even low-dose neuroleptics for thought disturbance, skilled monitoring and management of relationship issues before they get out of hand will be essential. Chronic pain is a lifelong proposition requiring formidable adjustments. The probability of interpersonal and affective attrition with borderline patients is markedly higher given their inherent instability of mood, cognition, and behavior. With these individuals the risk is quite high for analgesic abuse, doctor and pharmacy shopping, suicide gestures and serious attempts, as well as significant degradation of the medically treated condition requiring additional surgery and acute care.

Diabetes

Especially with a chronic, lifelong illness such as diabetes, where self-monitoring, self-discipline, and consistency is essential to managing this metabolic disturbance, borderline patients will face a constant challenge, as will their health care providers. Excessive emotionality will make it more difficult to maintain stable blood-sugar levels from a physiological standpoint, given emotion-related endocrine surges. Behaviorally, this instability can involve impulsive dietary indiscretion, substance abuse, smoking–nicotine consumption (that constricts the small blood vessels), and inattention to or neglect of insulin regulation because of emotional crises–interpersonal conflicts. Establishing a continuing sense of self-accountability concerning one's physical health requires well-developed psychological mechanisms lacking in the borderline character. These include a stable self-image, cohesive inner structures for internalizing experience, and especially modulating affect. Even in psychologically sound diabetic individuals, maintaining a resolve to resist temptation is a difficult psychological and behavioral accomplishment, often taken for granted by medical physicians.

The borderline patient may intellectually accept that the self-care requirements of diabetes are necessary to preserve health and prevent certain kinds of long-range organ damage during the contemplative phase. The planning phase for chronic illness management may not be necessarily problematic, unless the patient is a smoker or obesity is a primary contributor to the illness. The most certain prediction is that the borderline patient will have difficulty implementing and following the action component, those behaviors that need to be followed to ensure effective disease regulation. Likewise, even if behavior change is accomplished, relapse or departures from those established healthy behavior patterns would be predictable. Adverse physical consequences of poor control may have a transient sobering effect on these patients at the time the indiscretions occur, but they are less likely to serve as effective determinants of future health-related behaviors. Considering that the fundamental instabilities of individuals with borderline personalities are typically triggered by interpersonal vicissitudes, monitoring of this aspect of their lives will constitute an important element of their health care management. Self-neglect during a relationship conflict or termination could precipitate a diabetic crisis if these patients transiently decompensate and forget to take insulin, or do so deliberately to elicit guilt–remorse in their partners. Likewise, if the response is to binge eat or drink excessively, blood-sugar levels will become unstable. Knowledge that these scenarios are possible can promote consideration of compensatory, substitute responses that are healthier. For example, if a diabetic patient's relationships are typically tumultuous and fragile in nature, psychotherapy should be regarded as an essential feature of his or her medical management.

Neurological Diseases: Epilepsy, Multiple Schlerosis, Parkinson's Disease

Neurological conditions can represent both chronic, degenerative conditions and also disease processes such as epilepsy, which may be relatively well-controlled. Depending on the severity of seizures and the degree to which they can be controlled, this disease may play a comparatively minor or major role in the borderline patient's adjustment. What is most certain is that any neurological condition for the borderline personality will have an interpersonal manifestation. That is, it will present an opportunity for manipulation of family or significant others. A genuine medical condition may commit others to stay involved with the patient out of a sense of guilt or decency, affording some protection against abandonment and providing justification for emotional outbursts whose emotional antecedents may have little to do with the neurological disease process. Once the outburst has occurred, however, it certainly can alter the seizure threshold, and this can have consequences both obviously disruptive to the borderline patient's life and also beneficial in an indirect sense, by defusing or disengaging from interpersonal crises. There are also more obvious potential secondary gains deriving from escape from responsibility and avoidance of stressful experiences conferred by this condition, as manifested by real and pseudo-seizure attacks.

To the extent that these events become part of the learning experience of these patients and their disease process, then associations may be formed that consciously or unconsciously potentiate symptomatic manifestations of the condition. "Forgetting" to take anticonvulsant medications when it might be strategically beneficial from an interpersonal standpoint (i.e., neutralizing some interpersonal retribution) would represent operant social learning. Conditioned emotional responses (e.g., fear aroused at a threat of abandonment) could also change the seizure threshold and thereby exert a similar controlling influence. Where there are medically unexplainable changes in the patient's illness course, secondary gain influences of these kinds should be considered with these patients. Addressing them, however, will require considerable therapeutic skill given these patient's fragile defenses and vulnerability to emotional decompensation when confronted. A critical or judgmental confrontation would thus likely have destructive rather than constructive effect. Care would even have to be exercised in communicating psychogenic influences to the medical physician (e.g., neurologist), especially depending on the physician's capacity for diplomacy.

As a condition that can wax and wane with vague symptoms, multiple sclerosis represents another condition that the individual with borderline personality could use as a protection against interpersonal sanctions in response to untimely, aversive outbursts and emotional instability. Unlike epilepsy, where stress can be a precipitant to be avoided, there is not the immediate coercive requirement that emotional tranquillity is needed to prevent triggering an attack. Exacerbations of multiple sclerosis can persist for longer periods of time, however, and these can serve to modify interactive patterns, assigned responsibilities for instrumental activities, and caretaking. The most general effect of a prolonged episode of multiple sclerosis would be to create and justify greater dependency on the part of the patient and inhibit any expression of resentment on the part of caretaker. The vague and shifting nature of multiple sclerosis symptoms makes it difficult to distinguish the subjective from true central nervous system (CNS) pathology (even with expensive medical testing), and thus symptoms complaints can easily come under operant influences. In more extreme instances this can raise suspicions on the part of the caretakers, personal and medical, and then become a source of resentment and threat to the patient, who justifiably feels vulnerable. As with epilepsy, interventions that are nonconfrontive will likely generate the greatest yield.

Parkinson's disease offers similar secondary gain from those seeking justification for greater caretaking and satisfaction of dependency needs. However, as a more unremitting and degenerative chronic condition, it places a greater toll on the individual in terms of confining him or her to his or her existing psychosocial environment, which may include unsatisfactory relationships. Depression may thus intensify as a result of this factor and the disease progression itself, and this should be diagnosed and treated aggressively. Medications to treat the movement disorder may also potentiate psychotic symptoms more readily in these patients. It can be beneficial to consider atypical antipsychotics such as Clozaril and Olanzapine in conjunction with administration of Sinemet, especially for patients with advanced Parkinson's (Chacko, Hurley, Harper, Jankovic, & Cardosa, 1995).

Cardiac Disease

For patients with hypertension, occlusive artery disease, arrhythmia's, and risk for heart attack or stroke, sudden intense emotional distress is obviously undesirable. Misuse of substances or periods of self-neglect during acute decompensations are likely with cardiac patients with borderline personalities. For this reason it is important to consider ongoing mental health participation in the care plan early on. Fluctuations in the patient's cardiac status not readily explainable from the physical parameters of his or her disease could be the basis for counseling, use of antidepressants, or even low-dose antipsychotics to provide psychological stabilization. Beta blockers, which may already be in use, also may be considered for their tranquilizing as well as their cardiac effects. Periodic involvement of a mental health practitioner as part of the cardiac care plan can also monitor and anticipate relationship vicissitudes with these patients, which are the most likely source of their instability. When these patients have a heart attack or must undergo bypass surgery, they are then faced with a situation where there is dramatic change in their sense of physical well-being, starting with weakness and pain and an increased sense of mortality. All of this will intensify their sense of vulnerability and dependence on others for caretaking and reduce their opportunity to escape relationships and regulate their ambivalence over intimacy. They will be forced to remain in contact with and deal with those immediately involved in their care and those existing relationships that provide instrumental supports during their time of incapacity. This only heightens the likelihood of interpersonal distress in those relationships where the borderline patient feels caught, either by the intensity of his or her vulnerability, increased dependency needs, or the conflicts those needs engender, especially with dissatisfying relationships that previously were marginally tolerated.

Cardiac rehabilitation interventions that involve restriction and self-denial may produce resentment, reducing the patient's resolve to participate in the treatment regimen. During the acute phase of recovery, involvement of a behavioral health specialist could provide the borderline patient with some individual advocacy that might lessen any interpersonal distress during this high-risk time. It is perhaps ironic that expensive cardiac monitoring immediately around the time of heart attack or during the physical stress of exercise rehabilitation is a given, where great justification would be required for monitoring and modulation of interpersonal–emotional stresses despite their well-established relationship to cardiac functioning and recovery.

Stressors of an interpersonal nature will influence follow-up after the acute and immediate recovery stages of the illness, which are largely generated by the borderline patient's own inherent instability. Especially where their significant others show an investment in their well-being, threats to compromise their health by not taking medications or by placing their heart at risk through introduction of toxic agents (e.g., an alcohol or cocaine binge) may emerge as coercive, punishing reactions to inflict on loved ones. Unless there is some management of these processes, this risky behavior could get out of hand as a result of predictable escalation in these patients' acting out. This will set in motion the consequent process of exhaustion–disaffection–disgust that represents the destructive self-perpetuation process of the borderline condition.

Cancer

Detecting cancer in the borderline patient will not derive from his or her mature consideration of risk and a consequent desire to enhance the likelihood of maintaining a state of physical health. These individuals are too fragmented in their sense of self and chronically diverted from focused pursuit of long-range goals by the immediacy of their interpersonal crises and conflicts to develop a habitual sense of concern about their well-being that would motivate early disease detection–risk prevention strategies. If there is a strong family history and immediate family member afflicted with this disease, such individuals' exposure to these experiences in a contemporary with whom they share a common risk (e.g., a sibling) could induce at least a transient state of concern or vigilance until that concern is overshadowed by the next interpersonal crisis. For the most part, however, left of their own devices, early detection will represent a serendipitous event.

In addition to dread and a sense of mortality, the diagnosis of cancer represents an anticipation of pain and suffering, prospect of diminished capability and attractiveness, and an inherent state of dependency. These concerns are universal to all patients, irrespective of their personality type. For individuals with borderline personalities, however, these issues take on special meaning considering their triple ambivalence on all three polarities: interpersonal relationships (individuation versus nurturance), mode of coping (active versus passive), and their pleasure–pain orientation. These issues are relevant to all chronic medical conditions afflicting these patients, but may be brought out more strongly by a diagnosis of cancer, which invariably involves a patient's utter reliance on experts and a multitude of others to treat the disease if there is to be any hope of prolongation of life.

Assuming that care will extend over a considerable length of time, it is likely that some relationship intimacy will be established. The difficulties maintaining boundaries between individuals with borderline personalities and others creates the potential for conflict and antagonism. As the number of caretakers increase this might heighten the probability of a natural personality conflict, which might then expand and encompass others. Conversely, with only a few practitioners involved, this might intensify the degree of intimacy leading to conflict triggered by feelings becoming too intense and consequent dependency conflicts. Either way, the potential for some relationship conflagration would be high with this type of patient.

For this reason early recognition of patients who seem interpersonally fragile, who exhibit overidealization of the relationships they are establishing or devaluation of other past relationships (especially if other practitioners are vilified in an emotionally primitive fashion), will be important. Given their usually adequate interpersonal skills, borderline patients at times can elicit rescue fantasies in those oriented to giving help, who then become dismayed and angry when their efforts are invariably not enough. The most prudent strategy for dealing with such cases is early diagnosis of the patient's characteristics and prompt involvement of a skilled behavioral health–mental health practitioner. In particular, efforts should be made to avoid confounding of medical–physical care with these patients' interpersonal needs. A therapist aware of but separate from the medical care process can promote adequate boundary maintenance. Psychotropic medication management may be an important component of such care to stabilize mood, especially if chemotherapy treatments have central nervous system effects that could contribute to mental confusion or even mircopsychotic episodes. The best assumption is that there will be emotional turbulence for these patients in dealing with their disease, that this will be more than the cancer treatment team can and should attempt to deal with, and that behavioral–mental health involvement should be an integral part of their care plan.

CONCLUSION

The interaction between the individual with borderline personality and the health care system will reflect the nature of the patient's personality organization: tumultuous and unstable. Although infrequent contact with these individuals may go uneventfully if there is no serious illness, the practitioner may still see their behavioral excesses in the form of substance abuse, self-destructive behavior, and disorganized symptom presentations during episodic decompensations. Contacts of this kind, such as to an emergency room, may represent the onset of these patient's subsequent mental health history, when they are referred for psychiatric care. It is when prolonged illness strikes that the pathology of the individual with borderline personality will be evident. The major features of the interplay is shown in Figure 8.1. Initially the social skills of these individuals may be engaging or charming, but as relationships become more intense or complicated, and especially if there is team involvement, any care regimen will become confounded or diverted by the borderline patient's tendency to fragment relationships with his or her splitting and help-seeking, alternating between displays of desperate dependency and accusatory rage attacks. The borderline patient's acute interpersonal sensitivity to others' vulnerabilities (e.g., nurses, professionals) will draw him or her into conflicts as a consequence of his or her erratic efforts to balance dependency needs with fears of intimacy–trust conflicts. Preventive health behavior efforts may be haphazard, ranging from the extremes of overidentification with pursuit of wellness or abandonment of any concern about health and self-destructive indulgence. Disease detection may be accidental or incidental occurrences, because most of the borderline personality's attention will be consumed with relationship or personal identity conflicts.

Once disease is diagnosed, illness representations, if even accurate, will be highly affectively charged and vulnerable to distortion by subsequent relationship vicissitudes. Adhering to treatment regimens will also be erratic

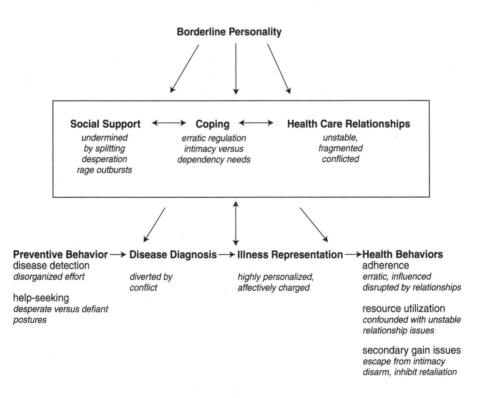

Figure 8.1. Borderline personality.

and often characterized by noncompliance acting out in protest of relationship dissatisfactions. The same will be true of their under and overuse of health care resources as seemingly straightforward interpersonal transactions become confounded with their conflicts from other arenas. Secondary gain may take the form of escape from intimacy–trust conflicts, use of the illness to escape retribution for provocative interpersonal behavior, and even a perverse satisfaction of engendering muted anger–rage in providers frustrated by the irresponsible behavior of their patients. The severity of the borderline personality's psychopathology and the extremes it may take behaviorally dictate that medical care providers not trained in psychotherapy *not* attempt to manage the intimacy–transference issues when they emerge, but rather seek expert consultation from a mental health practitioner who may need to become a consistent member of the medical management team. Even then, the course of medical care may be bumpy at best with these patients.

9

DEPENDENT PERSONALITY

The Cluster C dependent personality disorder is characterized by an overriding concern about being cared for, a submissive, clinging orientation dominated by fears of separation, evident in early adulthood in five or more of the following contexts, according to *DSM–IV* (American Psychiatric Association, 1994) criteria: (a) requires excessive reassurance or advice to make commonplace decisions; (b) seeks others to take responsibility for most aspects of life; (c) is hesitant to disagree or challenge others out of fear of disapproval or loss of support; (d) is hindered from initiating independent or new activities by a lack of confidence, not by a lack of interest or motivation; (e) excessive need for nurturance and support motivates willingness to engage in unpleasant activities; (f) burdened by excessive fears of helplessness and inability to care for oneself when alone; (g) the end of a close relationship will elicit desperate efforts to replace that loss; and (h) overly preoccupied with the idea of being left alone to care for oneself without any assistance.

Dependent individuals, as the term implies, are dominated by a need for validation, approval, and regard from others, and will sacrifice greatly to meet that need. They will subordinate their desires, make few demands, and tolerate great discomfort, even physical or emotional abuse, to ensure that a relationship endures. Such a passive posture not surprisingly leaves them feeling interpersonally weak, emotionally fragile, and vulnerable. From the polarity model, dependent personalities are clearly extreme on the accommodation side of the active–passive pole. They are strongly oriented toward nurturance on the self–other polarity and conversely weak on the individuation pole. An average and balanced combination of pleasure–pain (enhancement or preservation) features are present on the remaining pole that defines different personality types.

CLINICAL DOMAIN FEATURES

The most predominant features of the dependent personality on a behavioral level include first a helpless, accommodating and passive, interpersonally dependent orientation dominated by submission, subassertiveness, and avoidance of competition. To avoid offending others, dependent individuals may minimize their accomplishments and demean themselves while heaping praise and gratitude onto others, who are viewed as more capable of providing them desired gratifications they are unable to attain on their own. Beneath their obsequious and acquiescing presentation is likely an underlying anxiety characterized by fears of loss–abandonment, leading them to behave in a clinging or helpless manner. Because they are willing to sacrifice any autonomy or individuality, they are vulnerable to exploitation, and thus may endure deprivation and hardship at the expense of belonging, with the result that they are apprehensive and depressed over the cost of their need for acceptance. When in relationships, they may seek reassurance or become unusually distressed at any competition for their partners' attention. This mode of adaptation will in turn be manifest through expressively incompetent behavior in the form of displays of a mild, timid, or submissive manner, inhibition of emotions (especially anger), and a weak interpersonal presentation. Such behaviors may serve to escape adult responsibilities, which are taken over by others who rescue those who act in a helpless, ineffectual manner. Anxious, apprehensive, or doleful displays may be evident when the dependent individual is separated from those to whom he or she is attached.

From a phenomenological perspective, the individual with dependent personality on a functional–interactive level will present as cognitively naive—that is, easily influenced, gullible, overly trusting, and rarely given to doubt about others' intentions. Inconsistencies and warning signs of duplicity are ignored, and the attachment needs of dependent individuals motivate a self-reassurance even in the face of contradictory or obvious information suggesting that they are being exploited. Their generosity is likely motivated by the goal of keeping others engaged, and even reliant on them, which reduces the likelihood of abandonment. Structurally, the dependent personality's self-image is that of ineptness. These individuals view themselves as incompetent, unable to problem-solve or resolve conflicts, especially of an interpersonal nature. When faced with compliments about any competency, they may become anxious and belittle their accomplishments or capabilities, because this would threaten their position of having to rely on others. Although viewed by others as considerate and cooperative, these characteristics may emerge in situations where an assertive or competitive orientation may be appropriate.

Stable internal object representations may be undifferentiated, at times idealized, seemingly experienced from a childlike perspective. Although all humans maintain infantile impressions of relationships, these are typically modified and refined by later experience. The individual with dependent personality in contrast appears to encode later relationships and interactions in the same immature manner, reflecting a fixation with a childlike orientation of admiration and subservience to others, who are cast in parental roles or as "rescuers." Positive early experiences of nurturance leave them well-equipped to interact in a loving, caring manner, and often they are successful in earning the affection and loyalty of those to whom they may become attached. However, because their fundamental representation of the relationship is one of subservience, the likelihood is that their needs will be subordinated and in turn not satisfied.

Because of their sense of vulnerability to abandonment or loss, dependent personalities must defend against anxieties of being left alone. On an intrapsychic level this will involve use of introjection, a process by which such individuals take on the values, beliefs, attitudes, and capabilities of their partners, in that way reassuring themselves that they are not as vulnerable to the competitive, predatory adult world and its demands that threaten to expose their sense of incompetence. Denial is a common defense that serves to minimize or remove from awareness potential conflict or interpersonal threats. In particular, repression of feelings of anger and hostility, natural responses to frustrated dependency needs, serve to eliminate these potential threats to the relationship and the security obtained by it.

Having subordinated oneself to others and incorporated their characteristics, the dependent personality can be said to be functioning with "borrowed" attributes mixed in with their own underdeveloped or poorly differentiated capacities for modulating emotions and managing interpersonal relationships. Their internal organization is largely made up of preadult coping skills and a confidence that is reliant on the strength and introjected components of the significant other. Their forgiving, accommodating nature is also applied to their own self-appraisals, which allow dependent individuals to tolerate and excuse shortcomings or deficiencies that, if addressed more critically, might lead to personal growth and maturation.

On the biophysical level, Millon characterized dependent personalities as temperamentally passive, as having a tender, tolerant, accepting manner. However, when experiencing loss or the threat of dissolution of a relationship, anxiety, agitation, despair, and depression will emerge. It is at such times that the dependent patient will typically manifest somatic or emotional concerns, leading to access of health care providers.

The dependent personality typically enjoys warm, caring relationships during childhood, and experiences little frustration or disappointment because the powerful, caring parent figure always provides comfort. This prototypical relationship then becomes a model for the child, adolescent, and then adult: a more capable, powerful other on which to rely for one's needs being met. Because of their failure to develop competitive skills and autonomous modes of functioning, dependent personalities are typically less successful than peers in many endeavors, and may thus genuinely feel less competent. They will be more successful, however, at eliciting support and nurturance from adult figures and also their companions, through their displays of incompetence or helplessness or by being so accommodating, accepting, admiring, complimentary, and deferential to others who indeed appreciate such behavior.

DEPENDENT PERSONALITY SUBTYPES

Individuals with dependent personality subtypes include those with avoidant character traits. These individuals typically are anxious and apprehensive about rejection and easily alarmed at fluctuations in the level of support from those they depend on. Compared to the other dependent variants, there may be a more pervasive tendency to withdraw, not just out of preference to be solely with their loved one but because of anticipation of rejection or not being accepted by others. In a sense, the protectors of dependent personalities with avoidant traits are less effective in providing for their security needs. This causes underlying feelings of tension, resentment, and even anger, which may periodically surface and find expression when these individuals are feeling neglected or ignored by their significant other. Their fear of rejection and humiliation may combine with their inherent passivity with an *active* avoidance of new and unfamiliar situations, thereby complicating efforts to promote more independent functioning.

Individuals with dependent personalities with masochistic traits carry their submissiveness to the extreme, whereby they are sacrificing to the point of inviting mistreatment or neglect. In these individuals, it seems as if they do not feel safe in a relationship unless there is some degree of acceptance of discomfort or sacrifice in exchange for acceptance and nurturance. It is as if they are seeking roles of inferiority and are not comfortable when treated "too well" by others who might be willing to meet their needs. Nurturing, reassuring individuals who are too complementary may cause dissonance with these individuals' low self-esteem. Paradoxically this reassurance could be threatening to individuals with this dependent personality type, who may be more familiar and comfortable with a companion who demeans or devalues them.

In dependent personalities with schizoid characteristics there is a prominent lack of concern over evident deficiencies in adaptive functioning, especially in social spheres of adjustment. Such individuals are expressively flat, interpersonally ineffectual, passive and seemingly unconcerned or oblivious to what is happening around them. Unlike individuals with schizoid personalities who prefer to be alone and preoccupied with their own inner musings, these individuals need close personal involvement but lack the social skills to connect and maintain sufficiently effective social interchange necessary to attract and keep benefactors. A clinging dependency may coexist with a disorganized, disengaged lifestyle in which any adult responsibility is overwhelming and dealt with in an ineffective manner.

Dependent personalities with depressive traits are characterized by a readiness to subject their identities to "be at one" with those persons designated for their primary need fulfillments. There is an extreme deference to the designated other, a virtual living through the other person, with little interest or motivation in pursuing personal expression or differentiation of any sense of self. Individual capabilities and potentials are abandoned in favor of the security seemingly afforded by incorporating another's identity and relying on that person to carry out the adult responsibilities. The achievements of another thus become fulfilling, but the other's failures and crises also take on undue personal significance. Given the precarious and vulnerable nature of such an adjustment, it is not surprising that these individuals are prone to depression, as the world ultimately recognizes and responds to the active participant in the relationship. In the end, the individual with dependent–depressive personality type is chronically at risk of lack of recognition and indeed abandonment, because they are likely to be experienced as uninteresting, even boring, except by the most narcissistic of individuals who would resonate to the mirroring of such partners.

PERPETUATING FEATURES

Although generally successful in securing gratification of their security needs and maintaining contact with social reality, their one-dimensional coping style leaves individuals with dependent personalities vulnerable to self-perpetuating life experiences and vicious circles that maintain dysfunctional adjustment patterns and prevent emotional and personal growth. First, their constant acquiescence to others, avoidance of competition, and subservience often occurs at the expense of development of personal capabilities that would permit more independent functioning. To the extent that others' inherent limitations also fail to satisfy the dependent personality's different needs, this can lead to disappointment or chronic states of deprivation. Dependent patients' lack of success in using their constricted repertoire of social behaviors in turn can reinforce their sense of ineffectuality and helplessness, confirming the negative self-image that stifles any ventures into unknown modes of behavior. In contrast, nondependent individuals, who can tolerate disappointment and rejection, refine their adaptive skills after each failure to enhance their probability of success.

Second, because of their fear of assuming adult responsibilities and demands, dependent personalities steer away from learning experiences that would broaden their horizons and foster development of more diversified social and instrumental adaptive skills. Given that displays of helplessness and incompetence are necessary to gain escape from adult responsibilities, dependent individuals reinforce in themselves their worst image as deficient, helpless, and ineffective. Some will respond to them, providing nurturance and relief from burdensome demands, but others will react by restricting them from opportunities. And those of a more predatory or exploitive nature will correctly size up a dependent personality as an easy mark to be used, abused, and discarded. Such experiences will only intensify such individuals' timidity and view that the world is too dangerous to venture out except under the auspices of a more competent protector. As their needs are frustrated or as they feel threatened, they may become excessively obsequious, clinging, and covertly demanding, exasperating or repelling those on whom they may rely. This predictably can lead to even more desperate behavior and eventual loss, with consequent depression and despair.

INTERPERSONAL ASPECTS OF DEPENDENT PATIENTS IN THE MEDICAL CARE SETTING

With health care providers patients with dependent personalities may prove seductive in their positive responses to the professional interest shown in them. Dependent patients may initially have a favorable impact on the primary care provider, because they will be attentive, approving, grateful, and even obsequiously compliant with the physician's requests. This may lead providers into assuming that these patients' seeming enthusiasm will be matched by their responsiveness to a treatment regimen. They will thus be disappointed when these patients begin to exhibit their typical dependency behaviors, particularly over assumption of any responsibility for self-care. Depending on the nature of the illness, this can be quite serious and exasperating, especially to a busy medical or primary care specialist with limited tolerance and less time for the transactions these patients are likely to engage in with their caretakers. Signs of annoyance or rejection will only aggravate the difficulties by intensifying the helplessness and incompetence displayed by the individual with dependent personality. Involvement of a family member with a healthy appreciation for these dynamics, utilization of a nurse skilled in patient management interaction problems, or, in more refractory or complicated cases, a behavioral health care provider, will be called for.

The stress of either an acute or chronic illness will predictably elicit a regression or reversion to more primitive forms of adjustment, in this instance increased dependence and loss of any fragile sense of self-reliance that may have developed, especially concerning health-related issues. At such times dependent patients will be predictably anxious and clinging, and their repetitive efforts to obtain reassurance and clarification of instructions may become aggravating to busy health care providers. Especially the threat of abandonment at such times could precipitate a secondary Axis I emotional condition involving manifestation of significant anxiety, depression, or both. This affective distress in turn could aggravate the medical condition itself (e.g., in the case of hypertensive crisis), creating a self-perpetuating viscous cycle between both the patient and health provider.

Given the dependent personality's preference for submission–dominance relationship asymmetries, there is the potential that physicians particularly confident in or committed to some form of intervention (e.g., surgery over more conservative medical management) may elicit "informed consent" from these patients on the basis of their imposing personality rather than rational consideration on the patient's part. When this occurs and is contrary to the benefit or need of the patient, it is often the family members or some other party who will raise serious objections (even threat of legal action), to the surprise and dismay of an overzealous but well-intentioned practitioner. Dependent patients, in their desire to please their physicians, may also selectively share with them only positive information and experiences concerning their illness, omitting critical complaint information concerning important side effects or atypical treatment responses. In doing so, they will undermine their physician's efforts to appropriately modify–refine the treatment plan based on its true impact on the patient.

Given that dependent personalities are inherently subassertive and reliant on typically one close relationship for nurturance and protection, it would be expected that they can independently generate few resources on their own. Their agreeable, accommodating nature would make them pleasant to deal with, but ordinarily their support would come from those beneficent relationships they had already established. When required to mobilize resources for themselves when also faced with the stress of an illness, they may well become paralyzed with fear and inaction. If the illness is a serious one requiring hospitalization and specialized care these individuals will require the assistance of social services to do problem-solving for them. The challenge for the health care providers in this instance may be that dependent patients are so passive and unknowing about the resources required for their support that they will not be able to adequately anticipate or articulate their needs. If hospitalized, careful discharge planning will be required. When shifting to an ambulatory status, concrete specification regarding follow-up must be undertaken. For example, the physician–nurse may assume dependent patients can drive or have transportation back to the clinic, only to discover critical follow-up visits are missed because they were unable to secure transportation for themselves. It may be vital to involve a family member or a designated patient advocate to problem solve as needed and even anticipate the dependent patient's needs concerning use of supports.

One resource that should not be overlooked is that of spiritual assistance, especially with religiously oriented patients. Particularly where mortality is an issue and the fear of the unknown are concerns, reference to a higher being can provide these individuals a needed perspective that they are not alone. If there is a church the patient is affiliated with, a diplomatic call from a nurse or social worker can potentially mobilize support if the patient is reticent about placing the call her- or himself. If away at a strange hospital, there are priests–ministers of different denominations trained in working with medical patients who can help, both by mobilizing volunteers and by offering personal religious and scriptural guidance. Most important will be the personalized interaction such intervention can offer, given the dependent personality's strong social needs. Once a commitment for such contact is made, the party involved must be prepared to provide adequate continuity of contact and some follow-up, especially during any acute phase of the illness.

MEDICAL MANAGEMENT ISSUES

In the case of individuals with dependent personalities, the challenge for their health care providers will be to elicit any real measure of autonomous participation in their treatment plan, as their nature will be to place all responsibility on the idealized caretaker. Their overly accommodating nature will also inhibit constructive and even critical feedback their providers will rely on to guide treatment, out of fear of being considered annoying. These will be recurring issues practitioners will encounter with the dependent patient, which can be addressed only partially with a very modest successive approximation strategy for increasing self-management behaviors.

Preventive Interventions, Lifestyle Choices

Concerning risk factor modification, such as alcohol or smoking cessation and dietary change, dependent personalities may find themselves in severe conflict between pleasing the medical provider and their inherent incompetence concerning self-mastery over basic oral gratification impulses they are loath to give up. The consequence of these dynamics might be initial displays of placating enthusiasm on the part of these patients, followed by obsequious displays of anxious contrition when confronted with failures to attain treatment regimen goals of healthy behavior. Labeling these individuals as simply noncompliant will cast them in an antagonistic role in relation to their medical caretakers, further injuring the nature of the patient–physician relationship. Paradoxically, although the physician may feel devalued by the patient's failure to do what was requested, he or she is likely the most powerful influence for change given the dependent patient's orientation toward dominant authority figures. The challenge is to translate this influence into motivating action.

A primary care–specialist physician who has the time, patience, and an interactive style that is firm but nonpunitive and nonjudgmental in nature can promote patient striving to give up appetitive–addictive behaviors, by offering substitute gratifications in the form of approval and other relationship benefits. More frequent follow-up and lengthier visits to reinforce efforts for change, combined with judicious use of medications to reduce cravings, can mobilize patients to make changes and participate in support or behavior change groups that specifically teach self-management skills. To the extent that substitute gratifications can be introduced, this will facilitate these individuals' efforts to comply with the authority figure with which they have aligned themselves.

Stages of Change

Individuals with dependent personalities, with their external, other orientation as a fundamental frame of reference, initially would likely be at a precontemplative level concerning appetitive–addictive behavior patterns, unless the need for diet, alcohol, or smoking cessation had been a previous issue or recommendation in relation to the health problem being addressed. In adult smokers who are overweight with a long history of hypertension or diabetes, it would be surprising if they had not been previously confronted with such medical advice. For this reason, it would be important for any current intervention to review past history in this regard. This inquiry should be done in a friendly, inquisitive manner, emphasizing recognition of the difficulties of such change, to encourage and reinforce frank disclosure of mental, physical, or situational barriers to behavior change that occurred previously or that could present as obstacles at this time. Knowing that a spouse or significant other smokes; insists on high-carbohydrate, fat-intensive foods; or has a drinking partner can be the basis for a sympathetic alliance with dependent patients, who can then anticipate understanding and sympathy rather than scorn in discussing their struggles to change.

This can open the contemplative phase in a constructive, empowering fashion, where realistic motivational issues and situational constraints can be identified and targeted for problem solving. Fears and reservations against change can be identified and reframed, expectancies challenged and clarified (e.g., the assumption that not drinking with a companion will lead to rejection). Where the situational pressures and influences identified during contemplation appear to be formidable, it may be necessary to consult with a behavioral medicine specialist even before enrolling the patient in a group endeavor where the primary focus will be on implementing change. In psychologically sound patients who have a reasonable repertoire of coping and interpersonal skills, identifying these barriers can occur in group contexts where problem solving can readily occur. With a dependent patient positive attitudes and expectations must first be engendered to make possible an effective and comfortable preparation phase. A hierarchy of pre-action tasks may need to be identified, such as assertive skills training or even conjoint marital sessions to identify and align support in anticipation of the action phase, where the objective is actual initiation and implementation of change.

Even if interpersonal and situational obstacles are addressed and surmounted, the patient will still be left with powerful internal cravings or anxiety-reducing rituals—habit patterns that will be a challenge to overcome. The greater the awareness of these forces, the more opportunity for successful efforts at overcoming them. It may be worthwhile to preemptively discuss relapse as possible in the change process. Emphasizing that such eventualities need not be a source of shame and self-esteem-damaging recrimination but rather can represent useful information about unappreciated barriers to change can maintain a constructive focus on future goal attainment. This approach should exploit the positive qualities of individuals with dependent personalities, their interest in seeking direction, their desire for approval and a nurturing relationship, which can help to overcome specific health risk behaviors targeted for change. To the extent that they may experience mastery from any success, this can foster more independent, autonomous functioning. For a successful maintenance phase, the health care team and other supports must continue to remain engaged and reinforce treatment gains, given the inherent risk of relapse and regression posed by the basic personality structure of dependent patients.

Utility, Cost–Benefit Considerations of Preventive Interventions

As with other patients with personality disorders, a greater investment of professional time and effort is likely with the dependent personality. However, with dependent patients their orientation to health care authorities will be a positive and enduring one, given their strong attraction to powerful individuals. Unlike therapy, where the goal is more autonomous, independent functioning, change to healthy behavior patterns is a more circumscribed objective supported by continuing involvement with an authority figure and decision maker whose role is to act in the patient's best interests. To the extent that family and peer influences outside the medical arena can join in this orientation, then behavior change may be feasible. On the other hand, where there are competing negative influences that exert a strong hold on the patient (e.g., an alcoholic husband, girlfriend who insists on having a smoking partner, obese husband threatened by his wife's weight loss), their history of accommodation to these negative influences may represent insurmountable obstacles, at least until competing relationships can be strengthened. In these instances, it may be better to back off for the moment with the patients, to not shame them for their weakness or condemn them for the behavior, but maintain a respect for their "choice" while emphasizing that such health behavior risk reduction is important to their long-term well-being. This maintains an active state of contemplation, which may bear fruit later on if there is some erosion in those relationships, as is often the case.

Secondary and Tertiary Care of Acute and Chronic Illness

For patients with dependent personalities the matter of illness detection and personal wellness are secondary considerations to their preoccupation with relationship security. Illness detection as a manifestation of self-preservation concerns would be relatively unimportant compared to securing and maintaining a relationship. Unless this was an important issue to a concerned partner, the dependent patient is likely to remain more focused on relationship preservation than self-preservation. Were some important prodromal symptom to develop, disease denial might persist for a prolonged time until a more attention-getting, ominous manifestation of a disease was to emerge. Although the illness might represent a relationship opportunity with a health care provider for an unattached dependent patient, it is also plausible that the illness could threaten a loss of personal attractiveness (either physical or instrumental) that would be threatening to the security needs of a dependent patient. The latter proposition would initially be associated with denying or delaying behaviors concerning early illness identification and treatment.

Even when diagnosed and under treatment, the individual with dependent personality's deferential, subordinating nature may have important consequences for his or her illness management. Where medical authority figures may recommend a particular course of action, patient decision making may be determined more by the perceived stature of the recommending party than the rational cost–benefit considerations that should determine such choices. The desire to please and accommodate the physician may also lead to the patient distorting or even misrepresenting their illness status for the purpose of ensuring the physician will be satisfied. When problems come to light because symptoms went unreported, serious consequences (from illness progression) may create disenchantment between physician and patient, which can be threatening for either party.

Given their poorly differentiated inner psychic organization, dependent patients' illness representations are likely to be reasonably childlike or primitive. Similarly, their rather unformed sense of self will make it difficult for these individuals to incorporate disease knowledge and disease management issues as personal knowledge. Rather, this information is likely to be identified with the all-powerful healer and embedded in the relationship rather than internalized by the afflicted individual. Although this may prove workable provided the physician is available, attentive, and consistent, these conditions may be relatively rare for public sector care settings or even managed care environments where patient–specialist contacts are rationed or the continuity of care contact is fragmented. The dependent patients' deferential orientation may also make it likely that they may, out of a fear of courting disapproval, indicate they understand illness-related information or treatment regimen instructions when in fact they do not. It can be anticipated that they will be generally uncritical and especially unchallenging about what they hear.

If their disease is likely to stress or negatively affect their primary relationships (e.g., as in breast cancer), this may add an element of desperation above and beyond the ordinary threats that confront typical patients with these diagnoses. For that reason, the practitioner will have to remain alert to the meaning and significance of these relationships to their patients, so that couples' counseling or supportive interpersonal substitutes to threatened relationships can be provided in these patients' time of need. Anxiety and depression are likely consequences at such times, requiring pharmacological support.

Coping With Illness

Individuals with dependent personalities, by virtue of their childlike orientation, can be expected to rely on others to identify as well as address problem-focused issues. Their ability to function in this regard may be extremely limited. Likewise, these patients will most probably be preoccupied with addressing their interpersonal security needs during periods of infirmity. They may seem oblivious to readily apparent specific disease-related emotional issues (e.g., postoperative pain, disability that they may assume the idealized, powerful physician will protect them from). When such eventualities occur, this will only increase their sense of vulnerability and lack of personal control. Such experiences may also be anxiety provoking from the standpoint that they shatter dependent patients' expectations that they will be well-cared for by their providers, whom they have cast in omnipotent roles. As their displays of helplessness and excesses of reliance continue over time, those in a caretaking role may feel increasingly drained and resentful. When this threshold is reached, the dependent patient may experience an abrupt withdrawal of support and may even be confronted with exasperated, even hostile caretakers, who justifiably may point out that there are others more physically infirm who deserve their attention. The result will be that these patients in fact will experience their greatest fear, interpersonal abandonment at a time when they are confronted with a requirement to cope with illness-related demands.

In acute medical contexts, where a time-limited resolution can be anticipated, improving the emotional course of the illness for the dependent patient may involve coping by proxy—in other words, a provider doing the work for him or her. Following this strategy where there is a chronic phase following the acute illness can be more problematic. Although doing for the patient may represent modeling of potentially useful behavior patterns, the clinician should not be seduced that the dependent patient's perhaps initially favorable response to such intervention may mean it has been internalized. Rather, these individuals may regard the clinician as omnipotent and better suited to do for them given their posture of incompetence and deficient autonomous functioning. Gentle but firm insistence that the patients carry out concretely defined tasks (e.g., making a phone call to initiate contact with some agency that may provide charity assistance) early on following medical diagnosis can establish an interaction pattern that can be maintained for the duration of care. This will require both vigilance on the part of clinicians that no substantial erosion occurs with this strategy and also that there are judicious choices made concerning what these patients can manage, so that they experience success and increases in confidence rather than frustration and reinforcement of low self-esteem.

Medical Compliance

The chief impediment to compliance with the treatment regimen for patients with dependent personalities will not be disinterest in securing approval of the medical–caretaker authority (although this may be diminished with the dependent–schizoid variant). Rather, such individuals' lack of experience and deficient capacity for assuming responsibility will contribute primarily to failures of omission. The individual with dependent personality will simply appear incompetent in the ability to address even simple requirements that call for initiative and responsibility. Displays of frustration and criticism that might signify rejection or dismissal may only intensify their fearfulness that they may do something wrong. Basically, the goal will be to foster and encourage greater patient participation in their care in a manner that does not challenge their basic dynamics but rather promotes a sense of confidence and need for security when they engage in an act of self-management.

If the dependent personality senses that effective self-care will result in their being cut loose to fend for themselves, then compliance will only stimulate their greatest fear—that of being abandoned to be truly on their own. On the other hand, failure to comply conversely might mean dismissal as a noncompliant patient, an avoidance–avoidance paradigm. By using successive approximation in compliance training, the patient remains in the subordinate role, performing manageable tasks that can win approval but also continued practitioner involvement. This will require more monitoring and positive feedback to patients than may be desired by busy providers, but it represents a strategy that will keep dependent patients positively engaged while they are assuming more self-care, at the same time feeling reassured that there is close attention to their needs and caretaking immediately at hand. This approach should also encourage sharing of important symptom complaint information that these patients may be unaware of or may feel reluctant to share, out of concern that this would annoy the practitioner. For his or her part, the provider will need to invest some time personally communicating in a concrete, graded, repetitive manner, the compliance requirements and symptoms to be monitored. If this seems like educating a child, this is in fact what will be taking place, because such individuals have been overprotected and deprived of a sense of confidence in functioning autonomously.

IMPACT OF DISEASE STATES ON THE DEPENDENT PATIENT

Apart from the obvious relationship issues between dependent patients and their physicians already discussed, serious illnesses can have profound effects on individuals with dependent personalities. If their disease deprives them of the ability to function in a role satisfying to their relationship partner on whom their security depends, then they are faced with a dual crisis: loss of health and their emotional well-being, issues that require consideration for treatment to be successful.

Somatoform, Stress-Related Conditions: Headache, Diseases of the Digestive System

For dependent personalities, somatoform conditions may serve to defend against unacceptable impulses while acting to limit or avoid burdensome responsibilities and gain nurturance and caretaking from others. Whereas individuals with depressive or avoidant personalities may suffer the somatoform condition in relative privacy, the dependent individual may develop a condition that is readily visible and thus attention-seeking. Given strong social norms to respond to physical suffering, these individuals may reclaim the interest and support they may have felt deprived of earlier, when their needy and helpless interpersonal maneuvers were rejected

Dependent personalities under stress, particularly social tensions, threats of relationship loss, or maturity demands (e.g., caring for others without reciprocal nurturance) may also manifest their distress largely through physical channels. Headaches, upset stomach, digestive motility disorders, and stress-related fatigue may be common complaints. Typical behaviorally oriented interventions, however, may require active self-management techniques involving home practice, generally of a solitary nature that dependent patients may find unpalatable, particularly if they are alone at such times. Techniques such as relaxation training can be effective in providing symptom relief during treatment sessions, but generalization to real-life contexts may be more problematic and may require social skills training or insight-oriented techniques. If their source of tension results from being pressed to function beyond their means (e.g., look after a busy, demanding husband, children with special needs, caretaking a difficult parent), the obvious antidote of setting limits by saying no may be beyond their repertoire of assertive behavior.

Their social naivete and general lack of interpersonal guile may leave dependent patients' unaware of the motives and intentions of those who show interest in them. When they feel bound to individuals who are demanding or exploitive, the tensions these pressures can generate may nonetheless be less painful than recognition that one is being exploited by someone who does not really care.

When dependent patients are interpersonally bereft, the practitioner will often be cast as a substitute for the missing relationship. If treatment expectations are structured such that contact is maintained until the patient experiences symptom reduction, the motivational barrier to a successful outcome is obvious. Thus, it will be important to emphasize that when treatment goals are achieved, this should not signify the end of treatment and contact but simply a transition to regular follow-up contact, so that these patients can always anticipate additional interaction with their health care partners. If they seem deficient in their homework in between clinical contact, it may be necessary to model self-monitoring and use of specific exercises to encourage internalization or introjection of this behavior in the patient. It may be unrealistic to expect these patients will experience a real sense of self-efficacy, especially if that reduces relationship contact.

However, lessened use of basic medical and drug services in return for assured—if limited—practitioner contact would represent a favorable cost-effective trade-off.

Pain Management

Given the importance of relationship security to individuals with dependent personality, it should not be surprising that the presence of acute or chronic pain will be modified by interpersonal dynamics in dependent patients' lives. Although dependents will probably chose to endure physical over psychic pain if it ensures relationship security, their passivity and ineffective coping may make them overreliant on medications to ease their discomforts, especially given their propensity to somatically experience their anxiety. As a result they may be addiction-prone where long-term, chronic pain management is required. In the short run acute pain will doubtlessly secure caretaking given that there are few more powerful social cues to elicit such behavior. As time progresses, however, those individuals dependent patients come to rely on may begin to feel overburdened, disenchanted, even manipulated and angry over the coercive preemption of their freedom, which their companions' chronic pain imposes on them. Because it is viewed as cruel and inappropriate to challenge physically based sources of distress, companions or family of these individuals will also be inhibited from asserting their needs, especially if this causes intensification of the dependent personality's emotional discomfort (which would likely be expressed through physical complaints). Indeed, individuals with dependent personalities in patient roles may gain some degree of relationship dominance never before enjoyed when they were more physically capable of serving their partner's needs. These influences can be highly corrosive to these relationships, especially if the previously dominant partner begins to feel controlled and placed in an unfamiliar caretaking posture that changes the fragile balance in the relationship that previously had been "workable" for both parties.

The challenge for the clinician will be to anticipate and address these potential risks for dependent patients with chronic pain. Decreasing their pain behavior and increasing their activity level to restore their interpersonal attractiveness is an obvious goal. Changes in the patients' instrumental value to their partners could alter relationship satisfactions, especially sexual and companionship functions (e.g., accompanying their partners to their favored activities). Dependent patients' passivity and their history of subordination to the interests–desires of others may leave them at a disadvantage if their conditions preclude previously shared activities. Treatment of any consequent depression would be incomplete with only mood-elevating drugs; relationship counseling would also be necessary.

Diabetes

Because diabetes represents a lifetime demand where patient self-management is an inescapable requirement, this is an especially difficult condition for the dependent patient. Ordinarily acts of effective self-monitoring, self-denial, and self-regulation actions are likely to be taken for granted or ignored, giving the dependent patient little incentive to behave in this way. Therefore, from the onset of a diagnosis of diabetes, contemplative activity should introduce the notion of self-discipline as a particular feature of the illness management, to elicit whatever apprehensions and concerns such a notion may engender. This should be done in a specific fashion, emphasizing warmth and support for expressions of concern, so that strivings in this regard earn reward and recognition and this mode of functioning is strengthened for the later, preparation and action stages. This may help reduce any fear that failure to engage in new behaviors foreign to them will result in disapproval and threats to the relationship.

Expectations or demands placed on the dependent patient must be manageable and achievable so that success is relatively assured each step of the way during the later stages. Where difficulties arise, these can be viewed as not failures but opportunities for joint problem solving, which can enhance the sense of closeness needed for a long-term medical relationship. This strategy in a sense represents a reversal of what typically takes place in medicine—in other words, that the absence of a symptom or health problem means a reduction in contact with the nurturing authority figure. For individuals seeking security and caretaking, this constitutes a negative paradigm for illness management. Thus, opportunities to report success and effective regulation of blood-sugar levels will be needed, especially in the early stages of promoting wellness-behavior patterns.

Considering that introjection for the dependent personality is a primary coping mechanism for dealing with threat, then the more that illness-regulating behaviors can be identified with the medical authority who provides for the patient's security needs, the better the chance of such behaviors being incorporated into the patient's behavior patterns. Treating the illness as a shared concern and joint undertaking will also exploit these individuals' needs to feel a part of a security-providing enterprise. Emphasizing periodic follow-up where enthusiastic recognition can be given to the maintenance of health in the face of a potentially serious disease can help perpetuate dependent patients' positive attitudes toward a disciplined approach to illness management. It is also a useful vehicle for engendering a greater sense of self-efficacy in a circumscribed context where their security needs are assured, even enhanced with their active participation in the treatment plan.

Neurological Diseases: Epilepsy, Multiple Schlerosis, Parkinson's Disease

Epilepsy for the dependent patient can perpetuate and intensify his or her natural reliance on others, especially the earlier the condition develops in the individual's life, as in childhood. Even for adults, poorly controlled seizures can limit cognitive functioning, educational opportunities, and the right to drive, forcing these individuals to maintain their passive, helpless adaptation.

Multiple sclerosis may begin with innocuous motor and sensory systems, remain as a fluctuating illness, or develop into a progressive degenerative process. Even during periods of remission where comparatively normal functioning may be possible, the subjective nature of the motor and sensory symptoms are quite conducive to emotional or characterologically determined amplification. This can be confusing to the medical or behavioral–rehabilitation expert or even an earnest but suggestible patient with regard to what level of functioning is possible. Thus a patient with a natural aversion to independent functioning could tend to manifest weakness or reduced sensory competence as a result of lack of confidence in his or her ability to function, and it would be difficult to distinguish between subjective and objective determinants of any need for assistance.

Similar considerations apply to Parkinson's disease, although perhaps more objective tests of bodily rigidity and motor dysfunction are possible in this case. Individuals with this condition, because of the consequence of motoric freezing, impairments in balance, and progressive decline in cognitive functioning, are of necessity more reliant on others for assistance. Those with a strong expectation of being cared for, having been overly protected and nurtured during their early years, may regress from any premorbid tenuous attempts at mature functioning as an adult.

Cardiac Disease

As a potentially life-threatening illness, cardiac illness represents a diagnosis likely to intensify dependency issues with virtually any patient, especially one characterologically predisposed to reliance on others. It also represents a context wherein dependent, helpless behavior can easily be justified and caretaking readily coerced, on the basis that these patients would be endangered were they to exert or have to deal with stress on their own. Because for the dependent personality, independent functioning is stressful, this may represent a perfect rationale for avoiding any autonomous, independent functioning, where there is an identifiable threat of stroke or heart attack. Here a vigorous education concerning the patient's health status—in other words, how well they are in addition to the risks associated with their disease—should be imparted, especially to those others (e.g., family) who may be held hostage for the caretaking, nurturing responsibilities. The role of exercise, stress-management techniques, and other coping techniques that can augment the cardiac medications should be emphasized. Detailed communication of this information personally transmitted by the medical authority will promote more accurate, less fear-driven illness representations, which can be reinforced by educational materials that will then be associated with the authority figure.

Heart attack or bypass surgery obviously represents direct exposure to an individual's true vulnerability and his or her mortality that can induce a major regression in any patient and also intensify caretaking preoccupations with those related to them. Rehabilitation can in turn be impeded, especially if exertion or activities involving physiological arousal (e.g., sex) is viewed as a threat. Pain following bypass may be magnified by fears or become reinforced by overly solicitous family members. Involving dependent patients in educational classes and rehabilitation groups, with personalized follow-up with team members (including both the patient and their family members–significant others), can alleviate some of these concerns through reassurance that expert care is immediately at hand. Demands made on these patients must be accompanied by the availability of expertise and opportunities for approval from the medical authority on which their health needs depend.

Cancer

For dependent personalities the salience of cancer is likely to be remote before its diagnosis, unless an important individual in their lives was grappling with the condition, at which point it would become a threat to their own security needs. Given their inherent lack of initiative and reliance on others, ignorance of what some symptom may mean, and what an individual should do when it is present may not represent disease denial, which reflects an active suppression–repression of perceived risk or danger. Notwithstanding issues of informed consent–medical decision making discussed earlier, acute disease management involving surgery, radiation, and chemotherapy are all well mapped out interventions requiring a comparatively passive patient role. In these medical decision-making areas, the dependent personality is unlikely to be actively concerned. Rather, it is the interaction between the illness and the socioemotional context of the patient and his or her relationships that may be of concern.

Although caretaking, sympathy, and solicitude are all predictable social consequences of this dread disease (responses a dependent personality would particularly welcome), the threat of surgical disfigurement or chronic infirmity that might alter personal relationships represents a special threat. These individuals may be at greater risk of entering into exploitive relationships in which their partner's sense of loyalty or commitment may be contingent on particular needs getting met. If a cancer diagnosis and its treatment makes the dependent patient no longer useful to his or her exploitive partner, this can have devastating effect on morale and tolerance to the interventions required to treat this disease. The relationship the cancer patient is in, the needs of his or her significant other, and the likely way in which the relationship could change and affect the patient over the course of treatment may be important in determining how he or she will participate in the care and his or her emotional tolerance of treatments needed.

Early assessment of the spouses or significant others for their capacity to support dependent cancer patients is thus indicated. Where a potential for relationship fragmentation is sensed, referral for relationship counseling to clarify and counter such a possibility should be undertaken as soon as possible. Introducing substitute support for the cancer patient, in the form of groups, individual counseling, and involvement of allied health professionals, can buffer subsequent loss of support from the primary relationship. Much of this analysis may have to be accomplished by the health care team independent of these patients' awareness, given their social naivete that may leave them the last to know about relationship threats or changes.

The acute phase of cancer treatment, surgery and debilitating inpatient treatments, may leave these patients too ill to attend to relationship issues ordinarily of great concern to them. During this time education of family members concerning appropriate supportive roles will be important. Information concerning the patients' probable illness course will also help family members–significant others to prepare for what may come next. For the providers this also represents an opportunity to assess the commitment those close to the dependent patient may be willing or able to make. If a terminal illness course is forecast, then planning for anticipatory grieving and hospice care with patient and family can be initiated. Where a more favorable prognosis and long-term care is anticipated, consideration of possible relationship changes or losses may be appropriate. Considering the likelihood that the dependent patient's primary relationship involves marked asymmetry in dominance–submission patterns, any enduring disruption of this balance will likely require renegotiation of the relationship if it is to endure. This is a matter beyond the medical experts, and would require the early involvement of a mental health professional experienced in working with medical patients and their families.

CONCLUSION

For health care providers, dependent patients will be refreshingly accommodating and flattering until there is real work to be done. Then their passive, overreliant nature and lack of initiative will become a source of aggravation in proportion to the demands placed on these patients. As represented in Figure 9.1, their coping will be characterized by displays of incompetence that effectively ensure that caretaking is always available. Social supports if lacking may have to be engineered by professionals (e.g., social workers), because these patients' help-seeking will be ineffectual and lacking in good discrimination of their needs and those best to provide for them. Preventive health behaviors will only occur as long as they secure the attention and (on-going) approval of strong, protective authority figures. They will not be internalized as self-beneficial given the overwhelmingly other orientation of these individuals. Likewise, disease diagnosis will depend on the vigilance and acumen of these patients' providers. Once illness is identified it will be conceived of in primitive terms and will largely serve to provide secondary gains in the form of coercing continued interpersonal

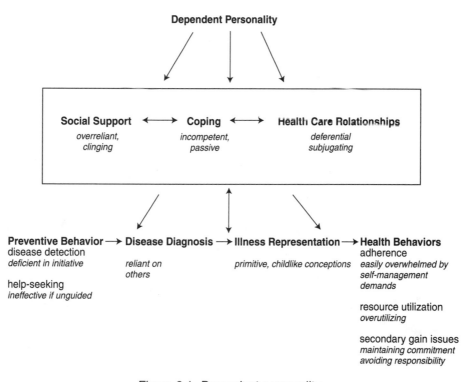

Figure 9.1. Dependent personality.

contact with important relationships or neutralizing expressions of anger from frustrated caretakers. Compliance will depend on the difficulty of the task and the approval available for successful effort.

Although frustrating to deal with during protracted illnesses, dependent patients will remain in relationships with their providers and will be responsive patients provided their limited capacity for independent functioning is not exceeded. Successive approximation in learning self-reliant behaviors will be essential, and combined with approval and assurance this will only strengthen the patient–provider relationship.

10

AVOIDANT PERSONALITY

Avoidant personality disorder represents a Cluster C disturbance, defined in the *DSM–IV* as "a pervasive pattern of social inhibition, feelings of inadequacy, and hypersensitivity to negative evaluation, beginning by early adulthood and present in a variety of four or more of the following contexts" (American Psychiatric Association, 1994, p. 664): the individual (a) avoids work activities involving considerable contact with others, to prevent disapproval or rejection; (b) hesitates or fails to establish relationships unless certain of acceptance; (c) is inhibited when intimate out of apprehension over being shamed or ridiculed; (d) is preoccupied in social contexts with criticism or rejection; (e) feels inadequate, which inhibits social behavior in new contexts; (f) has low self-esteem and feels socially incompetent and inferior to others; (g) fears interpersonal risk-taking out of fear of being embarrassed.

To the observer an individual with avoidant personality may be hard to distinguish from an individual with schizoid disorder in that both may appear emotionally constricted or flat, withdrawn and unresponsive when engaged. However, the individual with avoidant personality in fact is quite different than the individual with schizoid personality on the three basis polarities. Individuals with avoidant personality are strongly preservation-oriented or pain-avoidant and relatively weak on the opposite pleasure-seeking or enhancement polarity pole, whereas individuals with schizoid personality are weak on both. Unlike individuals with schizoid personalities, those with avoidant personalities are strongly on the active pole of the accommodation–modification continuum. The third polarity for the avoidant personality is the least defining of adjustment, because such individuals are equal on self–other, individuation–nurturance motivations, whereas the schizoid individual is more self-oriented. Thus, the prominent feature of the avoidant individual is his or her active pursuit of escaping social and psychic pain.

CLINICAL DOMAIN FEATURES

Considering the specific clinical domains of individuals with avoidant personalities, they can be characterized on a behavioral level by their experience of social phenomena as interpersonally aversive, so that there is an active avoidance of social interaction unless there are absolute assurances of acceptance. From an expressive standpoint these individuals are overly ill at ease in social contexts, hesitant and timid, and guarded about criticism or disapproval.

On a phenomenological level the individual with avoidant personality is characterized as being cognitively distracted, selectively concerned with the social environment for potentially aversive encounters, or distracted by inner ruminations over past or anticipated humiliations and rejections. These preoccupations only aggravate their discomfort in communicating effectively and projecting an attractive image to others. Their self-image is in turn one of social incompetence and inadequacy, perceptions that perpetuate negative schemas about themselves as being unworthy and unattractive. As a consequence, they feel alienated, unwanted, and isolated, which can give rise to feelings of depersonalization and futility.

The internalized representations of social experience of these individuals include a repository of negative memories of humiliation, rejection, and feelings of being unwanted by primary early figures in their lives. Largely absent are pleasant, comfortable interactions with others that would give rise to positive rather than negative anticipation. Other than intense anxiety and a need for escape, these recollections and associations do little to help individuals with avoidant personalities develop inner coping mechanisms, which would also depend on a positive sense of self.

Intrapsychically individuals with avoidant personalities may daydream, privately experiencing deep-felt desires or fulfillment needs of acceptance and social gratification. When reality intrudes, however, the contrast between these circumscribed, pleasant reveries and the anxious, tense anticipations they may experience in normal social discourse can be quite distressing. As a result, they structurally may manifest a fragile personality organization. What needs, goals, and drives that might have facilitated coherent, organized strivings have been undermined by fears, pain, and multiple avoidance tendencies. Their primary mechanism of functioning is thus escape from humiliation and rejection rather than a more typical accumulation of gratifications accompanied by some disappointments and frustrations, which are then reworked to maintain self-esteem and confidence.

Preventing such structures and mechanisms from development may be, on a biophysical level, a temperamentally determined sensitivity to embarrassment and social anxiety that characterizes the individual with avoidant personality's existence. A vacillation of feelings is typical, involving an oscillation between fear (of rejection and humiliation) and anger and sadness (over frustrated longings for acceptance and affection from others). It seems likely that there are fundamental temperamental or neural hormonal features to individuals with avoidant personalities' genetic makeup that predispose them to such chronic social anguish.

AVOIDANT SUBTYPES

In individuals with avoidant personalities with negativistic traits, underlying pessimism, anger, and resentment accompany their fears and social anxieties. Such individuals may periodically criticize or complain of social injustices, real or imagined, then exhibit mortification and apprehensive withdrawal for their outbursts. Not surprisingly, individuals with avoidant personalities may also develop prominent paranoid features, wherein a pervasive suspiciousness and a sense of mistrust characterize their social interactions. Such individuals may find it difficult to trust or positively respond to encouragement and self-esteem-enhancing maneuvers given the sense that others cannot be trusted. A mixture of avoidant with dependent character features describes individuals caught between longings for close personal relationships and a dread of abandonment combined with fears of intimacy and a sense of mistrust. The interplay of these dynamics often generates intense anxieties displaced into phobic concerns and fears that can be circumscribed or compartmentalized so as to be more manageable. In addition, specific fears can be more socially acceptable than pervasive social anxieties, and in turn elicit some degree of solicitousness and sympathy from others, with less risk of rejection. The individual with avoidant personality with depressive traits will exhibit not only marked social aversion but profound self-devaluation. Whereas other avoidant personality types may maintain comparatively rich compensatory fantasy lives, these individuals may feel disconnected from themselves, given their intolerance of their own negatively viewed personal characteristics. To ease the burden of psychic pain, they may disconnect from themselves, and if allowed, maintain a role of passive observer of what limited social interactions are allowed.

PERPETUATING FEATURES

The primary coping mechanisms used by individuals with avoidant personalities, that of vigilance and anticipation of social threat, ensures maintenance of negative belief systems of a dangerous and rejecting world. This in turn generates additional avoidant behavior patterns that maintain a vicious cycle of approach–avoidance conflicts. The constriction that naturally ensues essentially removes the individual with avoidant personality from opportunities for positive social events that could serve as corrective experiences disconfirming the negative schemas built up from early traumas. Whereas individuals without such personality disorders would routinely be immersed in social experience and interaction, individuals with avoidant personalities would have little distraction from their inner world of fears and anticipations. What actual social experiences they may have had are generally remote, providing little opportunity to update meager social skills. This lack of any new social input or experience leaves them unable to identify with groups or individuals who might provide different perspectives from the alienation produced by their social history.

Not only do individuals with avoidant personalities create self-perpetuating cognitive schemas and internalized social scenarios that self-maintain their primary personality features, but their behavior may also elicit social reactions reinforcing those views, by attracting individuals who experience gratification at the humiliation and suffering of others. Individuals with avoidant personalities may also invite rejection by openly sharing their self-contempt and anticipation of rejection. Although this might initially gain some reassurance from others, eventually others retreat or reject in response to the insatiable needs for complete reassurance.

Conventional psychological treatment of individuals with avoidant personalities is to reduce their tendency to anticipate social–emotional pain and pursue gratifications, overcoming the terrible approach–avoidance conflicts that have left them miserable and desperate. A supportive, even unrestrained empathic and nurturing orientation may be needed to overcome the deep-seated mistrust and hesitancy manifested in their interpersonal relationships. Given their fears of rejection or disapproval, these individuals may be reluctant to share experiences that in their minds might invite ridicule, humiliation, or contempt from others. Because of their low self-esteem, mistreatment on the part of others toward them may be construed as deserved and therefore an unfavorable reflection on them rather than the perpetrators of their pain.

Increasing positive experiences requires first reducing the anticipation of pain so that sufficient approach behavior occurs to elicit some reinforcing event. For the individual with avoidant personality this will require taking chances, an antithetical consideration. Only if bolstered by unconditional acceptance and encouragement is the individual with avoidant personality likely to risk additional rejection and social pain to create opportunities for a different mode of social functioning. This requires use of both potentiating and synergistic techniques, combinations of support, encouragement, modeling, social skills training, and pharmacotherapy.

INTERPERSONAL ASPECTS OF AVOIDANT PATIENTS IN THE HEALTH CARE SETTING

For the primary care provider the individual with avoidant personality may be seen as a quiet, passively compliant patient who is socially responsive but who also maintains a distance or remoteness that makes establishing a comfortable patient–physician relationship unlikely. Provided that there are no complicated medical conditions to contend with, such individuals may blend in with the unremarkable, unnoticeable, or innocuous part of the practitioner's patient load. Like the individual with schizoid personality, individuals with avoidant personality characteristics may be difficult to discern in the superficial medical contexts given their quiet, unassuming natures. However, as a relationship with a care team evolves, they will emerge as much less self-absorbed and if anything, overly attentive to interpersonal nuances that may signal disapproval or rejection. They will likely be responsive to the simple requests made by health care providers but may experience uncertainty and discomfort when confronted with the sometimes impatient or gruff interpersonal style of physicians interacting with them. Given their discomfort with any form of confrontation that could court criticism or rejection, they may try to hide their discomfort. These interpersonal concerns and issues could dominate the clinic contacts and interfere with the patients' processing of important instructions concerning their treatment regimen.

With medical conditions requiring extended interactions, emotional exchange, and monitoring of behavior, problems can emerge that are vexing or perplexing to the practitioner. At such times the typical defensive maneuvers of the individual with avoidant personality may come into play in his or her efforts to avoid ridicule or rejection. To keep from being viewed as stupid, the avoidant patient may passively acknowledge comprehension of medical treatment regimens even if he or she does not really understand them. Communications of frustration or disapproval over consequent noncompliance (often errors of omission) may be experienced as interpersonal injury for which the patient may abandon treatment or leave that practice to escape additional rejection.

Another problem may arise when the avoidant patient, out of a concern not to be viewed as a bother, may fail to report important complaint information necessary for symptom monitoring or effective medical management. Unless the behavioral medicine practitioner recognizes that such noncompliance is an inadvertent feature of the personality they are dealing with, the irritation that this naturally engenders in turn may be perceived as confirmation of the individual with avoidant personality's fears. The supportive, tolerant, and patient orientation that is called for may be beyond the capacity of many busy primary care providers. A nurse who can invest greater time and interest in such patients can be invaluable if he or she adopts an interested, sympathetic orientation.

Individuals with avoidant personalities are poorly equipped to go out and generate social support for themselves. Except for their preexisting inherent resources (insurance for medical payments, income for ancillary logistical support) and long-standing relationships, they will likely maintain their typical degree of social isolation to avoid any risk of rejection. In hospital environments, they will be superficially accommodating to staff and authority figures, hiding their internal concerns out of fear of courting disapproval. Some with negativistic features may episodically complain bitterly of their treatment or plight, although the nature of their complaints may be exaggerated by their excessive sensitivity. However, such displays may only elicit overt or covert negative feedback from staff, which will then inhibit such individuals from attempting meaningful communication.

MEDICAL MANAGEMENT ISSUES

The central concern for the practitioner in dealing with patients with avoidant personalities is their staying engaged with the health care system. Primary care prevention or treatment of illness cannot be accomplished if they are retreating from anticipated or imagined rejection. Recognizing their sensitivity to disapproval and criticism will be essential to establishing and maintaining a productive patient–physician relationship.

Preventive Intervention, Lifestyle Choices

Like all other personality types, individuals with avoidant characteristics can become addicted to tobacco or unhealthy eating habits. These can represent gratifications to be enjoyed privately without the apprehensions of socializing. Denial of these pleasures can represent an irreplaceable loss and source of personal suffering. When there is no immediate threat to their well-being, this can certainly represent a motivational barrier that must be addressed.

Stages of Change

The individual with avoidant personality would likely be at a precognitive level concerning these demands for change, given his or her chronic fretfulness and preoccupation with minor events, past humiliations and rejections, and sense of personal alienation. These same preoccupations would interfere with efforts to induce contemplative thought concerning the behavior changes in question. Unlike individuals with schizoid personality, which is comparatively impervious to social influence, avoidant patients' fear of disapproval could provide some leverage if a relationship has first been established and the provider is sensitive to their fears of rejection–disapproval. Here extensive work may be required preparing for the later stages, providing a supportive framework to build confidence, allay fears, recognize and address any sense of loss of important gratifications. For example, the obese individual with an avoidant personality may be sensitized to ridicule and rejection concerning his or her condition and may need considerable empathizing and support to undergo participation in weight loss groups and help with his or her anticipations of failure—the likely event of some relapse in pursuing weight loss.

Behavioral rehearsal, desensitization, and familiarization with the actual intervention phase may constitute the preparation phase. Here uncertainty can be reduced, a relationship forged with the behavioral medicine interventionist based on a shared understanding that detours and setbacks in the treatment process will be treated as constructive events that help refine and guide additional changes in the treatment plan. In this way there is no prospect of failure or rejection—only acceptance and productive learning from experience.

This preliminary work will provide important groundwork for the crucial stage of action, where the avoidant patient must anticipate a probable series of new social encounters involving many interpersonal comparisons eliciting performance anxiety and fears of failure. It is well known that to the extent that there are multiple apprehensions of this kind, regression to old behavior patterns, especially those that are anxiety-reducing, is likely. Smoking, drinking, and eating all serve such purposes. Therefore, instruction in impulse-control techniques—for example, using relaxation training and drugs that reduce anxiety or attenuate urges (e.g., to smoke)—will be crucial. For a drinker, selecting a supportive mentor–sponsor with whom the avoidant individual is comfortable would potentiate participation in group contexts that would otherwise be aversive. An important component of maintenance is to ensure that there are substitute pleasures and gratifications in the place of those lost, especially an improved self-image in which the behavior change (e.g., abstinence) is incorporated.

Utility of Preventive Interventions

Reducing the health risks inherent in tobacco use and alcohol- and eating-related conditions assumes that communication of commonsense knowledge of behavior and disease will motivate individuals to modify their habits using the behavior change-facilitating barrier-reducing (personal and situational) techniques that are taught. For individuals with avoidant personalities, absorbing this behavioral technology and, particularly, implementing it, may require additional skills that they are lacking, such as assertive behaviors to influence friends and family not to smoke in their presence. Insisting on use of condoms with sexual partners may be more frightening to the individual with avoidant personality (who may rightly anticipate disapproval or conflict if this is made a condition to intercourse) than some probability of being infected with a transmittable sexual disease. Group-based programs such as weight loss that have some monitoring and reporting goal attainment may be experienced as a risky situation where shortcomings might be exposed and unfavorable comparisons made. The anticipation of rejection or humiliation in such circumstances may be so great that meetings are missed, setting in motion avoidance of the interpersonal consequences of those actions (e.g., addressing their absences to the group leaders, their physician), even loss to medical follow-up of the original medical condition. Even when participating, avoidant patients may be so apprehensive about the social context that they are not focused on the important information being transmitted in the meeting.

In this instance, risk–benefit consideration for the medical recommendation (to participate in some program) can involve the prospect of a particular patient being so threatened or intimidated by the preventive program that he or she flees the health care arena altogether. Where patients may exercise some freedom of choice in selecting physicians, the avoidant patient may simply drop out and plan to seek additional medical contact with a new provider if some future illness were to occur, defeating the purpose of the original behavioral medicine intervention. Although the notion of personal responsibility has been advanced in relationship to the escalating costs of health care associated with disease-related health behavior, simply assigning blame for disease development ignores the reality of the patient–provider (health care system) interaction and its influence on health behavior change.

Recognizing prominent avoidant tendencies in a particular patient thus can constructively sensitize the clinician to the need to address the feelings and fears patients have concerning procedures and intervention they may need and their propensity to escape uncomfortable social situations to avoid rejection. A warm, unconditionally supportive orientation with an avoidant patient can keep alive the practitioner's influence to potentiate change. By encouraging these patients to think about making change, encouraging expression of fears, rather than prescribing (in effect, to avoidant patients ordering) action they are ill-prepared for keeps open the possibility for change that otherwise is foreclosed by their anticipatory anxiety.

Secondary and Tertiary Care of Acute and Chronic Illness

Illness detection and disease management for patients with avoidant personalities will be influenced by their social apprehensions. Concern over being perceived as a bother, hypochondriacal, or demanding could lead avoidant patients' withholding important complaint information crucial to diagnosis of a condition or its treatment, including adjustment of medicines and selection of future interventions. This same inhibition may keep avoidant patients from seeking clarification concerning their role in the treatment process. This may result in noncompliance errors that are frustrating to the busy physician, whose expressions of such impatience may only generate additional anxious, disruptive cognitions that interfere with the clarity of their thought processes. Where feasible, training in assertive behavior may be beneficial, as well as in vivo desensitization of specific interpersonal fears and anticipated rejections or humiliations.

To the extent that internalization of disease knowledge and treatment requirements into the patient's self-concept and sense of efficacy represents the ultimate goal of the patient–physician process, it will be important to examine avoidant patients' private illness representations. Given their disturbed self-image and sense of personal inadequacy, this can represent a significant undertaking that may only partially be accomplished. However, gaining some sense of the degree of integrity or disturbance of their self-concept may offer a means of understanding these individuals' inherent fragilities and their susceptibility to being overcome by external influences. For example, if the avoidant patient has an inaccurate or incomplete understanding of his or her disease and its potential impact (e.g., disfigurement, reduction in mobility), these misconceptions will need to be clarified. If an illness is likely to elicit self-devaluation and additional fears of rejection, these disruptive, fear incubating, or distracting anxiety-avoiding cognitions may undermine confidence in self-management efforts. To the extent that the clinician can create high probability opportunities for these patients to succeed in some compliance or treatment objective, this can contribute to their sense of self-efficacy, which can be the basis for healthier self-esteem and self-confidence and greater future cooperation.

Coping With Illness

For the individual with avoidant personality, the consequences of an illness may involve coping with different stresses that involve both emotion-focused disease-related issues and fears and problem-focused matters (e.g., planning when to go into the hospital, covering work-related responsibilities). The social skill deficits of such individuals make it likely that there is an interpersonal adjustment burden also incurred by their illness, because it automatically places them in a dependent posture with strangers, on whose good will their lives may seem to depend. Being removed from one's carefully contrived, insular social environment and thrown into a busy, impersonal system (e.g., health care environment–clinic or hospital) is itself more than most individuals can manage, especially when they are in fear of some debilitating disease. For the avoidant patient whose social fears exceed all others, this may mean that they will be coping with an additional hidden stressor—that of the health care system itself. To the extent that there is only so much time and energy to struggle with adaptive demands exceeding one's ordinary coping, it would be no surprise that illness-related issues, unless they are compelling and immediate, get insufficient attention from such individuals, who are overwhelmed by the competing interpersonal stresses confronting them.

Because the individual with avoidant personality is typically in hiding, it may be difficult to recognize his or her anguish, because it will be generally internalized. The effect of their personality on their functioning will be seen in their haphazard, fragmented response to medical treatment demands and their erratic compliance efforts. Rather than a confrontive approach to such difficulties, a supportive, empathic orientation, recognizing the probable difficulties that face them, may help them focus on the threats they must address. Otherwise they may be prone to engage in purposefully disruptive mental activity described as "intentional interference" (Millon, 1999, p. 318), which momentarily protects them from perceiving threat but also prevents effective emotion and problem-focused activity. Where important medical decision making must be accomplished rapidly, individuals with avoidant personalities may lack the assertive skills to ask appropriate questions or articulate personal concerns when confronted with an impatient surgeon or busy medical specialist. A behavioral medicine practitioner may be needed to run interpersonal interference by communicating directly with members of the patient's health care team for direct clarification of their situation. This may involve helping these patients construct a hierarchy of concerns, questions, and compliance requirements related to their illness management. These patients can also be assisted in dealing with specific interpersonal encounters by interpreting aberrant patient behavior to prevent punitive reactions and suggesting interpersonal strategies to providers for gaining patient confidence and facilitating relationship building.

Medical Compliance

For individuals with avoidant personalities, medical compliance can signify an illness that further diminishes their sense of attractiveness by restricting them from sharing in certain activities (e.g., drinking). It also creates an interpersonal context in which they may incur disapproval or outright rejection by disappointing a powerful authority figure cast in a beneficent role (the physician) if there is a compliance failure. The medical model contributes to this characterization by focusing on noncompliance, the failure to follow medical recommendations, rather than learning healthy behaviors to replace unhealthy habits. It also promotes too dogmatic a view of failures of adherence to treatment as patient deficiencies or contrariness, ignoring consideration of possible situational barriers and extenuating circumstances. For avoidant patients fearful of failure and condemnation, there is little incentive to remain in contact with individuals who are thus looking critically at their actions.

Where a patient is known to be particularly relationship-sensitive and fearful of criticism and rejection, the most appropriate strategy for promoting compliance is one oriented toward success and approval rather than failure and censure. Given that many treatment regimens may involve relatively complex combinations of medicines, schedules to take them, and side effects to watch for, it would be anticipated that the distracted, internally preoccupied individual is at risk for mistakes because of inattention at the times compliance behavior must take place. It would follow that emphasizing healthy behavior patterns and how they may be most readily attained might have more benefit on promoting compliance. For the avoidant patient the easier the task can be defined, and the greater the likelihood of success, the better. In addition, small, incremental changes may be more valuable, in that great accomplishments may be dissonant with the patient's self-esteem or run the risk of creating expectations of future success that the patient may feel is unrealistic and doomed to failure.

Emphasis on the process of changing behavior from unhealthy to healthy practices may also reduce the sense of performance anxiety these patients may have, while providing excellent opportunities for identifying important (social) barriers to change and how they might be overcome. Recognizing that compliance failures, properly analyzed, provide far more valuable information about the different aspects of behavior change can provide an important sense that patients can redeem themselves when they fall short. Predicting that compliance mishaps are inevitable but correctable can preempt a patient's anticipatory anxiety. Constructively addressing the difficulties that can occur will help create a sense that there will be acceptance no matter how imperfect the patient's efforts to effect change.

IMPACT OF DISEASE STATES ON THE AVOIDANT PATIENT

Confrontation with a serious illness for patients with avoidant personalities represents another instance where their sense of unacceptability and unworthiness is activated. Beyond the anguish this causes, it can create significant disruptions to these patients' earnest attempts to participate in their treatment and recovery efforts. An accepting, supportive orientation from those providing their care will be an important part of overcoming these influences.

Somatoform, Stress-Related Conditions: Headaches, Diseases of the Digestive System

Individuals with avoidant personalities may use or develop physical symptoms as a means of escaping from situations perceived as threatening rejection and humiliation, thereby protecting fragile self-esteem and perpetuating low self-worth. Sensitive and temperamentally nervous by nature, avoidant individuals may be vulnerable to stress-sensitive conditions such as headache, gastrointestinal distress, and the like, which, with their many fears, may become features of complex clinical syndromes. Once stress is identified as a component, it will be important for the medical practitioner *not* to make referral to a mental health specialist as if his or her role is complete. The fact that the patient's illness conception is that of a physical cause should justify an orientation of interest and the view that mind–body conditions are inseparable. An argument that evidence of serious bodily disease is absent but that additional investigation of the patient's distress is clearly indicated will be far more reassuring than the unfortunately familiar message, "its all in your head," and with it the rejecting addendum that the patient needs to "see a shrink."

The anxiety proneness of individuals with avoidant personalities, their worry and anticipation of harm or attack, leave them hypervigilant and subject to chronic sympathetic nervous system arousal. In somatically vulnerable individuals this background arousal will interfere with gastric motility digestion, promote sustained muscle contraction, or vasospasms of the blood vessels. Although relaxation training may be beneficial, the distractibility and pervasive anxiety-proneness to social stimuli of such individuals make effective generalization of these techniques problematic. Use of medications such as a short-acting benzodiazapine, or a beta-blocker, to tone down nervous system reactivity may be necessary. Instruction in self-management techniques in relative isolation away from immediate social stressors or distractions is important to strengthen the relaxation response and promote a mind-clearing component to reduce the fragmented, intruding distracting thoughts that can disrupt these individuals' coping efforts.

Once an effective relaxation response is acquired, careful review of the different stressors, typically social fears, will be important to establish a hierarchy of commonly encountered situations that presumably provoke the psychosomatic response. Considering social skills training, particularly assertive skills, may be important to support self-relaxation efforts that will be of little benefit if the individual is susceptible to coercion or intimidation through lack of interpersonal competence. Rehearsing effective interaction strategies and responses may increase predictability concerning what the avoidant patient is supposed to do in difficult situations, and this will help diminish the anticipatory anxiety that can incubate and distort expectations of future social encounters. A cognitive–behavioral orientation can help link these component elements of stress-management treatment into an individualized, effective treatment package paced to the tolerance level of the given patient.

Pain Management

Given that individuals with avoidant personalities are actively pain- and harm-avoidant by nature, to have chronic physical discomfort added to their psychic suffering seems particularly cruel and unfortunate. For them, their dynamic that life may get worse rather than better in fact is realized by the added burden of chronic pain. To those with a particularly damaged sense of self-esteem, however, this may seem their just desserts, consistent with a destiny devoid of the social rewards and pleasures taken for granted by others. Given their alarmist nature, their tendency may be to experience any fluctuation in pain as acute, a signal of potential harm to the body rather than an unfortunate consequence of a resolved injury. Education may have to be repetitive and patient, recognizing the source of their complaints as stemming from their anxiety and chronic state of vulnerability.

In one sense, chronic pain and the inactivity and social withdrawal it naturally promotes is consistent with the basic avoidant personality adaptation. The physical disability associated with it may serve to justify alleviation of burdensome or fear-provoking responsibilities. Other secondary gain might include increased caretaking from those few close relations, such as family, where the pain–disability justifies special consideration and sympathy. Over the long-term, however, such benefits may erode and be replaced by covert resentment from caretakers tiring of the unchanging nature of these individuals' response to their conditions and the roles they are forced to take. Nonetheless because their chronic pain adaptation does provide a potential structure around which some social uncertainties can be reduced, the avoidant patient may cling to this adjustment, which provides them an acceptable basis for eluding uncomfortable situations.

Participating in chronic pain treatment programs, especially inpatient settings, may be anxiety-provoking for these individuals, given the intense interpersonal nature of most programs and their reliance on group processes and interpersonal reinforcers to produce reductions in pain behavior. Avoidant patients' fretful expressive style may produce displays of restless discomfort. Lacking any versatility in social skills, their injury and chronic pain condition likely has been incorporated into their social behavior and self-image, which are then inextricably tied up with their self-esteem. Intentional ignoring of pain behavior may be particularly impactful to them, given their hyperreactivity to any feedback that they might be doing something to incur disapproval. Unresponsiveness to their displays may thus be experienced as rejection, generating feelings of social panic, humiliation, and disorganized apprehension rather than a reduction in the pain behavior itself. The effect may be hurt withdrawal from the staff who ignored them; those treatment team members are thus avoided and thereby lose their potentially reinforcing properties. Accordingly with avoidant patients, it will be crucial to ensure that they have learned alternative well behaviors to substitute for their pain behaviors and have a means of securing the acceptance and approval of their care providers.

Although addiction to analgesics is a common risk for chronic pain patients, these agents also serve other purposes, such as sedation and mood alteration. For patients with avoidant personalities, anxiety reduction and diminishment of their typical state of hyperarousal may be an important effect, especially needed if they are thrown into a controlled social environment where withdrawal is not tolerated and participation in socially based activities is mandatory. Anxiety management training may be helpful, but particularly so if it is accompanied by addressing the avoidant patient's social anxiety, skill deficiencies, and low self-esteem. A patient advocate–interpreter of the treatment process who always remains in a nonjudgmental, supportive role may be essential to diminishing some of the potential barriers faced by these individuals.

In addition to reducing pain behavior, the goal of treatment is obviously rehabilitation. For avoidant patients, this can mean return to responsibility and social environments that were previously aversive or punishing when they were fully healthy. They may anticipate the prospect of returning to a similar situation in a diminished and presumably less capable state. Preparatory goal setting involving selection of modest objectives where there is a high probability of success will be necessary to contain their anxiety level. Rehearsing anticipated situations and work-hardening experiences with supportive, encouraging staff who are well informed about the patient's sensitivities and characteristics will help minimize the avoidant patient's tendency to become deflected with minor setbacks and interpersonal distractions. It must be remembered that these individuals are especially sensitive to false prospects of improvement in their lives. For them to regain some functioning from an injury or illness in the face of persisting negative aftereffects (pain) represents a significant challenge for the health care provider. Prognostic forecasts should not be overly optimistic, because this likely will only be threatening. Rather, recognition, even emphasis of significant remaining handicaps, particularly during periods of gain, may be important to give the avoidant patient a sense that lack of progress and setbacks are acceptable and not a basis for derision or rejection. For these individuals, to feel there is an acceptable explanation for any lack of success in regaining normal functioning and that effort, not success, is (socially) rewarded may serve as protection from the intense fear of failure that otherwise may consume them.

Diabetes

Being anxiety-prone, stressful situations for individuals with avoidant personalities could contribute to altered glucose metabolism. Dealing with fluctuations in the illness that are not diet-caused can be a source of interpersonal tension and recrimination with the health care providers, who may not initially consider alternative causes and attribute the difficulty to patient misbehavior. The risk is that such misunderstanding by health care providers can result in a sense of rejection potentially strong enough that the severely avoidant patient might exit the care setting. Once rejected, they may remain fearful about seeking alternative care, which they would anticipate as also ultimately rejecting. Like individuals with schizoid disorders, individuals with avoidant personalities might drop out of contact not out of indifference but to escape from a potentially noxious social situation. A patient, accepting orientation by the physician combined with discussion and monitoring of the different contributing factors in problematic blood-sugar regulation should help counter these potential risks to the care of the avoidant individual.

Neurological Diseases: Epilepsy, Multiple Schlerosis, Parkinson's Disease

Epilepsy for avoidant patients could represent a convenient escape from burdensome anxieties and responsibilities, justifying social withdrawal, but it would also likely increase their social and self-alienation, making them feel even more vulnerable and inadequate, limited and restricted. Public episodes would be experienced as particularly humiliating. Such patients' chronic anxiety might also make their seizure thresholds lower and conditions more difficult to manage given their stress-proneness. Erratic medication monitoring caused by their ruminative, distractible cognitive style might also contribute.

Multiple sclerosis may be an unobtrusive illness that creates a chronic sense of uncertainty to the patient, who may experience episodes of sensory or motor dysfunction (e.g., blurred vision, weakness) disruptive to functioning. Any experience of this kind may produce more intense feelings of vulnerability, inadequacy, and self-loathing. Organic personality changes may produce exaggeration of preexisting anxiety-prone characteristics, creating an even more unstable, overreacting individual, phobic and prone to behavioral and emotional paralysis. Depression can intensify the withdrawal of such individuals, whereas organic mania can cause out of character boldness, irritability, effusiveness, and behavioral excess later mortifying to these individuals.

Parkinson's disease for the avoidant patient would represent a more visible reminder of his or her unacceptability to others. The depression common with this condition would likely intensify such individuals' moments of acute anguish, interspersed with their more typical chronic, numbing sense of despair. As frontal lobe functioning may be affected, this can produce a behavioral apathy or ruminative, anxious inertia that makes decision-making and initiative problems already prominent in the avoidant patient even more severe. Conversely, the characteralogical response to a debilitating illness such as Parkinson's can also produce emotional–behavioral responses that suggest greater organic involvement than may actually be present.

In contrast to individuals with schizoid personalities, avoidant patients may be more actively affected by their illness and involved in their treatment regimen, although their inner preoccupations and distracted nature may make them vulnerable to confusion concerning their treatment regimen, especially when given oral messages by busy, intimidating, impersonal authority figures (e.g., their neurologist). As the disease becomes more progressive, requiring treatment with dopaminergic agents, there can be periods of freezing, where movement is particularly difficult and activities such as driving can be quite hazardous. Such episodes can be particularly frightening to anxiety-prone, self-conscious individuals, who may become even more reclusive and phobic as a result, experiencing additional reduction in the quality of life. Special attention to such features of the disease, and specification of a plan about how to anticipate wearing off of medication and what to do when an attack occurs at inopportune times can mitigate the devastating effect of these events.

Cardiac Disease

To the extent that central and sympathetic nervous activity play a role in cardiac functioning, the hypervigilant, fearful state of the avoidant patient could serve as psychological hindrances to stabilization of cardiac abnormalities (Haines, Imeson, & Meade, 1987). In addition, the vulnerability of such individuals to generalized anxiety and panic attack disorders could contribute symptoms of a noncardiac nature confusing to the internist or cardiologist treating the patient. There is in fact a high prevalence of anxiety disorders in patients with noncardiac chest pain (e.g., Kane, Stroehlein, & Harper, 1991; Wielgosz et al., 1984), as determined by expensive and invasive procedures (e.g., angiograms). Many of these patients paradoxically receive prescriptions of nitroglycerine even if there is no physiological indication for it, reinforcing false illness representations concerning their symptoms (Kane et al., 1991). Relatively few are ever referred out for psychological–psychiatric evaluation. The behavioral medicine practitioner thus should be sensitive to psychological conditions masquerading as cardiac disease in anxiety-prone patient personality types, apart from the well-described Type A pattern.

The extent to which avoidant patients with hypertension can be sensitized to accurately detect fluctuations in blood pressure levels without direct monitoring has not been directly studied, although it would seem their distractible, jumpy nature would not facilitate such an objective. Because different cardiac medicines can have significant side effects, including depression, reporting important symptoms indicative of undesired drug effects can be important to successful management. Avoidant patients, however, will be inhibited and anxious not to be seen as difficult to manage. Or they may be distracted by the interpersonal intimidation of visiting with a busy physician to remember to mention some symptom associated with drug taking. As a consequence, such individuals may be at greater risk for privately suffering unintended drug effects that could be easily resolved.

Coronary artery disease ending in heart attack is one of the most feared health events, as are stroke and diagnosis of cancer. Many of the symptoms of panic attack are so similar to the prodromal manifestations of heart attack and so intense that it can be very difficult to reassure a patient, particularly an anxiety-prone one, that the next occasion of chest pain, diaphoresis, shortness of breath, or a sense of indigestion might not signify the "real thing." In truth, it must be recognized that even if such patients are diagnosed with an anxiety disorder, there is no absolute assurance that the next attack might not *be* real. Many "cardiac neurotics" are disabled by their fears.

Serious illness such as heart attack or coronary artery blockage requiring bypass surgery could represent an occasion, during the acute phase, where there is sufficiently organized and structured caretaking that avoidant patients need fear little rejection. They might thus enjoy some degree of privately longed for interpersonal attention, which might even be seen as secondary gain. For the avoidant patient, getting well can represent a resumption of responsibilities and assumption of new ones, involving sacrifice and deprivation (e.g., eschewing high-cholesterol foods, giving up cigarettes). A sick role can thus be attractive, reinforced by secondary gain through alleviation of responsibility and avoidance of anxiety-provoking demands (e.g., work).

Even during the early phases of recovery, however, there may be performance requirements in the form of rehabilitation and educational heart-healthy groups addressed at changing lifestyle. These could represent approach–avoidance situations for these individuals, given their longing to belong and be approved of and their stronger fear of rebuke–rejection over disappointing others. Difficult-to-break habits involving unhealthy behaviors may be anticipated as a situation where avoidant patients will receive criticism and disappointment in their performance. The distracting influence of anticipated rejection at such times will only impede their acquiring and retaining important information concerning the process of changing behavior, which are the fundamental ingredients for accomplishing and maintaining it. These considerations would suggest that part of the initial education of such cardiac patients in recovery should include what it means to be mortal and vulnerable in this way, to be sick and then faced with the responsibility of recovery, which can involve sacrifices and effort involving potential failure. Although such an approach is not likely to inoculate the individual with avoidant personality from deeply ingrained conditioned emotional fear responses, it can provide a context where feelings and behaviors typically hidden can be addressed in a more constructive manner that will indeed potentiate learning healthy behaviors and lifestyle changes.

As previously mentioned, the clinician should be sensitized to symptoms of depression at this time in particular, not only because of the biological shock inherent in heart attack but also the many psychological losses associated with it (e.g., loss of a sense of wellness, cessation of previous pleasure). Treating affective disturbance can remove an immobilizing influence in moving into the action phase of cardiac recovery change.

Cancer

Individuals with avoidant personalities' heavy loading on the preservation–pain-avoidance and active polarities leaves them ill-suited to the catastrophic stresses associated with diagnosis of cancer. Added to their chronic sense of interpersonal vulnerability is a condition that threatens to make them feel even more unattractive and wretched than they already perceive themselves to be. Some, who have come to view social acceptance, regard, and the good things of life as undeserved or beyond their reach would only feel more so now with a dreaded physical disease to contend with. Added to this is the intensification of interpersonal contact that acute treatment of their illness would require, with stranger–specialists on whom their lives depended. These patients' deficient social skills, their tendency to be deflected in their thinking by their intruding preoccupations and inner conflicts, would certainly produce the complex clinical syndromes involving the depression and anxiety conditions common in cancer patients.

With respect to early detection, avoidant patients' preoccupied with pervasive troubled memories and anticipations would have little energy or focus to proactively exercise concern over their physical well-being. Confrontation with a threat of increased vulnerability in the form of some screening program or cancer prevention activity at work might elicit a brief flurry of concern or fearful apprehension, but this would predictably be replaced by a more immediate internal or external conflict in their lives. If identified as being at high risk from family heredity or ethnic background, this type of patient may require aggressive follow-up by the primary care physician or managed care organization responsible for providing care, to ensure preventive early detection is periodically carried out (e.g., colon examinations, routine skin cancer screening). The stronger a sense of an accepting relationship with the primary care physician, the more likely an individual with avoidant personality would respond to such announcements. Conversely, if the physician is busy and impatient, this would likely be taken personally by the patients, who would thus avoid contact with his or her provider except when prompted to seek care for some acute illness.

The propensity for avoidant patients to become deflected by their inner preoccupations and situational–interpersonal crises may contribute to procrastination or unfortunate delays in obtaining specialized referral when a condition is detected or suspected. This is especially likely to be true if the health care system is impersonal, busy, and emotionally remote. Their cognitive distractions and threat-reduction defenses may also interfere with effective decision making concerning treatment options. Avoidant patients lacking assertive skills may be intimidated into agreeing to procedures favored by the medical authority figure involved in their care. Obviously, where the outcome if good, there is little fallout. However, if adverse events occur, then there may be more recrimination and potential for accusations of failure to give informed consent.

The avoidant patient's anxious, fretful nature may also contribute to his or her erratic reporting of symptoms, some of which may be anxiety-related and confused for important complaint information related to medicine side effects or the disease course. These and other distractions could contribute to confusion concerning the treatment regimen and efforts to carry it out. Detecting compliance mistakes may be difficult because they will be hidden by the avoidant patients' fear of censure.

Although support groups could potentially be helpful, group leaders would have to be attuned to these patients' sensitivities to any kind of interpersonal tension, lest that divert their focus from illness-related coping and disease education. Emotion-awareness or abreaction activities could unintentionally amplify the idiosyncratic and complex aspects of these patient's complex clinical syndromes rather than effectively address what for others would be disease-specific symptoms of anxiety and depression.

CONCLUSION

Patients with avoidant personality characteristics, as with other patients, will have good intentions to do "what is right" in health care contexts. However, their primary goal rather than good health care will be avoiding censure and disapproval of those with whom they are dealing. Where there is little to do, then practitioners will be pleased and these patients will be reasonably comfortable. However, if the interactive requirements and the treatment regimen for effective health care management is complex or difficult or aversive (a brusque practitioner), then the natural apprehensiveness and fear of rejection of these patients will emerge as a complicating factor. These patients' coping responses are predominated by escape–avoidance behavior, reducing communication opportunities to seek needed support, clarification of needed medical information, and efficient tracking of symptoms. Under threat these individuals will retreat into a private, anxious world cut off from corrective opportunities, distracted by fears of rejection, thoughts of unworthiness and self-loathing. Individuals with these characteristics have little opportunity to generate needed social support for

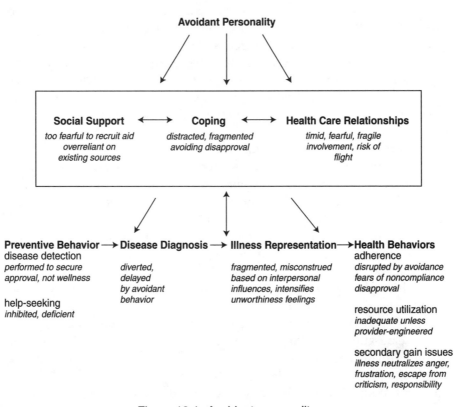

Figure 10.1. Avoidant personality.

themselves. Unless their symptoms are so severe as to overcome avoidance motivation, help-seeking is delayed or reduced, lessening the possibility of early disease detection. Illness representations will be infused with anxious preoccupations, perhaps notions of deservedness and heightened fears of unacceptability, hardly views conducive to accurate understanding of the disease process and management. Underuse of resources is more likely, given that these individuals will shy away from unfamiliar social contact, especially group-based experiences. Secondary gains will center around relief from anxiety stemming from aversive social contact or performance situations where failure is possible and, in turn, censure. These considerations are schematically depicted in Figure 10.1.

These individuals will be difficult to recognize as patients given their retiring nature. Once identified, patience and an accepting, nurturing orientation will be necessary to ensure contact is maintained. Even so, their anxious, private ruminations will likely remain an interfering influence, requiring ongoing monitoring to ensure their understanding and participation in their health care management.

11

COMPULSIVE PERSONALITY

The *DSM–IV* describes obsessive–compulsive personality, a Cluster C disorder, as "a pervasive pattern of preoccupation with orderliness, perfectionism, and mental and interpersonal control, at the expense of flexibility, openness, and efficiency, beginning by early adulthood and present in a variety of contexts" (American Psychiatric Association, 1994, p. 672), with an individual demonstrating at least four of the following: (a) preoccupation with details, rules, lists, schedules of such magnitude that the purpose of the intended activity is subverted or lost; (b) perfectionism that consistently impedes completion of tasks; (c) devotion to work and perceived productivity that excludes enjoying leisure activity and friendships; (d) inflexibility and overconscientiousness about moral issues not explainable by religious convictions or cultural (subcultural) influences; (e) hoarding and inability to dispose of objects of no present or future value; (f) difficulty delegating to others without reassurance that tasks will be performed exactly according to specifications; (g) excessive conservation of money for future anticipated catastrophes at the expense of self and others; and (h) rigidity and stubbornness in dealing with matters.

From an evolutionary personality standpoint, the individual with compulsive personality is fundamentally beset with a core ambivalence between polarities on the self (autonomy) and other (dependent) interpersonal orientations. Conflicts between submission (other orientation) and defiance (self-orientation) are typically resolved by channeling aggressive and oppositional impulses into an inflexible conformity and adherence to rules and social conventions. Although admirable in many respects, compulsive personalities can also be experienced as rigid, emotionally cold and unresponsive, and out of touch with their own feelings. Industrious and concerned about organization, compulsive individuals can delay gratification and suffer frustration, but will become anxious or agitated when confronted by a loss of structure, control, and predictability. Spontaneity is rare and they may be accused of lacking imagination and tending to miss the forest for the trees. Sensitive to criticism and guilt-prone, they may have excessive needs for reassurance and approval from authority, in response to which they will be quite loyal and protective. Often they will manifest unusual concern and sensitivity to potential mishaps causing harm to others, which may be viewed as reaction formation, a defense against actual expression of the very impulse being defended against.

Individuals with compulsive personalities are more strongly oriented toward preservation (pain avoidance) than enhancement (pleasure-seeking) polarities. They are strongly accommodating or passive in their adaptation, rarely taking initiative or an active stance in dealing with the environment. As one of the ambivalent personality types in Millon's formulations (Millon, 1999), individuals with compulsive personalities have resolved their conflicts between development of self and autonomy (individuation) and the antagonistic–oppositional impulses that accompany that adaptation by shifting strongly to an other-nurturance, caretaking role, overcompensating for those underlying impulses to rebel and defy authority.

CLINICAL DOMAIN FEATURES

In terms of the prototypical diagnostic domains, individuals with compulsive personalities on a behavioral–expressive level are possessed with a serious sense of purpose, a disciplined, self-denying orientation, emotional reserve and constriction, and concern about propriety and appearance. Preoccupations with perfectionism may leave them indecisive and unable to realize objectives in a fashion where expedience and timely completion are more important than quality and flawlessness. On an interpersonal level, compulsive individuals typically convey a respectful orientation, especially to those in authority, with whom they may be overly deferential and ingratiating. Conversely, with subordinates they may adopt a somewhat rigid, authoritarian stance, reflecting their preoccupation with status or rank. Manners and etiquette, adherence to formality, and loyalty are important relationship issues, anxiously adhered to around superiors and rigidly uncompromising with subordinates.

From the phenomenological perspective, individuals with compulsive personalities on a cognitive level may be tightly rule-bound and conventional in their consideration of things, rarely deviating from well-established bounds. Their views, perspectives, and modes of thinking may be considered constricted, contained, conventional, and unimaginative. Conversely, they may be overcritical of seemingly impulsive or spontaneous behavior on the part of others, especially where that deviates from the prevailing social norms, which they unconsciously resent. To the extent that these qualities result in trustworthy and efficient actions, individuals with compulsive personalities are likely to be appreciated by others, but they may also elicit irritation or disapproval for their stubbornness or seemingly relentless perseverance in completing assignments and responsibilities.

Supporting this orientation is the self-image of the compulsive personality, which is that of a conscientious, responsible individual, willing to make personal sacrifices for the good of others. Identifying with the rules and authoritarian strictures to control their own impulses, compulsive individuals can perceive themselves as virtuous beyond others. The assumption is that good deeds and behavior will be rewarded; they can thus feel secure that they are safe from disapproval. However, when the world behaves in an arbitrary and unfair way, they may be unprepared to deal with such events, experiencing disillusionment or unproductive self-recrimination and doubt because their experience was inconsistent with their virtue. In that way they can be harsh and self-punitive in their own judgments, and in turn become superstitious and overly cautious concerning decision making and risk-taking, failing to appreciate that they are not necessarily in control. Unknown forces and events beyond them can exert arbitrary negative influence no matter how hard they may strive and how carefully they may adhere to rules.

The internalized representations of relationships of individuals with compulsive personalities are generally confined to images and experiences that are censored, so that only socially acceptable recollections are accessible to conscious retrieval. Misconduct, expression of selfish, base impulses, and conflicts between needs and impulses and societal conventions that place the individual in an unfavorable light are excluded from consideration. True introspection into feelings and attitudes are thus rejected as interfering with goal attainment and efficiency, because it might undermine rational effort and expose the individual to loss of self-control.

Intrapsychically, individuals with compulsive personalities use reaction formation extensively to regulate or manage oppositional impulses and tendencies. Their relentless pursuing of virtue and avoidance of all impropriety hides underlying feelings of anger, opposition, or rebellion. To consciously experience these feelings would be quite stressful and conflictual to them. Their overly accommodating orientation may reflect the opposite, a longing to resist, put selfishness first and pursue shameless self-gratification. Other means of dealing with unacceptable impulses can involve identification with authority figures, wherein feelings of hostility are expressed through reproach and punishing others for being tempted and engaging in the forbidden, longed for behavior. Sublimation of hostile drives may be a more adaptive, socially acceptable regulatory mechanism, by pursuing roles such as combat soldier, police officer, prison guard, medical surgeon, or judge, all of whom have some degree of power and the potential to judge and inflict some form of suffering or discomfort onto others. Isolation of affect as a defense can also prevent hostile or negative impulses from coming forth in situations that would ordinarily elicit such feelings but that would incur sanctions or disapproval from authority. Finally, undoing, repetitive acts of atonement for perceived wrongdoing or failure to meet one's standards can help the compulsive individual restore his or her sense of righteousness and moral fitness. Not surprisingly, individuals with compulsive personalities tend to be serious and sober in their mood and temperament, purposeful and controlled rather than spontaneous in their expression of feelings. The energy expended in their rigid maintenance of a proper façade may leave the compulsive individual vulnerable to fatigue and prone to psychophysiological disorders. Constitutionally, such individuals may be on a biophysical level prone to anhedonia, lacking in a capacity for joy and pleasure capable of other personality types. Compulsive individuals are also particularly vulnerable to anxiety and depressive disorders, given their high standards and emotional inhibitions, which make them vulnerable to chronic feelings of inadequacy.

COMPULSIVE PERSONALITY SUBTYPES

Individuals with compulsive personalities with dependent features are the prototypically conscientious individuals, given their combination of rule-abiding, fear–disapproval-avoiding compulsive traits and their need to subjugate and sacrifice to the expectations and desires of others in return for safety and emotional acceptance. This adaptation is the antithesis to independent, self-directed functioning. Unambitious, duty-bound, self-effacing, and looking to others for initiative, individuals with this compulsive personality pattern variant typically will become attached to large institutions with predictable environments that minimize the possibility of risk and making a mistake. Perfectionism is pursued more out of a fear of rebuke and rejection than from the standards themselves that might not be met. Competition, let alone confrontation, is avoided at all costs, as conformity and agreement offer the only perceived safety of approval and acceptance.

If placed in benign, supportive environments (e.g., church organizations), such individuals will be seen as loyal, devoted, sacrificing, and trustworthy employees. However, the likelihood is that most ordinary social settings are not entirely benign but competitive and even in some instances ruthless. In these situations, the compulsive individual with dependent features is at the mercy of others who may behave assertively, even aggressively in pursuing their needs and hidden agendas, of which individuals with this variant will be virtually unaware. Making the fundamental mistake that others are like themselves, helpful and cooperative, they will be oblivious to their exploitative intent, exhaust themselves doing others' work or supervisors' bidding, no matter how unreasonable or unfair. Eventually, they may become overwhelmed with anxiety or depressed or despondent at being unable to perform to what constitute unreasonable expectations, yet driven to do so out of fear of rejection and letting others down. Compulsive–dependent individuals may be hesitant to seek clarification if they do not understand, to avoid being perceived as inadequate or unaccommodating of their valued care providers.

The compulsive personality with paranoid features involves a combination of authority-oriented, rule-abiding characteristics and overcontrol of anger, with a more suspicious, judgmental orientation reflecting a projection of intense feelings to resentment on to others, who are in turn viewed as potentially harmful or dangerous. Individuals with this variant of compulsive personality are likely to be fearful that any negative thoughts or feelings deviant from prevailing social conventions may be publicly exposed unless they remain vigilant against any internal leakage. This adaptation may be seen in individuals who are highly puritanical, hyperreligious, and zealous about monitoring others and enforcing rules and regulations. Anger, sexual desires, self-aggrandizement, and longing for materialistic comforts are potential threats to one's virtue and a basis for finding shortcomings in others, about whom individuals with compulsive personality with paranoid features would feel righteously indignant. These individuals may seem bigoted and dogmatic yet are also privately or unconsciously terrified that their own moral weaknesses will result in their being shamed. Their anger over these conflicts between conformity and self-gratification is channeled into a harsh, punitive orientation to others.

Another common variant of the compulsive personality are those individuals with narcissistic features. These individuals identify strongly with authority, rules and regulations, and find comfort and self-importance in conforming to them, using sanctioned power and influence. Association with an organization endowing authority to act (e.g., a governmental agency, the military, the judicial system) provides a structure by which to harness and contain poorly recognized aggressive impulses stemming from unconscious oppositional feelings. Certainty conferred by highly prescribed routines and procedures is valued and depended on. The "system" and its perpetuation is more important than fundamental fairness and a regard and sympathy for those who might be treated unfairly by it. The narcissistic features of individuals with this compulsive personality variant leave them characterologically prone to devalue the opinions and feelings of those they cannot identify. A hard, stern orientation to administration and disciple predominates these individuals' adjustment.

Because their self-esteem seems dependent on a rigid and officious adherence to their authority role, they are vulnerable to becoming unsettled whenever situations confront them that exceed their inflexible mode of functioning. Threats and challenges of this kind can create emotional crises, because the basis to their sense of well-being is undermined. Not surprisingly, these threats can elicit a sense of outrage and anger frightening to their surface, overcontrolled adaptation, producing anxiety-related and psychophysiological responses. The fear of being shamed and publicly repudiated by the organizational structure their esteem relies on can create inflexibility in adhering to procedures and requirements and paralysis when there is not a formula on which to rely. Failing to act appropriately and judiciously on these occasions can be emotionally devastating and depleting to their sense of self, because their self-regard is dependent on efficient administering of rules and appropriate execution of authority. In these instances, the compulsive–narcissistic individual has both failed to upkeep the system by inaction and the system has failed him or her by not providing a ready prescription as to the appropriate courses of action.

A different adaptation can be seen with the individual with compulsive personality with schizoid traits, whose adjustment is characterized by an apparent paucity of pleasure or intensity of experience and instead a preoccupation with protection against loss through self-isolation to a restricted, barren, predictable existence, insulated and distanced from the demands and involvement of others. These individuals also share a common fear of public exposure of underlying conflictual oppositional impulses and the shame that accompanies such a discovery. In the clinical context, these individuals require a formality and impersonal, reserved interactive style from the provider to feel comfortable; efforts to gain rapport from intimacy will likely be anxiety-producing for them, experienced as intrusions into their personal lives that threaten to reveal inadequacies. Motivational communications that are most effective or impactful will emphasize maintaining their status quo and capacity to function on a level comfortable to their premorbid state.

A final variant of this personality pattern is the compulsive–negativistic personality. These individuals more intensely experience the core conflict between conformity–accommodation and approval-seeking from others and oppositional striving for "selfish" needs and impulses. The negativistic features of their adjustment will create a state of inner confusion and ambivalence between individualistic and conforming tendencies, resulting in a chronic tension and self-torment, which may manifest in periodic obsessions and compulsions that attempt to bind this unstable confluence of competing impulses.

PERPETUATING FEATURES

For the individual with compulsive personality, change threatens pain and discomfort, avoidance of which is the primary purpose of the compulsive adaptation. Fear of mistakes and risks and a pervasive rigidity is central to the compulsive personality's strategy of functioning. They seek a comfort zone of predictability, conventionality, and certainty in action and result. Even when faced with a seemingly obvious requirement for change, sheer force of habit may perpetuate routines and rituals that no longer apply. The obvious cost is stagnation, loss of imagination and emotional richness that comes with spontaneity. In addition, even in the nonemotional, instrumental aspects of life, they risk being passed by when new trends and social paradigm shifts occur. Over time the lack of creative outlets block potential discharges of natural tensions. Their inflexible manner will also fail to protect against the unexpected, generating mistakes and failures that may leave the individual with compulsive personality feeling shattered and pervasively anxious following this ruinous loss of control. The old adage, "he (she) who would save his (her) life must lose it," applies all too well to the dysfunctional extremes of this adaptation.

The virtue that generates self- and other-admiration so important to the compulsive individual also exacts a price in the form of a rigid, demanding, and punitive superego that gives him or her no respite from responsibility and expectations of self and others. Companion to this structural personality feature is the propensity of individuals with compulsive personalities to create requirements and rules for themselves. This helps them deal with unacceptable impulses striving for expression and provide safe formulas for action that generate predictable consequences of approval from authority. However, these tendencies generate ever bigger lists of prohibitions that begin to suffocate and constrict these individuals, preventing any legitimate expression and gratification of personal needs.

Patients with compulsive personalities commonly seek medical care for physical symptom complaints generated by their psychophysiological manifestations of conflicts, anxieties, and emotional tensions. Immobilizing anxiety or fatigue, sexual impotence, and gastrointestinal distress are common complaints. Like histrionic patients who have repressed the emotional source of their physical symptoms, compulsive individuals are unaware of their ambivalences and unrecognized resentments and hostilities that are likely to be activated by situational stressors and demands of daily living.

Their unconscious fears that to have unacceptable impulses is to act on them and thereby engender punishment is a major impediment to addressing the emotional underpinnings of their symptom complaints.

Given that the self–other polarity imbalance conflict is central to the compulsive personality, emphasizing the importance of personal needs over those internalized expectations stemming from authority figures or external rules and regulations is critical in treatment. Identifying all the rules and requirements impinging on them will make it easy to infer how "normal" personal needs are cramped, likely in ways unrecognized by the compulsive individual. Although such exploration may be initially baffling or anxiety-provoking to the compulsive patient, this strategy can create a climate where identification of unacceptable feelings (especially anger or resentment) may become easier. Gradually, the focus may shift to personal needs and their fulfillment and perhaps how others' expectations and responsibilities are overexaggerated, as are the assumed negative consequences for being selfish.

The practitioner can model a more flexible mode of functioning that can help reduce the need for rigid formulas that the compulsive individual will attempt to devise during this time. Encouragement to express ideas and feelings spontaneously and elicit similar reactions from others can be presented and modeled as the most effective and efficient way for individuals to regulate interaction, because it requires no forethought or anticipation, simply a comfort with the feeling states communicated and confidence that anger (when properly expressed), will not automatically generate punishment.

Cognitive–behavioral techniques can directly address the constricted modes of thought characteristic of the compulsive individual by identifying important schema and implicit assumptions, operating in a more cerebral domain initially, which will be more comfortable for individuals with this personality type. Changes in expectations that ensue can reduce perfection-istic needs and behavior patterns. A more flexible outlook can also facili-tate a lightening up of the compulsive personality's often driven, somber orientation.

INTERPERSONAL ASPECTS OF COMPULSIVE PATIENTS IN THE MEDICAL CARE SETTING

The compulsive patient, because of his or her poorly recognized inner tensions between repressed–suppressed hostilities and fears of punishment, may be frequently subject to a variety of somatic complaints such as tension headache, gastrointestinal distress, diarrhea, and experience of fatigue. They will typically present as earnest, somber, deferential, and proper in their interpersonal manner. They may generally make a good impression with their polite demeanor and careful responsiveness to the health care team. Their exacting nature, however, may make them at times irritating in their repetitive questions and their efforts to seek absolute clarity concerning what they are told, in hopes of obtaining total certainty about their condition or diagnosis and what they should do. As is usually the case, where genuine ambiguity may exist in the medical diagnosis, they may become anxious or agitated, if there are no clear answers. When such answers are not available, this may make the provider uncomfortable to disappoint such a conscientious patient, a good person, or alternatively frustrated if these patients are anxious and still relentlessly pestering in their seeking of assurance.

In pursuing treatment, compulsive individuals will seek to reduce their anxiety about ill-health and the loss of control it may portend by quickly seeking formulas for success. Treatment regimens may be rigidly and over-anxiously adhered to, resulting in anxious, annoying behavior vexing to the primary care provider and his or her staff. Unexpected adverse events in the medical course of such individuals' illnesses may lead to guilty self-recrimination or disillusionment in the health care team. The desire to be perceived as a model patient may create fears, which will in turn generate underreporting of illness symptoms important to regulating treatment (e.g., side effects of medicines or discomforts signaling early or subtle change in the disease state that need to be addressed).

In their relationship with the health care team, compulsive patients will exert every effort to be the good patient, especially compliant with all treatment recommendations. The greater the authority figure, the more the deference and obedience. In their rigidity, compulsive patients may become overly anxious when unclear about their role in treatment. Their tendency to be uncertain in such matters may reflect a lack of confidence that to outsiders seems remarkable for such seemingly orderly, exacting individuals. But it may reflect their basic dynamic of competing longing to be in a dependent, cared for role and to enjoy autonomy unfettered by external authority and control.

Their need to be viewed as good patients will differ from that of a dependent patient, whose chief concern is approval as a signal of personal liking and regard. In the avoidant patient, approval signifies that he or she is safe interpersonally from criticism, repudiation, or humiliation. But for compulsive patients, what is important is being correct in their actions, being right, doing the right thing. Approval from others is secondary to the fear of punishment, sanctions against the self in the form of censure that signifies worse to come. In their efforts to avoid this, they will seek out and internalize, often concretely and rigidly, whatever rules they can divine that will ensure their interpersonal and medical safety and comfort.

Unfortunately, with disease there are instances where even if everything is done right, there can still be an adverse outcome. It would seem a basic assumption of individuals with this personality type, learned very early in dealing with the world, that good behavior will ensure fair treatment, the obsessional contract discussed by Freedman (1997). This is considered to be a contract negotiated unilaterally, wherein the assumption is that if the individual with compulsive personality follows all the rules, there will be guaranteed fairness and safety from mishap. When fate, individuals, or circumstances produce unfairness, such as illness, there may be a sense of confusion, even vague guilt over presumably having done something wrong to deserve the particular event. Even self-recrimination may occur, wasting valuable time and energy needed for more positive coping with the disease.

In their compensated state, individuals with compulsive personalities will evidence a strong need for mastery, control, and predictability. Where they cannot function because of illness and are left confused and uncertain about the future, depression will set in. More significant for their functioning, there is a hopelessness and regression into a state of helpless dependency associated with this depression. When confronted with serious illness, such patients may present as being more incapacitated than their condition warrants, a distinction that may be difficult to make. The longer they remain in this state, the more they will be refractory to rehabilitation, and a state of psychological incapacitation will persist.

Compulsive personalities' pain-avoidant, precautionary, preservation-oriented adaptive style would make it likely that they would strive to have decent health care insurance and material resources to protect them against unexpected perils. Concerning interpersonal supports, this would be less certain. Although compulsive individuals have inner longings to be dependent and cared for, their compensated adaptation is to be autonomous and self-sufficient, typically in a caretaker role. In the relationships they establish, this may tend to bring them into contact with others who are in search of caretakers. Because these individuals are not particularly disposed to reverse roles and care for others, there may be disappointments in store for compulsive individuals when they find themselves in a needy, dependent role. Even when offered help, this may make them feel uncomfortable and indebted, especially if the help comes from others who are freely giving, not reciprocating from some previous obligation. These may be emotionally difficult issues for these patients to deal with in negotiating support issues when they are confronted with serious illness.

MEDICAL MANAGEMENT ISSUES

Individuals with compulsive personalities have a strong need to be in control and low tolerance for ambiguity. They will find it difficult to be in a dependent helpless stance defined by the patient role. When faced with threat, they also will harbor many recurring doubts requiring repetitive clarification and reassurance. Understanding their apprehensions and providing compulsive patients with some sense of predictability about their care and information may serve to restore a sense of control and reduce anxieties that may otherwise escalate.

Preventive Interventions, Lifestyle Choices

Compulsive individuals are particularly suited characterologically to receive communications regarding risk factors and unhealthy habits and to then feel compelled to act on the advice given. Their concern is security and safety, minimizing risk and maximizing certainty. Threats of any kind receive prompt attention and action, because their propensity to anxiety and alarm will affix to communications about health risks. The problem is that when there is addiction, such as nicotine or alcohol, then there are powerful physiological and psychological influences competing with these tendencies. Indeed, they may come to serve important regulatory functions for the individual's anxiety management. In addition to reaction formation, compulsive individuals can engage in rationalization, as do most smokers, overeaters, and alcoholics, to justify this persisting behavior. When confronted with a medical recommendation to diet or stop smoking or drinking, compulsive patients may seem to embrace such recommendations and commit to them, without actually implementing the action component treatment recommendations. In effect they will identify with the importance of the changes to take place, but then procrastinate in altering their behavior. This will be done while maintaining a posture of virtuous intent, but with much excuse and explanation for the delay. Over time if there is no change, then genuine distress may occur over failure to curb impulses and appetitive urges. However, this may take the form of unproductive self-recrimination and self-flagellation that is depressogenic, diverting the patient to potentially paralyzing self-image and emotional issues, straying from the task at hand.

Stages of Change

In the compulsive patient, the notion of change is likely to be threatening because it portends an attempt to undo a fragile balance between contrary impulses and a need for conformity, safety, and acceptance. It may be necessary to spend considerable time characterizing and operationalizing change proposals in nonthreatening ways that the compulsive patient can see will be beneficial and not unsettling of delicate balances. Emphasis on small, comfortable steps in a process such individuals can feel is under their control may be necessary to gain continued commitment to a difficult process. For these individuals, risk-taking is what therapy or treatment constitutes; they must be able to see and anticipate the benefit to productively participate in the process—and in so doing, adjust to the challenges they face in addressing their illnesses.

These considerations aside, individuals with compulsive personalities are among the most likely of the personality types to be engaged in general precontemplation concerning their health and perceived need for change. Like other individuals of all personality types, there are compulsive patients who overeat, smoke, and drink too much, knowing they are doing something unhealthy. Their awareness of a need to correct this, however, takes the form of vacillation and anxiety-ridden rumination, guilt over not controlling impulses, and procrastination in a recurring cycle. Their capacity for contemplation without action is remarkable, and they are expert at drawing out their personal deliberations with endless speculation and planning, without taking any actual steps forward toward real progress.

With this personality type contemplative activity will have to be guided or directed. Minimal time and focus should be spent discussing the decision to commit to change, because doing the right thing is an implicit value for these individuals. Rather, addressing the unspoken oppositional aspects of their personality and resistances that block them from taking constructive action should receive the greatest attention. These are likely subconscious resentments that represent their hidden desire to rebel against their conformity tendencies, which are driven by fear of punishment. Given that they are by nature anxious and guilt-prone, compulsive personalities have developed considerable tolerance for mental tension and anguished recrimination, unpleasant feeling states that might motivate other personality types to action.

Addressing hidden motivational and attitudinal barriers to behavior change initially may involve no more than introducing the idea that there are such things as oppositional tendencies, resistances, and subconscious resentments that influence action or inaction. This notion will be incompatible with compulsive patients' sense of virtue and threatening to them, in that such feelings and impulses are perceived as bad. It would be unrealistic to assume that all the resistances could be identified and worked through, to prepare the compulsive patient for smooth passage thereafter. Rather, the contemplative stage represents the first opportunity to introduce a systematic, more constructive self-critical appraisal process that will occur continuously throughout the later stages where change takes place and new healthier habits perpetuated.

The preparation stage can take into account those identified intra-individual (attitudinal, motivational) or interindividual, situational–psychosocial barriers to change (e.g., a spouse or friends that still drink and smoke), followed by planning how to address them. For example, an alcoholic will need to plan social contacts and activities away from bars and alcohol-serving establishments. The obese patient will need to make arrangements to remove tempting foods from easy access while not depriving other family members from desired foods. It will be important to discuss the procedure to be followed when treatment objectives are not met. This should involve identifying constructive, problem-solving-oriented responses to replace ruminative, counterproductive activity that would impede change.

By the time the patient is ready for the action stage, there should thus be some problem-solving mechanisms in place to constructively deal with difficulties in carrying out the change plan. The focus will be on developing new, healthy, and flexible behavior patterns to substitute for old health-risk activities, integrating them into established habit patterns, and modifying problematic barriers. As change takes place, the ambivalence of the compulsive patient will periodically resurface and a motivational battle will be taking place to curb poorly recognized rebellious impulses in favor of conformity to authoritative medical recommendations. These recurrences should be acknowledged as a predictable part of a natural struggle that even virtuous individuals cannot escape. This can provide an opportunity to set into place a more analytical and anxiety-minimizing approach for identifying threats to behavior change, where positive recognition and respect are gained from the sense of honest introspection involved in this process.

As change takes place, maintenance stage issues will emerge, where substitute gratifications to curb appetitive behavior patterns will need to be identified and put in place. Internalization of these changes should be facilitated in a more conscious, flexible manner to avoid rigidities that would court destructive, underlying feelings of rebellion that might erode consolidation and perpetuation of these changes. Planning for instances of relapse is critical. For individuals with this personality type, it will be important that the change process does not represent another form of self-denial and reflexive capitulation to external authority. That is the tyrannizing feature of the compulsive personality. Rather, the intervention should be presented and managed in a fashion that promotes increased personal flexibility, an opportunity to feel genuinely benefited from change rather than merely relieved to be spared some future punishment for the sacrifices made.

Utility, Cost–Benefit Considerations of Preventive Interventions

Compulsive individuals are inherently motivated to reduce risk given their strong loading on the preservation polarity, and threats to their health signify potential loss of control. Where adoption of healthy behaviors do not impinge on previously well-established appetitive urges (food, alcohol, tobacco), they should be readily adopted (e.g., use of condoms) by individuals oriented to prudence and safety. Many such individuals likely practice such precautionary behaviors. Those not addicted to tobacco or certain potential food types will be dispositionally sensitized to attend to and heed such health warnings.

The compulsive patient's propensity to readily incorporate and internalize directives from authority figures also will make medical recommendations likely to be well received with this population. As conformists, group intervention experiences involving monitoring and specific goal setting and attainment exploit the dominant tendencies of these individuals. The risk of punishment through public exposure to wrongdoing (e.g., overeating, relapsing in a smoking-cessation program) should provide strong incentive to motivate and maintain change. Support from other group members for their virtuous efforts also will play to their need to maintain a conscientious self-image.

Preventive measures may prove characterologically difficult for this personality type when willful, volitional actions may not be helpful. Doing volitional, effortful activity such as exercise or restraining impulses involve strengths of compulsive patients. Risk reduction in certain diseases, such as cardiovascular conditions, for which meditative modes of functioning are most beneficial, will run counter to the individual with compulsive personality's rigid, rule-bound, control-oriented mode of functioning, which is antithetical to the "letting go" of self-relaxation approaches. The compulsive personality is a self-vigilant individual, quick to suppress natural impulses and control feelings that will build up somatic tensions, which will be channeled into vulnerable organs of those constitutionally disposed to psychosomatic conditions. The desire to get it right will generate performance anxiety that will interfere with self-relaxation. Fortunately, the compulsive patient will generally remain motivated to overcome these tendencies, so that with individual treatment, mastery of these risk-reduction techniques should be possible.

Secondary and Tertiary Care of Acute and Chronic Illness

The compulsive individual by nature is vigilant and concerned about threats to his or her well-being and motivated to do what is possible to prevent them. Although this orientation should in theory keep these individuals alert to early manifestations of disease and prompt to respond to danger signals, compulsive patients are also notorious for being preoccupied with a variety of concerns, so that they often miss the forest for the trees. Their interest in maintaining their health by early identification of diseases will have to be focused and guided by their care providers, otherwise it may be misdirected. Compulsive individuals' anxiety-proneness and tendency to develop somatic complaints may create a myriad of symptoms that could falsely mimic the prodrome of many conditions. If they are under stress and feeling vulnerable, they could become hypochondriacal and overwhelm themselves and their health care advisors with their concerns.

In promoting development of accurate illness representations, practitioners will need to address these patients' rigidity, their tendency to concretely interpret information in a way that robs them of flexibly relating to changing circumstances. Compulsive personalities by nature tend to be sensitizers rather than repressors. They will benefit from information that provides them with predictability. However, where illness courses do not follow predicted scripts or where there are unexpected adverse events, this would involve a loss of control that could be overwhelming for these patients. Monitoring their anxiety level when distressing information is imparted concerning the probable course of the illness and its treatment (e.g., disfigurement) will be important to ensure that such patients do not overwhelm themselves with responses to their questions, having generated more information than they can handle.

Compulsive individuals' need for control can make them interpersonally trying to caretakers, because they may become overinvolved with their care, monitoring everyone's activities, asking repetitive and endless questions, and sometimes seeking to take over their care by anticipating treatment activity and attempting to do some of it themselves, to the consternation of those responsible for their treatment. In some instances, they may make adjustments to their medicines based on their rudimentary understanding because of unpleasant side effects or certain effects they wish to obtain. If they are caught engaging in such behavior, they may be predictably mortified but also may stay anxious if they are not also reassured everything is being done to help them. They may also experience unrecognized feelings of resentment when their efforts at autonomy, however unwise, are thwarted. Although their presentation will be that of a conscientious, obedient patient, when the treatment course or drug effects take an unusual turn, the possibility of such patients meddling with their treatment may be a consideration. Accusing patients who view themselves as being virtuous and conscientious may create an interpersonal crisis. If mistaken, the caretaker has wrongfully conveyed a lack of confidence in the patient, undermining his or her sense of being part of a team.

Even if such accusations are correct, this may leave the patient contrite or guilt-ridden and anticipating punishment in the form of adverse events in the illness course, rather than focused on actions that promote healing and recovery. Thus, where overzealous participation in treatment is suspected, the best strategy may be initially to share information with the patient in a factual, nonaccusatory fashion about how the effect (the patient is suspected of causing) can occur—for example, certain drug interactions if the dose level is modified. Monitoring the patient's condition more closely and administering drugs under supervision of clinic visits may also be strategies to make the point without relationship-damaging confrontation. In this way, the incentives for the patient to retain a virtuous image is kept intact. Obviously, the practitioner will need to exercise all necessary precaution to prevent such patients from harming themselves, and if other behavior persists where these patients are exceeding their role, then confrontation at that time can take place.

Coping With Illness

When dealing with threats to their health, problem-focused coping is likely more comfortable to individuals with compulsive personalities than the emotional issues associated with a disease process. By nature constricted in the kind and range of affects they can comfortably experience, compulsive individuals would have difficulty dealing with the emotional states involved with loss and grief (over disfigurement, loss of function), especially those that involve anger. Nonetheless, their passive rather than active stance on the accommodation polarity may make it difficult to engage in more proactive, innovative problem solving rather than using overlearned habitual routines approved of by authorities. Because such individuals are other-oriented, their functioning during times of illness will be to look to authority outside themselves for the ways to respond, rather than focus on inner work having to do with poorly recognized conflicts and feelings stemming from the stress of being removed by illness from their constricted comfort zones.

Initially in the course of a serious illness, they may feel overwhelmed by the pain or discomfort of the illness itself. At the same time, they may also feel anxious about any ambiguities and in need of clarification that may not be available (concerning their exact diagnosis, prognosis, and illness course, which may require further diagnostic tests). As a result, they may end up overwhelming themselves with information, adding confusion to uncertainty, and increasing their own sense of diminished control and predictability caused by their illness.

Being in a patient role where the normative expectations are that they will be cared for, rather than doing the caring, may be a challenge for compulsive individuals, given their discomfort with taking from others. Busy nurses and hospital aides may find these patients' efforts to do for themselves annoying if they involve delays in efficient administration of care to individuals with many needs to look after. This may in turn cause the compulsive patient to become upset or confused when he or she is rebuffed for efforts to be a cooperative, good patient—when he or she is, in effect, getting in the way of routine caretaking by health care staff. To the extent that this causes visible consternation on the part of staff, this will be an additional stressor for the patient who is sensitive to disapproval for doing something wrong.

What these individuals may most need in times of acute illness phases is an advocate or guide to their illness, to provide appropriate information, reduce uncertainty, and help them maintain a sense of control. From the patient's standpoint, the best person in this role would be the ultimate authority, the physician in charge of his or her care. However, given the probable limited availability of the physician, an articulate nurse or other assistant should suffice, provided such individuals are seen as the appropriate link in the chain of command and can communicate sufficient information to the patient. Thus, a combination of a big-picture daily report by a confident, well-informed physician and periodic interim communications by support staff should minimize patient anxiety and provide a sense of predictability. This ensures that there is not a vacuum of empty time to incubate fears and unnecessary worry. If compulsive patients are to cope effectively, they need to know what they are facing as early as possible. Even where uncertainties are unavoidable, information about what is planned, how the procedures will work, and the time frame involving uncertainty (about a test result) can provide some sense of control. This context also is consistent with the compulsive patient's basic passive–accommodation mode, where he or she knows what is happening and what to do. Even when the only instruction is to patiently wait, this can be nonetheless construed as doing something.

Once an illness course becomes apparent, individuals with compulsive personalities may respond well to a script concerning their role, based on the treatment plan and expected course of the illness. If they are clear on what they can appropriately do, how they interact with the medical authority, and the technical and medical details necessary to have a sense of predictability, they can fortify themselves with this information while facing potential pain and suffering.

Where an unfavorable course is anticipated or emerges from the disease process, these patients may need assistance in processing the implications of such changes to their illness representations. This should be done in a judicious fashion, because preserving the compulsive defenses of such individuals will be an important goal, so long as there is not overreliance on avoidance coping modes that impedes necessary emotional work from eventually taking place. The care provider must be sensitive to where the patient is emotionally and offer counseling or pharmacological aid for depression or anxiety as it develops. Premature introduction of psychological treatment may preempt these patients' efforts to cope on their own and cast them in a dependent role that could foster regression into a helpless dependency rather than stabilize them emotionally.

Medical Compliance

Because compliance with authority is what ensures safety and freedom from punishment in the minds of individuals with compulsive personalities, it should follow that they would be highly motivated to adhere to their treatment regimens. As is well known, however, motivation and intent increase the likelihood of successful goal attainment but does not guarantee it. For example, if compulsive patients are struggling with well-established habit patterns based on strong appetitive–addictive urges, they will experience anxiety and guilt when they transgress. In addition, in their exactness and in their eagerness to comply and be seen as responsive, compulsive patients may not seek clarification of complicated regimen instructions, out of fear of being perceived as uncooperative. They may thus get the instructions wrong, especially if dealing with busy, impatient providers. Conversely, they may deviate to the other extreme by attempting in a piecemeal fashion to seek clarification and concretization of every little detail, which they may then assemble in an incorrect, confused fashion. Although desirable with any patient, unambiguous, carefully written out instructions with concrete, full-proof examples will work best for this population. The anxiety to get it right may otherwise disrupt the communication process, which is often abrupt and incomplete.

Beneath this conscious veneer of fanatical adherence to conformity, compulsive patients also will harbor longings for defiance, not to indulge or pursue immediate gratifications but to establish their own sense of autonomy. This underlying ambivalence toward authority represents compulsive patients' own rigid introjections of earlier experiences of punishment for deviations from parental expectations. An overly stern presentation of compliance requirements can activate many earlier conflicts or old schemas, which can then distort or intrude on new learning and more flexible, creative courses of action to adhere to treatment regimens. For this reason, with compulsive patients, a discriminating orientation to the treatment regimen requirements may be helpful. This may involve a more casual presentation of the ordinary self-care routines, alternating with carefully reasoned discussions of the more critical aspects of their compliance requirements. Such an approach can engender a less rigid approach to their self-management, which helps counter the more dysfunctional perpetuating features of their adjustment. Above all, an approving attitude from the treatment authority conveying recognition that the patient wants to comply and be a good patient is necessary, even if barriers and difficulties interfere with perfect performance. When deviations from perfect treatment adherence do inevitably occur, emphasis on a problem-solving approach to any difficulties is needed, not a condemning response that will only paralyze the compulsive patient with guilt or anticipatory performance anxiety.

IMPACT OF DISEASE STATES ON THE PATIENT

Compulsive patients will be most sensitive to any condition that reduces their ability to be of value or makes them beholden to others. Treatment planning for these individuals should where possible involve their participation and opportunities to demonstrate their mastery and contribute to their care and restoration of functioning.

Somatoform, Stress-Related Conditions: Headache, Diseases of the Digestive System

These are relatively common conditions among compulsive personalities given their rigid adaptive style, self-generated pressures to conform, and inner tensions generated by their poorly recognized oppositional impulses. Techniques focused on self-control will have appeal but may be difficult for these individuals, who have little concept of letting go. Their response to listening to relaxation tapes may be, as with other tasks, to order themselves to relax, exactly the opposite maneuver needed for tension reduction. If needed, biofeedback may serve as a guide for conditions such as tension headache. Muscle relaxants should be a last resort, because this would rob these patients from the benefit of experiencing success that they can master their nervous systems responses to external stresses. Assertive training may prove beneficial for those individuals with compulsive personality variants who have difficulty saying no and who find themselves overcommitted and overwhelmed, struggling to maintain their conscientious self-image at all costs. A cognitive–behavioral focus can help them to examine their self-perpetuating tendencies to create tensions in themselves by internalizing other's expectations as requirements for themselves, fulfillment of which is necessary to maintain their self-esteem.

Pain Management

Acute pain, provided it is accompanied by predictions of relief and recovery of functioning, should be a reasonably manageable proposition for individuals with this personality type. Forecasting recovery should be conservative rather than optimistic, however, because compulsive personalities will be sensitive to the unexpected—for example, delays in the healing process, more pain and less function than anticipated. These medical setbacks risk internalization by compulsive patients, who may remain polite and accommodating to their physicians, all the while hiding their sense of betrayal–loss of confidence that the authority has failed to reward their obedience and sacrifices. To the extent that trust in the physician and positive expectations also promote healing and recovery, then these elements may be lost and not readily recovered.

If the illness course is a brief one, then not much may be at stake. However, if recovery becomes more problematic, or as is often the case with back injury, the intervention fails to provide enduring relief and the picture shifts to chronic pain, then disillusionment may set in. Loss of function and control, combined with episodes of debilitating pain, is a formula for regression into an abhorred, helpless dependency that promotes additional despair, which can even lead to suicide. If there is a risk of some continuing pain without full recovery of functioning, better the compulsive patient know early on rather than develop false hopes and then a sense of betrayal. A thorough explanation of not only the immediate treatment *and* the possible outcomes accompanied by a discussion of additional measures that can address any unplanned eventualities can be reassuring. Compulsive patients can then be psychologically preparing themselves to a range of outcomes with confidence that their physicians have at hand different strategies for whatever does occur.

As soon as possible after the surgical or other medical intervention, rehabilitation involving routines and structure will provide the basis of the compulsive patient's recovery. These should be designed for easy integration into work or at-home activity patterns. Resumption of even a few minor old routines may help maintain morale, as well as praise for the sacrifice and suffering involved in efforts to get better. Rapid restoration of a sense of control and reestablished mastery and a virtuous conscientious self-image for dutiful recovery efforts will play to the strengths rather than weaknesses of this patient's character structure. As needed, use of antidepressants, anxiolytics, and analgesics for pain control can support these efforts.

Diabetes

Among the personality types considered, the compulsive patient is perhaps constitutionally best suited to deal with a chronic illness such as diabetes, which requires lifelong self-monitoring, discipline, self-denial, and self-regulation. Provided that diabetic self-care measures are well-integrated into daily routines and habit patterns, they will become part of the patient's rigid mode of functioning. Where difficulties may emerge is initially establishing these changes if the diabetic condition first develops in an older individual whose routines are deeply ingrained and who may have strong appetites that must be curbed, such as for sweets, alcohol, and tobacco. Such requirements will place in conflict unhealthy but automatic overlearned routines that will be at odds with the compulsive individual's good intentions to preserve their health and conform to medical recommendations.

Because diabetes is a lifelong condition with serious consequences for noncompliance, there are ample incentives for these harm-avoidant individuals to reduce their risk behaviors. Adopting too harsh a response to early deviations from the treatment regimen as these patients are struggling to conform may be counterproductive from the standpoint of intensifying preoccupation with punishment, leading to greater rigidity inherent in their constricted modes of coping. If their experience of shame is too intense, then their earnest efforts to change may be replaced with fear-avoiding behaviors designed to elude detection of noncompliance. This will be accompanied by nonproductive guilty self-recrimination and distancing from their health care providers or defensive encapsulation of their transgressions, where those behaviors are excluded from normal self-image considerations of being conscientious and "law-abiding." For this reason, it will be important to convey an accepting, supportive orientation toward these patients, recognizing their struggles and poorly recognized conflicts, while conveying a sense of confidence that they will do enough to manage their illness, even with occasional compliance mishaps.

Neurological Diseases: Epilepsy, Multiple Schlerosis, Parkinson's Disease

Epilepsy will represent for the individual with compulsive personality a disruptive influence that threatens his or her sense of control because of the potential of loss of consciousness and regular bodily function and prospect of cognitive alteration and decline, if the symptoms are poorly controlled. Such individuals' capacity to engage in self-regulation and self-monitoring should be beneficial in promoting good medication compliance and exercise of precaution. However, their need for control, order, and anxiety proneness will leave them more vulnerable to stress, which could potentially affect and lower their seizure threshold. To the extent that this neurological condition could place restrictions on their range of functioning and opportunities for expression of self-mastery and worth to others, it could have a differentially negative impact on the self-image of individuals with this personality type.

Multiple sclerosis, depending on the physical systems and the disease's progressive nature, can take a particular emotional toll on the compulsive patient, given the disease's common off-again and on-again course, which can force the patient to seek assistance from others during periods of exacerbation. Given that such individuals are ordinarily most comfortable functioning as caretakers, such role reversals will challenge their rigid adaptive style. Unless or until this disease affects cognitive functioning, its more typical impact on motor systems may leave these individuals still able to function vocationally if they are white-collar workers. However, they will find themselves publicly diminished in the eyes of others by their weakness or the requirement for canes and physical assistance. Unlike other personalities such as the dependent or histrionic personalities, this attention-generating spectacle will be a realization of compulsive patients' worst nightmares—such an individual prided on self-reliance, trapped in a betraying body that forces him or her to be increasingly reliant on help. Depression and anxiety conditions are not uncommon responses to this condition, which may also bring shame and embarrassment to these control-oriented individuals. Preemptive counseling, even if dismissed initially, may create a context for later grieving, some loss of emotional control, and opportunities for resolution.

A similar scenario also applies to Parkinson's disease, except that the patient generally is much older and some degree of diminished functioning is expected with aging. Advanced years also confers some respectability to slower movement, and there is less of a dramatic contrast between these patients and others of similar age, unless the movement disorder is severe. However, there are also the influences of subcortical changes affecting the affective state of the patient, producing depressive affect, reduced executive cognitive competence, and the impact of anti-Parkinsonian medications on mental and emotional stability. There may even come a time when treatment of the movement disorder induces disruptive psychotic conditions, such as hallucinations. Careful neuropsychiatric monitoring and skilled titration of dopaminergic and antipsychotic medications can, however, permit use of these medications with reduced psychiatric side effects (Chacko et al., 1995).

Cardiac Disease

For those compulsive patients with a strong heredity and history of coronary artery disease, the hope is that virtuous adherence to these precautionary measures will prevent those dreaded events that have afflicted other family members who have experienced heart attack, stroke, or painful operative procedures for occlusive artery disease. When these measures are not successful, there will be an understandable demoralization for any individual. For compulsive patients, this may represent a violation of their obsessional contract, a betrayal that brings into question their rigid adherence to authority and, indeed, the credibility of authority itself. Accompanying this will be a sense of vulnerability and apprehensiveness that may permeate their daily routines. When a heart attack strikes or there is a requirement for bypass surgery, the loss of control imposed by those circumstances will make these patients particularly vulnerable to depression and paralyzing anxiety that is conducive to a regression into a state of helpless dependency. This will be especially true if their recovery is complicated, placing them in a patient role for a prolonged period of time.

The rigid nature of individuals with compulsive personalities will make it difficult for them to accept their hereditary vulnerabilities and the uncertainties associated with them. Their temptation will be to reassure themselves that prudent action on their part will be protective, not just merely risk-reducing. When disappointed or disillusioned, their poorly recognized contrary, defiant tendencies may be intensified, contributing to a rejection of the wisdom of the authorities and intense conflict or apprehension when momentary rebellious impulses surface, activating their predictable fear of punishment at a time when they are feeling vulnerable from the condition that has violated their preventive efforts.

Especially when heart attack occurs or bypass surgery is required, it will be important to aggressively promote restitution of a sense of control to the compulsive patient. A component to this may include pharmacotherapy for depression and anxiety conditions. These may not be readily apparent, because compulsive patients are emotionally constricted and poor at recognizing their own feeling states. Having failed to prevent expression of their risk factor, these patients may be fearful of exercise and activity lest this stress their cardiovascular system further and court even more serious health consequences. Rehabilitation efforts with monitoring in a medical setting where help is immediately nearby may provide needed reassurance. Information concerning their condition may also prove fortifying against lingering apprehensions. Ultimately, the passage of time, whereby resumption of normal functioning, particularly sexual arousal and activity and previously enjoyed strenuous pursuits is tolerated without incident, will help promote a sense of recovery. However, because a heart attack or bypass surgery patient is forever changed by his or her experience, frequent reassurance that there is a carefully laid out plan for any future mishaps may be required to reduce this patient's sense of chronic vulnerability.

Cancer

Cancer for the individual with compulsive personality represents a cruel punishment for efforts to conduct a life of virtue and conformity, involving delay of gratification and a self-denying, saving for the future approach to life. With a single diagnosis all that effort and concern is potentially negated, brought to an end with a prospect of pain, suffering, and premature death. Properly informed, compulsive personalities ordinarily will be conscientious in performing early detection routines, but only provided these are integrated into their lifestyle patterns. Some, for example, may be such workaholics that regular medical appointments are ignored and their health is assumed, ignored in favor of their immediate concerns over productivity and maintaining a can-do image in the eyes of their superiors at work. With these individuals, even once a problem is identified, as long as they feel reasonably well, they may remain consumed with their sensed obligations, partially because they may be stuck in their routines, but also because they are not equipped to deal with the feelings of helplessness inherent in the prospect of being cancer patients fighting for their lives.

For the most part, these individuals should be responsive and attentive to their physicians and their recommendations. Their nature will lead them to cooperate under the assumption that this will bring the best possible result. Although this will be true, the uncertainty and lack of predictability that comes with the disease, and the suffering associated with treatments (chemotherapy, radiation), ensures a succession of demoralizing events before any favorable news. At the least, careful preparation concerning treatments planned, the risk or likelihood of mutilation, and the side effects of chemically based treatments will provide information that can help reduce anticipatory anxiety and uncertainty about the illness course. Support groups may be important to provide reassurance that they are being correct, virtuous, and courageous (if not for themselves, for their loved ones) in their choice to fight the disease, even if their actions are essentially based on faith (i.e., that the interventions, however horrific, will work).

This conviction will be tested by the vagaries of a disease like cancer. The individual with compulsive personality has cast his or her lot with conformity to authority as a means of providing security, predictability, success, and freedom from punishment or adversity. Affliction with a potentially fatal illness violates these precepts and may create a crisis of understanding more difficult to reconcile for individuals with this type of personality than many others whose personal meaning is less tied up with issues of fairness. As a consequence, such individuals' faith may be challenged, and with it inner resources needed to combat their illness on that level. Out of habit, they will probably stoically persist in their adherence to recommended interventions, but with little confidence that things will go well for them, having already once been betrayed. To the extent that positive outlooks contribute to favorable medical outcomes, this is not good. Accordingly, spiritual or philosophical guidance may be an important resource to explore issues that may only be on the periphery of these patients' awareness.

CONCLUSION

Individuals with compulsive personalities will represent the earnest, good patients in primary care providers practice, steeped in virtue and respectful of authority. Under most ordinary circumstances the patient–physician relationship will be especially satisfying for them. The exception will be when there are threats to these patients' security from illness. If

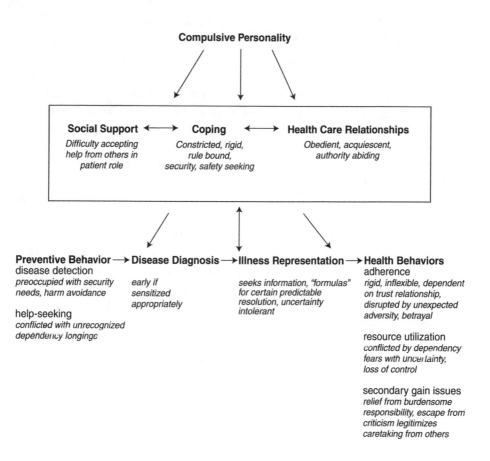

Figure 11.1. Compulsive personality.

there is no immediate formula or plan for a cure, then uncertainty and ambiguity will generate anxiety and a press for clarity that the physician may not be able to provide. In turn the physician may become frustrated and project anger in reaction to these anxious demands that exposes their inadequacy in not adequately serving their model patients. Because of their conflicts concerning dependency needs and reversal of their caretaking role imposed by their illness, help-seeking and use of social support will be difficult for them to accept. Because they may have associated with takers rather than givers who will be unaccustomed to reciprocating, compulsive patients may also be demoralized by failure of their obsessional contract. Figure 11.1 highlights the characteristics of individuals with compulsive personalities in the different health care contexts.

Disease diagnosis should occur early if these patients are properly sensitized or if it serendipitously occurs in the context of persistent anxiety-generated false alarms that are tiring to the practitioner. Compulsive patients' illness representations may be characterized by a jumble of anxiety-ridden, overideational concerns and overly concrete conceptions, all centered around fears of loss of mastery and control. To the extent possible they will attempt to develop self-reassuring schemas or frantically seek special formulas by which they can protect themselves from what medicine and science may be able to only partially address. This will lead to rigid, inflexible adherence to treatment objectives unless in their anxiety they try to themselves manage their treatment, often to their detriment in terms of the disease process and relationship with their specialists. Compulsive patients may vary from discomfort in using resources given their conflicted dependency longings to fruitless overuse of health care services to foster an illusion of control where none may be possible. Secondary gain, as with other patient types, will come from relief of burdensome responsibility and fears of failure and may also legitimize repressed longed for caretaking from others.

Recognition by providers that some sense of control can come from patient explanation and sharing of information, especially that there are measures that can be taken if the unexpected occurs, and a willingness to put up with repetitive, annoying questions seeking reassurance, can do much to restore these patients' defenses so that they more effectively participate as the good patients they desire to be.

12

PERSONALITY DISORDERS
NOT OTHERWISE SPECIFIED

This chapter is devoted to an awkward phase in personality nosology, stemming from the consensual decision by the *DSM–IV* committee to exclude the *DSM–III* category of passive–aggressive personality. Although sadistic and masochistic (self-defeating) personality disorders were also considered in the third version, they also failed to be included in version *IV*. Millon (1999) has persuasively argued for a characterologically based depressive disorder. Especially because these personality type features are present in variants of the other, currently accepted *DSM–IV* personality disorders already described in previous chapters, these need to be considered, at least in more abbreviated form.

DEPRESSIVE PERSONALITY

Previously considered as a dysthymic adjustment, enduring depressive trait characteristics of certain individuals were argued to be included as personality disorders when the *DSM–IV* personality workgroup was conferring. This personality prototype included not only distinct mood disturbances with somatic and neurovegetative symptomology but also distinct cognitive and interpersonal features. In terms of the polarity schema outlined by Millon (Millon & Davis, 1996), the depressive personality prototype is dominant on the preservation or pain pole and conversely weak on the enhancement–pleasure domain. A passive or accommodating orientation characterizes the depressive personality on the second domain. This is in contrast to the avoidant personality that is also dominant on the preservation domain side but is proactive and modifying in efforts to avoid pain. The self–other polarity is relatively balanced for the depressive personality. Translated into a lay perspective, the individual with depressive personality in effect has accepted emotional pain or deprivation as a feature of his or her existence, and in effect has acquiesced in terms of any struggles to modify the subject of the experienced misery and discomfort. It is this difference that distinguishes the depressive individual from the avoidant individual, where there is an active effort to escape or minimize the experience of pain and distress.

Clinical Domain Features

On an observable behavioral level the depressive individual conveys a disconsolate presentation characterized by an enduring sense of hopelessness, at times wretched desperation, a forlorn demeanor. On an interactional, interpersonal level, individuals with depressive personalities convey a sense of vulnerability and defenselessness, that they are at the mercy of others, as a consequence of which they may act in a helpless, unprotected manner to secure protection or nurturance. Given their strong fears of abandonment, they may behave also with passive withdrawal and retreat or in a needy fashion that serves to coerce affection and reassurance from others. Their mood state and expressions of distress do have instrumental value in securing interpersonal aid, even professions of loyalty from others. The same behaviors can also serve to escape responsibility by conveying inadequacy and incompetence, which can serve as justification for the depressive individual's inability to do things. Implicit in this posture may be a sense that if others had been more forthcoming and supportive, greater capability may have been possible. Although depressive individuals may seek nurturing and caretaking from others, their self-absorption and preoccupations create little opportunity for their reciprocating interpersonally, leaving others feeling drained and in time used. In response such others may become angry, manifesting signs of rejection to which depressive individuals are exquisitely sensitive.

On a phenomenological level the depressive individual can be described as cognitively pessimistic, a functional–interactive domain in which a fatalistic and defeatist orientation pervades all thought, past, present, and future. The worst is always anticipated and neutral or positive events are reinterpreted to fit with negative schema, in keeping with the depressive individual's general sense of despair. On a structural level such individuals' self-image is dominated by a sense of inadequacy and worthlessness, which likely also serves to elicit reassurance or to justify a lack of accomplishment. This self-denigration may also inspire a feeling of desperation and hopelessness, which can inspire genuine self-destructive impulses. Another enduring structural feature of individuals with depressive personalities is their repository of internal representations of object relationships and important past events. These are diminished in terms of their capacity to evoke a sense of pleasure, joy, accomplishment, or self-reassurance. As such, there are no internalized positive recollections to counter the natural feelings of loss, abandonment, and aloneness that will occur.

On an intrapsychic level the depressive individual is self-punitive, self-denying, and functions in a manner as to be deprived of pleasures or rewards, while exacting penalties or penitence for shortcomings and failures. This mode of action reflects and also contributes to a structural depletion of those intrapsychic structures that ordinarily would mobilize action, effectively regulating emotion to maintain a positive sense of self-esteem, and moderate impulses or external conflicts, to ensure that life remains tolerable. Depressive individuals lack the capacity for effective coping and have meager defenses against threats or assault on their self-esteem.

Finally, on a biophysical level, it is likely that individuals with depressive personality are predisposed to a melancholic temperament involving a morose orientation, a propensity for worry, and a brooding dysphoria accompanied by a lack of energy. It seems probable that there is a physiological basis for the difficulty sleeping, experience of chronic fatigue, diminished sex drive, poor appetite, and neurovegetative complaints.

Perpetuating Features

The self-perpetuation process for the depressive individual involves repeating experiences of disappointment and suffering. Recollecting past experiences and future expectancies are distorted by negative cognitive schema. Minor events of a negative nature are amplified to conform to negative anticipations, reinforcing a sense of discouragement, despair, or incompetence. Initially a sad, helpless, defeated demeanor may elicit well-intended expressions of sympathy or interest. But in time the persistence of the depressive displays of suffering and such individuals' lack of responsiveness to reassurance and nurturance will alienate even the most committed supporters, creating resentment in immediate family and those who cannot escape the relationship. This will be sensed by depressive individuals as rejection, consistent with their own self-loathing and fears of abandonment.

Depressive individuals' anger turned inward may manifest in chronic self-depreciation, self-negation, or self-accusation, which only intensifies their emotional pain and sense of depletion and deprivation. A viscous cycle is thus set up in which pleasurable experiences become more infrequent and unfamiliar, facilitating an adaptation to a barren and unrewarding existence, from which the only escape is self-destruction. The sense of hopelessness engendered by this adaptation undermines any active striving to change things, reinforcing a sense of failure in never gaining change or improvement. In the extreme, depressive individuals may exhibit complete apathy representing a giving up on their own sense of self.

Generally the first target of intervention of the depressive individual is the passive polarity pole. This is what creates the inertia, lack of action, and state of deprivation, which makes it virtually impossible for such individuals to experience any reinforcement or gratification of a need state that would create a sense of accomplishment or worth that might counter the self-perpetuating dysphoric mode of functioning. Antidepressants may be useful in energizing depressive patients and potentiating activity that might generate events of a positive nature. These experiences themselves are unlikely to alter depressive individuals' basic adjustment, however. They do nonetheless provide a basis for addressing distortions of their experiences caused by negative schema. There may be a synergistic benefit from medication and psychotherapy, especially cognitive therapy that specifically addresses the depressive individual's belief system and negative self-worth.

Depressive individuals will rely on their interpersonal presentation of misery and wretchedness to secure some degree of sympathy and support from others. They will need active caretaker involvement to provide the initiative they are lacking, given their passivity and helplessness in dealing with problems. Although this manner of interpersonal functioning may secure some of their needs in the short run, it will be draining of others and ultimately alienating. When support erodes, the depressive patient may fall back into an increasingly dysphoric and despairing stance that undermines efforts to instill greater patient self-responsibility. Particularly in the course of long-term illness management, these individuals may require an outside advocate organizing and orchestrating support to ensure necessary problem solving is accomplished.

NEGATIVISTIC PERSONALITY

The individual with negativistic personality is most similar to the passive–aggressive type formulated for *DSM-III-R* (American Psychiatric Association, 1987). Considering the basic polarities, the individual with negativistic personality, like the compulsive individual, is oriented toward the preservation–pain-avoidance pole as opposed to the enhancement–pleasure-seeking counterpoint. An active, modifying mode is adopted contrary to the accommodating, passive orientation of the compulsive individual. The negativist individual is also more oriented to the self (individuation) pole than the nurturance (other) position, but this polarity dimension is quite conflicted and characterized by marked ambivalence, which accounts for the seemingly contradictory, vacillating behavior patterns that are invariably aversive to others and ultimately costly to such an individual's strivings to avoid pain. Theoretically (Millon 1969, 1981, 1990) both the compulsive and negativistic personalities have in common similar basic conflicts concerning ambivalence about self and others. Such individuals' response to this is what differs. Compulsive individuals bind their oppositional, contrary impulses behind a stringently defended adaptation of conformity to authority. In contrast, negativistic individuals are unable to resolve these ambivalences and conflicts and may oscillate between being grudgingly accommodating and conciliatory or engaging in a resisting posture to conventions while (often anxiously) pursuing their own personal needs. The negativistic personality also oscillates erratically between an active and passive mode of functioning. Such behavior is normal in young children exploring their need for expression and interacting with adult expectations, defiantly "bad" one moment and contritely, anxiously dependent the next. Over time children gain a sense of predictability and can discriminate when prosocial and individualistic interests may be pursued. When feedback is inconsistent concerning this, confusion, anger, frustration, and anxiety are a consequence, producing childlike behavior patterns in adults, who are viewed as being capricious, impulsive, moody, changeable, pessimistic, and complaining. Typically, they are unhappy and discontented with themselves and others.

Clinical Domain Features

Among the most obvious of the characteristics of individuals with negativistic personalities for the behavioral level is such individuals' manifest resentment expressed in their interpersonal and instrumental behavior. Nonverbally this might be seen in a scowling or sullen expression conveying a begrudging, oppositional orientation expressed in the form of negative, covert aggressive behavior that is indirect, difficult to prove or to punish for. Procrastination or an unenthusiastic, ineffective, half-hearted effort that frustrates the expectations or realizations of others is a common means by which the negativistic individual gains satisfaction with a minimal likelihood of overt retaliation or punishment. Their contrary interpersonal behavior is evidenced in the context of vacillation between anxious accommodation reflecting a dependent–other polarity position and an independent polarity orientation involving hostile impulses suppressed by an anticipation of frustration or defeat over expression of any autonomy. Commonly, negativistic individuals are quite vulnerable to feelings of envy that give rise to resentments over others being perceived as more fortunate and a disgruntled attitude that life has not treated them fairly. This interactive style that is not overtly aggressive or conspicuously anxious and dependent can keep others off balance with inconsistent displays of accommodating, solicitous, and demanding, disapproving behavior.

The predominant phenomenological, cognitive style feature of negativistic individuals is a mistrusting, disparaging, cynical, or pessimistic orientation, reflecting an anticipation of dissatisfying outcomes. Their inherent ambivalence may be seen in their oscillation between pursuit of seemingly positive courses of action and contrary, disruptive, or undermining positions that impede realization of gratifications for others. They perceive themselves as unfortunate, mistreated, misunderstood, not appreciated, and destined to be cheated of the benefits of life accorded to others, perceptions that generate feelings of envy, resentment, pessimism, and bitterness. Insight into the nature of their behavior is invariably lacking, because this would serve to inhibit expression of their discontent by realization of hostile impulses unnerving to them.

The early, prototypical experiences of negativistic personalities are predominated by conflicting feelings, frustrations, and expectancies, which give these individuals little basis for consolidating a core set of object representations as the basis for future relationships. Erratic parental discipline prevents development and internalization of self-controls, which accounts for the often impulsive reactions to events.

Because of their contradictory nature, negativistic individuals on an intrapsychic level evidence incompatibility of different personality elements and an inadequate capability for reconciling them. The vacillation between accommodation and opposition that is felt in virtually every encounter gives rise to relatively extreme feelings of ineffectuality, frustration, guilt, and then anger. This inner turmoil contributes to such individual's chronic sense of instability and vulnerability to confusing surges of contradictory emotions (e.g., anger, then anxiety and guilt) they cannot modulate effectively. Ambivalence about overt expression of hostility, especially toward authority figures who have thwarted them, make displacement of their anger onto substitute targets less threatening. Introjection, or turning one's feelings against the self, may also be a defense mechanism that varies with use of projection, attributing covert feelings of hostility onto others, who in turn are viewed as malicious and harmful, reinforcing their view of the world as unsafe and unfulfilling.

In addition, on a biophysical temperamental level, the negativistic personality is typically sensitive, irritable, short-fused, hypersensitive, and overreactive to events. The extent to which these characteristics are biologically determined or are conditioned emotional responses to an inconsistent reinforcement history is unclear.

Perpetuating Features

Unlike individuals with other personality disorders in which there are some tenuous periods of tranquility, individuals with negativistic personalities are unable to attain moments of peace because their character features generate chronic discontent. Most evident are their negative and unpredictable behavior patterns that disrupt their efforts to achieve their needs by alternatively appeasing then upsetting and alienating others with their vacillating emotions and shifting attitudes or by second-guessing themselves and reversing their own pursuit of objectives. Even tolerant friends or family will grow weary of the negativistic individual's sulking, sullen, complaining orientation. Eventually others may become angry and rejecting when their efforts to ameliorate these individuals' distress is ineffectual in reducing their inconsolable, pitiful manner. Such predictable reactions only intensify the negativistic individual's sense of distress and alarm, generating additional displays of dismayed, hapless, or resentful, spiteful behavior.

Given such experiences, it is not surprising that negativistic individuals develop expectations that their efforts (or those of others trying to help) will be fruitless, even pointless in achieving success or happiness. This anticipation of frustration and disappointment may even cause the negativistic individual to create impediments where none exist, causing pseudo-turmoils, baffling but aversive to the objective bystander, who typically exits the scene when such self-inflicted defeat is then followed with resentment, disillusionment, or bitterness. Negativistic individuals' low self-esteem creates cognitive dissonance with any successes experienced, which prompts them to interrupt their effort, in anticipation of failure, when success may be nearly within their grasp. In so doing, they effectively nullify any possibility for corrective experiences in the form of growth-promoting positive outcomes.

What accidental successes negativistic individuals may experience places them in effect on partial reinforcement schedules that strengthen the resistance to extinction of their most disruptive and aversive behavior patterns. In pursuing relationships these individuals may test their new companions with annoying, demanding behavior, to determine the depth of commitment and gain reassurance that past disappointments (particularly, rejection or inconsistent acceptance by a parent) will not recur. In so doing, they engender the antipathy of their new relationship hope, whose natural reaction to this confusion is to withdraw, confirming their worst fears of betrayal and abandonment. This recreating of past failures–disappointments is a crippling feature of this adjustment pattern.

Typically, negativistic personalities will enter treatment only in response to some external pressure or crisis, because their natural tendency would be to flee any situation that would require self-examination or assumption of responsibility for their chronic discontent. Contracting for specific behavior change can also alter expectations from previous prototypical inconsistent experiences with parental authorities. It is important to enlist the negativistic patient as an involved observer of situations where their basic ambivalence between self–other, assertion–submission conflict can foster a collaborative approach between therapist and patient, promoting a healthy reexamination of long-held schemas that have driven their behavior for so long.

The characteristics of negativistic individuals ensure that those stable figures involved in their lives are largely inured to many of their most unpleasant features. Even so, the stress of illness may present new challenges, because as patients these negativistic individuals will have coercive influence on their supports, who may feel unable to detach from them at their time of crisis. They may even feel constrained from taking needed respite "vacations" from those difficult relationships that may have been a feature of the pre-illness relationship. Where there is serious illness requiring extended hospitalization and support resources to augment the lengthy treatment process, there are risks of caretaker alienation and exhaustion, given these patient's cantankerous, "difficult" presentation and the confounding and contradictory nature of their demands. For serious illness management an "advocate" with experience in dealing with these individuals may be needed to orchestrate resources and minimize the interpersonal damage the patient might inflict on their relationships with the health care team.

SADISTIC PERSONALITY

Given the appalling growth of violent, hateful behavior in not only social organizations, individual adults, and even teenagers and children, it is important to consider sadism as a condition to be better understood. Whereas the natural propensity of individuals is that of seeking love, pleasure, and joy, sadism is the antithesis of these things, and it is important to recognize malevolence, even evil in individuals, and not mistake it for something else. In the sadistic individual the dominant polarities are the preservation (pain) and modification (active) components. The self is of average strength, whereas the polarity dimension of nurturance is weak.

Clinical Domain Features

On a behavioral level, sadistic individuals are truly dangerous. They are frequently precipitous and reckless in their actions, often drawing others into dangerous circumstances where there is a high likelihood of inflicting or receiving pain or injury. Sadistic individuals seek to interpersonally humiliate, demean, or even physically harm others, not as a means to some other end but as a source of gratification in its own right. From a phenomenological perspective the sadistic individual cognitively maintains an authoritarian orientation, rigid and unyielding, closed-minded and prone to prejudicial attitudes and intolerance. Individuals with sadistic personality types perceive themselves as dominant and aggressive in pursuing their needs and views, and their self-image reflects a valuation of intimidation and exercise of power as a pursuit in its own right. Internalized object relations based on early prototypical experiences are associated with aggressive impulses, attitudes, and images. Absent are feelings of tender sentimentality, as well as shame, guilt, self-recrimination, or a propensity to feel conflict about actions taken and their consequences on others. Relationships are dominated by power and coercion, not empathy, caring, or reciprocity.

Intrapsychically sadistic individuals use the defense of isolation of affect wherein they can adopt a detached orientation to the punishing, harmful, or hurtful consequences of even excessive actions. Objects of wrath are devalued and viewed as deserving of suffering at the hands of harsh justice. These individuals' morphological organization, although generally integrated and modulated to manifest these characteristics in a controlled manner, periodically is subject to disruption by expression of powerful intruding aggressive and sexual impulses. This may stem from a biophysical makeup constituted by an irritable temperament and volatility, which predisposes a combative, belligerent orientation toward others.

Perpetuating Features

Individuals with sadistic personality characteristics share an expectation that relationships are characterized by cruelty and abusiveness rather than consideration and gentleness, such that one must demonstrate greater dominance and aggressive potential to discourage aggressive acts against them. Their anticipation of attack and derogation and propensity to beat others to the punch makes it likely they will sabotage opportunities to experience kindness and empathy by distorting social experiences and overtures by others by seeing such actions as potentially dangerous and derogating.

Conversely, sadistic individuals will harbor a mistrust and disrespect for gentle, kind, empathic behavior, which are viewed as sentimentalities dangerous to their welfare, given their assumption that others are basically out to dominate or harm them. Their assumed early experiences of being punished, often arbitrarily, have in their case left them hardened to mistreatment and contemptuous of feeling states that only caused them pain and demoralization. The consequence of their harsh, intimidating posture, however, is to drive others away, especially those most likely to provide contrary, potentially corrective experiences or to elicit counterhostility that reinforces their distorted social reality.

Under ordinary circumstances most sadistic individuals will have selected roles and vocations that place them in some relative power over others, where they can exercise dominance and control and at least benignly mistreat their subordinates at home or at work. Where this behavior becomes excessive, even abusive such that it is challenged, then sadistic individuals may end up confronted with their deviance. Especially in corporate workplace environments, political correctness requires that harassment, especially of lower status individuals, cannot be tolerated from a legal standpoint. Because of their inherent lack of empathy, individuals with sadistic personalities are unlikely to be concerned about their behavior being hurtful; rather, this may be experienced pleasurably as an indicator of their power and dominance. Insight into their actions may thus be restricted to their gaining an appreciation that continued interpersonally abusive behavior will only result in punishment and sanctions, including loss of their power and influence. At best, such contingencies may restrict the behavior from situations where it can be monitored and where requirements for appropriate social behavior are enforced.

Based on theory, the goal of treatment of the sadistic individual would be to reverse the pain–pleasure polarity, where inflicting discomfort on others does not generate a sense of satisfaction or gratification through dominance and coercion. Successful interventions should provide these individuals with experiences where nondestructive, even superficially considerate behavior is rewarded by others and not necessarily treated as a sign of weakness. In doing so, awareness of previously disregarded needs and feelings of others may be emphasized as an alternative means of exerting positive influence to gain respectful, even affectionate behavior from others that is not coerced or achieved through intimidation. Specific prohibitions against pathology-perpetuating abusive behaviors may be required (especially where external sanctions have already occurred). Alternative, substitute behaviors may have to be directly taught and role-played. Consideration of their implicit or explicit assumptions about the motives and meaning of other's conduct toward them will require examination, especially about how that contributes to actually court counterhostility from others in a self-fulfilling fashion. Modulation of their tendency to experience surges of aggressive impulses and emotions will be particularly important.

It would be presumed that the domineering nature of individuals with sadistic personalities hardly serve to spontaneously generate new support, especially when they are in a relatively powerless position. If anything, their frailty or vulnerability might embolden some of their oppressed preexisting supports (e.g., family), especially if the illness is certain to have a weakening or diminishing effect. If overly belligerent and threatening, such patients may elicit passive–aggressive forms of counteraggression that could be potentially harmful (e.g., delays in authorization to perform important diagnostic or treatment procedures by antagonized insurance care managers). In such instances, some member of the treatment team, such as a hospital social worker, may be invaluable in smoothing out ruffled feathers and coordinating ancillary health care activity, insulating staff from these difficult patients.

MASOCHISTIC PERSONALITY

Although also not a personality subtype provided for in the *DSM-IV*, the masochistic type (Millon, 1999) has features that overlap with the self-defeating personality referenced in *DSM-III-R*, along with mention of the sadistic type (American Psychiatric Association, 1987). Individuals with these characteristics are self-denigrating and will undo any accomplishments, as if they seek to embrace mistreatment or failure and undermine any external efforts to build competence, self-esteem, or self-reliance. Polarity theory views these individuals as manifesting a reversal between pleasure and pain, the latter representing the preferred state (provided the pain is not too extreme, such as in physical torture). It is assumed that this results from repetitive experiences that some degree of discomfort and negative states serve to protect from more significant and unbearable unpleasantness. Masochistic individuals are more oriented to nurturance (other) concerns than self-enhancement. They are also passive on the accommodation–modification pole. Unlike the depressive individual, who is hopeless and reconciled to defeat and suffering, the masochist individual's passivity represents more an adaptive choice to accept the lesser of two evils, where only those alternatives exist.

Clinical Domain Features

On the behavioral–interpersonal level, masochistic personalities are expressively self-denying and minimizing. They eschew positive experiences, diminishing their value or accomplishment and avoiding the limelight, maintaining a deferential subservient demeanor that permits if not encourages mistreatment or exploitation by their more sadistic counterparts.

Phenomenologically their cognitive representations and activity reflect a reluctance to view events and themselves in a positive self-enhancing manner, because this would elicit anticipation of punishment. There is thus a propensity for negative expectations to protect from more unfavorable outcomes. In turn this promotes a self-image in which failure is expected, generating mistreatment and some degree of suffering that is viewed as one's due for disappointing others but also protection from greater harm and punishment. Their internalized object representations consist of a repository of failure experiences and relationship disappointments, blunted or punished pleasure impulses, images and feeling states that intensify rather than reduce conflict and internal dissonance.

The masochistic individual's intrapsychic regulatory mechanisms serve to amplify rather than diminish the experience, expression, or recollection of psychic pain. These individuals seem to evidence a need to maintain, even create a distress level in keeping with their accustomed sense of discomfort. This may represent a form of control, whereby pain can be anticipated, disappointment made predictable. This affords protection against the uncertainty of greater pain and distress that comes with unexpected failure that those without such personality disorders have learned to tolerate as natural consequences of achievement striving, interpersonal relationship risk, and physical endeavors.

On the affective level, masochist individuals are often anxious when experiencing favorable events or attempting to pursue pleasure. Inner torment may be a more comfortable state that superstitiously represents safety against some greater trauma. This posture of suffering and misery does have the interpersonal effect of implicitly communicating a state of being mistreated, which may then justify claims of nobility that may protect against further depredations and even legitimize in their minds (and elicit from others) deserved transitory reprieves from this state of misery. By contrast, individuals without this personality disorder would seek pleasure in a straightforward fashion, require no justification for it, and would find discomfort unacceptable and a stimulus to remedial action.

Perpetuating Features

It is not difficult to see how masochistic behavior contributes to a self-perpetuating process. Such individuals' undoing of any positive actions and their verbal self-disparagement establishes a low opinion of themselves that is communicated to others. Although this maintains a needed but safe state of misery, their self-devaluating manner places them in a default position of complete reliance on others for a sense of acceptability. When their behavior fails to elicit sympathy, caretaking, or nurturance, this may elicit what they truly dread, fears of abandonment and isolation, what their convoluted interpersonal maneuvers seek to escape but only invite. Masochistic individuals confronted with threatened abandonment may be willing to accept greater abuse and mistreatment in return for social contact and acceptance, if even of a punitive or disparaging nature. This pattern may induce increasingly greater needs to heighten their sense of mistreatment.

However, amplifying comparatively innocuous events into great injustices may alienate those individuals who are made into unwitting perpetrators.

An obvious treatment goal would be to begin to undo the pain–pleasure reversal. A process of slow bolstering of self-esteem (so as not to elicit self-defeating anxiety) combined with insight into their reinforcement history involving anxiety reduction through displays of suffering and experience of discomfort can slowly interrupt the vicious cycle outlined. Mood elevators may alleviate dysphoric affect and guilt feelings that engender feelings of unworthiness and that punishment is deserved. More difficult to address will be the unconscious courting of mistreatment from others.

INTERPERSONAL ASPECTS OF PERSONALITIES NOT OTHERWISE SPECIFIED IN THE HEALTH CARE SETTING

What will characterize depressive personality patients presenting to the clinic will be their generally passive orientation to their condition, their seeming acceptance of their misfortune, and their demeanor, which conveys a sense of helplessness and misery. It is these very behaviors that serve the depressive patient to solicit caring and nurturance from others, often in a subtle coercive fashion that leaves others initially disarmed, then eventually resentful. Because health care providers are sanctioned only to act in a caring and not rejecting manner (or face consequences from peers and perhaps attorneys), a medical setting is a good environment for the depressive individual to enjoy the experience of caring, nurturing interpersonal behavior. The depressive individual may thus become a "regular" among patients, but can be experienced also as a draining, interpersonally aversive force in a physician's life. Their inability to take responsibility or initiate any self-management activity will frustrate those attempting to help if there is anything but an acute, time-limited illness to deal with. With a busy physician hurriedly transmitting treatment regimen information, depressive patients' passive communication style may be misconstrued as hearing what the provider intended to communicate, which is unlikely. Their mood disturbance from a cognitive standpoint may impede their ability to even encode and recall important information. In either instance, these individuals may come to be perceived as unmotivated or noncompliant about their illness, contributing to prejudicial, pejorative attitudes that may feed into their illness.

In the medical setting, negativistic patients will present either because they are somatizing their emotional distress and seeking some alleviation of symptoms or because of actual illnesses requiring either acute care or long-term management. Relying on others for caretaking and nurturance may intensify their anxious anticipation of disappointment and lead to recreation of unsatisfactory prototypical relationships disruptive to treatment. In this state negativistic patients may behave in a more active but childlike, provocative manner that only serves to antagonize the support system on which they may rely heavily. They may procrastinate on implementing treatment regimens, failing to report important information necessary to monitor treatment, missing appointments, and then complaining about the inevitable negative consequences of their behavior, as if it is someone else's fault. Even when the best that can be hoped for is an adversarial relationship, treatment complications may be minimized by the provider maintaining a professional, straightforward manner. Accompanying this orientation should be a task orientation emphasizing discrete goals and objectives, with clear delineation of the benefits as well as the side effects and the consequences of noncompliance (e.g., acute or gradual deterioration of organ function or symptom intensification). Where medications that provide emotional symptom relief are being used, caution may have to be exercised against excessive use, because these individuals may overreact to frustration and setbacks in their care and display intense anxiety for which they will seek immediate relief. Dutiful scheduling of brief follow-up visits at shorter intervals may be important to guard against important deviations from their treatment plan and the natural tendency of the provider to avoid contact altogether, given the aversive nature of the interaction.

The patient with a sadistic personality may initially present as a somewhat guarded individual whose intimidating tendencies are muted by situational constraints—in other words, the medical practitioner represents a potentially more powerful figure in a better position to inflict than receive harm or abuse. Efforts to project a caring or sensitive persona on the part of health care providers may be treated with silent disdain or even mistrust, an orientation that may affect treatment selection and decision making through doubt about the genuineness of the medical diagnosis and intent behind medical recommendations. If the practitioner exhibits discomfort with this type of patient, this could elicit efforts to dominate the patient–physician relationship. An interpersonally neutral presentation where the factual aspects of care (e.g., objective medical findings, laboratory studies) supporting the recommendations may reduce but not eliminate the significance of some of these undercurrents that may not be evident until prolonged care is required.

The masochistic patient, in contrast, may present as overly self-effacing and deferential, all too ready to embrace a negative medical forecast or agree to some uncomfortable procedure. Over time their behavior may subtly invite actions from their care providers that in effect cast the practitioners in punitive roles that such patients are comfortable with but that is distressing to the provider. Efforts to treat them in the caring fashion that patients would respond to might be anxiety-arousing to these masochistic patients, who would invite disapproval or punishment through incompetent compliance behavior or potentially harmful administration of self-managed treatments. In reaction, the frustrated provider may understandably experience guilt-inducing antagonistic or confused feelings hardly conducive to clear-headed medical decision making.

The individual with masochistic personality, in addition, is likely to be helpless and ineffectual in activating any support. The propensity to accept or perhaps even embrace discomfort may even contribute to his or her sabotaging efforts to use resources that may indeed be important to a favorable clinical response. The nature of personal relationships of such individuals and "partner-selection" also increases the likelihood that others in their lives may tend to be "takers" rather than "givers," individuals less likely to step forward with time and effort to provide essential instrumental assistance. These patients will require professional advocacy to mobilize support and to ensure that sufficient physical and psychological comfort is provided to counter their potential decompensation from illness-related stresses that may exceed even their "required" level of discomfort.

MEDICAL MANAGEMENT ISSUES

In the following subtopics, the problems posed by each of the personalities described in this chapter will be considered, in juxtaposition with each other. This should highlight even more the different adaptive stances patients with different personality disorders may take in their interactions with the health care system.

Preventive Interventions, Lifestyle Choices

For depressive individuals, there is essentially no intrinsic motivation for changing appetitive–addictive behavior patterns, given their pervasively gloomy outlook that would anticipate ill health or some other misfortune in the future. Warnings would likely be only mood-congruent and consistent with their existing negative schemas. Confrontation with medical recommendations that require behavior change may be taken personally by negativistic individuals, who would react with dismay that they are to be denied what few pleasures they are able to secure out of life. They may not express their discontent directly, but their antipathy will be skillfully expressed in passive–aggressive forms of behavior or manifestations of interpersonal grievance that will be guilt-inducing and, over time, vexing, even infuriating, to the providers. This may alternate with seemingly appeasing and accommodating behavior that may give rise to hope of a more cooperative stance that will not last, leaving the providers feeling confused and powerless to manage the interaction and emotional undercurrents taking place.

Busy physicians used to exercising their expertise and authority as a means of influence may be unprepared to deal with sadistic individuals, who have come to experience relationships as "dominate or be dominated" and who may adopt a belligerent stance in response to the perceived threat of medical recommendations. This is likely to elicit antagonism on the part of the physician unaccustomed to such defiance. Given that masochistic patients have established unhealthy habits and routines that provide some gratification of need states, new health behavior demands may present unwelcome requirements for change that are not part of their dynamic of passivity and discomfort. Their pathology typically involves acceptance of interpersonal suffering in return for escape from greater (relationship) pain. Their response to these unwanted medical recommendations may be helpless or incompetent behavior that is seemingly accommodating yet ineffectual in meeting the medical recommendation. This may be accompanied by an unnerving acceptance, even embracing of any provider reaction that is punitive in nature.

Stages of Change

The individual with depressive personality will be at a precontemplation level concerning modification of unhealthy behavior given his or her inability to adopt a prospective orientation to life's challenges or demands. Simply communicating that such individuals may be at increased risk for some health problem may have little motivational impact given that they are inherently passive in their orientation to pain avoidance and lacking in initiative to engage in rational self-preservation. Efforts to move into the contemplation stage will have to take into account the patient's general state of psychic depletion and behavioral inertia. Use of mood-elevating drugs to activate the depressive patient should be combined with a supportive, caring orientation emphasizing that treatment goals are to be collaboratively achieved by patient and the health care team, that they will be led through the change process. The practitioner must therefore engage in considerable preparation with the depressive individual, where probable barriers are identified and a timetable set that will orient the patient to the tasks to come. Emphasizing the principal of successive approximation in pursuing clearly defined, modest (achievable) objectives, the therapist can better move into the action phase. This may initially require participation of a family member to identify unhealthy behaviors to be changed and what behaviors to replace them with. Monitoring the change process will be important to ensure these patients experience believable incremental improvement at a rate not so rapid as be excessively dissonant with the patient's low self-esteem. Whereas for other personality types, doing for the patient would be countertherapeutic, for depressive individuals this will appropriately recognize and address their sense of hopelessness–helplessness and inertia, while demonstrating tangible progress that may counter their negative schema that they are eternally mired in a static, powerless, unhappy existence. The maintenance phase may take considerably longer to achieve in this group, given the characterological barriers to be overcome. By this point, the depressive individual should have incorporated and internalized the behavior pattern changes acquired during the earlier phases. However, an added requirement may be integration of the changes into the patient's self-concept, in which there is a deeply ingrained sense of worthlessness. Depressive individuals maintain an orientation of self-punishment that must be replaced with a capacity for self-reinforcement, a sense of worthiness.

Negativistic individuals' preoccupation with their litany of daily discontents and anticipated dissatisfactions place them at the precontemplation level concerning behavioral lifestyle change. Negativistic patients will be too consumed with resisting or opposing existing directives or demands from others to seriously appreciate any appetitive behavior patterns as being excessive and potentially harmful. Indeed, the concept of doing something wrong to themselves may be rather foreign, given their fundamental preoccupation that others have or will bring harm to them. The contemplation stage will likely consist of preoccupation with contrary sentiments and attitudes elicited by the medical recommendation for behavior change, which leave little opportunity for any rational consideration about the potential benefits of such self-management interventions. Their sense of antagonism toward any authority figures with power to withhold benefit will displace any sensible arguments for reduction of health-risk behaviors. The preparation phase will require the practitioner to actively propose a behavior change plan that may be argued, demeaned, protested, and resented. It is also possible it may be passively or grudgingly accepted, but this may represent only a placating form of stalling, a prelude to later inaction. As such, the action phase may be anything but, manifesting instead as a perplexing battle between the harried provider charged with implementing the change and a patient whose attitudes, expressions, and behavior seem to continually shift from passive obstruction to promises of accommodation that is only partially actualized and then is undone. The best-case scenario may be that healthy behaviors become habitual and automatic as a result of recurring demands, rather than a result of attitude change and premeditated intentions. Most likely attitude change would follow, not precede, behavior change as a means of reducing cognitive dissonance. These dynamics will continue to apply for the maintenance stage, which will have to consist of others—the patient's family, spouse, or support group—providing the initiative, monitoring, and situational influences necessary to sustain the targeted behavior changes to the point they become habitual parts of the negativistic patient's everyday routine.

Movement from the initial precontemplation to contemplation phase for the sadistic individual will need to involve consideration of his or her sensitivity to being controlled, especially emasculated or dominated. A problem may be that even discussion of such vulnerability may be unacceptable in that it would reflect potential weakness and a lack of authority. Rather, a consultative orientation that acknowledges, implicitly or explicitly, the (sadistic) patient has final say on implementing the change may be helpful. This may begin with impersonal discussion that emphasizes the medical implications of continued smoking, overeating, or alcohol consumption, and risk for personal diminishment if not modified. This future threat alone may elicit considerable bluster and belligerence, but the extent that this venom can be directed at the requirement for change and not toward the provider responsible for conveying the recommendations will be crucial to facilitating constructive dialog during this phase and later stages. During the planning stage consideration of barriers and obstacles to change may require diplomatic discussion of how individuals who will be viewed as subservients can be enlisted (and supported) to facilitate the change process. It can be anticipated that there may be considerable potential for displacement of aggressive impulses and relationship abuse during the action stage. The practitioner implementing change may need to anticipate and preemptively address the likelihood of such displaced wrath with both the patient and supporting health care cast. By anticipating such provocations, the health care team can be interpersonally inoculated so that natural countertransference reactions may be replaced with a more temperate professional orientation. The hope would be that by the maintenance stage, many or most of the problematic interaction patterns would be sufficiently worked out and that unhealthy practices are replaced with health-promoting habit patterns.

Masochistic personalities are characterologically oriented to be submissive and acquiescing, so it is likely they will be initially at a precontemplative stage but tacitly agreeable rather than belligerent to proposals for change. Agreeing that change may be needed cannot be treated as a behavioral intention that ordinarily would potentiate change. For the masochistic individual, it may simply represent a reflex appeasement response to an authority demand. The masochistic individual's attitudes and considerations during contemplative stage thus may be misleading to the practitioner in that change will not be as easy as it seems. This may lead to disappointment and disapproval, which will then activate masochistic interpersonal behavior patterns that only further disrupt targeted behavior change. The planning and action stages may prove quite frustrating in the change process, given that the masochistic personality has a need to maintain a certain state of discomfort or distress so as not to feel anxious. Positive reinforcement for astute planning or demonstrated resolve will not elicit greater effort but perhaps the reverse. To the extent that there are others (e.g., spouses, significant others) who are available to play a role in implementing change (e.g., preparing healthy foods, removing alcohol from the home, discouraging smoking), this may be a more effective route to pursue rather than attempt to motivate or enable these individuals to become change agents themselves. If their psychosocial environment promotes smoking, drinking, or overeating, overcoming these situational influences and one's own appetitive urges and temptations may be impossible without group or psychotherapeutic intervention. If the maintenance stage can be achieved, this will have involved most probably a protracted effort removing situational obstacles, especially those with relationship implications, so that new habit patterns can be developed around which to integrate the healthy behaviors.

Utility, Cost–Benefit Considerations of Preventive Interventions

In an individual with a relatively severe case of depressive personality, the prospect of promoting enduring change in relation to a theoretical risk of later health problems is not an attractive cost–benefit ratio from a behavioral medicine standpoint. Nonetheless, targeting weight control in a depressive individual with obesity and strong family history of heart disease and diabetes may in the long run be worth strenuous efforts from the standpoint of lifetime health care costs. The presence of a family member suffering some consequence of an unhealthy lifestyle may serve as a motivating influence, although the family member's behavior may have been a negative model for the patient's own problematic behavior (e.g., smoking).

For negativistic patients the benefit of change will have to be considerable to justify the persistence, patience, and energy entailed in arguing for, implementing, and then providing adequate follow-up to ensure the patients and their families do not revert to old patterns. A high risk for heart disease, stroke, diabetes, and examples of family members afflicted with serious health problems may be necessary to provide tangible evidence of the damage that smoking, overeating, and excessive alcohol consumption can cause to vulnerable persons. Even so, the mistrust of negativistic individuals and their anticipation of things going wrong in their life can diminish the motivating fear that a person with more positive life experiences and outlooks—in other words, someone with something to lose—otherwise might experience as a basis for his or her behavior change. For such individuals, threat is not a call to action but simply another instance to anticipate something going wrong, the negativistic patient supplying the self-fulfilling behavior consistent with those expectations.

Considering sadistic patients, practitioners must counter being mistreated or dominated while negotiating and motivating change. With masochistic patients they must avoid being cast in an abusive role while facing sabotage and undoing of positive change by seemingly well-intended individuals.

Secondary and Tertiary Care of Acute and Chronic Illness

For depressive individuals, development of a symptom may initially represent another complaint of not feeling good, which is experienced as their consistent lot in life. Given that depressive individuals are beset with a generalized malaise and may have a variety of somatic complaints, neurovegetative manifestations of depression associated with their affective disturbance (e.g., changes in bowel habit, increased fatigue), it may be difficult for them to distinguish those from legitimate early symptoms of physical illness (e.g., colon cancer). Once a serious illness is diagnosed this will be experienced as yet another misfortune in a life of unending mishaps, losses, and disappointments. It may represent validation of their basic position—that life for them remains unfair. It can also serve as justification to maintain their helpless, complaining stance, compelling support and nurturance from others. If they have tired or alienated their family or close relationships with their previous litany of complaints, now they may have something by which to generate a sense of guilt and additional inhibition of anger–resentment in others. In this sense the depressive individual may be disease-embracing. A second purpose served may also be avoidance of burdensome responsibilities, which are justified away because the individual is too ill to assume previously assigned duties. This is an especially important issue, because these secondary gain incentives will certainly undermine efforts to engender a healthy sense of self-mastery in these patients. They may see that they have more to lose than gain in attaining greater competence in managing their illness, if that means a return to old, unwelcome routines. Because they are determined to suffer, they may magnify their symptoms, which can bias the practitioner to disregard potentially important complaint information interspersed between symptoms that are distorted or irrelevant in nature.

Negativistic individuals, by virtue of their turbulent inner tensions and negative feeling states, are familiar with a variety of physical ailments that are stress-related, which combine with their anxious, dysthymic nature to reinforce their sense of dissatisfaction and misery. The negativistic individual's inherent skepticism may combine with his or her mistrust of others, to create an unstable, changing set of impressions of health status, which will be unfavorably confounded with his or her relationship with health care providers. Initial health warnings may be dismissed as misdiagnosis because of physician incompetence and laboratory–device error. This could result in delays in treatment and follow-up to control the disease process, which ironically then is blamed on the health care providers whose very diligence was thwarted.

For the sadistic individual, interaction with the medical authority may be experienced as a power struggle for control and domination of the interaction process. Medical decision making involving patient consent may be a threatening experience for the individual with sadistic personality and a frustrating one for the care provider, whose authority may be challenged or demeaned in a fashion reminiscent of some of the more brutal clinical rotations they went through with supervising attending physicians. The challenge for the practitioner will be to remain neutral while this tedious interpersonal play unfolds, because to interfere or engage in counterefforts to assert dominance would only delay decision making and implementation of treatment. In contrast, the masochistic patient may be overly willing to adopt a suffering role in which there is too much deference to the recommendations simply because they are offered by an attractive authority figure. Informed consent in this instance may thus also be distorted by the patient's personality dynamics.

The process of forming illness representations by depressive individuals will reflect their basic negative schema and sense of worthlessness, such that they may have a personalized, rather distorted view of their condition, especially negative expectations that any constructive, proactive effort on their part will be of benefit. Education concerning the disease, how it is manifested, its typical course, how it might be aggravated or ameliorated, may be a repetitive, frustrating process for the medical practitioner, especially if he or she is diligent enough to verify these patients' understanding of their communications, which may well be incomplete or distorted. Where these distortions are serious and persistently undermine adherence to the treatment regimen, then behavioral medicine consultation may be indicated. With a patient with severe depression, the objective of complete self-management is likely unrealistic, although modest gains in self-confidence in personal illness management and self-efficacy may be a reasonable goal, provided the patient does not feel that this will seriously reduce the social nurturance and contact the illness may have provided.

Given the flux their internal turmoil and changing object representations keep them in emotionally and cognitively, it is unlikely negativistic patients will form stable illness representations. Written materials concerning disease processes may only partially offset the distortions that may occur as problematic relationship issues doubtlessly emerge and become confounded with the patient's beliefs and expectations about their illness. The sensitivity of the negativistic individual to feelings of resentment and bitterness may divert him or her from systematic self-management or treatment regimen requirements, such failures in turn contributing to growing acrimony with frustrated providers.

The sadistic individual's illness representations will likely contain elements of apprehension that his or her momentary weakness may represent an opportunity for others to gain advantage rather than provide care. Thus there may be mistrust of some of the information provided, or it may not be fully heard, given these distracting considerations. Written materials outlining the disease process, the treatment alternatives, and even encouragement to seek second opinions may help defuse some of these latent concerns. The authoritarian nature of sadistic personalities may also be exhibited in their menacing attitude while demanding absolute assurances that the procedure will be successful. In their illness representations, masochistic patients by comparison may assume matters will go awry or experience discomfort when the outcome is regarded as uniformly positive. Providing educational–instructive materials for the masochist patient can provide an objective basis for a more mature dialogue in which patient responsibilities can be discussed as part of the treatment process and any anticipated or actual difficulties in carrying them out can be dealt with in a neutral but firm manner. Discussion of treatment options involving the physician recommending a second opinion (or even psychological evaluation of the patient's motivation for surgery) may be appropriate before embarking on expensive or controversial forms of care.

Coping With Illness

Depressive individuals' predisposition to accept misfortunes into their general sense of misery and malaise that make up their self-image may prevent them from regarding aggravations as unwanted and undeserved, the motivational basis for doing something about them. Indeed, their response to illness-related stresses may be to incorporate them into their negative schemas. This can make the patient a poor source of information concerning potentially modifiable illness-related issues even for a patient advocate called in to help. Their coping may consist of maintaining a defenseless interpersonal style, which has the effect of coercing assistance. As an illness will represent an additional burden for the depressive individual's fragile adjustment, it should not be surprising that there may be some regression or intensification of his or her basic characteristics. The practitioner should accept this and seek initially to educate and model coping for depressive patients, by essentially doing it for them, then gradually getting them to take over, with monitoring and reinforcement for doing so.

It is somewhat of a misnomer to talk of negativistic patients as coping, given that they are inherently shifting and inconsistent in their object representations, moods, dispositions, and actions. Displacement is identified as their most prominent defense, where typically anger is directed away from the original source onto others, even at times themselves. With this constellation of characteristics, negativistic individuals' response to stresses beyond their adaptive capacities, the original definition of coping given in this book is thus to behave in a way that is erratic and counterproductive, especially with respect to the expectations of others. This disorder is primarily a disturbance involving ambivalence of interpersonal relations, self and other. Aiding negativistic individuals in coping will essentially mean countering their worst self-perpetuating tendencies. This will involve stabilizing their behavior to include tendencies for interpersonal conflict, erratic, vacillating actions and moods. These individuals are unable to establish or maintain a focus to address their problems. They need to be helped to concretely and specifically adhere to treatment plans, participating in their illness management as constructively as possible or with minimum destructive or obstructing effect. It will be no small feat for the practitioner, given the basic nature of this personality type to skeptically anticipate disappointment or harm and therefore actively engage in opposition to those influences that are mistrusted.

The sadistic individual's natural tendency to attack when vulnerable or threatened, as an assumption of how others are disposed to act toward him or her or projection of his or her own behavior, is hardly conducive to engaging caretakers at a time of true need. Although their behavior may elicit counterhostility in those not used to being intimidated, they may still attempt to bully their physicians, who are typically used to at least polite deference if not adulation for their curative skills. Experienced physicians with presumably high self-esteem will be more immune to such obnoxiousness than novice medical staff or lower-status caretakers (e.g., nurses, physical therapists) who typically carry out rather than issue orders. These individuals may be more vulnerable to the intimidation and abusive behavior of individuals of this personality type. If not involved in a team management approach where their abusive experiences can be reported and their esteem repaired or bolstered by recognition of their professionalism, caretakers' motivation and effectiveness in contributing to the treatment plan will be diminished.

Coping with illness for the masochistic individual is likely to present more covert problems to the health care provider. The patient may present as a quietly suffering individual ready to accept punishment as if it seems to be his or her fate of destiny to do so. Discomforts will be accepted and tolerated up to a certain point, but extreme illness or severe pain will elicit genuine distress and protest. Masochistic patients' unconscious assumption is that in passively and uncomplainingly accepting a certain degree of misery or mistreatment, they will have paid their dues and thereby gain exemption from more extreme misfortunes. Their reinforcement history has emphasized dependence and subservience to others as the only safe posture, because any competent–independent or successful–adaptive modes of functioning have been punished or undermined by powerful (e.g., parental) authority figures. The result will be that these individuals will be ill-equipped to take charge of their illness management and proactively identify and problem solve difficulties in implementing their care. This will be especially true for barriers in their personal life, where some degree of assertiveness would be involved with individuals who are likely to be more domineering. Masochistic patients are also prone to self-neglect, especially where discomforts, self-inflicted or otherwise, would maintain a comfortable (or familiar) level of distress. If these characteristics emerge during an illness in a fashion persistently disruptive to that patient's care, then special attention to the patient's self-management routines may be needed to protect against sabotage.

Medical Compliance

Medical compliance for depressive patients represents an unwanted burden to those beset with pessimism, helplessness, and hopelessness. Where appetitive–addictive behavior patterns are involved, change may involve denial of presumably one of their last few pleasures. Although drinking or some consummatory response such as smoking or overeating may initially serve to allay negative affect, it can also aggravate it by increasing the depressive individual's self-condemnation for giving in to such impulses. The depressive individual may be particularly frustrating for health care professionals to work with concerning compliance issues, given their behavioral inertia and apathy. Unlike the avoidant patient who is motivated to escape disapproval, the depressive patient is reconciled to criticism and censure, which only causes him or her to wilt further into ineffectuality. Indeed, such individuals may neutralize negative responses by declaring their incompetence and worthlessness first to those seeking to motivate corrective action. Their natural pessimism may also leave them skeptical that any compliance in fact will be beneficial, because they may feel doomed that treatment will in fact be ineffective in any event. Initially medication may be needed if the patient is too apathetic and immobilized.

Depressive patients can readily become suicidal, especially if they feel life has cast them another intolerable burden. In such instances their noncompliance could take the form of self-destructive neglect that either serves to elicit caretaking and solicitation from others or that may represent a genuine desire to end it all. Ultimately, involvement of a family member and close follow-up to maintain accountability for compliance may be required to ensure satisfactory long-term maintenance of therapeutic regimens.

Requirements to do something prescribed by a medical authority figure represents a natural conflict situation for the negativistic individual, especially given the sacrifices, discomfort, or inconveniences this may entail.

Compliance also may involve establishing new habit patterns, such as regular exercise. These expectations feed into the natural tendency of negativist individuals to anticipate disappointment or frustration, or harm, and respond with resistance, obstruction, avoidance, or procrastination, even if such behavior is contrary to their rational side, which recognizes certain actions may be necessary to maintain or restore one's health. The pervasive sense of resentment these individuals feel toward external expectations and demands is reflected in their propensity to turn relationships, even unambiguously helpful ones, into conflictual encounters where disappointment or harm is anticipated. For providers it may seem as if there is no set of circumstances where the treatment regimen will not seem to be an imposition and source of difficulty and complaint for these patients. However, the goal is not to gain these patients' approval or praise for the care being provided, it is simply to get them to carry out their part of the treatment plan with minimal incident or disruption to the effort, although some is to be expected. This means not giving in to the understandable temptation to convey some hostility, frustration, or disapproval, any more than is possible. Although they will always likely interact in a complaining fashion, what may benefit the patient would be a neutral interpersonal environment in which the patient has no interpersonal grievances to react to, only the relevance of his or her own behaviors as important determinants of physical well-being.

For sadistic individuals, adjusting to the loss of health and the compromises involved in treatment may represent unacceptable vulnerabilities antithetical to their view of a harsh, cruel world of survival of the fittest. Efforts to empathize with these individuals' difficulties in making change may only elicit belligerence or contempt, reflecting their discomfort with feeling states and any focus on their sense of vulnerability. For them compliance must be seen as a means of restoring and sustaining their power that their illness denies them. The more the change or treatment required represents a direct means to that end, the better it will be tolerated and adhered to. Medications that produce prolonged fatigue, even dysphoria (e.g., interferon) that diminish these patients' sense of aggressiveness and ability to control may be poorly tolerated, especially if there is the perception that this could confer some advantage to competitors in their social environment–dominance hierarchy. Criticism from the physician for sadistic individuals may activate status–power concerns, especially if these patients feel the practitioner is lecturing, scolding, or talking down to them. Where this occurs, efforts to improve compliance will likely be derailed by a power struggle involving these patients' efforts to reexert their sense of control–autonomy. In some instances the power struggle may be overperformance of the compliance behavior itself. Communicating in a neutral, analytical, fact-oriented view the natural consequences of noncompliance may represent the best strategy.

In contrast, with masochistic patients noncompliance is likely to stem from inaction or incompetence rather than active resistance to avoid a state of perceived submission. Masochistic patients are naturally disposed to submit to authority, but they are also attuned to punishment. Criticism from a practitioner for ineffectuality may well not represent a motivating aversive event (for adherence to treatment) but an acceptable social punishment consistent with the need to feel downtrodden. Efforts to promote a sense of efficacy may be anxiety-provoking. The consequence is that the medical practitioner may become frustrated, angry over the loss of his or her authority, and then conflicted or guilty over the negative feelings the masochistic behavior will engender. Eventually caretakers may withdraw from these patients, writing them off as hopeless. If there is danger of this occurring, the best strategy may be referral for psychological–behavioral intervention. This will permit the physician to retain his or her authority role by assigning the responsibility for dealing with noncompliance issues to designated consultants, who have the expertise and skill to address these patients' self-defeating health care behaviors.

IMPACT OF DISEASE STATES ON DEPRESSIVE, NEGATIVISTIC, SADISTIC, AND MASOCHISTIC PATIENTS

As seen in the previous section, each personality type discussed in this chapter requires an understanding of the personal *and* interpersonal meaning and significance that medical management issues can have for both the patient and treating clinician. Understanding the phenomenology of the following medical conditions from the perspective of different personality disorders also will lead to varied strategies and expectations for following even standardized clinical pathways to treating different illnesses.

Somatoform, Stress-Related Conditions: Headaches, Diseases of the Digestive System

In the case of depressive individuals, a somatoform condition can represent an internalization of anger directed at oneself, in the form of physical symptoms that punish or reduce rewarding experiences for the patient. This is in keeping with the negative schema and low self-esteem of the individual. Initially, depending on the symptom presentation, it may take some time to identify the emotional etiology. Especially complaints of fatigue, gastrointestinal distress, and weakness may mimic viral (e.g., Epstein-Barr) or autoimmune conditions (e.g., chronic fatigue). If the primary care provider takes the time to explore for neurovegetative manifestations of depression (e.g., sleep disturbance, appetite loss) and prevailing mood state, the affective component may be recognizable. However, it may take time and repetitive patient contact to establish an emotional component. In addition, because the depressive condition is characterologically based and the symptoms interwoven into the patient's adjustment matrix, a rapid response to antidepressants may not be forthcoming. Persistent complaints that do not conform to medical etiology thus may require involvement of a mental health professional and a strategy of coordinated medical–psychological care. The individual with depressive personality, with deficient coping and few or no psychological resources to resist stress, is ill-equipped to overcome stress-induced symptoms when they occur. The most common behavioral treatment of these conditions places a heavy emphasis on self-management. Active, even proactive patient behavior is required, which may go beyond the capacity of individuals with depressive personalities who may be immobilized by their dysphoria, passive nature, and pervasive helplessness and hopelessness. With most depressive patients extensive behavioral homework assignments may exceed their self-monitoring capacities and limited self-discipline, at least initially. If behavioral techniques are to be used with these patients, cognitive work may have to precede programmed assignments to determine their true readiness for change and for commitment to a therapeutic program. To the extent feasible, pharmacological treatment of symptoms may be required to reduce the level of distress and increase the capacity for activation in these patients. In addition to learning stress reduction, depressive individuals will undoubtedly require some social skills training, especially in assertive techniques, to deal with the common interpersonal stresses that likely are the primary sources of their tensions. Developing the ability to say no, to represent one's interests, and to more gracefully deflect inappropriate interpersonal behavior can be esteem-enhancing and create a sense of confidence, the best antidote to anticipatory apprehension or defeat.

The natural irritability and covert hostility and resentment characteristic of individuals with negativistic personalities leave them at greater risk for psychosomatic ailments. Panic attack, mimicking a cardiac symptom or gastric motility disorder, when precipitated by signal anxiety in individuals constitutionally ill-disposed to experience or manifest hostility overtly, could fall into this category of disturbance. Although in theory these conditions should be readily treated given the psychogenic mechanisms involved, the passive–aggressive features of this personality disorder is so pervasive and nonspecific that anger-based tensions would not be consciously or interpersonally acknowledged. This lack of awareness of feelings would then perpetuate the tension-producing symptoms from which these patients might genuinely desire relief.

Another even more predictable difficulty posed by the negativistic personality type is the oppositional orientation to behaviorally oriented interventions that would represent their having to accept some responsibility for the symptom. For them to do this explicitly would involve in a sense a repudiation of their core position, that they are being unjustly mistreated by others. For this reason, it seems prudent to combine any purely behavioral approach (e.g., biofeedback, progressive muscle relaxation) with a cognitive–behavioral orientation that diplomatically addresses dysfunctional perceptions and attitudes toward others, their pervasive negative expectations, and those environmental stressors generating their tension-related condition. Although these patients by definition may be skillful at covert expressions of hostility, they may also be deficient in their capacity to behave truly assertively, expressing their rights and defending their needs in a fair, effective way that does not court retaliatory hostility or alienation from others.

Where easily recognizable stress-related symptoms in patients with sadistic personalities are identified by medical providers, they may be perplexed and put off by belligerent denial of such a possibility. This could even lead to a questioning of their physician's competence or paranoid alarm about some malicious causation (e.g., poisoning by a perceived enemy). Obviously, if there is no agreed-to diagnosis, then treatment can hardly proceed. Even if this could be overcome, behavioral techniques such as relaxation training might be difficult for a hypervigilant, aggressive person to tolerate, because by definition it teaches a state antithetical to a readiness for action, especially preemptive attack or counterattack that the sadistic individual is continually anticipating. The implication of these considerations is that considerable education would need to take place in a contemplative stage where the diagnosis is introduced. It might serve the primary care physician to emphasize the consideration of truly serious conditions any patient, the sadistic type included, would be relieved to rule out (e.g., a brain tumor in the case of headache; stomach or colon cancer in the case of gastrointestinal distress). This could precede judicious discussion of the subclinical physiological disorders that can develop if there is a state of unremitting preparedness for action. The idea would be to embrace the patient's dynamic and conceptual language in a fashion that would meaningfully but not threateningly portray the symptom and its cause, to invite consideration of possible solutions. A planning phase would also be important to carefully desensitize patients to psychologically oriented interventions. One could certainly involve medication to alleviate the physical component of the symptom (e.g., aspirin for headache pain), but also self-mastery techniques for conservation of energy and action preparation. In effect, the script most behaviorists would provide to psychosomatic patients would need to be significantly altered to accommodate such patients' need to maintain a sense of power and mastery.

In contrast, a diagnosis of "stress" for masochistic patients would fit with their sense of subjection to external noxious influences, although they might have difficulty accepting and particularly acting on the notion that they have power to alter the source of stress. Where there would be the promise of some alleviation of tolerable symptomology, this would disrupt the masochistic individual's pain–pleasure schema, creating a disincentive to get well because that would create anxiety over the anticipated and unknown misfortune that would replace the known one. This may require counseling and medication to reduce such apprehensiveness before there can be gradual institution of self-control methods. These techniques and the comfortable feelings they may induce will be unfamiliar and potentially frightening to individuals with a long reinforcement history of punishment whenever they did something to improve their circumstances.

Pain Management

Depressive individuals confronted with chronic pain would be particularly prone to problematic reactions involving complex clinical syndromes, where preexisting patterns of suffering are merged with newfound misery from chronic pain. The depressive individual is already deficient in terms of experiencing energizing and fulfilling reinforcements of life. Chronic pain will only be an additional limiting factor preventing any change. Although initially there may be caretaking and secondary gain in the early or acute phases of injury or pain, as time progresses, these individuals and their conditions may become a source of resentment and annoyance to their family members or relatives. Because of their apathy and tendency to withdraw, follow-up with these patients may be difficult. Use of analgesics, especially unsupervised, may occur as the depressive individual medicates his or her dysphoric state, sometimes with agents that only aggravate the underlying mood disturbance. For this reason, treatment of these individuals in highly controlled environments with carefully monitored reinforcements and caretaking contingent on reduction of pain behavior may be beneficial. However, the treatment staff will need to be prepared for very slow, vacillating progress from these individuals, recognizing that this is a feature of their depressive characterological makeup and not deliberately obstructionistic and confounding behavior. It will be important that the dysphoric, passive nature of these individuals' adjustment not be attributed exclusively to the depressogenic effect of their chronic pain, because this will lead to disappointment or frustration as interventions that help other patients may be transformed into more negative or convoluted treatment courses with this personality. Use of activating antidepressants and required involvement in groups with increased physical activity must be insisted on. Especially with these patients, the rule for staff working with them will be to track what they do, evaluate their behavior, rather than determine the worth of interventions from what the patient says based on their subjective analysis of its benefit. This approach may interrupt the vicious cycle of their negative expectations and evaluations. The more family can be involved in these programmatic changes and maintain a relentless posture of reinforcing appropriate levels of activity and social involvement with reduced pain behavior, the greater the likelihood that modest but beneficial gains will be maintained. Especially important will be the family's learning to ignore the complaints and negativism that will accompany these individuals' response to any intervention, while maintaining a focus on what the patient does, not says.

Chronic pain would represent a maximum provocation to negativistic patients, generating feelings of resentment and mistreatment, by fate or fortune (for the condition producing the chronic pain), by the health care establishment (for failing to keep them pain-free and restore their health), and by family and other relationships (for indifference to their suffering). During rehabilitation, complaints about being pressured to exercise or about withholding of increased analgesics, conveying a sense of disapproval or unspoken questions about the competence of the providers, can be anticipated. As a result, providers could give up, which could undermine the recovery or process of restoration of functioning (e.g., the patient is left with a permanently reduced range of motion). Once the patient's physical rehabilitation reaches a plateau with no real prospect of improvement and the limitations in activity are determined, future medical care becomes relatively static and necessarily oriented to conservative, nonaddictive approaches to pain management. This represents a shift in emphasis from things being done for the patient to the patient having to take the initiative for self-management and maintenance of whatever chronic pain-coping strategies he or she has been able to develop. In the case of individuals with negativistic personality, it is clear that their internal psychic organization is so competitive and contradictory that their capacity for coping with a difficult situation would be minimal. The predictable response from such patients would be to continue to make demands and have expectations for relief from their caretakers, whose role would then shift to that of a withholding orientation (e.g., pain medications). Some relief in the form of antidepressants or other psychotropic medications may be available rather than the narcotics typically administered by the surgeons that may have been responsible for the care up to that point. Certainly involvement in a chronic pain program would be indicated if that has not taken place. Professionals in that context would also need to be aware of these patients' baseline personality characteristics and their propensity for procrastination, contrariness, and resentful contemptuousness toward those who disappoint them. Attention should also be paid to negativistic patient interactions with other patients, whose morale is at risk from the negativistic individual's skeptical, cynical, orientation.

Although sadistic individuals' combative orientation and heightened arousal when in an attack mode doubtlessly protects them from transient acute pain, intractable pain represents a different matter. Where threats of physical harm to spouse, children, or weaker members of the sadistic individual's social sphere were once credible, injury and chronic pain will eliminate or reduce the potential for these forms of intimidation. A sense of vulnerability may create a chronic tension and apprehension that complicates efforts to maintain a more relaxed state conducive to effective pain management. For some in the sadistic patient's social environment, their lives may ease if they are less vulnerable to being bullied (e.g., a maturing teenage son who can physically hold his own). However, others who remain lower in the dominance–submission hierarchy may be subject to increased mistreatment because of the greater irritation of the chronic pain patient who transfers his or her aggression to those available targets. There may also be more exposure to these potential victims (e.g., nonworking spouse, a child) when the sadistic patient is disabled and homebound. Displacement of intimidating, aggressive behavior as a vehicle driver may also occur, raising the risk of mishap to these patients and those innocents who may cross their paths. When physical power is no longer a credible threat, alternative, even more dangerous means of coercion (e.g., firearms) may come into play. In addition, the potential for misusing analgesic agents or other treatments (e.g., steroids) could have an amplifying and disinhibiting effect on emotional lability. In a chronic pain program with other patient members, the sadistic patient could also transfer his or her personality style to this environment, where competitive, bullying, and aggressive behavior and a mean-spirited, callous orientation would be highly disruptive and maladaptive. The need by such individuals to dominate others through aggressive behavior would also extend to demanding, intimidating interactions with lower status staff. Unless this pattern were addressed by a unified team approach, supported by firm limit-setting, even confrontation by the physician authority figure, the treatment milieu could be critically affected. Some such patients must ultimately be asked to leave these programs.

Chronic pain for masochistic patients would fit with their general world view that life is to be endured rather than enjoyed. The effect of their illness on their psychosocial environment would initially be to disarm others from mistreating them and to magnify their role as martyr. This and their persisting wretchedness, combined with ineffectuality and outright sabotage of intervention efforts, could erode the enthusiasm of health care professionals. If in formal programs, other patients might also experience diminished enthusiasm for rehabilitation when exposed to others that seem to embrace suffering. Recognizing that their behavior is perversely self-protective may permit maintenance of a more charitable attitude toward these patients, who will require a special strategy of conservative goal setting to facilitate assimilation of discrete but modest progress within the comfort tolerance they display.

Diabetes

If one expects the worst to occur from a disease process (e.g., retinal deterioration, kidney failure, vascular disease), the incentive for forestalling it lessens. The depressive individuals' negative schemas must be addressed, especially those that perpetuate a perspective of unremitting unhappiness and misfortune. Such precontemplative assumptions and views must be modified to facilitate appropriate nondepressive contemplative activity, in advance of the planning stage, wherein education and treatment regimen information are provided. From a motivational standpoint, if private expectations concerning a disease process and the prospects of self-management are negative, it would be contrary to human nature for one to then energetically reorganize his or her eating, exercise, and self-care habits if that were only an exercise in futility. The tenacity of depressogenic thought and mood in these individuals will make it important for an extended action period of training and consolidation of critical self-maintenance behaviors, so that they may become habitual in nature. In turn, this will make them less likely to be disrupted by transitory events that typically derail depressive individuals, overwhelming their fragile coping. If the dietary changes and blood sugar self-monitoring can become well-established, integrated into patients' daily routines and family patterns, then the maintenance stage can be more secure. Especially with depressive personalities the concept of self-management must be tempered with the reality that they will need as much support as can be made available to them.

For negativistic individuals, diabetes may represent a re-creation on a physical basis of many aspects of their basic prototypical interpersonal paradigm, where minor efforts at autonomy (e.g., self-indulgence) are punished, in this case, with physical sickness. It should not be surprising that confrontation with a diagnosis, implying a lifelong battle to conform to the constraints of their metabolic aberration, would tend to activate self-perpetuating, destructive behavior. When the practitioner assumes or conveys a sense of responsibility for introducing the concepts of self-care and management with these patients, this will invite a long sequence of conflictual interactions, conducive to an antagonistic relationship over the noncompliance that inevitably follows. For negativistic individuals, it is mistrust and opposition to the relationships that activate their problematic behavior. This of course can take the form of resistance to expectations and even partially internalized and incompletely adopted demands from an authority figure. To the extent possible it will be important to remove the medical practitioners as unwanted elements in these dynamics, where they can play more of an observer role in the struggles these patients have with their illness. An extended period of contemplation may be required for these individuals when first diagnosed to identify dysfunctional attitudes, resistances, and begin to work through contrary feelings and oppositional tendencies. The goal should not be to take care of all these problems before moving to the planning and action phase but to establish those as issues for ongoing dialogue as these patients struggle to implement the changes imposed by their illness.

The immediate and long-range health threats posed by diabetes would likely be a particularly frustrating burden to the power-oriented sadistic individual, given the limitations and restrictions the disease places on an individual. Managing the disease also creates an interpersonal context in which there is a risk of power struggle with the health care provider. The wise practitioner will try to manage the potentially difficult interpersonal aspects of these inevitable interactions by maintaining an interpersonally neutral and fact-oriented posture. This might start with introducing a written scenario of the disease course of diabetes, a flow chart of treatment requirements given certain stages of the illness, and a time frame. Included in this would be what these patients can do to help their condition, the most obvious being smoking cessation, reduced alcohol consumption, weight reduction, and strict dietary controls. This review of "what might happen" places the physician in the role of counselor–educator–advisor rather than authority figure with the patient. If there are problems or unwanted progression of the disease, the physician can reference the written materials and previous forecasts that the patient may have had some time to digest and anticipate, along with the treatment–self-management responses to such events. This process should ideally be initiated during the contemplation phase of change following diagnosis of the disease.

The physician will encounter no resistance in being authoritative or acting authoritatively with masochistic patients, but it may turn out to be a frustrating experience when behavior change is not forthcoming. Anger will be a natural consequence, but this will only feed into masochistic patients' natural proclivity to fall into a martyred, abused role. The physician in turn will be confounded and left with unresolved feelings of resentment and the discomfort that induces. Because masochistic patients are used to having things done to them, involvement of others in their medical management who serve as agents of the physician can be helpful. This would include spouses, significant others, parents, all individuals who are present during much of the patient's daily lives and who can influence behavior change, monitor behavior, and create barriers to unhealthy behaviors. Although this strategy will not transform these patients into responsible, proactive problem-solving managers of their own health, it would substantially reduce those occasions where their passivity, ineptitude, or need to suffer some discomfort could occur, undermining their disease management. Whereas educational process-oriented group approaches would likely be unpalatable to sadistic individuals, they could prove beneficial to their masochistic counterparts by modeling healthy behavior and exposing their self-destructive behavior patterns that could facilitate examination and change of their maladaptive behavior, at least in this important context.

Neurological Diseases: Epilepsy, Multiple Schlerosis, Parkinson's Disease

For the depressive individual, epilepsy may provide some opportunity to elicit caretaking, sympathy, and alleviation of some responsibilities, but it also represents a paradigm of helplessness, given the potentially unpredictable nature of the condition. Memory and other cognitive impairment, often a concomitant of this condition, can be aggravated by depression and add to these patients' sense of ineffectiveness, in turn undermining medication compliance. Multiple sclerosis with its fluctuating course and variegated symptoms can also represent a learned helplessness paradigm for patients who already feel betrayed by their interpersonal and physical misfortunes. As noted previously, organic personality changes can either produce a more labile, impulsive adjustment or increase the passivity and lack of initiative associated with demyelinization in the frontal lobes. Parkinson's disease, a subcortical degenerative disorder, begins as a movement disorder and typically progresses to produce cognitive slowing and depression, a combination that can only aggravate the depressive disorder state. Conversely, the depressive personality pattern can present with symptoms of apathy and dysphoria, mimicking some of the behavioral features of Parkinson's, confounding monitoring of progression of the neurological condition. Careful observation of the patient's interpersonal style, however, should reveal differences. In the Parkinson's patient, depression will be evident in a mood disturbance and lack of initiative. These features will be present in the personality disorder pattern, but there will be additional features of pessimism, worthlessness, ineffective coping, and a self-denigrating orientation that will become evident with extended interaction.

Epilepsy can represent an additional reason for justify negativistic patients' sense of embitterment, to maintain their aggrieved posture, and serve as a basis for not living up to others' expectations or personal responsibilities. The vulnerability from unpredictable episodes of loss of control and the cognitive impairment that can be a consequence of poorly controlled seizures would serve as a special source of discontent for individuals predisposed to such feelings. Where their condition is not well controlled, this may be a source of resentment toward the neurologist treating them. Given that emotional and physical influences do alter seizure thresholds and can cause them, this can serve as a coercive weapon to justify many expressions of their psychopathology. Difficulties in discerning neurological causation from fluctuations in motivation and emotional state can provide opportunities for negativistic patients with multiple sclerosis to justify many forms of behavior with impunity. With Parkinson's disease, when the patients are elderly and widowed, with children not intimately involved in their lives, their caustic, complaining, and obstructionistic behavior can cause them difficulty at their care setting and with new practitioners who may not know their baseline mode of interpersonal interaction.

Epilepsy for the sadistic patient would represent a perceived vulnerability and potential opportunity for others to gain advantage during periods of debilitation. Provided their seizures were controlled, it would not necessarily pose a major impediment to their ordinary adjustment. However, their propensity to emotional arousal and uncontrolled outbursts could affect the seizure threshold, making control more difficult. In addition, persistent or prolonged seizures could cause organic personality changes, producing even more disinhibited, aggressive behavior and emotional arousal, in turn contributing to a potentially degenerative vicious cycle. Multiple sclerosis will represent an unpredictable threat to these individuals, where the waxing and waning and progressive nature of this neurological condition will necessarily force adjustments given the dependence on others this condition ultimately imposes. The problem is whether patients' behavior and interpersonal style that produces either alienation or intimidation will undermine the availability of such support or indeed embolden those who have been oppressed to exhibit counteraggression when their condition deteriorates. The same considerations apply to Parkinson's disease, where movement is restricted, affect blunted, and cognitive decline are inevitable consequences of the disease process.

For masochistic individuals, seizures can represent an aspect of their suffering to elicit sympathy and neutralize others from more punitive behavior, to the extent that it could aggravate their neurological condition. Their tendency for self-neglect could also contribute to poor medication monitoring and more complicated medical management. Similarly, multiple sclerosis and Parkinson's disease for masochistic individuals can generate sufficient but not unbearable discomfort to satisfy their need for suffering and induce guilt and inhibition of aggression in others, thereby gaining some indirect benefit from this illness.

Cardiac Disease

Many antihypertensive medications have depressive side effects, and with patients with depressive personalities, substitutes should be considered or these medications should be used with careful assessment for this side effect. Self-monitoring for blood pressure requires initiative and attentiveness, qualities lacking in brooding, preoccupied, passive, depressive patients. The absence of obvious symptoms associated with blood pressure changes thus leaves individuals with depressive personalities vulnerable to poor control or dangerous variation in blood pressure levels. Where this is a significant risk, extra monitoring may be the only option, either through increased health services use, enlistment of family members, or a combination of both. Depressed mood has long been implicated as a risk factor for recovery in heart disease (Bennett & Carroll, 1997) as well as perhaps a biological consequence of the physical and psychological shock of heart attack or bypass surgery. Although acute physical illness can briefly disrupt depressogenic behavior patterns and even stimulate rudimentary coping efforts, chronic ill health only reinforces depressive patients' expectations that pain and diminishment will always find them in life. The added burden of chronic heart disease could intensify their dysthymia into a truly disabling and health-threatening depression.

Post-heart attack education for occlusive artery disease management will need to recognize that these individuals' mood states may interfere with effective encoding and consolidation of new information necessary to undertake dietary and lifestyle change requirements. Rehabilitation from heart attack, bypass surgery, or stroke may require a level of activity and energy difficult for these individuals. Vigorous rehabilitation efforts may be beneficial to postmyocardial infarction or recovering bypass patients experiencing reactive depressions by activating and energizing them. With depressive individuals following myocardial infarction, stroke, or bypass, the health care team in contrast will be undoubtedly dealing with a complex clinical syndrome where characterological patterns are intermixed with the reactive depression to the illness. Mistaking their characterological mode of functioning for transient, illness-related depression may lead to frustration and misplaced expectations. The patient then may be viewed as volitionally noncompliant and dismissed as uncooperative, without recognizing that there are potentially treatable aspects to their problematic adjustment to their cardiac illness with appropriate mental health referral. In addition, for the depressive individual, recovery from heart disease may promise a loss of secondary gains (caretaking) and the return of unwanted, threatening demands as the endpoint of getting well. For change to be negotiable the negative incentives of improvement or recovery must be recognized in a nonjudgmental fashion, in the context of the depressive individual's unhappy history of losses and disappointments that has produced maladaptive behavior patterns. Otherwise, these individuals will find themselves regarded in a pejorative fashion, which only reinforces their lack of self-worth and polarizes their estrangement from a care system whose mission is to heal, not condemn.

The physical debilitation and consequent dependence on others imposed by heart disease can have a greater demoralizing effect on negativistic patients, who feel chronically beset and imposed on by any expectations or constraints, especially at times of misfortune. Dietary and lifestyle changes, medications with negative side effects, and invasive procedures (e.g., catheterization), especially surgery, are likely to elicit protest and bitter invective. The timing of interventions is an important consideration. If the patient views what is offered as a means by which to restore his or her health or sense of control, it may be adopted more readily. The naturally irascible, dissatisfied, and distressed state of mind and mood of these individuals will also generate negative psychophysiological environments for cardiovascular functioning, placing these individuals at continuing risk for psychological influences adversely affecting their health. To the extent that some antihypertensives can have depressogenic effects, it is important to carefully monitor changes in these patients' mood state (from their characteristic negative state) for medication-induced aggravation of dysfunctional patterns. Even though hypertension, heart attack, or occlusive artery disease represents in a sense an individual's battle against his or her own bodily frailties, negativistic patients may transform this into more familiar, prototypical antagonistic interpersonal (self–other) encounters, typically in such a fashion as to draw caretakers into these conflicts. As long as such processes can be recognized by the provider, this can afford some opportunities for recasting the basic dilemma of these patients—that their health problem is not interpersonal but intrapersonal. If successful in maintaining this distinction, then the provider can interact in a more supportive, advocative role rather than in the adversarial position assigned by the negativistic patient.

Blood pressure medicine side effects may be pertinent to compliance for sadistic patients if their sense of aggressiveness is muted by the drug, which could make them feel weak. This would be especially true if there were depressive effects with the medication. Nonuse of antihypertensives in these individuals could be potentially hazardous given their basic temperamental aggressiveness and volatility, which would likely exacerbate any genetic predisposition to respond to stress and challenge with blood pressure elevation. Selection of medications that minimize this effect are important to facilitating compliance. Once out of danger, following heart attack a patient with sadistic characteristics would be likely to attempt to impose his or her will on the care team in conspicuous displays of forceful interpersonal behavior. Channeling some of these patients' resurgent aggressivity into appropriate physical rehabilitation activity may be helpful, although assurance of physiological monitoring may be important to allay fears that exertion could precipitate another attack. Group education experiences, especially those that are feeling-oriented rather than problem-focused, could prove provocative to the sadistic individual, whose contempt for sentimentalities could unnerve the discussion leaders and detract from the potential benefit of self-disclosure by other members.

With masochistic patients, antihypertensives with depressant effects could increase passivity and apathy about self-management issues (e.g., monitoring their blood pressure, regulating salt intake, etc.). Their subsequent passivity and seeming apathy during rehabilitation efforts might be construed as a depressive reaction. Although they may be differentially at risk for affective disturbance given their dynamics, the anticipation of improvement after mood elevators are introduced may be followed by consternation on the part of the care team when it is undermined. On the other hand, group experiences for the masochistic patient could model healthy behavior patterns, help expose their self-defeating tendencies in a supportive context so as to elicit mobilizing rather than sabotaging behavior.

Cancer

Although depressive individuals may feel doomed to enduring life's misfortunes, their broodings will most likely center around past painful experiences generally of a social nature, rejection or loss, defeat in achievement strivings, and anticipations of disappointment or future failure. Cancer may represent an unexpected danger of loss and suffering. One likely result will be an intensification of helplessness, despair, and behavior that will serve to enlist the caretaking of others and alleviate unwanted responsibilities. These will become issues that will affect the behavior of these patients and their care following the acute phase of the illness. Concerning measures to detect cancer early, it would be expected that any initiative would come from the patient's doctors or family. Simply providing pamphlets concerning periodic screening intervals and signs and symptoms to observe will hardly ensure that these goals will actually be accomplished proactively. For these preventive behaviors to have any likelihood of being incorporated by this personality subtype, they would need to be initially part of the context of caretaking by the health care providers. Symptom screening would then represent an opportunity to connect with the clinic, where patients report in and interact in a fashion to elicit a supportive, nurturing response. Knowledgeable providers who maintain reminder card lists could note the importance of this type of reinforcement so that it is emphasized in follow-up care activities. The acute phases of treatment will predictably overwhelm depressive patients' negligible coping skills, and this will be a time for family or providers to mobilize all available support and resources on behalf of these individuals. If chemotherapy is used in treatment, consideration should be given if depression or cognitive impairment is a side effect, so that these discomforts can be addressed in advance and countered to the extent possible.

Given their inherent pain-avoidant orientation, severe physical discomfort should be addressed aggressively, to minimize its predictable effect of demoralization and despair on individuals so vulnerable in this respect. Support groups, especially those involving family members, may be particularly helpful for the acute phase. For the long-term, the group leaders may have to be sensitized to these patient's depressive interpersonal style and the probable negative effect on others. Specifically, their vulnerable, morbid, pessimistic orientation may have an undermining influence on other patients' coping or may compete for available attention and nurturance from leaders to be cumulatively alienating to other members. Even professional staff may feel some disgust or resentment at these individuals' displays of helplessness and pity-seeking contrasted with the more admirable coping of their more psychologically sound fellow patients.

Negativistic patients would not be expected to be reliable concerning early-risk detection of cancer. For individuals with family histories placing them at risk for the disease, their distractions of petty grievances and the consequences of their contentious behavior would likely interfere with developing a consistent pattern of self-examination—early detection measures, such as for skin changes or lumps. Recognizing early internal symptoms (e.g., changes in bowel habits, digestive functioning) might be delayed because of their propensity to experience so many psychosomatic manifestations of the stress they generate for themselves. In addition, their pessimistic anticipation that consultation with a specialist would lead to bad news would likely also increase their tendency to procrastinate concerning personal preservation responsibilities to self and family.

When confronted with a diagnosis of cancer, negativistic patients, contradictory intrapsychic mechanisms would give them virtually no capacity for coping and containing the stress they would experience. Initially there may be a state of shock or period of depression and grieving (the loss of health), but then reversion to the pattern of erratic, provocative, complaining behavior could be expected. Judicious preemptive use of tranquilizers or analgesics would be worthwhile to reduce any discomfort and alarm that these patients would predictably experience. Although support groups are potentially helpful to any patient afflicted with cancer, negativistic patients are more likely to be experienced as interpersonally toxic to the efforts to generate positive expectations and constructive coping in a group context. Educationally oriented or problem-focused sessions may elicit little damage to a group environment, but involving negativistic patients in sessions emphasizing emotion-focused coping could be risky for other group members, especially if they are fragile to begin with. Rather, if there are family members who might buffer or mediate stresses these patients are experiencing, preferential use of known resources may produce better results, at the same time protecting others in need of morale-bolstering.

Sadistic patients' propensity to gain dominance and control over others would suggest that they are not likely to be particularly vigilant over their physical health. Consideration of preventive–detection measures would more likely come from individuals close to them, physicians aware of special (family history) risk factors, or even their medical plans if they required employer-sponsored mandatory well-visit schedules for annual physicals. Cancer for these individuals would represent an ironic turnabout, one's own body inflicting pain on one disposed to derive pleasure from causing suffering in others. This could influence the medical decision making of these individuals, which will be based on distorted beliefs that health providers may harbor malice toward them and wish them pain and continued debilitation. Their self-image, based on a tough-minded, hard-nosed philosophy that primes them to counterattack in anticipation that others will exploit any disadvantage or weakness, is an adaptation best suited for a wartime context, not a caretaking environment that would be viewed with mistrust and even contempt. To accept such assistance would be a sign of weakness, inviting others to take advantage. Because caretakers tend to be sensitive individuals who find gratification in alleviating suffering, it would be stressful to be confronted with belligerent, contemptuous rejection of their good will. Although educationally focused, task-oriented meetings where didactic approaches are used could be beneficial, the sadistic individual's tendency to dominate interaction might be disruptive even in that situation. Where this occurs, then strategic removal of those individuals from those contexts and, when appropriate, use of individual meetings would be indicated.

Masochistic patients might be considered unlikely to exercise prudence in health prevention efforts because their bent is to court discomfort and suffering in keeping with their inverted pleasure–pain polarity. External demands and structured appointments might generate timely contact with physicians, but their tendency for self-neglect and passivity would not be conducive to developing initiative in pursuing self-examination–early detection measures. Although disposed to experience discomfort as a seeming prerequisite for a sense of safety from greater harm, cancer doubtless exceeds this requirement for masochistic patients. Their orientation to the martyr role would tend to make them superficially deferential and uncomplaining and less inclined to complain of pain or seek relief from it. Although they might view this new misfortune of a potentially terminal physical disease as one more instance of their unworthiness, the purely physical nature of the anguish could represent a different, more intense form of suffering that would produce depression in need of pharmacological treatment. Their typical presentation of wretchedness, however, might mask the manifestations of depression, which would alert practitioners to initiate pharmacological and psychological care measures. Support groups could be helpful in countering some of the tendencies of masochistic patients by making them more visible and creating more opportunities for gentle confrontation where the behavior interferes with potentially effective treatment. In clearly terminal cases, the issue would be one of reducing unnecessary suffering (with appropriate introduction of analgesics) that their martyr-prone orientation might incur.

CONCLUSION

By summarizing these final personality types together in this one chapter, it is possible to show how these adjustment patterns are manifested differently in the behavioral medicine context. The depressive patient's incompetent, helpless coping style and the masochistic patient's self-effacing posture is in marked contrast to the aversive, caustic, complaining posture of the negativistic patient and threatening–punitive orientation of the sadistic patient. Under the stress of illness, these individuals will respond differently. Depressive and masochistic individuals will coerce caretaking but over time insidiously build up resentment from providers frustrated at either their inability to take charge of their illness management or seemingly even sabotage their care, their wretched interpersonal presentation inhibiting direct expression of disapproval or rejection. In contrast, the negativistic and sadistic individuals will present as contentious during protracted illness management, the former as a complaining, bitter, and aggrieved individual whose discontent is a basis for poor cooperation and complaining, negativistic manner. The latter will attempt to establish dominance and intimidation wherever possible, if even over subordinates of the primary provider, generating power struggles and ill-will disruptive to the care process.

Recognizing these different personality types will vary as a function of their interpersonal style. Naturally, the abrasive individuals will be more apparent given their more obvious need to control the interaction. The depressive and masochistic individuals will be less visible given their more obsequious and accommodating manner of interacting. Their deficiencies in health care behavior will be subtle and reflected by errors of omission, inappropriate decision making, and inability to effect new health care behaviors. The negativistic and sadistic patients will seem more oppositional and contentious, even mistrustful in their receiving medical treatment recommendations and guidance, whereas the depressive and masochistic patients will uncritically and unquestioningly show passive acceptance but then inability to fulfill their responsibilities in treatment without extensive support. Resource use may tend to be excessive for the more needy types (depressive and masochistic patients), whereas negativistic and sadistic patients may tend to misuse health care in the sense of disrupting services or making them less efficient.

All of these personality types may experience difficulty with preventive health behaviors. The depressive and masochistic patients will exhibit deficiencies in their ability to mobilize themselves and make change, especially where interpersonal assertion is necessary. The negativistic and sadistic patients will show more oppositional and antagonistic behavior, either because of their pessimistic anticipation of mistreatment or need never to be in an acquiescing role. Disease diagnosis may be delayed by their own particular personality-generated distractions. Their illness representations will be similarly distorted or incomplete, contaminated by pessimistic assumptions or fears that harm is forthcoming given their weakened state. Differences in management strategy will also be dictated by those personality types. For example, where a kind orientation will be essential to engage a depressive patient in treatment, such behavior will be viewed as a sign of weakness and opportunity for exploitation by a sadistic individual.

13

FUTURE DIRECTIONS

The preceding chapters represent a preliminary effort to relate the features of personality disorders to the setting of behavioral medicine. This can be considered an extension of Millon's pioneering work matching different mental health treatment modalities to specific patient types (Millon, 1999). The goal of applying this approach to behavioral–medical health care is to more systematically consider both the different adjustment challenges posed by medical conditions on patients with different personality characteristics and reciprocally the challenges these different patients pose for their health care providers. Although to health economists it might seem that this only introduces unwanted complexity to the consideration of patient management and clinical pathways for well-known medical conditions, experienced health care practitioners recognize that these patients and the problems they pose for treatment paradigms are real. Just as better understanding of a disease process should result in better treatment, so should a greater understanding of patient characteristics lead to improved overall health care delivery. The difficulty these individuals pose is not a theoretical one or a matter of inconvenience to providers. The costs a few difficult patients may incur represents a real threat to all who rely on finite health care resources.

In the current health care environment, providers are confronted with limited financial resources to provide services. This makes it even more important to get it right, which is often defined in dollar cost per disease, excluding any consideration of the afflicted host. Personality disordered patients will represent outlier cases, unwanted by insurance plans. They will especially constitute an enemy to any capitated plan. Conscientious providers will become frustrated and demoralized over the barriers to good health care delivery posed by these patients' psychopathology.

In the traditional medical model, the physician is viewed as the all-knowing authority who dispenses care to be followed exactly by a grateful patient. With health care costs skyrocketing, the notion of patient responsibility has emerged, as well as monitoring of provider behavior in managed care plans. Documentation that health care is appropriately being administered is an ongoing focus of these efforts. Less attention has been paid to patient response to interventions. This is the other half of the health economics equation. As yet most health care plans are segmented into major medical, or physical problems, and mental health issues, typically administered by separate management organizations devoted only to mental health care. Separately funded, there is no incentive for representatives of the major medical plans dealing with medical diagnoses to be concerned about the behavioral component in care. To address patient personality needs would only be adding front-end costs that would look bad to auditors, even if it might result in dramatically reduced final expenditures for given conditions.

Even when well, most individuals experience some degree of aversion or dread visiting a health care practitioner over the implicit fear that something might be discovered that is wrong and over the prospect of some degree of suffering or sacrifice. In uncomplicated medical care the patient and practitioner will have a generally shared focus on disease diagnosis, treatment, and the necessary adjustments required for the care plan to be successful. Apart from depression, anxiety, and other Axis I conditions that complicate medical problems or develop from them, personality disorders add a distinct interpersonal aspect that can disrupt health care. These can be considered in terms of the specific agendas different patients will bring to the health care setting. Table 13.1 provides a rough outline of the different features of the primary disorder types discussed in this volume. It should not be difficult to consider how these would complicate providing effective and efficient care, especially factoring in variations in provider personality characteristics that might clash with the patient agendas.

Caring for these individuals effectively will require recognition of their agendas and their importance to the patient. This will involve tolerantly addressing the dysfunctional interaction patterns identified and contentious behaviors as they occur and establishing an interaction history with the patient. This can provide reference points where these patients can be gently or firmly reminded of their personality-driven excesses so that these can be better countered in future medical care crises. The alternative is often dismay and then outrage by the provider that his or her earnest efforts to cure are being disrupted or sabotaged. Interpersonal style strategies for dealing with different patient types are suggested in the right-hand column of Table 13.1.

If care is to be administered efficiently and rationally, primary care providers will have to pay more attention to their patient characteristics. Such patient profiling could occur in the natural course of care provided. Although understanding of the particular dynamics of the patient does not predispose that behavior change can be effected, it does suggest that there may be certain kinds of management strategies and the potential for some influence on the providers' part. Depending on the personality type, this influence may take the form of engaging the patient in a fashion that always promotes trust but does not necessarily produce greater intimacy that for some types would be threatening (e.g., paranoid, schizoid, antisocial, schizotypal), and for others would create boundary problems (e.g., borderline, dependent). In addition, if practitioners can come to view aberrant patient behavior as potential opportunities to provide better care then the annoying nature of patient distortions and his or her failure to understand and incorporate adequately presented details concerning the illness, such episodes can provide key insights into the patient's personological barriers to effective self-management. As such, these observations can be viewed as important clinical information rather than aggravating manifestations of stupidity, noncompliance, or resistance, views that undermine constructive communication efforts.

This rationale presupposes that there is opportunity for a patient–provider relationship to develop. Unfortunately, the danger in current health care delivery is that patients may cycle through different insurance plans and always remain new to their primary care providers, and they will be most prone in those circumstances, especially if stressed and insecure, to revert to their basic agendas. Without continuity of care there will be no opportunity to establish a personal relationship where some mutual understanding and trust can be developed on which a less convoluted care plan can unfold. Especially where there are significant long-term illness and management issues, the relationship between patient and health care provider will be paramount for establishing appropriate illness or representations, rational medical decision making, and optimal adherence to treatment regimens. Where medical service is necessarily rationed, as in the case of organ transplant, patient characteristics may play a significant role. If vulnerability to stress or noncompliance with life-preserving posttransplant regimens is related (as suggested by Chacko & Harper, 2000; Chacko, Harper, Gotto, & Young, 1996), then there is good reason to be concerned about this phenomena. Better understanding of patient characteristics from an ethical standpoint should result in patient behavior and patient choices (e.g., to continue smoking or drinking when confronted with a need for

TABLE 13.1
Personality Type Agendas

Personality type (cluster)	Primary agenda	Interpersonal impact	Defensive style	Management approach
Schizoid (A)	Maintain distance, preserve inner world	Aloof, self-absorbed, unresponsive	Withdrawal, avoidance	Reserved but cordial, businesslike, manner, avoid intense emotions
Paranoid (A)	Preservation of superiority, autonomy	Guarded, suspicious, mistrustful	Projection of hostility onto others	Respectful, factual, focused on self-preservation issues
Schizotypal (A)	Fending off disorganization, especially from confusing social experiences	Peculiar, odd, disjointed	Undoing, fragmenting	Reserved, tracking, refocusing errant thought, social feedback, guidance
Histrionic (B)	Interpersonal attention, stimulation	Seductive, flighty, socially reactive, suggestible	Denial/repression, dissociation	Patient but focused, redirecting to treatment goals
Narcissistic (B)	Self-inflation, esteem-enhancement	Arrogant, presumptive, entitled	Rationalization, self-deception to protect fragile self-esteem	Professional, authoritative, no-nonsense but tolerant manner
Antisocial (B)	Self-aggrandizement, exploitation, maintaining independence	Charming, dishonest, manipulative, impulsive	Projection of blame	Authoritative, confrontive manner, conveying awareness of their motives
Borderline (B)	Regulation of intimacy, dependency conflicts	Unstable, impulsive, erratic, volatile	Splitting, regression to primitive defenses	Parental patience, perseverance, boundary-setting

322   PERSONALITY-GUIDED THERAPY IN BEHAVIORAL MEDICINE

Dependent (C)	Security support, care from powerful other	Admiring, accommodating but clinging, incompetent	Introjection of strong relationship figure	Promote, insist on gradually increased self-reliance with guaranteed contact
Avoidant (C)	Avoidance from rejection, disapproval, humiliation	Timid, interpersonally inadequate, distracted	Escape, avoidance behavior	Warm, engaging, uncritical, reassuring
Compulsive (C)	Rule-abiding, conforming to gain approval from authority, safety-seeking	Constricted, rigid, rule-bound, authority-sensitive	Reaction formation, conversion of anger into caretaking	Relaxed, reassuring manner, encouraging flexibity, self-indulgence

lung, liver, or heart transplant) being the primary determinant of continuing life and receiving the greatest potential benefit from a scarce resource.

The focus of this book has necessarily been on *disorders* of personality. By definition these are extreme variations of personality types that meet a threshold level of pathology that meet distinct diagnostic criteria. However, it is also evident to clinicians that occult or subclinical manifestations of these personality types can create problems as well in patients with no psychiatric history and seemingly reasonable pre-illness adjustment histories. Complicated treatment regimens with major adjustment requirements will tax even psychologically healthy patients. Potentially problematic trait characteristics may not become exposed or maladaptive until there is the stress of a serious health problem, at which time their care and medical outcome may become more problematic. Denial in some situations may be healthy and maladaptive in others, just as information-seeking and a need for control can result in greater distress and disrupted functioning.

Although most of the patients with Cluster B type personalities will generally be discernible given their rather visible interactive style and interpersonal presence, the other types may be more difficult to recognize. Where serious medical procedures with long-range medical consequences are being entertained (e.g., back surgery), prior knowledge of patient personality characteristics, especially as they may affect outcome, can represent information crucial to cost-efficient medical decision making and care planning. The Millon Behavioral Health Inventory (MBHI; Millon, Green, & Meagher, 1982; see also Everly & Newman, 1997) and its current successor, the Millon Behavioral Medicine Diagnostic (Antoni et al., 1997) are excellent instruments for this purpose, thoroughly discussed in the references cited. Their particular value is in maintaining the scope of Millon's personality types while providing dimensional analysis to permit useful descriptions of probable adjustment patterns in relation to health care problems (e.g., chronic pain, medical compliance, response to chronic illness). Individuals with no psychiatric history can be meaningfully described for those extreme situations where they can become dysfunctional in coping with their illness. Chacko et al. (1996) found that although *DSM–IV* diagnoses failed to predict heart transplant outcome, the MBHI successfully predicted survival. In addition, it showed good correspondence with threshold *DSM–IV* psychiatric diagnoses (Harper et al., 1998), and a variety of scale measures were found to correlate with other parameters of treatment outcome (Harper et al., 1998b). There are thus readily available means to identify individuals who may be at varying risk for problematic health outcomes. Where expensive medical interventions are planned, it may be a worthwhile investment to screen patients and identify those at risk for difficult treatment courses.

It is hoped that applying this knowledge of personality to behavioral health care will improve delivery of services, particularly from the standpoint of effective use of finite resources. This does not necessarily mean optimal care for each individual, especially patients with personality disorders. These are individuals who are already suffering from the consequences of their maladjustment, who are then confronted with physical discomfort and diminishment. In the health care arena both forms of suffering will likely be presented to the health care provider confounded with each other. Practitioners should be on guard not to be superhuman but realistic and philosophical in what they can accomplish. One should not expect a perfect outcome with a personality disordered patient even if the physical condition is successfully treated. Obviously, there is a need for much conceptual refinement to the ideas presented, as well as a great deal of empirical work to justify to health care financiers a different model of health care delivery than our present managed care environment permits. A starting point, however, is heightened consciousness about the characterological influences and determinants of health care delivery. If this effort serves this purpose in some measure, then it will have represented a worthwhile endeavor.

REFERENCES

Abramson, L. Y., Seligman, M. E. P., & Teasdale, J. D. (1978). Learned helplessness in humans: Critique and reformulation. *Journal of Abnormal Psychology, 87,* 49–74.

Adler, J., & Kalb, C. (2000). An American epidemic: Diabetes. *Newsweek, September 4,* 40–47.

Ajzen, I. (1985). From intention to actions: A theory of planned behavior. In J. Kuhl & J. Beckman (Eds.), *Action-control: From cognition to behavior* (pp. 11–39). Heidelberg: Springer.

Ajzen, I. (1988). *Attitudes, personality and behavior.* Chicago: Dorsey Press.

Akiskal, H. S. (1981). Subaffective disorders: Dysthymic, cyclothymic, and bipolar II disorders in the "borderline" realm. *Psychiatric Clinics of North America, 4,* 25–46.

Akiskal, H. S. (1983). Dyythmic disorder: Psychopathology of proposed chronic depressive subtypes. *American Journal of Psychiatry, 140,* 11–20.

Alexander, F. G. (1930). Emotional factors in essential hypertension: Presentation of a tentative hypothesis. *Psychosomatic Medicine, 1,* 175–179.

American Psychiatric Association. (1987). *Diagnostic and statistical manual of mental disorders* (3rd ed. revised). Washington, DC: Author.

American Psychiatric Association. (1994). *Diagnostic and statistical manual of mental disorders* (4th ed.). Washington, DC: Author.

Andersen, B. L. (1992). Psychological interventions for cancer patients to enhance the quality of life. *Journal of Consulting and Clinical Psychology, 60,* 552–568.

Andersen, B. L., Cacioppo, J. T., & Roberts, D. C. (1995). Delay in seeking a cancer diagnosis: Delay stages and psychophysiological comparison processes. *British Journal of Social Psychology, 34,* 33–52.

Andersen, B. L., Kiecolt-Glaser, J. K., & Glaser, R. (1994). A biobehavioral model of cancer stress and disease course. *American Psychologist, 49,* 389–404.

Antoni, M. H., Millon, C. M., & Millon, T. (1997). The role of psychological assessment in health care: The MBHI, MBMC, and beyond. In T. Millon (Ed.), *The Millon inventories: Clinical and personality assessment* (pp. 409–448). New York: Guilford Press.

Antonovsky, A. (1987). *Unraveling the mystery of health.* San Francisco: Jossey-Bass.

Antonovsky, A. (1993). The structure and properties of the sense of coherence scale. *Social Science and Medicine, 36,* 725–733.

Aspinwall, L. G., & Taylor, S. E. (1992). Modeling cognitive adaptation: A longitudinal investigation of the impact of individual differences and coping on college adjustment and performance. *Journal of Personality and Social Psychology, 63,* 989–1003.

Ayres, A., Hoon, P. W., Franzoni, J. B., Matheny, K. B., & Cotanch, P. H. (1994). Influence of mood and adjustment to cancer on compliance with chemotherapy among breast cancer patients. *Journal of Psychosomatic Research, 38,* 393–402.

Bandura, A., O'Leary, A., Taylor, C. B., Gauthier, J., & Gossard, D. (1987). Perceived self-efficacy and pain control: Opiod and nonopoid mechanisms. *Journal of Personality and Social Psychology, 53,* 563–571.

Baron, R. M., & Kenney, D. A. (1986). The moderator–mediator variable distinction in social psychological research: Conceptual, strategic, and statistical considerations. *Journal of Personality and Social Psychology, 51,* 1173–1182.

Baum, A. (1990). Stress, intrusive imagery, and chronic distress. *Health Psychology, 9,* 653–675.

Baum, A., Newman, S., Weinman, J., West, R., & McManus, C. (Eds.). (1997). *Cambridge handbook of psychology, health and medicine.* Cambridge: Cambridge University Press.

Baum, A., Revenson, T. A., & Singer, J. E. (Eds.). (2000). *Handbook of health psychology.* Mahwah, NJ: Erlbaum.

Becker, M. H., & Rosenstock, I. M. (1987). Comparing social learning theory and the health belief model. In W. B. Ward (Ed.), *Advances in health education and promotion* (pp. 245–249). Greenwich, CT: JAI Press.

Belar, C. D., & Deardorff, W. W. (1995). *Clinical health psychology in medical settings: A practitioner's guidebook.* Washington, DC: American Psychological Association.

Bennett, P. (1997). Irritable bowel syndrome. In A. Baum, S. Newman, J. Weinman, R. West, & C. McManus (Eds.), *Cambridge handbook of psychology, health and medicine* (pp. 515–516). Cambridge: Cambridge University Press.

Bennett, P., & Carroll, D. (1997). Gastric and duodenal ulcers. In A. Baum, S. Newman, J. Weinman, R. West, & C. McManus (Eds.), *Cambridge handbook of psychology, health and medicine* (pp. 464–465). Cambridge: Cambridge University Press.

Bennett, P., & Carroll, D. (1997). Coronary heart disease: Impact. In A. Baum, S. Newman, J. Weinman, R. West, & C. McManus (Eds.), *Cambridge handbook of psychology, health and medicine* (pp. 419–420). Cambridge: Cambridge University Press.

Bennett, P., & Wilkinson, S. (1985). A comparison of psychological and medical treatment of the irritable bowel syndrome. *British Journal of Clinical Psychology, 24,* 215–216.

Berkman, L. F., Leo-Summers, L., & Horowitz, R. I. (1992). Emotional support and survival after myocardial infarction: A prospective, population-based study of the elderly. *Annals of Internal Medicine, 17,* 1003–1009.

Beutler, L. E., Engle, D., Oro'-Beutler, M. E., Daldrup, R., & Meredith, K. (1986). Inability to express intense affect: A common link between depression and pain? *Journal of Consulting and Clinical Psychology, 54,* 752–759.

Billings, A. G., & Moos, R. H. (1981). The role of coping responses and social resources in attenuating the stress of life events. *Journal of Behavioral Medicine, 4*, 139–157.

Blazer, D. G. (1982). Social support and mortality in an elderly community population. *American Journal of Epidemiology, 115*, 684–694.

Blumer, D., & Heilbronn, M. (1981). The pain-prone patient. A clinical and psychological profile. *Psychosomatics, 22*, 395–402.

Bonica, J. J. (1986). *The management of pain* (2nd ed.). Philadelphia: Lea & Febiger.

Bowman, B. J. (1996). Cross-cultural validation of Antononovsky's Sense of Coherence Scale. *Journal of Clinical Psychology, 52*, 547–549.

Buchanan, G. (1995). Explanatory style and cardiac disease. In G. Buchanan & M. E. P. Seligman (Eds.), *Explanatory style* (pp. 225–232). Hillsdale, NJ: Erlbaum.

Bundy, C., Carroll, D., Wallace, L., & Nagle, R. (1998). Stress management and exercise training in chronic stable angina pectoris. *Psychology and Health, 13*, 147–155.

Buss, D. M. (1987). Selection, evocation, and manipulation. *Journal of Personality and Social Psychology, 53*, 1214–1221.

Butler, R., Damarian, F., Beaulieu, C., Schwebel, A., & Thorn, B. E. (1989). Assessing cognitive coping strategies for acute post-surgical pain. *Psychological Assessment: A Journal of Consulting and Clinical Psychology, 1*, 41–45.

Carmelli, D., Halpern, J., Swan, G. E., Dame, A., McElroy, M., et al. (1991). Twenty-seven-year mortality in the Western Collaborative Group Study: Construction of risk groups by recursive partitioning. *Journal of Clinical Epidemiology, 44*, 1341–1351.

Carney, R. M., Freedland, K. E., Rich, M. W., & Jaffe, A. S. (1995). Depression as a risk factor for cardiac events in established coronary heart disease: A review of possible mechanisms. *Annals of Behavioral Medicine, 17*, 142–149.

Cassileth, B. R., Lusk, E. J., Strouse, T. B., Miller, D. S., Brown, L. L., et al. (1984). Psychosocial status in chronic illness: A comparative analysis of six diagnostic groups. *New England Journal of Medicine, 311*, 506–511.

Chacko, R. C., & Harper, R. G. (2000). Psychiatric predictors of organ transplant outcome. *Directions in Clinical Psychiatry, 20*, 17–25.

Chacko, R. C., Harper, R. G., Gotto, J., & Young, J. (1996). Psychiatric interview and psychometric predictors of cardiac transplant survival. *American Journal of Psychiatry, 153*, 1607–1612.

Chacko, R. C., Hurley, R., Harper R. G., Jankovic, J. J., & Cardoso, F. (1995). Clozapine in the treatment of psychosis in Parkinson's disease. *Journal of Neuropsychiatry and Clinical Neurosciences, 7*, 471–475.

Chamberlian, K., Petrie, K., & Azariah, R. (1992). The role of optimism and sense of coherence in predicting recovery from surgery. *Psychology and Health, 7*, 301–310.

Chesney, M. A., & Folkman, S. (1994). Psychological impact of HIV disease and implications for intervention. *Psychiatric Clinics of North America, 17,* 163–182.

Cioffi, D. (1991). Beyond attentional strategies: A cognitive–perceptual model of somatic interpretation. *Psychological Bulletin, 109,* 25–41.

Contrada, R. J., & Guyll, M. (2000). On who gets sick and why: The role of personality and stress. In A. Baum, T. A. Revenson, & J. E. Singer (Eds.), *Handbook of health psychology* (pp. 59–84). Mahwah, NJ: Erlbaum.

Cox, D. J., & Gonder-Frederick, L. (1992). Major developments in behavioral diabetes research. *Journal of Consulting and Clinical Psychology, 60,* 628–638.

Cramer, J. A., Scheyer, R. D., & Mattson, R. H. (1990). Compliance declines between clinic visits. *Archives of Internal Medicine, 150*(7), 1509–1510.

Creer, T. L., & Holroyd, K. A. (1997). Self-management. In A. Baum, S. Newman, J. Weinman, R. West, & C. McManus (Eds.), *Cambridge handbook of psychology, health and medicine* (pp. 252–258). Cambridge: Cambridge University Press.

Cummings, J. L. (1992). Depression in Parkinson's disease: A review. *American Journal of Psychiatry, 149,* 443–454.

Cummings, J. L. (1988). Intellectual impairment in Parkinson's disease: clinical, pathologic, and behavioral correlates. *Journal of Geriatric Psychiatry and Neurology, 1,* 24–36.

Dahlstrom, W. G., Welsh, G. S., & Dahlstrom, L. E. (1972). *An MMPI handbook: Vol I. Clinical Interpretation.* Minneapolis: University of Minnesota Press.

Dakof, G. A., & Taylor, S. E. (1990). Victims' perceptions of social support: What is helpful from whom? *Journal of Personality ad Social Psychology, 58,* 80–89.

Dekker, F. W., Kapein, A. A., Van der Waart, M. A. C., & Gill, K. (1992). Quality of self care of patients with asthma, *Journal of Asthma, 29,* 203–208.

Dew, M. A., Roth, L. H., Thompson, M. E., Kormos R. L., & Griffith, B. P. (1996). Medical compliance and its predictors in the first year after heart transplantation. *Journal of Heart and Lung Transplant, 15,* 631–645.

Digenio, A. G.,. Padayachee, N., & Groeneveld, H. (1992). Multivariate models for compliance with phase 3 cardiac rehabilitation services in Johannesburg. *Annals of the Academy of Medicine, Singapore, 21,* 121–127.

Doll, R., & Peto, R. (1981). *The causes of cancer.* New York: Oxford University Press.

Duncan, J. (1991). Modern treatment strategies for patients with epilepsy: A review. *Journal of the Royal Society of Medicine, 84,* 59–162.

Dupont, S. (1997). Multiple sclerosis. In A. Baum, S. Newman, J. Weinman, R. West, & C. McManus (Eds.), *Cambridge handbook of psychology, health and medicine* (pp. 538–539). Cambridge: Cambridge University Press.

Ell, K., & Dunkel-Schetter, C. (1994). Social support and adjustment to myocardial infarction, angioplasty, and coronary artery bypass surgery. In S. A. Shumaker & S. M. Czajkowski (Eds.), *Social support and cardiovascular disease* (pp. 301–302). New York: Plenum Press.

Ell, K., Nishimoto, R., Mediansky, L., Mantell, J., & Hamovitch, M. (1992). Social relationships, social support and survival among patients with cancer. *Journal of Psychosomatic Research, 36,* 531–541.

Ellertsen, B. (1992). Personality factors in recurring and chronic pain, *Cephalgia, 12,* 129–132.

Ellertsen, B. (1997). Headache and migraine. In A. Baum, S. Newman, J. Weinman, R. West, & C. McManus (Eds.), *Cambridge handbook of psychology, health and medicine* (pp. 492–494). Cambridge: Cambridge University Press.

Ellertsen, B., Troland, K., & Klove, H. (1987). MMPI profiles in migraine before and after biofeedback treatment, *Cephalgia, 7,* 101–108.

Engel, G. L. (1959). "Psychogenic" pain and the pain-prone patient. *American Journal of Medicine, 26,* 899–918.

Engel, G. L. (1977). The need for a new medical model: A challenge for biomedicine. *Science, 196,* 129 –135.

Engel, G. L. (1980). The clinical application of the biopsychosocial model. *American Journal of Psychiatry, 137,* 535–544.

Everly, G. S., & Newman, E. C. (1997). The MBHI: Composition and clinical applications. In T. Millon (Ed.), *The Millon inventories: Clinical and personality assessment* (pp. 409–448). New York: Guilford Press.

Falk, A., Hanson, B. S., Isacsson, S-O., & Ostergren, P-O. (1992). Job strain and mortality in elderly men: Social network, support, and influence as buffers. *American Journal of Public Health, 82,* 1136–1139.

Fawzy, F. I., Cousins, N., Fawzy, N. W., Kemeny, M. E., Elashoff, R., et al. (1990). A structured psychiatric intervention for cancer patients: I. Changes over time in methods of coping and affective disturbance. *Cancer Intervention, 47,* 720–725.

Fawzy, F. I., Fawzy, N. W., Hyun, C. S., Elashoff, R., Guthrie, D., et al. (1993). Malignant melanoma: Effects of an early structured psychiatric intervention, coping, and affective state on recurrence and survival 6 years later. *Archives of General Psychiatry, 50,* 681–689.

Fawzy, F. I., Kemeny, M. E., Fawzy, N., Elashoff, R., Morton, D., et al. (1990). A structured psychiatric intervention for cancer patients: II. Changes over time in immunological measures. *Archives of General Psychiatry, 47,* 1729–735.

Flor, H., Birbaumer, N., & Turk, D. C. (1990). The psychobiology of chronic pain. *Advances in Behaviour Research and Therapy, 12,* 47–84.

Flor, H., & Turk, D. C. (1988). Chronic back pain and rheumatoid arthritis: Predicting pain, and activity levels of chronic pain patients. *Journal of Psychosomatic Research, 31,* 251–259.

Florian, V., Mikuliner, M., & Taubman, O. (1995). Does hardiness contribute to mental health during a stressful real-life situation? The roles of appraisal and coping. *Journal of Personality and Social Psychology, 68,* 687–695.

Fordyce, W. E. (1976). *Behavioral methods for chronic pain and illness.* St. Louis, MO: C. V. Mosby.

Frasure-Smith, N., Lesperance, F., Gravel, G., Mason, A., Juneau, M., et al. (2000). Social support, depression, and mortality during the first year after myocardial infarction. *Circulation, 101,* 1919–1924.

Frasure-Smith, N., Lesperance, F., Juneau, M., Talajic, M., & Bourassa, M. G. (1999). Gender, depression, and one-year prognosis after myocardial infarction. *Psychosomatic Medicine, 61,* 26–37.

Frasure-Smith, N., Lesperance, F., & Talajic, M. (1993). Depression following myocardial infarction. *Journal of the American Medical Association, 270,* 1819–1825.

Freedman, D. A. (1997). *On infancy and toddlerhood.* Madison, CT: International Universities Press.

Friedman, M., Thoresen, C. E., Gill, J. J., Ulmer, D., Powell, L. H., et al. (1986). Alteration of type A behavior and its effect on cardiac recurrences in postmyocardial infarction patients: Summary results of the Recurrent Coronary Prevention project. *American Heart Journal, 111,* 653–665.

Funch, D. P., & Marshall, J. (1983). The role of stress, social support, and age in survival from breast cancer. *Journal of Psychosomatic Research, 27,* 77–83.

Funk, S. C. (1992). Hardiness: A review of theory and research. *Health Psychology, 11,* 335–345.

Gallacher, J. E. J., Hopkinson, C. A., Bennett, P., Burr, M. L., & Elwood, P. C. (1997). Effect of stress management on angina. *Psychology and Health, 12,* 523–532.

Gill, J. J., Price, V. A., & Friedman, M. (1985). Reduction of Type A behavior in healthy middle-aged American military officers. *American Heart Journal, 110,* 503–514.

Gonder-Frederick, L. A., & Cox, D. J. (1991). Symptom perception, symptom beliefs, and blood glucose discrimination in the self-treatment of insulin-dependent diabetes. In J. A. Skelton & R. T. Croyle (Eds.), *Mental representation in health and illness* (pp. 220–246). New York: Springer-Verlag.

Green, M. F. (1996). What are the functional consequences of neurocognitive deficits in schizophrenia? *American Journal of Psychiatry, 153,* 321–330.

Haines, A. P., Imeson, J. D., & Meade, T. W. (1987). Phobic anxiety and ischemic heart disease. *British Medical Journal, 295,* 297–299.

Hanson, C. L., Henggeler, S. W., & Burghen, G. A. (1987). Social competence and parental support as mediators of the link between stress and metabolic control in adolescents with insulin-dependent diabetes mellitus. *Journal of Consulting and Clinical Psychology, 55,* 529–533.

Harper, R. G., Chacko, R. C., Kotik-Harper, D., Young, J., & Gotto, J. (1998a). Detection of psychiatric diagnosis in heart transplant candidates with the MBHI. *Journal of Clinical Psychology in Medical Settings, 5,* 187–198.

Harper, R. G., Chacko, R. C., Kotik-Harper, D., Young, J., & Gotto, J. (1998b). Self-report evaluation of health behavior, stress vulnerability, and medical outcome in heart transplant recipients. *Psychosomatic Medicine, 60*(5), 563–569.

Harper, R. G., & Steger, J. C. (1978). Psychological correlates of frontalis EMG and pain in tension headache. *Headache, 18,* 215–218.

Helgeson, V. S., Cohen, S., Schulz, R., & Yasko, J. (1999). Education and peer discussion group interventions and adjustment to breast cancer. *Archives of General Psychiatry, 56,* 340–347.

Helmers, K. F., Posluszny, D. M., & Krantz, D. S. (1994). Association of hostility and coronary artery disease: A review of studies. In A. W. Siegman & T. W. Smith (Eds.), *Anger, hostility, and the heart* (pp. 67–96). Hillsdale, NJ: Erlbaum.

Herbert, T. B. B., & Cohen, S. (1993). Stress and immunity in humans: A meta-analytic review. *Psychosomatic Medicine, 55,* 364–379.

Hilsop, T. G., Waqxler, N. E., Coleman, A. J, Elwood, J. M., & Kan, L. (1987). The prognostic significance of psychosocial factors in women with breast cancer. *Archives of General Psychiatry, 56,* 340–347.

Holmes, T. H., & Rahe, R. H. (1967). The social readjustment rating scale. *Journal of Psychosomatic Research, 11,* 213–218.

Holt, P., Fine, M. J., & Tollefson, N. (1987). Mediating stress: Survival of the hardy. *Psychology in the Schools, 24,* 51–58.

Holtmann, G. Armstrong, D., Poppel, E., Clasen M., Witzel, L., et al. (1992). Influence of stress on the healing and relapse of duodenal ulcers. A prospective, multicenter trial of 2109 patients with recurrent duodenal ulceration treated with ranitidine. *Scandinavian Journal of Gastroenterology, 27,* 917–923.

Houston, B. K. (1994). Anger, hostility, and psychophysiological reactivity. In A. Siegman & T. W. Smith (Eds.), *Anger, hostility, and the heart* (pp. 212–253). Hillsdale: NJ: Erlbaum.

Hui, W. M., Shiu, L. P., Lok, A. S. F., & Lam, S. K. (1992). Life events and daily stress in duodenal ulcer disease. *Digestion, 84,* 165–172.

Ingram, K. M., Corning, A. F., & Schmidt, L. D. (1996). The relationship of victimization experiences to psychological well-being among homeless women and low-income housed women. *Journal of Counseling Psychology, 43,* 218–227.

Jahanshahi, M. (1997). Parkinson's disease. In A. Baum, S. Newman, J. Weinman, R. West, & C. McManus (Eds.), *Cambridge handbook of psychology, health and medicine* (pp. 545–547). Cambridge: Cambridge University Press.

Jenkins, C. D., Stanton, B A., & Jono, R. T. (1994). Quantifying and predicting recovery after heart surgery. *Psychosomatic Medicine, 56,* 203–212.

Johnston, D. W., Gold, A., Kentish, J., Smith, K. J., Vallance, P., et al. (1993). Effect of stress management on blood pressure in mild primary hypertension. *British Medical Journal, 306,* 963–966.

Kane, F. J., Stroehlein, J., & Harper, R. G. (1991). Noncardiac chest pain in patients with heart disease. *Southern Medical Journal, 84,* 847–852.

Kasl, S. V., & Cobb, S. (1966). Health behavior, illness behavior, and sick role behavior. II. Sick role behavior. *Archives of Environmental Health, 12,* 531–541.

Kernberg, O. F. (1975). Borderline conditions and pathological narcissism. Northvale, NJ: Aaronson.

Kiecolt-Glaser, J. K., Malarkey, W. B., Chee, M., Newton, T., Cacioppo, J. T., et al. (1993). Negative behavior during marital conflict is associated with immunological down-regulation. *Psychosomatic Medicine, 55*, 395–409.

Kobasa, S. C. (1979). Stressful life events, personality, and health. *Journal of Personality and Social Psychology, 37*, 1–11.

Larsson, G., & Setterlind, S. (1990). Work load/work control and health: Moderating effects of heredity, self-image, coping and health behavior. *International Journal of Health Sciences, 1*, 79–88.

Lavey, E. D., & Winkle, R A. (1984). Continuing disability of patients with chest pain and normal coronary arteriograms. *Journal of Chronic Diseases, 32*, 191–196.

Lazarus, R. S. (1975). A cognitively oriented psychologist looks at biofeedback. *American Psychologist, 30*, 553–561.

Lazarus, R. S., & Cohen, F. (1973). Active coping processes, coping disposition, and recovery from surgery. *Psychosomatic Medicine, 35*, 375–389.

Lazarus, R. S., & Cohen, J. B. (1977). Environmental stress. In L. Altman & J. F. Wohlwill (Eds.), *Human behavior and the environment: Current theory and research, 2* (pp. 89–127). New York: Plenum Press.

Lazarus, R. S., & Folkman, S. (1984). Coping and adaptation. In W. D. Gentry (Ed.), *Handbook of behavioral medicine* (pp. 282–325). New York: Guilford Press.

Lee, D., Mendes de Leon, C. F., Jenkins, C. D., Croog, S. H., Levine, S., et al. (1992). Relation of hostility to medication adherence, symptom complaints, and blood pressure regulation in a clinical field trial of anti-hypertensive medication. *Journal of Psychosomatic Research, 36*, 181–190.

Leiker, M., & Hailey, B. J. (1988). A link between hostility and disease: Poor health habits? *Behavioral Medicine, 3*, 129–133.

Lepore, S. J. (1995). Cynicism, social support, and cardiovascular reactivity. *Health Psychology, 14*, 210–216.

Lerman, C., Miller, S. M., Scarborough, R., Hanjani, P., Nolte, P., et al. (1991). Adverse psychologic consequences of positive cytologic cervical screening. *American Journal of Obstetrics and Gynecology, 165*, 658–662.

Lerman, C., Schwartz, M. D., Miller. S. M., Daly, M., Sands, C., et al. (1996). A randomized trial of breast cancer risk counseling: Interacting effects of counseling, educational level, and coping style. *Health Psychology, 15*, 75–83.

Leventhal, E A., & Crouch, M. (1997). Are there differences in perception of illness across the lifespan? In K. J. Petrie & J. A. Wienman (Eds.), *Perceptions of health and illness: Current research and applications* (pp. 77–102). London: Harwood Academic.

Leventhal, H., Leventhal, E. A., & Cameron, L. (2000). Representations, procedures and affect in illness self-regulation: A perceptual–cognitive model. In A. Baum,

T. A. Revenson, & J. E. Singer (Eds.), *Handbook of health psychology* (pp. 19–47). Mahway, NJ: Erlbaum.

Leventhal, H., Zimmerman, R., & Gutmann, M. (1984). Compliance: A self regulation perspective. In W. D, Gentry (Ed.), *Handbook of behavioral medicine* (pp. 369–436). New York: Guilford Press.

Levy, S., Morrow, L., Bagley, C., & Lippman, M. (1988). Survival hazards analysis in first recurrent breast cancer patients: Seven-year followup. *Psychosomatic Medicine, 50,* 520–528.

Ley, P. (1989). Improving patients' understanding, recall, satisfaction and compliance. In A. Broome (Ed.), *Health psychology.* London: Chapman & Hall.

Ley, P. (1997). Compliance among patients. In A. Baum, S. Newman, J. Weinman, R. West, & C. McManus (Eds.), *Cambridge handbook of psychology, health and medicine* (pp. 281–287). Cambridge: Cambridge University Press.

Linton, S. (1985). The relationship between activity and chronic back pain. *Pain, 21,* 289–294.

Loof, L., Adami, H.-O., Bates, S., Fagerstrom, K. O., Gustausson, S., et al. (1987). Psychological group counseling for the prevention of ulcer relapses. A controlled randomized trial in duodenal and prepyloric ulcer disease. *Journal of Clinical Gastroenterology, 9,* 400–407.

Lorig, K., Chastain, R. L., Ung, E., Shoor, S., & Holman, H. R. (1989). Development and evaluation of a scale to measure perceived self-efficacy in people with arthritis. *Arthritis and Rheumatism, 32,* 37–44.

Maes, S., Leventhal, H., & DeRidder, D. T. D. (1996). Coping with chronic diseases. In M. Zeidner & N. Endler (Eds.), *Handbook of coping: Theory, research, applications* (pp. 221–241). New York: Wiley.

Magnani, L. E. (1990). Hardiness, self-perceived health, and activity among independently functioning older adults. *Scholarly Inquiry for Nursing Practice: An International Journal, 4,* 171–174.

Margalit, M., & Eysenck, S. (1990). Prediction of coherence in adolescence: Gender differences in social skills, personality, and family climate. *Journal of Research in Personality, 24,* 510–521.

Matarazzo, J. D. (1980). Behavioral health and behavioral medicine: Frontiers for a new health psychology. *American Psychologist, 35,* 807–817.

Matarazzo, J. D. (1984). Behavioral health: A 1990 challenge for the health sciences professions. In J. D. Matarazzo, N. E. Miller, S. M. Weiss, J. A. Heard, & S. M. Weiss (Eds.), *Behavioral health: A handbook of health enhancement and disease prevention* (pp. 3–40). New York: John Wiley.

McCrae, R. R., & Costa, P. T., Jr. (1990). *Personality in adulthood.* New York: Guilford Press.

McCrae, R. R., & Stone, S. V. (1997). Personality. In A. Baum, S. Newman, J. Weinman, R. West, & C. McManus (Eds.), *Cambridge handbook of psychology, health and medicine* (pp. 29–34). New York: Cambridge University Press.

McKay, J. R. (1991). Assessing aspects of object relations associated with immune function: Development of the affiliative trust–mistrust coding system. *Psychological Assessment: A Journal of Consulting and Clinical Psychology, 3*, 641–647.

Medalie, J. H., Strange, K. C., Zyzanski, S. J., & Goldbourt, U. (1992). The importance of biopsychosocial factors in the development of duodenal ulcer in a cohort of middle-aged men. *American Journal of Epidemiology, 136*, 1280–1287.

Meichenbaum, D. (1997). Cognitive behavior therapy. In A. Baum, S. Newman, J. Weinman, R. West, & C. McManus (Eds.), *Cambridge handbook of psychology, health and medicine* (pp. 200–202). Cambridge: Cambridge University Press.

Melzack, T., & Casey, K. L. (1968). Sensory, motivational and central control determinants of pain: A new conceptual model. In D. Kenshalo (Ed.), *The skin senses* (pp. 423–443). Springfield, IL: Thomas.

Meyer, D., Leventhal, H., & Gutmann, M. (1985). Common-sense models of illness: The example of hypertension. *Health Psychology, 4*, 115–135.

Meyerink, L. H., Rietan, R. M., & Zelz, M. (1988). The validity of the MMPI with multiple sclerosis patients. *Journal of Clinical Psychology, 44*, 764–769.

Millon, T. (1969). *Modern psychopathology—A biosocial approach to maladaptive learning and functioning*. Philadelphia: Saunders.

Millon, T. (1981). *Disorders of personality: DSM–III, Axis II*. New York: Wiley-Interscience.

Millon, T. (1990). *Toward a new personology: An evolutionary model*. New York: Wiley-Interscience.

Millon T. (1999). *Personality-guided therapy*. New York: John Wiley.

Millon, T., & Davis, R. D. (1996). *Disorders of personality. DSM–IV and beyond*. New York: Wiley-Interscience.

Millon, T., Green, C., & Meagher, R. (1982). *Millon Behavioral Health Inventory* (3rd ed.). Minneapolis: National Computer Systems.

Milne, B., Joachim, G., & Niedhart, J. (1986). A stress management programme for inflammatory bowel disease patients. *Journal of Advanced Nursing, 11*, 561–567.

Mokdad, A. H., Ford, E. S., Bowman, B. A., Nelson, D. E., Engelgau, M. M., et al. (2000). Diabetes trends in the U.S.: 1990–1998. *Diabetes Care, 23*, 1278–1283.

Moos, R. H., & Schaefer, J. A. (1984). The crisis of physical illness: An overview and conceptual approach, In R. H. Moos (Ed.), *Coping with physical illness: New perspectives* (Vol. 2, pp. 3–25). New York: Plenum Press.

Morrill, A. C., Ickovics, J. R., Golubchikov, V. V., Beren, S. E., & Rodin, J. (1996). Safer sex: Social and psychological predictors of behavioral maintenance and change among heterosexual women. *Journal of Clinical and Consulting Psychology, 64*, 819–828.

Murray, H. A. (1943). *Thematic Apperception Test*. Cambridge, MA: Harvard University Press.

National Center for Health Statistics & Koch, H. (1986). The management of chronic pain in office-based ambulatory care: National Ambulatory Care Survey. In *Advanced data from vital and health statistics* (No. 123, DHHS Publication No. PHS 86–1250). Hyattsville, MD: Public Health Service.

National, Heart, Lung, and Blood Institute. (1992). International consensus report of diagnosis and treatment of asthma. Washington, DC: U.S. Department of Health and Human Services.

Neale, A. V., Tilley, B. C., & Vernon, S. W. (1986). Marital status, delay in seeking treatment and survival from breast cancer. *Social Science and Medicine, 23*, 305–312.

Ogden, J. (2000). *Health psychology*. Philadelphia: Open University Press.

Ouelette, S. C. (1993). Inquiries into hardiness. In L. Goldberger & S. Breznitz (Eds.), *Handbook of stress: Theoretical and clinical aspects* (2nd ed.) New York: Free Press.

Parker, S., Tong, T., Bolden, S., & Wingo, P. (1997). Cancer statistics, 1997. CA-*A Cancer Journal for Clinicians, 47*, 5–27.

Parkes, C. M. (1997). Coping with death and dying. In A. Baum, S. Newman, J. Weinman, R. West, & C. McManus (Eds.), *Cambridge handbook of psychology, health and medicine* (pp. 91–94). Cambridge: Cambridge University Press.

Pendleton, D., Schofield, T., Tate, P., & Havelock, P. (1984). *The consultation: An approach to learning and teaching*. Oxford: Oxford Medical.

Pennebaker, J. W., & Beall, S. K. (1986). Confronting a traumatic event: Toward an understanding of inhibition and disease. *Journal of Abnormal Psychology, 95*, 274–281.

Pennebaker, J. W., Gonder-Frederick, L., Cox, D. J., & Hoover, C. W. (1985). The perception of general versus specific visceral activity and the regulation of health-related behavior. *Advances in Behavioral Medicine, 1*, 165–168.

Pennebacker, J. W., Kiecolt-Glaser, J., & Glaser, R. (1988). Disclosure of traumas and immune function: Health implications for psychotherapy. *Journal of Consulting and Clinical Psychology, 56*, 239–245.

Pennebaker, J. W., Mayne, T. J., & Francis, M. E. (1997). Linguistic predictors of adaptive bereavement. *Journal of Personality and Social Psychology, 72*, 863–871.

Peterson, S., Seligman, M. E. P., & Valliant, G. E. (1988). Pessimistic explanatory style is a risk factor for physical illness: A thirty-five year longitudinal study. *Journal of Personality and Social Psychology, 55*, 23–27.

Pettingale, K. W., Morris, T., & Greer, S. (1985). Mental attitudes to cancer: An additional prognostic factor. *Lancet, 1*, 750.

Phillips, W. T., Kiernan, M., & King, A. C. (2000). The effects of physical activity on physical and psychological health. In A. Baum, T. A. Revenson, & J. E. Singer (Eds.), *Handbook of health psychology* (pp. 627–657). Mahwah, NJ: Erlbaum.

Pomerleau, G. F., & Brady, J. P. (1979). *Behavioral medicine: Theory and practice*. Baltimore: Williams & Wilkins.

Prochaska, J. O., & DiClemente, C. C. (1984). *The transtheoretical approach: Crossing traditional boundaries of therapy*. Homewood, IL: Dow Jones Irwin.

Prochaska, J. O., DiClemente, C. C., Velicer, W., & Rossi, J. S. (1993). Standard-ized, individualized, interactive, and personalized self-help programs for smok-ing cessation. *Health Psychology, 12,* 399–405.

Reed, G. M., Kemeny, M. E., Taylor, S. E., Wang, H-Y, J., & Visscher, B. R. (1994). Realistic acceptance as a predictor of decreased survival time in gay men with AIDS. *Health Psychology, 13,* 299–307.

Reynolds, P., & Kaplan, G A. (1990). Social connections and risk for cancer: Prospective evidence from the Alameda County study. *Journal of Behavioral Medicine, 16,* 101–110.

Rich, V. L., & Rich, A. R. (1987). Personality and burnout in female staff nurses. *Image, 19,* 63–66.

Richardson, J. L., Shelton, D. R., Krailo, M., & Levine, A. M. (1990). The effect of compliance with treatment on survival among patients with hematologic malignancies. *Journal of Clinical Oncology, 8,* 356–364.

Rogers, R. W. (1975). A protection motivation theory of fear appeals and attitude change. *Journal of Psychology, 91,* 93–114.

Rogers, R. W. (1983). Cognitive and physiological processes in fear appraisals and attitude change: A revised theory of protection motivation. In J. R. Cacioppo & R. E. Petty (Eds.), *Social psychology: A source book* (pp. 153–176). New York: Guilford Press.

Rogers, R. W. (1985). Attitude change and information integration in fear appeals. *Psychological Reports, 56,* 179–182.

Rose, J. H. (1990). Social support and cancer: Adult patients' desire for support from family, friends, and health professionals. *American Journal of Community Psychology, 18,* 439–464.

Rosen, T. J., Terry, N. S., & Leventhal, H. (1982). The role of esteem and coping in response to a threat communication. *Journal of Research in Personality, 16,* 90–107.

Rosengren, A., Orth-Gomer, K., Wedel, H., & Wilhelmsen, L. (1993). Stressful life events, social support, and mortality in men born in 1933. *British Medical Journal, 307,* 102–105.

Rosenstock, I. M. (1966). Why people use health services. *Millbank Memorial Fund Quarterly, 44,* 94–124.

Roth, H. P. (1979). Problems in conducting a study of the effects of patient compliance of teaching the rational for antacid therapy. In S. J. Cohen (Ed.), *New directions in patient compliance* (pp. 111–126). Lexington, MA: Lexington Books.

Sardell, A. N., & Trierweiler, S. J. (1993). Disclosing the cancer diagnosis. *Cancer, 72,* 3355–3365.

Scambler, G. (1997). Epilepsy. In A. Baum, S. Newman, J. Weinman, R. West, & C. McManus (Eds.), *Cambridge handbook of psychology, health and medicine* (pp. 457–459). Cambridge: Cambridge University Press.

Scambler, G., & Hopkins, A. (1986). Being epileptic: Coming to terms with stigma. *Sociology of health and illness, 8*, 26–43.

Scheier, M. F., & Bridges, M. W. (1995). Person variables and health: Personality predispositions and acute psychological stress as shared determinants for disease. *Psychosomatic Medicine, 57*, 255–268.

Scheier, M. F., & Carver, C. S. (1985). Optimism, coping and health: Assessment and implications of generalized outcome expectancies. *Health Psychology, 4*, 219–247.

Scheier, M. F., & Carver, C. S. (1992). Effects of optimism on psychological and physical well-being. The influence of generalized outcome expectancies on health. *Journal of Personality, 55*, 169–210.

Scheier, M. F., Matthews, J. A., Owens, J. F., Magovern, G. J., Lefebre, R. C., et al. (1989). Dispositional optimism and recovery from coronary artery bypass surgery: The beneficial effects on physical and psychological well-being. *Journal of Personality and Social Psychology, 57*, 1024–1040.

Schwartz, G. E., & Weiss S. M. (1977). *Yale Conference on Behavioral Medicine.* Washington DC: U.S. Department of Health, Education, and Welfare; National Heart, Lung, and Blood Institute.

Schwartz, J. L. (1987). *Review and evaluation of smoking cessation methods: The United States and Canada, 1978–1985.* Bethesda, MD: U.S. Department of Health and Human Services.

Schwarzer, R. (1992). Self efficacy in the adoption and maintenance of health behaviors: Theoretical approaches and a new model. In R. Schwarzer (Ed.), *Self efficacy: Thought control of action* (pp. 217–243). Washington, DC: Hemisphere.

Seyle, H. (1956). *The stress of life.* New York: McGraw-Hill.

Seyle, H. (1984). *The stress of life* (Rev ed.). New York: McGraw-Hill.

Shapiro, A. P. (2000). Nonpharmacological treatment of hypertension. In A. Baum, T. A. Revenson, & J. E. Singer (Eds.), *Handbook of health psychology* (pp. 697–708). Mahway, NJ: Erlbaum.

Shaw, L., & Erlich, A. (1987). Relaxation training as a treatment for chronic pain caused by ulcerative colitis. *Pain, 29*, 287–293.

Shepperd. J. A., Maroto, J. J., & Pbert, L. A. (1996). Dispositional optimism as a predictor of health changes among cardiac patients. *Journal of Research in Personality, 30*, 517–534.

Shontz, F. C. (1975). *The psychological aspects of physical illness and disability.* New York: Macmillan.

Siegal, J. M. (1984). Type A behavior. Epidemiologic foundations and public health implications. *Annual Review of Public Health, 5*, 343–367.

Siegler, I. C. (1994). Hostility and risk: Demographic and lifestyle variables. In A. Siegman & T. W. Smith (Eds.), *Anger, hostility, and the heart* (pp. 199–214). Hillsdale: NJ: Elbaum.

Slater, M. A., Hall, H. F., Atkinson, J. H., & Garfin, S. R. (1991). Pain and impairment beliefs in chronic low back pain: Validation of the Pain and Impairment Relationships Scale (PAIRS). *Pain, 44,* 51–56.

Smith, T. W., & Gallo, L. C. (2000). Personality traits as risk factors for physical illness. In A. Baum, T. A. Revenson, & J. E. Singer (Eds.), *Handbook of health psychology* (pp. 139–173). Mahway, NJ: Erlbaum.

Spiegel, D. (1996). Cancer and depression. *British Journal of Psychiatry, 168,* 109–116.

Spiegel, D., & Bloom, J. R. (1983). Pain in metastatic breast cancer. *Cancer, 52,* 341–345.

Spiegel, D., Bloom J., Kraemer, H., & Gottheil, E. (1989, October 14). Effect of psychosocial treatment on survival of patients with metastatic breast cancer. *Lancet, ii,* 888–891.

Stanton, A. L., Collins, C. A., & Sworowski, L. (2000). Adjustment to chronic illness: Theory and research. In A. Baum, T. A. Revenson, & J. E. Singer (Eds.), *Handbook of health psychology* (pp. 387–404). Mahway, NJ: Erlbaum.

Steptoe, A., Sutcliffe, I., Allen, B., & Coombes, C. (1991). Satisfaction with communication, medical knowledge, and coping style in patients with metastatic cancer. *Social Science in Medicine, 32,* 627–632.

Stern, M. J., Pascale, L., & McLoone, J. B. (1976). Psychosocial adaptation following an acute myocardial infarction. *Journal of Chronic Diseases, 29,* 523–526.

Stewart, A. L., Greenfield, S., Hays, R. D., Wells, K., Rogers, W. H., et al. (1989). Functional status and well-being of patients with chronic conditions: Results from the Medical Outcomes Study. *Journal of the American Medical Association, 262,* 907–913.

Styra, R., Sakinofsky, I., Mahoney, L., Colapinto, N. D., & Currie, D. J. (1993). Coping styles in identifiers and nonidentifiers of a breast lump as a problem. *Psychosomatics, 34,* 53–60.

Suls, J., Wan, C. K., & Costa, P. T., Jr. (1995). Relationship of trait anger to resting blood pressure: A meta-analysis. *Health Psychology, 14,* 444–456.

Sutton, S. (1997). Transtheoretical model of behavior change. In A. Baum, S. Newman, J. Weinman, R. West, & C. McManus (Eds.), *Cambridge handbook of psychology, health and medicine* (pp. 180–183). Cambridge: Cambridge University Press.

Taylor, S. E., Lichtman, R. R., & Wood, J. V. (1984). Attributions, beliefs about control, and adjustment to breast cancer. *Journal of Personality and Social Psychology, 46,* 489–502.

Temoshok, L. (1987). Personality, coping style, emotion, and cancer. Towards an integrative model. *Cancer Surveys, 6,* 545–567.

Topf, M. (1989). Personality hardiness, occupational stress, and burnout in critical care nurses. *Research in Nursing & Health, 12,* 179–186.

Tuckett, D., Boultron, M., Olson, C., & Williams, A. (1985). *Meetings between experts.* London: Tavistock.

Turk, D. C. (2000). Physiological and psychological bases of pain. In A. Baum, T. A. Revenson, & J. E. Singer (Eds.), *Handbook of health psychology* (pp. 117–137). NJ: Erlbaum.

Turk, D. C., & Rudy, T. E. (1988). Toward an empirically derived taxonomy of chronic pain patients: Integration of psychological assessment data. *Journal of Consulting and Clinical Psychology, 56,* 760–768.

Turk, D. C., & Salovey, P. (1984). "Chronic pain as a variant of depressive disease:" A critical reappraisal. *Journal of Nervous and Mental Disease, 172,* 398–404.

Uchino, B. N., Cacioppo, J. T., & Keicolt-Glaser, J. K. (1996). The relationship between social support and physiological processes: A review with emphasis on underlying mechanisms and implications for health. *Psychological Bulletin, 199,* 488–531.

Van't Spijker, A., Trijsburg, R W., & Duivenvoorden, H. J. (1997). Psychological sequelae of cancer diagnosis: A meta-analytical review of 58 studies after 1980. *Psychosomatic Medicine, 59,* 280–293.

Velcier, W., Prochaska, J. O., Bellis, J. M., DiClemente, C. C., Rossi, J. S., et al. (1993). An expert system intervention for smoking cessation. *Addictive Behaviors, 18,* 269–290.

Weinman, J. (1987). Diagnosis as problem-solving. In J. Weinman (Ed.), *An outline of psychology as applied to medicine* (2nd ed.). London: J. Wright.

Wiklund, I., Sanne, H., Vedin, A., & Wilhelmsson, C. (1984). Psychosocial outcome one year after a first myocardial infarction. *Journal of Psychosomatic Research, 28,* 309–321.

Wiebe, D. J., & Williams, P. G. (1992). Hardiness and health: A social psychophysiological perspective on stress and adaptation. *Journal of Social and Clinical Psychology, 11,* 238–262.

Wielgosz, A. T., Fletcher, F. H., McCants, C. B., McKinnis, R. A., Haney, T. L., et al. (1984). Unimproved chest pain in patients with minimal or no coronary disease: A behavioral self-management phenomenon. *American Heart Journal, 108,* 67–72.

Williams, R. B., Barefoot, J. C., Califf, R. M., Haney, T. L., Saunders, W. B., et al. (1992). Prognostic importance of social recourses among patients with CAD. *Journal of the American Medical Association, 267,* 520–524.

Williams, J. E., Paton, C. C., Siegler, I. C., Eigenbrody, M. L., Nieto, F. J., et al. (2000). Anger proneness predicts coronary heart disease risk: Prospective analysis from the athlerosclerosis risk in communities (ARIC) study. *Circulation, 101,* 2034–2039.

Wills, T. A. (1985). Supportive functions of interpersonal relationships. In S. Cohen & S. L. Syme (Eds.), *Social support and health* (pp. 61–82). Orlando, FL: Academic Press.

Wills, T. A., & Filer Fegan, M. F. (2000). Social networks and social support. In A. Baum, T. A. Revenson, & J. E. Singer (Eds.). *Handbook of health psychology* (pp. 209–234). Mahway, NJ: Erlbaum.

AUTHOR INDEX

Abramson, L. Y., 12, 327
Adami, H.-O., 335
Ajzen, I., 25, 327
Akiskal, H. S., 179, 180, 327
Alexander, F. G., 9, 327
Allen, B., 44, 340
Andersen, B. L., 43, 44, 327
Antoni, M. H., 7, 327
Antonovsky, A., 11, 327
Armstrong, D., 333
Aspinwall, L. G., 11, 327
Atkinson, J. H., 36, 339
Ayres, A., 9, 328
Azariah, R., 11, 329

Bagley, C., 10, 335
Bandura, A., 36, 328
Barefoot, J. C., 341
Baron, R. M., 10
Bates, S., 335
Baum, A., 19, 328
Beall, S. K., 21, 337
Beaulieu, C., 36, 329
Becker, M. H., 25, 328
Belar, C. D., 5, 328
Bellis, J. M., 341
Bennett, P., 34, 35, 41, 42, 312, 328, 332
Beren, S. E., 336
Berkman, L. F., 28, 328
Beutler, L. E., 35, 328
Billings, A. G., 21, 329
Birbaumer, N., 36, 331
Blazer, D. G., 329
Bloom, J. R., 27, 36, 340
Blumer, D., 35, 329
Bolden, S., 43, 337
Bonica, J. J., 35, 329
Boultron, M., 31, 340
Bourassa, M. G., 41, 332
Bowman, B. A., 336
Bowman, B. J., 11, 329
Brady, J. P., 5, 337
Bridges, M. W., 9, 339

Brown, L. L., 329
Buchanan, G., 10, 329
Bundy, C., 41, 329
Burghen, G. A., 27, 332
Burr, M. L., 41, 332
Buss, D. M., 10, 329
Butler, R., 36, 329

Cacioppo, J. T., 27, 44, 327, 334, 341
Califf, R. M., 341
Cameron, L., 25, 334
Cardoso, F., 200, 329
Carmelli, D., 9, 329
Carney, R. M., 10, 329
Carroll, D., 34, 41, 42, 312, 328, 329
Carver, C. S., 11, 339
Casey, K. L., 35, 336
Cassileth, B. R., 24, 329
Chacko, R. C., 41, 200, 272, 321, 329, 332
Chamberlian, K., 11, 329
Chastain, R. L., 37, 335
Chee, M., 334
Chesney, M. A., 24, 330
Cioffi, D., 37, 330
Clasen, M., 333
Cobb, S., 25, 333
Cohen, F., 334
Cohen, S., 20, 27, 333
Colapinto, N. D., 44, 340
Coleman, A. J., 333
Collins, C. A., 23, 340
Contrada, R. J., 9, 330
Coombes, C., 44, 340
Corning, A. F., 11, 333
Costa, P. T., Jr., 9, 13, 335, 340
Cotanch, P. H., 9, 328
Cousins, N., 27, 331
Cox, D. J., 24, 25, 36, 330, 332, 337
Cramer, J. A., 28, 330
Creer, T. L., 3, 330
Croog, S. H., 334
Crouch, M., 334

Cummings, J. L., 40, 330
Currie, D. J., 44, 340

Dahlstrom, L. E., 34, 127, 330
Dahlstrom, W. G., 34, 127, 330
Dakof, G. A., 27, 330
Daldrup, R., 35, 328
Daly, M., 334
Damarian, F., 36, 329
Dame, A., 329
Davis, R. D., 277, 336
Deardorff, W. W., 5, 328
Dekker, F. W., 28, 330
DeRidder, D. T. D., 24, 335
Dew, M. A., 28, 330
DiClemente, C. C., 30, 31, 52, 337, 338, 341
Digenio, A. G., 9, 330
Doll, R., 3, 330
Duivenvoorden, H. J., 24, 341
Duncan, J., 39, 330
Dunkel-Schetter, C., 24, 330
Dupont, S., 40, 330

Eigenbrody, M. L., 341
Elashoff, R., 331
Ell, K., 24, 28, 330, 331
Ellertsen, B., 33, 34, 331
Elwood, J. M., 333
Elwood, P. C., 41, 332
Engel, G. L., 5, 35, 331
Engelgau, M. M., 336
Engle, D., 35, 328
Erlich, A., 34, 339
Everly, G. S., 324, 331
Eysenck, S., 11, 335

Fagerstrom, K. O., 335
Falk, A., 27, 331
Fawzy, F. I., 27, 44, 331
Fawzy, N. W., 27, 331
Filer Fegan, M. F., 26, 27, 341
Fine, M. J., 11, 333
Fletcher, F. H., 341
Flor, H., 36, 331
Florian, V., 11, 331
Folkman, S., 20, 24, 330, 334
Ford, E. S., 336

Fordyce, W. E., 35, 331
Fox, M. J., 40
Francis, M. E., 21, 337
Franzoni, J. B., 9, 328
Frasure-Smith, N., 10, 41, 332
Freedland, K. E., 10, 329
Freedman, D. A., 260, 332
Friedman, M., 41, 332
Funch, D. P., 28, 332
Funk, S. C., 11, 332

Gallacher, J. E. J., 41, 332
Gallo, L. C., 10, 340
Garfin, S. R., 36, 339
Gauthier, J., 36, 328
Gill, J. J., 41, 332
Gill, K., 28, 330
Glaser, R., 21, 43, 327, 337
Gold, A., 333
Goldbourt, U., 34, 336
Golubchikov, V. V., 336
Gonder-Frederick, L. A., 24, 25, 36, 330, 332, 337
Gossard, D., 36, 328
Gottheil, E., 27, 340
Gotto, J., 41, 321, 329, 332
Gravel, G., 332
Green, C., 324, 336
Green, M. F., 92, 332
Greenfield, S., 340
Greer, S., 10, 337
Griffith, B. P., 28, 330
Groeneveld, H., 9, 330
Gustausson, S., 335
Guthrie, D., 331
Gutmann, M., 25, 29, 335, 336
Guyll, M., 9, 330

Hailey, B. J., 9, 334
Haines, A. P., 244, 332
Hall, H. F., 36, 339
Halpern, J., 329
Hamovitch, M., 28, 331
Haney, T. L., 341
Hanjani, P., 334
Hanson, B. S., 27, 331
Hanson, C. L., 27, 332
Harper, R. G., 33, 41, 200, 244, 321, 324, 329, 332, 333

Matheny, K. B., 9, 328
Matthews, J. A., 339
Mattson, R. H., 28, 330
Mayne, T. J., 21, 337
McCants, C. B., 341
McCrae, R. R., 8, 13, 335
McElroy, M., 329
McKay, J. R., 12, 336
McKinnis, R. A., 341
McLoone, J. B., 42, 340
McManus, C., 19, 328
Meade, T. W., 244, 332
Meagher, R., 324, 336
Medalie, J. H., 34, 336
Mediansky, L., 28, 331
Meichenbaum, D., 37, 336
Melzack, T., 35, 336
Mendes de Leon, C. F., 334
Meredith, K., 35, 328
Meyer, D., 25, 32, 336
Meyerink, L. H., 127, 336
Mikuliner, M., 11, 331
Miller, D. S., 329
Miller, S. M., 334
Millon, C. M., 3, 327
Millon, T., 3, 4, 5, 12, 15, 16, 17, 18, 48,
        49, 66, 92, 93, 113, 135, 136,
        209, 238, 252, 277, 281, 287,
        324, 327, 336
Milne, B., 34, 336
Mokdad, A. H., 38, 336
Moos, R. H., 21, 22, 329, 336
Morrill, A. C., 11, 336
Morris, T., 10, 337
Morrow, L., 10, 335
Morton, D., 331
Murphy, G., 12
Murray, H. A., 336

Nagle, R., 41, 329
Neale, A. V., 28, 337
Nelson, D. E., 336
Newman, E. C., 324, 331
Newman, S., 19, 328
Newton, T., 334
Niedhart, J., 34, 336
Nieto, F. J., 341
Nishimoto, R., 28, 331
Nolte, P., 334

O'Leary, A., 36, 328
Ogden, J., 3, 5, 19, 43, 337
Olson, C., 31, 340
Oro'-Beutler, M. E., 35, 328
Orth-Gomer, K., 28, 338
Ostergren, P.-O., 27, 331
Ouelette, S. C., 11, 337
Owens, J. F., 339

Padayachee, N., 9, 330
Parker, S., 43, 337
Parkes, C. M., 22, 23, 337
Pascale, L., 42, 340
Paton, C. C., 341
Pbert, L. A., 11, 339
Pendleton, D., 31, 337
Pennebaker, J. W., 21, 36, 337, 337
Peterson, S., 12, 337
Peto, R., 3, 330
Petrie, K., 11, 329
Pettingale, K. W., 10, 337
Phillips, W. T., 21, 337
Pomerleau, G. F., 5, 337
Poppel, E., 333
Posluszny, D. M., 9, 333
Powell, L. H., 332
Price, V. A., 41, 332
Prochaska, J. O., 30, 31, 52, 337, 338,
        341

Rahe, R. H., 20, 333
Reed, G. M., 10, 338
Revenson, T. A., 19, 328, 340
Reynolds, P., 28, 338
Rich, A. R., 11, 338
Rich, M. W., 10, 329
Rich, V. L., 11, 338
Richardson, J. L., 27, 338
Rietan, R. M., 127, 336
Roberts, D. C., 44, 327
Rodin, J., 336
Rogers, R. W., 338
Rogers, W. H., 25, 340
Rose, J. H., 27, 338
Rosen, T. J., 29, 338
Rosengren, A., 28, 338
Rosenstock, I. M., 25, 328, 338
Rossi, J. S., 31, 341
Roth, H. P., 31, 338

Roth, L. H., 28, 330
Rudy, T. E., 36, 341

Sakinofsky, I., 44, 340
Salovey, P., 35, 341
Sands, C., 334
Sanne, H., 42, 341
Sardell, A. N., 44, 338
Saunders, W. B., 341
Scambler, G., 39, 338, 339
Scarborough, R., 334
Schaefer, J. A., 22, 336
Scheier, M. F., 9, 11, 339
Scheyer, R. D., 28, 330
Schmidt, L. D., 11, 333
Schofield, T., 31, 337
Schulz, R., 27, 333
Schwartz, G. E., 5, 339
Schwartz, J. L., 42, 339
Schwartz, M. D., 334
Schwarzer, R., 25, 339
Schwebel, A., 36, 329
Seligman, M. E. P., 12, 327, 337
Setterlind, S., 11, 334
Seyle, H., 20, 339
Shapiro, A. P., 41, 339
Shaw, L., 34, 339
Shelton, D. R., 27, 338
Shepperd. J. A., 11, 339
Shiu, L. P., 34, 333
Shontz, F. C., 22, 339
Shoor, S., 37, 335
Siegal, J. M., 9, 339
Siegler, I. C., 9, 339, 341
Singer, J. E., 19, 328, 340
Slater, M. A., 36, 339
Smith, K. J., 333
Smith, T. W., 10, 340
Spiegel, D., 27, 36, 44, 340
Stanton, A. L., 23, 24, 340
Stanton, B. A., 9, 333
Steger, J. C., 34, 333
Steptoe, A., 44, 340
Stern, M. J., 42, 340
Stewart, A. L., 24, 340
Stone, S. V., 8, 335
Strange, K. C., 34, 336
Stroehlein, J., 244, 333
Strouse, T. B., 329
Styra, R., 44, 340

Suls, J., 9, 340
Sutcliffe, I., 44, 340
Sutton, S., 30, 340
Swan, G. E., 329
Sworowski, L., 23, 340

Talajic, M., 10, 41, 332
Tate, P., 31, 337
Taubman, O., 11, 331
Taylor, C. B., 36, 328
Taylor, S. E., 10, 11, 23, 27, 327, 330,
    338, 340
Teasdale, J. D., 12, 327
Temoshok, L., 9, 340
Terry, N. S., 29, 338
Thompson, M. E., 28, 330
Thoresen, C. E., 332
Thorn, B. E., 36, 329
Tilley, B. C., 28, 337
Tollefson, N., 11, 333
Tong, T., 43, 337
Topf, M., 11, 340
Trierweiler, S. J., 44, 338
Trijsburg, R. W., 24, 341
Troland, K., 34, 331
Tuckett, D., 31, 340
Turk, D. C., 35, 36, 37, 331, 340, 341

Uchino, B. N., 27, 43, 341
Ulmer, D., 332
Ung, E., 37, 335

Vallance, P., 333
Valliant, G. E., 12, 337
Van der Waart, M. A. C., 28, 330
Van't Spijker, A., 24, 341
Vedin, A., 42, 341
Velcier, W., 31, 341
Vernon, S. W., 28, 337
Visscher, B. R., 10, 338

Wallace, L., 41, 329
Wan, C. K., 9, 340
Wang, H.-Y., J., 10, 338
Waqxler, N. E., 333
Wedel, H., 28, 338
Weinman, J., 19, 31, 328, 341

Weiss, S. M., 5, 339
Wells, K., 340
Welsh, G. S., 34, 330
West, R., 19, 328
Wiebe, D. J., 11, 341
Wielgosz, A. T., 244, 341
Wiklund, I., 42, 341
Wilhelmsen, L., 28, 338
Wilhelmsson, C., 42, 341
Wilkinson, S., 35, 328
Williams, A., 31, 340
Williams, J. E., 41, 341
Williams, P. G., 11, 341
Williams, R. B., 28, 341

Wills, T. A., 26, 27, 341
Wingo, P., 43, 337
Winkle, R. A., 42, 334
Witzel, L., 333
Wood, J. V., 23, 340

Yasko, J., 27, 333
Young, J., 41, 321, 329, 332

Zelz, M., 127, 336
Zimmerman, R., 29, 335
Zyzanski, S. J., 34, 336

SUBJECT INDEX

Change model, 30–31. *See also individual personality types*
Chemotherapy, 9, 88, 108, 314
Childhood, 25, 157, 281
Cholesterol, 9, 41, 170
Chronic diseases
    adjustment to, 23–24
    illness representation, 24–26, 36
Chron's disease, 34
Church organizations, support from, 254
Cigarettes. *See* Smoking
Clinical domains
    of antisocial personality, 158–159
    of avoidant personality, 230–231
    of borderline personality, 180–182
    of compulsive personality, 252–254
    of dependent personality, 208–210
    of depressive disorder, 278–279
    of histrionic personality, 112–113
    of masochistic personality, 287–288
    of narcissistic personality, 134–135
    of negativistic personality, 281–282
    of paranoid personality, 66–68
    of sadistic personality, 284–285
    of schizoid personality, 48–49
    of schizotypal personality, 92–94
Cognitive behavior strategies, 37, 147, 259
Coherence, 11
Communication, 30
Comorbidity, 14–15
Compliance, to treatment regimen, 28–32. *See also individual personality types*
Compulsive personality
    biophysical level of, 254
    cancer, 273–274
    cardiac diseases, 272–273
    change model, 261–263
    clinical domains, 252–254
    coping with illness, 266–267
    defined, 251–252
    and dependent traits, 255
    diabetes, 270–271
    diagram of (figure), 275
    interpsychic level of, 253–254
    interventions, preventative, 260–264
    medical compliance, 268
    and narcissistic traits, 255–256
    and negativistic traits, 256–257
    neurological diseases, 271–272

    pain management, 269–270
    and paranoid traits, 255
    as patients, 258–260, 274–276
    perpetuating features, 257–258
    and schizoid traits, 256
    secondary/tertiary care, 264–266
    somatoform disorders, 269
    subtypes of, 254–257
Conversion Hysteria scale, 127
Coping, 14, 20–21, 22–24
    anticipatory, 20, 22
    and antisocial personality, 168–169
    and avoidant personality, 237–238
    and borderline personality, 192–193
    and cancer, 44, 129
    and compulsive personality, 266–267
    and dependent personality, 218–219
    and depressive disorder, 298
    and histrionic personality, 121–122
    and masochistic personality, 299–300
    and narcissistic personality, 144–145
    and negativistic personality, 298–299
    and paranoid personality, 78–79
    and sadistic personality, 299
    and schizoid personality, 55–56
    and schizotypal personality, 101
    styles of, 21
Coping Effectiveness Training Program, 24
Cost benefits, of intervention, 319–320
    and antisocial personality, 167
    and avoidant personality, 235–236
    and borderline personality, 190–191
    and compulsive personality, 263–264
    and dependent personality, 216–217
    and depressive disorder, 295
    and histrionic personality, 119
    and masochistic personality, 296
    and narcissistic personality, 142
    and negativistic personality, 295
    and paranoid personality, 76
    and sadistic personality, 296
    and schizoid personality, 53–54
    and schizotypal personality, 99
Counseling, 218

Death, 22
Demyelination, 40, 310

Emotion suppression, 9
Emphysema, 141
Epilepsy, 39. *See also* Neurological
     diseases
     and antisocial personality, 173
     and avoidant personality, 243
     and borderline personality, 199
     and compulsive personality, 271
     and dependent personality, 224
     and depressive disorder, 310
     and histrionic personality, 126–127
     and masochistic personality, 311
     and narcissistic personality, 150
     and negativistic personality,
          310–311
     and paranoid personality, 85–86
     and sadistic personality, 311
     and schizoid personality, 60
     and schizotypal personality, 106
Exercise, 6, 201
     and coping, 21
     and optimism, 11–12

Family support, 27, 40, 63, 139, 213, 293,
     295
Fear, 288. *See also* Anxiety

Group support, 27, 247
     and avoidant personality, 233, 247
     and compulsive personality, 274
     and dependent personality, 216
     and histrionic personality, 118–119,
          125, 128
     and narcissistic personality, 142,
          144, 152, 154–155
     and paranoid personality, 73
     and schizoid personality, 51

Hardiness, 10
Headache personalities, 33
Headaches, 33, 81. *See also* Somatoform
     disorders
Heart. *See* Cardiac diseases
Helplessness–hopelessness, 10, 22, 36,
     212
Histrionic personality, 18, 111–131
     antisocial features of, 114–115
     biophysical level of, 113

cancer, 129–130
cardiac diseases, 128–129
change model, 118–119
clinical domains, 112–113
coping with illness, 121–122
defined, 111
vs. dependent personality, 111
diabetes, 126
diagram of (figure), 130
interpsychic level of, 112–113
interventions, preventative, 117–119
and medications, 123
medical compliance, 122–123
and narcissistic traits, 113–114
and negativistic traits, 114
neurological diseases, 126–128
obsessive–compulsive, 114
pain management, 124–125
as patients, 116–117, 130–131
perpetuating features, 115–116
secondary/tertiary care, 120–121
somatoform disorders, 124
subtypes of, 113–115
Homelessness, 11
Hypertension, 25, 32
     anger–hostility and, 9
Hypnosis, 37
Hypochondria, 33, 138, 147, 237

Illness representation, 24–26, 36
     and antisocial personality, 168
     and avoidant personality, 237
     and borderline personality, 192
     and compulsive personality, 265
     and dependent personality, 218
     and depressive disorder, 297
     and histrionic personality, 121
     and narcissistic personality, 144
     and negativistic personality,
          297–298
     and sadistic personality, 298
     and schizoid personality, 54
     and schizotypal personality, 100
Immune functioning
     anger–hostility and, 9
     and stress, 20
Impotence, 257
Insulin pumps, 105
"Intentional interference," 238
Interactions, 17

Interventions. *See* Behavioral medicine; Cost benefits, of intervention; *individual personality types*

Irritable bowel syndrome, 34–35

Levodopa, 106, 173

Management, and coping, 20

Marital support, 28

Masochistic personality, 18, 287–289
    biophysical level of, 288
    cancer, 316–317
    cardiac diseases, 314
    change model, 294–295
    clinical domains, 287–288
    coping with illness, 299–300
    defined, 287
    diabetes, 309–310
    interpsychic level of, 288
    interventions, preventative, 292, 294–295, 296
    medical compliance, 302
    neurological diseases, 311
    pain management, 307–308
    as patients, 290–291, 317–318
    perpetuating features, 288–289
    secondary/tertiary care, 297
    somatoform disorders, 304–305

Medical compliance
    and antisocial personality, 168–170
    and avoidant personality, 238–239
    and borderline personality, 193–194
    and compulsive personality, 268
    and dependent personality, 219–220
    and depressive disorder, 300
    and histrionic personality, 122–123
    and masochistic personality, 302
    and narcissistic personality, 145–146
    and negativistic personality, 300–301
    and paranoid personality, 79–81
    and sadistic personality, 301
    and schizoid personality, 56
    and schizotypal personality, 102–103

Memory, and pain, 36
    polarity model, 12–13, 92

Millon Behavioral Health Inventory, 324

Millon Behavioral Medicine Diagnostic, 324

Millon's theory of personality, 12–14, 15–16, 18

Minnesota Multiphasic Personality Inventory (MMPI), 34, 127

Misery, 288

Mood elevators, 125, 146, 222, 289, 292

Morphological structures, 15–16

Multiple sclerosis, 23, 39–40. *See also* Neurological diseases
    and antisocial personality, 173
    and avoidant personality, 243–244
    and borderline personality, 200
    and compulsive personality, 271–272
    and dependent personality, 224
    and depressive disorder, 310
    and histrionic personality, 127
    and masochistic personality, 311
    and narcissistic personality, 150
    and negativistic personality, 311
    and paranoid personality, 86
    and sadistic personality, 311
    and schizoid personality, 60
    and schizotypal personality, 105–106

Myocardial infarction, 42

Narcissistic personality, 18, 133–156
    and antisocial traits, 135–136
    and avoidant traits, 136
    biophysical level of, 135
    cardiac diseases, 151–152
    change model, 140–141
    clinical domains, 134–135
    coping with illness, 144–145
    defined, 133–134
    diabetes, 149–150
    diagram of (figure), 155
    and histrionic traits, 136
    interpsychic level of, 135
    interventions, preventative, 140–142
    medical compliance, 145–146
    and negativistic traits, 136
    neurological diseases, 150–151
    pain management, 148–149
    vs. paranoid personality, 68–69
    as patients, 138–139, 155–156
    perpetuating features, 136–137
    secondary/tertiary care, 142–143
    somatoform disorders, 147–148
    subtypes of, 135–136

Parkinson's disease, *continued*
    and negativistic personality, 311
    and paranoid personality, 78, 86
    and sadistic personality, 311
    and schizoid personality, 60
    and schizotypal personality, 106
Patient profiling, 321
Personality. *See also individual personality*
    types
    disorder, defined, 17
    and illness, 8–10
    and interventions, 15–17
    Millon's theory of, 12–14, 15–16, 18
    type agendas (table), 322–323
    and wellness, 10–12
Potentiating pairings, 16
Promiscuity, sexual, 115, 165, 175
Psychosocial supports, 26–28

Relaxation exercises, 34
    and antisocial personality, 169
    and avoidant personality, 235
    and dependent personality, 221
    and histrionic personality, 125, 128
    and paranoid personality, 82
    and schizoid personality, 58
Religious support, 213
Risk behaviors, reduction of, 7, 151

Sadistic personality, 18, 284–287
    biophysical level of, 285
    cancer, 316
    cardiac diseases, 313–314
    change model, 294–295
    clinical domains, 284–285
    coping with illness, 299
    defined, 284
    diabetes, 309
    interpsychic level of, 285
    interventions, preventative, 292,
       294, 296
    medical compliance, 301
    neurological diseases, 311
    pain management, 307
    vs. paranoid personality, 69
    as patients, 290, 317–318
    perpetuating features, 285–287
    secondary/tertiary care, 297
    somatoform disorders, 304

Schizoid personality, 18, 47–64
    vs. avoidant personality, 48, 233, 244
    biophysical level of, 48–49
    cancer, 62–63
    cardiac diseases, 61–62
    change model, 52–53
    clinical domains, 48–49
    coping with illness, 55–56
    defined, 47
    and depression, 49, 50
    diabetes, 59–60
    diagram of (figure), 64
    interpsychic level of, 48–49
    interventions, preventative, 50,
       52–54
    medical compliance, 56
    neurological diseases, 60
    out-patient treatment, 58–59
    pain management, 57–59
    as patients, 50–51, 63–64
    perpetuating features, 49–50
    relaxation exercises, 58
    secondary/tertiary care, 54–55
    somatoform disorders, 56–57
    subtypes of, 49–50
Schizotypal personality, 18, 91–109
    vs. avoidant personality, 95
    biophysical level of, 94
    cancer, 107–108
    cardiac diseases, 106–107
    change model, 99–99
    clinical domains, 92–94
    coping with illness, 101
    defined, 91–92
    diabetes, 104
    diagram of (figure), 109
    interpsychic level of, 93–94
    interventions, preventative, 98–99
    medical compliance, 102–103
    neurological diseases, 105–106
    pain management, 103–104
    as patients, 96–97, 108–109
    perpetuating features, 94–95
    secondary/tertiary care, 99–100
    somatoform disorders, 103
    subtypes of, 95–96
Seizures, 39. *See also* Epilepsy
Self-examination, for cancer, 315
Self-management, of disease, 3–4, 80,
       297, 321. *See also* Coping
Self-mutilation, 180

Sleep hygiene, 9
Smoking
    anger–hostility and, 9
    and cancer, 43
    cessation of, 6, 41, 42, 52, 53, 84,
        98, 123, 141, 198, 261, 270
Social supports, 26–28. *See also* Family
    support; Group support
Somatoform disorders, 32–35, 42. *See also*
    Headaches; Stress
    and antisocial personality, 170–171
    and avoidant personality, 240–241
    and borderline personality, 195–196
    and compulsive personality, 269
    and dependent personality, 220–222
    and depressive disorder, 302–303
    and histrionic personality, 124
    and masochistic personality,
        304–305
    and narcissistic personality, 147–148
    and negativistic personality, 303
    and paranoid personality, 81–82
    and sadistic personality, 304
    and schizoid personality, 56–57
    and schizotypal personality, 103
Steroids, 307
Stress, 19–21. *See also* Somatoform
    disorders

Stress management, 34, 35. *See also*
    Coping
Substance abuse, 197, 198, 201. *See
    also* Alcohol abuse; Drug
    abuse
Suicide, 183, 197
Support. *See* Family support; Group
    support; Social support
Support groups. *See* Group support

T-cell ratios, 12
Temperament, 16
Thematic Apperception test (TAT),
    12
Tobacco. *See* Smoking
Transactions, 17
Type A personality, 10, 41
Type C personality, 9

Ulcers
    and stress, 34

Wellness, and personality, 6, 7, 10–12

ABOUT THE AUTHOR

Robert G. Harper, PhD, received an AB degree in psychology and economics from the University of California, Berkeley, in 1966. After military service, he attended the University of Texas at Austin, earning his doctorate in clinical psychology in 1971. After completing his pre- and postdoctoral training at the Department of Medical Psychology, University of Oregon Medical School, he has held faculty appointments at the University of Maryland Medical School and the University of Oregon Health Sciences Center. His current position is with the Menninger Department of Psychiatry at Baylor College of Medicine, where he is associate professor and conducts research and provides training in a behavioral medicine/neuropsychology predoctoral internship position.